The Independent Hostel Guide 2012

England
Wales
Scotland

Edited by
Sam Dalley

GW00482914

The Backpackers Press

ISBN 978-0-9565058-1-1

Dedicated to Bob Oldfield
5/9/1964 - 19/3/2011

Editor 2008 - 2011

He found treasures
where the crowd didn't look
and shared them with us.

Independent Hostel Guide 2012: England, Wales and Scotland

21st Edition
Editor : Sam Dalley

British Library Cataloguing in Publication Data
A Catalogue record for this book is available from the British Library
ISBN   978-0-9565058-1-1

ISBN 978-0-9565058-1-1

9 780956 505811

Published by: The Backpackers Press, Speedwell House,
Upperwood, Matlock Bath, Derbyshire, DE4 3PE
www.independenthostelguide.co.uk
Tel: +44 (0) 1629 580427

Printed by: Stering Solutions, www.sterlingsolutions.co.uk
Back Cover Photographs: Dalehead Bunkhouse pg 130, River House
Hostel pg 258, Flat Holm Farmhouse pg 252, Albatross Backpackers pg 230
Front Cover Photographs: Top and Bottom Right: Photography by Ian Dais-
ley www.iandaisleyphotography.com; Bottom Left: Gareth Robinson, Mountain
Biking Britain (MTB Forum).
Internal photographs: Provided by the Independent Hostels. Photos on
page 369 (Corran House) credited to Highland Photos and page 329 (Sgubor
Unnos) credited to Tony Jones.

Distributed in the UK by:-
        Cordee Books and Maps, 3a De Montfort Street,
        Leicester, LE1 7HD. Tel: (0116) 2543579

CONTENTS

Independent Hostels UK (IHUK) is a not-for-profit company providing a networking, coordinating and marketing platform for individual operators and managers of hostels, backpackers, camping barns and bunkhouse style accommodation. The organisation seeks to maintain and improve standards and quality as well as raise awareness of bunkhouses, hostels and group accommodation at all levels.

www.IndependentHostelsUK.co.uk

SYMBOLS

👫	Mixed dormitories
👫	Single sex dormitories
🅿	Private rooms
⊇	Blankets or duvets provided
▤	Sheets required
◈	Sleeping bags required
▥	Hostel fully heated (including common room)
▦	Common room only heated
⌂	Drying room available
☂	Showers available
▦	Cooking facilities available
▽	Shop at hostel
🍽	Meals provided at hostel (with notice)
🍽	Breakfast only at hostel (with notice)
🍽	Meals available locally
▣	Clothes washing facilities available
♿	Facilities for less-able people.
💻	Internet facilities
🚴 1m	Within 1 mile of a Sustrans cycle route
🚴 3m	Within 3 miles of a Sustrans cycle route
🚴 5m	Within 5 miles of a Sustrans cycle route
⚠	Affiliated to Hostelling International
Ⓢ	Simple accommodation. Clean, friendly and basic.
GROUPS ONLY	Accommodation for groups only

Bunkhouses, camping barns, backpackers hostels and group accommodation centres all offer friendly hostel style accommodation. These independent hostels have shared areas, large kitchens and some sleeping accommodation in bunks. Ideal for families, backpackers, outdoor enthusiasts and groups of all shapes and sizes, their unique qualities are:-

▲ No membership requirements

▲ Privately owned (5% are also affiliated to YHA or SYHA)

▲ Self catering facilities

▲ Private bedrooms, en-suite rooms and dorms,

▲ Groups, individuals and families welcome

▲ Can be booked completely (sole-use) for get-togethers

▲ Great locations for outdoor activities

▲ Central city locations for independent travellers

▲ Available for individual nights, weekends or weeks

▲ Eco-conscious and great value

▲ Updated daily on www.Independenthostelguide.co.uk

pp	per person
GR	Ordnance Survey grid reference

 VisitScotland Quality Assured

 VisitWales Quality Assured  Wales Cymru

VisitEngland Quality Assured

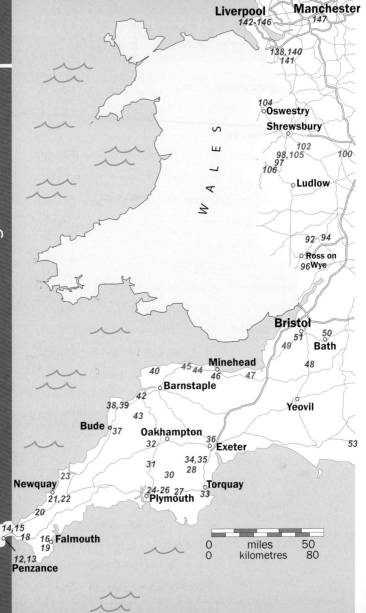

South England / Midlands

9

Sheffield — 132, 130, 128, 126, 124, 134, 135,136,137, 122, 118120, 116,117

Lincoln — 148

Skegness

Derby

Nottingham — 110

King's Lynn — 111, 114,115

Norwich — 112

Leicester

Peterborough

Birmingham — 109, 107,108

Coventry

Northampton

Cambridge

Ipswich — 88

Colchester

Luton

London — 71, 72 to 87

Oxford — 90

Reading

Canterbury — 64, 66

Dover

Salisbury — 52

Guildford — 60

Portsmouth — 68,69, 59

Brighton — 62

Hastings — 70

Bournemouth — 54,56, 58

KEY

45 - **Hostel page number**

45 - **Page number of group only accommodation**

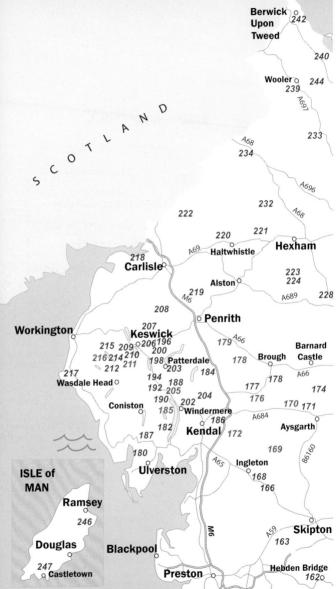

Berwick Upon Tweed 242

240

Wooler 244
239

A697

233

A68
234

A696

232

A68

222

220 221

A69 Haltwhistle

Hexham

218
Carlisle

Alston

223
224

228

219
M6

A689

208

Penrith

207
Keswick

179 A66

Barnard
Castle

215 209 206 196
200

178

Brough

A66

216 214 210
212 211

198 Patterdale
203

184

177 178

174

217
Wasdale Head

194

188
192 205

176

170 171

190 202 204

Coniston

185 Windermere
186

A684

Aysgarth

182

Kendal 172

169

B6160

187

180

A65

Ingleton

168

166

Ulverston

M6

A59

Skipton

163

ISLE of
MAN

Ramsey
246

Blackpool

Hebden Bridge
162

Douglas

247 Castletown

Preston

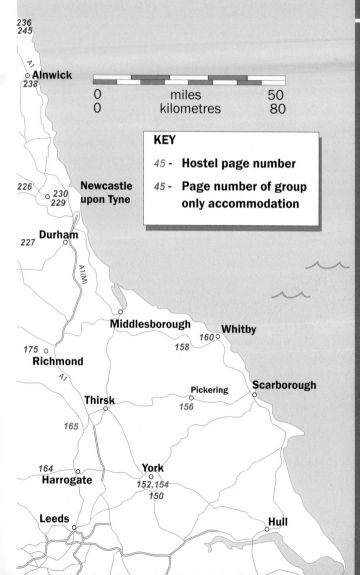

236
245

A1

238

Alnwick

0   miles   50
0   kilometres   80

KEY

45 - **Hostel page number**

45 - **Page number of group only accommodation**

226

230
229

Newcastle upon Tyne

227

Durham

A1(M)

Middlesborough

160

Whitby

158

175

Richmond

A1

Scarborough

Pickering

156

Thirsk

165

164

Harrogate

York

152, 154
150

Leeds

Hull

Y M C A CORNWALL
(PENZANCE)
ENGLAND

West Cornwall is famous for its rugged coastlines, secret coves and long sandy beaches. It offers the chance to relax and unwind, to surf, walk, deep sea dive, horse ride and to visit galleries, small harbours and villages. There are many attractions such as the famous Minack open air theatre.

The YMCA is more than just a hostel, it offers sporting and conference facilities as well as an internet café. The facilities provide the ideal location for school/ youth groups of any size, for short weekends or for longer holidays. The YMCA has been serving the community of Penwith since 1893, providing an ideal base for you to discover all the area has to offer.

Now available: Isle of Scilly parking from just £3.50 a day!!

DETAILS

- **Open** - All year, 8am to 10pm (except by prior arrangement)
- **Number of beds** - 54:
- **Booking** - booking not essential but advisable in Summer
- **Price per night** - Dorm from £15pp, single from £20, twin from £18pp, family rooms from £42. Discount for parties of 15+. 10% discount for students in dormitories.
- **Public Transport** - Penzance train station 15 min walk. Penzance bus station bus service numbers 6A and 6B. Taxi from Penzance centre approx £3.
- **Directions** - From the train / bus stations, turn left towards the centre of town onto Market Jew Street. Turn left and follow Market Jew Street until it becomes Alverton Road. Go straight over the roundabout until you see our sign on the left (approx 200m).

CONTACT: Reception Team
International House, The Orchard, Alverton, Penzance, TR18 4TE
Tel: 01736 334820
penzanceadmin@ymcacornwall.org.uk www.ymcacornwall.org.uk

PENZANCE
BACKPACKERS

ENGLAND

Penzance, with its mild climate, its wonderful location looking across to spectacular St Michael's Mount, with all the coach and rail services terminating here, is the ideal base for exploring the far SW of England and the Scilly Isles.

Whether you are looking for sandy beaches and sheltered coves, the storm lashed cliffs of Land's End, sub-tropical gardens, internationally acclaimed artists, the remains of ancient cultures, or simply somewhere to relax and take time out, Penzance Backpackers is for you. Situated in a lovely tree-lined road close to the sea front, with the town centre, bus station and railway station only a short walk away. Accommodation is mostly in small bunk-bedded rooms with bed-linen. Fully equipped self-catering kitchen, hot showers, comfortable lounge, lots of local information and a warm welcome all included.

DETAILS

■ **Open** - All year, 24 hours
■ **Number of beds** - 30: 2 double, 1x 4 (double + 2 bunks), 3x6, 1x7.
■ **Booking** - It's best to email or phone.
■ **Price per night** - From £16 per person.
■ **Public Transport** - Penzance has a train station and National Express service. 15 mins walk from train/bus station or catch buses 1, 1a, 5a or 6a from Tourist Information/bus/train station. Ask for top of Alexandra Road.
■ **Directions** - From Tourist Information/bus/train station either follow Quay and Promenade to mini-roundabout, turn right up Alexandra Rd, we are a short way up on the left; or follow main road through town centre until second mini-roundabout, turn left down Alexandra Rd; we are on right.

CONTACT:
The Blue Dolphin, Alexandra Road, Penzance, TR18 4LZ
Tel: 01736 363836
info@pzbackpack.com www.pzbackpack.com

THE OLD CHAPEL
BACKPACKERS

Zennor is a small picturesque village situated between St Ives and Land's End and is a haven for walkers, bird watchers and anyone who wants a taste of the rural way of life or just simply to relax! The hostel is located very close to the pub and St Ives is nearby for shopping, clubbing, cinemas, restaurants and some of the finest beaches in Cornwall.

The Old Chapel Backpackers has been converted to a very high standard and is perfectly situated for clear views over the sea and moorland. They have four rooms that sleep six people, one room that sleeps four and a family room with double bed. There are washbasins in every room and the hostel is centrally heated throughout. They can offer self-catering and can provide breakfast, packed lunches and evening meals if required. There is also a café on the premises serving delicious soup, rolls and cakes

DETAILS

- **Open** - All year (winter by prior arrangement), 10am - 9am
- **Number of beds** - 32: 4 x 6 : 1 x 4 : 1 x family room
- **Booking** - Booking is advisable, 50% deposit
- **Price per night** - From £18.50 per person all year
- **Public Transport** - There are train stations at St Ives (4 miles) and Penzance (10 miles). Local buses run to/from St Ives every few hours. The taxi fare from St Ives is approximately £8.
- **Directions** - Approximately 4 miles from St Ives on Coastal Road heading towards Land's End.

CONTACT:
Zennor, St Ives, Cornwall, TR26 3DA
Tel: 01736 798307
zennorbackpackers@btinternet.com www.zennorbackpackers.net

LOWER PENDERLEATH ¹⁵
FARM HOSTEL

Lower Penderleath Farm Hostel provides self catering accommodation in four twin rooms and a family maisonette, five miles from penzance. An additional room with an alpine sleeping platform for 12 will be available from Easter 2012. All the rooms are private and lockable, three rooms have single beds and the forth has a bunk bed. The hostel has a fully equipped kitchen with all crockery and utensils provided. There is a dining room adjoining the kitchen and plenty of showers and toilets. Heating in the common areas is by oil filled radiators and drying racks are provided. The self contained family maisonette has a small equipped kitchen and private shower and toilet. The water on site is natural mineral water defined in 1989 and sold as bottled mineral water. Now visitors can cook, drink and shower in it. There is a picturesque footpath to the village of Cripples Ease which has a pub which serves meals and is only a ten minutes walk. The village of Halsetown with its own pub is also reachable on foot.

DETAILS

■ **Open** - Easter to October inclusive , Open all day (except kitchen at some times)
■ **Number of beds** - 12 (24 from Easter 2012) : 4x2 plus 1x4 self contained family maisonette. Alpine platform providing 12 sleeping matts available from Easter 2012.
■ **Booking** - Phone to book. Pay on arrival.
■ **Price per night** - £12.50 per person. £25 for twin room. £50 for Maisonette. Key deposit of £20 refunded after inspection.
■ **Public Transport** - Local busses pass the road end three quarters of a miles from the hostel. Service runs four times a day between St Ives and Penzance.
■ **Directions** - Pass Penderleath camping park on left and 300m further on right hand side you will find Lower Penderleath Farm and Hostel.

CONTACT: Russell Rogers
Lower Penderleath Farm, Towednack, St.Ives, Cornwall, TR26 3AF
Tel: 0772 3014567
rusrogers@hotmail.com www.lowerpencampsite.4t.com

FALMOUTH
BACKPACKERS

Falmouth's beautiful natural harbour provides a picturesque background to the main street of charming shops, restaurants, cafés and pubs. Voted the 2nd best coastal town, Falmouth is renowned for its sandy beaches, Pendennis Castle, exotic gardens, Arts Centre and the Princess Pavilion. Go sightseeing on ferries to St Mawes, Truro, Flushing and the Helford Passage. On a rainy day visit National Maritime Museum and the Ships and Castle leisure pool. Take advantage of watersports, fishing trips, sailing, diving, with tuition and equipment hire. New owner Judi has moved back from Grenada in the West Indies, to take over Falmouth Lodge. Judi welcomes guests to enjoy all Cornwall has to offer and has added her own character and flavour to the hostel. Relaxed, friendly and clean, Falmouth Lodge Backpackers is just two minutes walk from the Blue Flag beach of Gyllyngvase and the South West Coast Path and eight minutes walk into town and the harbour. Free Wi-Fi and internet facilities. Free parking. No curfew. Complimentary tea, coffee and breakfast. Well-equipped kitchen and cosy lounge with TV/DVD and games.

DETAILS

- **Open** - All year, , 9am to 12pm and 5pm to 10pm
- **Number of beds** - 21: 1 x 2/3; 2 x 4/5; 1 x 6/7; 1 double en suite (some seaviews)
- **Booking** - Telephone or email in advance. Walk-ins also welcomed.
- **Price per night** - From £19 per person
- **Public Transport** -   Train - change at Truro for Falmouth Town Station 250 mtrs. National Express to Falmouth. By air - London Stansted/Gatwick to Newquay
- **Directions** - On A39 look for Gyllyngvase Rd on right, then left to Gyllyngvase Ter.

CONTACT: Judi
9 Gyllyngvase Terrace, Falmouth, Cornwall, TR11 4DL
Tel: 01326 319996, mobile 07525 722808
judi@falmouthlodge.co.uk www.falmouthbackpackers.co.uk

GRANARY
BARN / BACKPACKERS

Objective; quality accommodation at low cost.

Nantrisack Farm is on the B3302 holiday route, midway between Penzance and Lizard. The accommodation consists of a dormitory equipped with 8 new beds, sleeping bags can be hired (advise in advance). There is heating, toilet with H&C basin, shower room and communal kitchen with dining / lounge. There is a secure bike store / drying room, huge parking & BBQ area. B&B accommodation is also available.

The location is minutes from the beach at Portleven (surfing / shops / restaurants / pubs), Helston (Lidl store / pubs / restaurants). Pub up the road. Transport to and from Portleven and Helston - by arrangement and subject to availability. Receive a friendly welcome, access to a wealth of local knowledge and a commitment to make your stay one to remember for all the right reasons.

DETAILS

- **Open** - All year, all day
- **Number of beds** - 8
- **Booking** - Essential - call to check availability (24 hrs)
- **Price per night** - £7.50 per person. B&B with continental breakfast £15 per person.
- **Public Transport** - Train & bus stations; Camborne, Redruth and Penzance.
- **Directions** - Next to Sithney Primary School. GR OS Map 103 SW 638 298 on the B3302

CONTACT: Tom
Nantrisack Farm, Sithney, Helston, TR13 0AE
Tel: Mobile 07740 514188 (24hrs)
thomas-martin1@sky.com

Tregedna Lodge offers comfortable, spacious accommodation . The Lodge has been converted to a high standard, yet keeping much of its originial charm and character. There are 24 bedspaces in a range of five bedrooms - single occupancy or shared, You can book a little space or the whole lot. All the facilities have disabled access and include; a shared fully equipped kitchen and open dining area, a relaxing lounge with comfy chairs, laundry room with coin operated washer/dryer, separate showers and toilets. Bed linen is provided and towels are available to hire. There is ample parking for cars and boats and a secure area for bikes etc. The South West Coastal footpath is adjacent for walks with spectacular views and Maenporth beach, only half a mile away, offers a safe,clean,sandy beach. Nearby Falmouth has a wide range of restaurants, pubs, places of interest, ideally located to explore the many delights of Cornwall. Tregedna Lodge has a 4-star grading by Visit England.

DETAILS

- **Open** - All year, all day (please phone between 9am-8pm)
- **Number of beds** - 24: 1x8,1x6,1x2, 2x4 / family (double bed and bunk bed)
- **Booking** - Booking essential. 25% deposit.
- **Price per night** - £20pp in dormitory style rooms, Family rooms £50.
- **Public Transport** -   Trains at Falmouth (1.5 miles). Buses run past Tregedna hourly during summer months, less frequently during winter months.
- **Directions** - By car from Truro take the A39 to Falmouth. At the ASDA roundabout go straight across. At the Hillhead roundabout turn right, go straight over the next two roundabouts and continue on this road for approx 2 miles.Tregedna is on your right.

CONTACT: Liz
Tregedna Farm, Maenporth, Falmouth, Cornwall, TR11 5HL
Tel: 01326 250529
tregednafarm@btinternet.com www.tregednafarmholidays.co.uk/lodge.html

PORTHTOWAN
BACKPACKERS

For low budget accommodation near Porthtowan, look no further! Porthtowan Backpackers is a small, friendly, family-run place, ideal for surfers, body boarders, walkers, backpackers and students. On Cornwall's North Coast, it is only 300 yds from a Blue Flag beach, one of the best for surfing in Cornwall. At high tide there's lots of sand and at low tide you can walk to Chapel Porth, St. Agnes with a really nice cliff walk back to Porthtowan. Shops and bars are a short walk away. Accommodation comprises a 6 bed room, 4 bed room, double room, and a family room with single bed and triple sleeper (single bunk above a double bed). All rooms en suite. Also: a communal lounge with 32" TV and kitchenette; storage for surf boards and wetsuits; car parking; roof deck for sunbathing and a barbeque area. Pre-arranged pick-ups from train station £5.

DETAILS

- **Open** - All year, all day
- **Number of beds** - 16-19 : 1x6, 1x4, 1x2, en suite family room for 4 + futon settee bunk bed in lounge for larger groups (all rooms en suite).
- **Booking** - Booking is advised by phone or email, with booking fee.
- **Price per night** - Shared room: £21.50pp (4th April to 30 Sept), off peak £18.50pp. 4 nights Mon to Fri £75pp (£66 off peak). Double room: £26pp (£20.50 off peak); 4 nights Mon to Fri £90 (£75 off peak). Family room £82. Continental breakfast included. Sole use available for minimum of 2 days.
- **Public Transport** - Trains at Redruth (4 miles). Buses to village from Truro (Hopleys). Airport at Newquay , (Fly-be, Skybus, Lufthansa, Bmibaby).Taxis available.
- **Directions** - In the centre of Porthtowan village, between Newquay and St Ives.

CONTACT:
Porthtowan Backpackers, Seamyst, Beach Road, Porthtowan, TR4 8AA
Tel: 01209 891697, Fax: 01209 891697
info@porthtowanbackpackers.co.uk   www.sicklamelazy.co.uk

Newquay is about having fun - and the fun starts here! The Lodge has been open for fifteen years and still offers the same easy-going relaxed atmosphere. Newquay is an all year round mecca for surfers, students and travellers, with dramatic cliffs, idyllic beaches and attractions galore. The backpackers is situated at the highest point of the town, only five minutes walk from Central Square with its night life and shops. Fistral Beach and the Town beaches are all within ten minutes walk. All the rooms are clean and comfortable, many with sea view or en suite facilities. Rates include breakfast, tea /coffee all day and unlimited hot showers. There is a fully equipped kitchen, WiFi, no curfews, a licensed bar which has good music and 100s of DVDs, plus a games room with pool table and other games.

Free car park and secure surfboard and bike storage.

DETAILS

- **Open** - All year, 24 hours
- **Number of beds** - 49: 4 x 6 : 3 x 4 : 1 x 3 : 5 x twin/double
- **Booking** - Recommended for weekends and peak season, but not essential. First night's fee required as deposit.
- **Price per night** - From £10pp (or £12.50 for en suite sea view). From £15pp July, August and bank holidays. £45 per week available from September to June.
- **Public Transport** - Local train and bus station. Free pickup when available.
- **Directions** - From coach station walk up St George's Rd, turn right at top. From train station turn left and left again opposite Victoria Hotel onto Berry Rd which leads onto Mount Wise

CONTACT: Matt
110 Mount Wise, Newquay, Cornwall, TR7 1QP
Tel: 01637 874651
matt@surflodge.co.uk www.surflodge.co.uk

NEWQUAY SILVER
SPRAY LODGE

Newquay Silver Spray Lodge is located in the heart of Newquay, only two minutes walk from the town centre, with its pubs, clubs, surf shops, supermarket and take-aways. What's more it's a stone's throw from three great surf beaches - Towan, Great Western and Tolcarne.

The lodge has clean and comfortable dormitories and private rooms accommodating two to twelve people, four of these are en suite. All beds come with quilts, pillows and fitted sheets, but towels are not supplied. All guests have their own keys to the front door and room door and so are free to come and go as they please, with no curfew. A light breakfast which includes tea/coffee, fruit juice, cereals and toast is available free of charge every morning between 8:30am and 10:30am. Other facilities include safe secure storage for surfboards and wetsuits, a garden with barbeque, drying facilities and use of the kitchen between 8.30am and 9pm.

DETAILS

- **Open** - All year, 24 hours
- **Number of beds** - 38: 1x12,1x6, 4x4, 2x dbl
- **Booking** - Book with a deposit, online or by phone
- **Price per night** - From £16pp (£18 en suite) at low season rising through many stages to £27pp (£30) at peak times. Prices include a light breakfast and bed linen.
- **Public Transport** - Train station and coach station only 5 minutes walk away.
- **Directions** - Trebarwith Crescent joins directly onto East St (the main steet for shops, pubs etc.)

CONTACT: Reception
9 Trebarwith Crescent, Newquay, Cornwall, TR7 1DX
Tel: 01637 440031 / 07766 950212
Info@newquaysilverspray.com www.newquaysilverspray.com

Owned and managed by the National Trust, Beach Head Bunkhouse is a converted barn in a stunning coastal location (8 miles from Newquay and 5 from Padstow) providing comfortable accommodation for up to 14 people.

The South West Coast Path is just a few hundred yards away and the bunkhouse provides a perfect base for outdoor activities with beautiful scenery, high cliffs, glorious sandy beaches and moor land areas all nearby.

There are two externally accessed dormitories, each sleeping 6 in bunk beds, both with adjoining single-bedded leader's rooms. Mattresses are provided but visitors must bring sleeping bags, blanket and pillows. Below each dormitory is a washroom with showers, toilets and hand basins. There is a large common room on the ground floor, with a multi-fuel stove (logs not provided) and comfortable seating. Fully equipped kitchen with cooker, fridge and freezer, and a laundry with drying racks. Heated throughout with night storage heaters.

DETAILS

- **Open** - All year, 24 hours
- **Number of beds** - 14: 2x6, 2x1
- **Booking** - Booking essential with deposit. Booking address is: Old Farmhouse, Pentireglaze, St Minver, Wadebridge, Cornwall, PL27 6QY
- **Price per night** - £160 per night, Mon -Thurs. £180 per night, Fri - Sun.Contact for minimum stay requirements. Non refundable deposit £100.
- **Public Transport** - By rail: to Newquay Station approx 8 miles away. No bus from station. Newquay Airport approx 5 miles (details: www.newquaycornwallairport.com)
- **Directions** - Grid Ref SW 852708. Just off the B3276 8 miles N of Newquay.

CONTACT:
Park Head, St Eval, Wadebridge, Cornwall, PL27 7UU
Tel: 01208 863046, Fax: 01208 862805
Margaret.hosegood@nationaltrust.org.uk www.nationaltrust.org.uk/basecamps

PLYMOUTH
UNIVERSITY

From late June to early September Plymouth University offers low cost accommodation within the heart of Plymouth, a modern vibrant city with a fantastic waterfront. There are no single supplement charges or minimum night's stay. Self-catering accommodation offers double and single en suite rooms with a fully equipped kitchen. Room only offers single rooms with wash basins, arranged in flats containing 6 bedrooms with a shared shower, toilet and kitchen (no kitchen equipment is supplied). See website for details of 'special offers'. Breakfast is available Mon-Fri in one of the on-campus cafés with a wide choice of cooked and continental items or pastries and coffees to go. Free gym membership, free internet access and free use of cycle and wet room storage are included with the room rate.

DETAILS

- **Open** - 22nd June to 3rd September ,
- **Number of beds** - 100s of rooms
- **Booking** - Book online or by email, or phone (Mon-Fri 0900-1630).
- **Price per night** - Room only: £20, Self-catering £32.50 (single en suite), £25.00 (Single Standard), £56.00 (double en suite). Weekly rates available. Breakfast available Mon-Fri £5.85 (8 item breakfast).
- **Public Transport** - Reception is under a mile from train station and bus station.
- **Directions** - From the A38 follow signs to the city centre and university. At Charles Church roundabout take the 3rd exit to Hampton Street, turn left to Regent Street, then first right into Gibbon Street. Student village reception is on the right. Directions available from www.plymouth.ac.uk/location.

CONTACT:
Summer Village Recep.,University of Plymouth,Drake Circus,Plymouth,PL4 8BT
Tel: 01752 588599, Fax: 01752 588982
summeraccommodation@plymouth.ac.uk   www.plymouth.ac.uk/summeraccommodation

PLYMOUTH
GLOBE BACKPACKERS

Globe Backpackers Plymouth is located just five minutes walk from the ferry port, where boats leave for Roscoff and Santander. The hostel is close to all amenities and a short stroll to the famous Barbican waterfront, Mayflower Steps and city centre. Also near to the bus and railway stations. Excursions to Dartmoor, canoeing on the Tamar River, local boat trips, sailing and walking the coastal paths can be arranged from Plymouth. The theatre, sports/leisure centre, ice-skating rink and National Aquarium are a short walk from the hostel.

Globe Backpackers Plymouth has 4, 6 and 8 bedded dorms, plus 2 double rooms. Bedding and linen are included in the price. Fully equipped self-catering kitchen, TV lounge, separate social room and courtyard garden. Free WiFi. Free tea and coffee. Brits and Overseas all need to produce valid ID.

DETAILS

- **Open** - All year, reception 3.30-11pm, less in winter. No curfew.
- **Number of beds** - 38
- **Booking** - Phone ahead to secure booking
- **Price per night** - From £16pp. Weekly rates available. 50p surcharge for cards.
- **Public Transport** - National Express, local buses and various rail networks.
- **Directions** - From train station walk up Saltash Road to North Croft roundabout, turn right along Western Approach to Pavilions on your left. From bus station walk up Exeter Street, across roundabout to Royal Parade, cross road to Union Street, Pavilions on your left. From Plymouth Pavilions walk towards the Hoe, turn left up Citadel Road, the hostel is in 100 metres on the right hand side.

CONTACT:
172 Citadel Road, The Hoe, Plymouth, PL1 3BD
Tel: 01752 225158
info@plymouthbackpackers.co.uk www.plymouthbackpackers.co.uk

Harford Bunkhouse & Camping offers comfortable budget accommodation on the edge of South Dartmoor. An ideal choice if you are planning to start the Two Moors Way walk from south to north.

Run alongside a working Dartmoor farm, the bunkhouse offers dormitory style accommodation with bunk beds in each of the rooms. A kitchen, large seating area, toilets and showers are also within the bunkhouse.

The camp site is divided between two of our meadows. Campers can use the toilets and showers located within the camping barns' buildings and small campfires and bbqs are allowed at our discretion. Facilities include a wash up area, drying room, laundry facilities and disabled access.

Children and dogs welcome.

DETAILS

- **Open** - All year, Open all hours
- **Number of beds** - 40-50 beds
- **Booking** - Phone or email.
- **Price per night** - From £12pp
- **Public Transport** - Yes, train or bus nearby
- **Directions** - From Ivybridge take Harford Road, Bunkhouse is 1.5 miles from Ivybridge in The Dartmoor National Park.

CONTACT: Julie Cole
West Combeshead, Harford, Ivybridge, Devon, Pl210JG
Tel: 01752691883 or 07968566218
julie.cole6@btinternet.com www.harfordbunkhouse.com

DARTMOOR
EXPEDITION CENTRE

Great for walking, climbing, canoeing, caving, archaeology, painting or visiting places of interest nearby. Dartmoor Expedition Centre has two 300-year-old barn bunkhouses' with cobbled floors and thick granite walls.

Simple but comfortable accommodation for groups,with bunk beds and a wood burning stove, radiant heaters (two in each area) and night storage heating (one in each barn). Kitchen area equipped with 2 fridges, water heater, electric stoves and kettles. All crockery and pans provided, and there is freezer space available. Electric appliances are coin operated (£1 coins). Solar hot water system for free showers in wash rooms. House Barn has the living area downstairs and upstairs sleeps 9 plus 5 in an inner cubicle. Gate Barn sleeps 11 downstairs and 10 upstairs. There are two upgraded rooms (1 double, 1 twin). Beds provided with sheet/pillow/pillowcase, sleeping bags needed.

DETAILS

- **Open** - All year, , 7.30 am to 10.30 pm
- **Number of beds** - 37: 1 x 1 : 1 x 2 : 1 x 8 : 1 x 5 : 1 x 11 : 1 x 10
- **Booking** - Book in advance with 25% deposit.
- **Price per night** - £14 pp (£16 in upgraded room).
- **Public Transport** -   Newton Abbot is the nearest train station. In summer there are buses to Widecombe (1.5 miles from hostel). Taxi fare from station £30.
- **Directions** - GR 700 764. Come down Widecombe Hill into the village. Turn right 200yds after school and travel up a steep hill past Southcombe onto the open moor. Continue for one mile until you reach crossroads. Turn right and take first left after 400yds. Hostel is 200yds on left.

CONTACT: John Earle
Widecombe-in-the-Moor, Newton Abbot, Devon, TQ13 7TX
Tel: 01364 621249
earle@clara.co.uk www.dartmoorbase.co.uk

FOX TOR
CAFÉ AND BUNKHOUSE

Princetown in Dartmoor is an ideal base for anyone wishing to spend time on Dartmoor whether it is to walk, climb, cycle, kayak or just relax and enjoy the spectacular scenery. Fox Tor Café Bunkhouse is situated near the centre of the village and offers self-catering accommodation for up to 12, in 3 rooms of 4. It is newly decorated, has central heating and a kitchen equipped with microwave, fridge, kettle, toaster and sink. There are separate male and female showers and toilets with under-floor heating. Bunkhouse guests have the option to use the drying room / store room (big enough for bicycles) and can book packed lunches and breakfasts for an early start. The Cafe has Wifi, a wood burning stove and hosts seasonal events and activities such as Christmas wreath making. Guided walks and off road mountain biking are available and outdoor adventure holidays can be arranged to your requirements. Contact Abbie or Dave for more details.

DETAILS

- **Open** - All year, all day. Arrive from 4.30pm, leave by 10.30am.
- **Number of beds** - 12: 3 x 4
- **Booking** - Advisable with 50% deposit.
- **Price per night** - From £10.00 per person. Sole use £110.00.
- **Public Transport** - Trains at Exeter and Plymouth. Devon Bus 98 Tavistock-Princetown. Devon Bus 82 Exeter-Plymouth. First 272 Gunnislake-Newton Abbot.
- **Directions** - GR 591 735. Just off the mini roundabout in the centre of Princetown on the Two Bridges road (B3212). 20 mins drive from Tavistock, 15 mins Yelverton, 35 mins Ashburton.

CONTACT: Abbi or Dave
Two Bridges Road, Princetown, Dartmoor, Devon, PL20 6QS
Tel: 01822 890238
enquiries@foxtorcafe.com www.foxtorcafe.co.uk

Tavistock Bunkhouse is situated in the centre of Tavistock, nestled into the Dartmoor Hills close to the Tamar Valley, an area of outstanding natural beauty.

The bunkhouse is within easy reach of the Devon Coast-to-Coast Cycle Route and the Tavi Woodlands Downhill Mountain Bike Trails. It is a perfect destination to stop over if you are walking the coastal path, or to use as a base while you take part in outdoor activities in Dartmoor from canoeing to cycling and climbing.

The bunkhouse is located in the grounds of the Union Pub which offers breakfast, packed lunches and dinner in addition to a meeting room and pool table. The self-contained hostel accommodation includes three separate bunk rooms, sleeping up to 20 people, a drying room, toilet and shower facilities, a secure cycle storage area and a "wash down" area for cleaning muddy bikes.

Bedding & Towels are provided.

DETAILS

- **Open** - All year, all times
- **Number of beds** - 20
- **Booking** - Recommended
- **Price per night** - £20 pp. £25 pp with breakfast.
- **Public Transport** - Trains at Plymouth. Buses to Plymouth every 30 mins.
- **Directions** - From centre of Tavistock head up West Street (past the Church on the left). Take third turning on right onto King Street, bunkhouse is 200 yards on left.

CONTACT: Francis Jasper
The Union, King Street, Tavistock, Devon, PL19 ODS
Tel: 01822 613115
info@tavistockbunkhouse.co.uk   www.tavistockbunkhouse.co.uk

GALFORD SPRINGS
HOLIDAY FARM

Galford Springs Holiday Accommodation is situated in rural Devon on a 300 acre farm nestled in the Lew Valley, overlooking some of England's most stunning scenery. It is ideal for families, groups, schools and clubs.

Situated next to a 17th century Devon longhouse the hostel is a recent conversion and contained within the same building is a free-to-use 15m indoor swimming pool. The main area is large and ideal for holding meetings and events as the furniture can be moved into a variety of configurations. This area also contains bunkbeds for 10 people and a sofa bed for two. In addition there are two en suite double bedrooms. The hostel features all modern conveniences including a pool table and table tennis. Outside there is a basket ball and barbeque area. Breakfasts at the hostel are available by arrangement. Also available in the farmhouse is B&B in three double rooms, two en suite.

DETAILS

- **Open** - All year,
- **Number of beds** - 16: 1x10, 2x2 (double beds) & sofa bed (sleeping 2)
- **Booking** - Recommended
- **Price per night** - £15 pp. Minimum charge of £85 (6 persons or less). B&B £30pp.
- **Public Transport** - Bus route to Lewdown village which is about one and half miles from accommodation on the old A30.
- **Directions** - Turn left of A30 at Sourton Services. Turn right at end of slip road then immediately left towards Lewdown. Follow for 6 miles then turn left, signposted Chillaton. After reaching Lewtrenchard Manor, turn left and further down the road take the right turn to Lew Mill. Turn left at T junction, Galford Springs is on the right.

CONTACT: Mr F. Harding
Galford Farm, Lewdown, Okehampton, Devon, EX20 4PL
Tel: 01566 783264
claire_taylor1@btconnect.com   www.galfordsprings.co.uk

Torquay is on the English Riviera, famous for warm weather and Mediterranean atmosphere. Turquoise sea, red cliffs, long sandy beaches and secret shingle coves combine to create one of the UK's most beautiful coastlines. Torquay is renowned as a watersport mecca with sailing, water-skiing, windsurfing, diving and night life with pubs, clubs and restaurants a mere stagger from the hostel.

The hostel is in the heart of Torquay. Hostel activities include beach barbecues, cable TV, zorbing, international food nights and DVD evenings. There are also trips to Dartmoor exploring emerald river valleys where pixies dwell and the open tor-dotted moors. The hostel offers travellers a friendly, almost family atmosphere.

Those who find it hard to leave can easily find work.

DETAILS

- **Open** - Open all year, check in 9am-3pm and 6-9pm.
- **Number of beds** - 50: 1 x 12, 1 x 8, 1 x 6, 5 x 4, 1 x 2, 2 x pods.
- **Booking** - Advised at all times.
- **Price per night** - From £10per person.
- **Public Transport** - Torquay can be reached by coach or train from all major towns. From London take a train from Paddington/Waterloo or a coach from Victoria/Heathrow.
- **Directions** - Drivers: follow signs to sea front. Turn left. At junction with lights and Belgrave Hotel, bear left up Sheddon Hill. Next T junction is Abbey Road. Turn left. Hostel is 200m on right.

CONTACT: The Manager
119 Abbey Road, Torquay, Devon, TQ2 5NP
Tel: 01803 299924   Mob: 07912 426252
torquaybackpackers@yahoo.co.uk www.torquaybackpackers.co.uk

SPARROWHAWK
BACKPACKERS

Sparrowhawk is a small, friendly eco-hostel located within the breathtaking Dartmoor National Park. The hostel is situated in the village centre of Moretonhampstead, 14 miles west of Exeter and can be reached easily by frequent direct bus. Accommodation is in a beautifully converted, fully equipped stable. High open moorland is close by for great hiking, cycling and off-road mountain biking, while the rocky tors rising up on the hilltops offer climbers a challenge. Wild swims in the rivers amongst woodlands or out on the moor are a must for the adventurous traveller. Magnificent stone circles, dwellings and burial sites of ancient civilizations together with wild ponies, buzzards, flora and fauna are all here to be explored. Moretonhampstead has shops, cafés, pubs, good food, live music and an outdoor heated swimming pool. Dartmoor Way and CTC End2End cycle routes are on the doorstep. Sparrowhawk has solar-heated showers, waste recycling, a secure bike shed and a bus stop nearby.

DETAILS

- **Open** - All year, all day
- **Number of beds** - 18: 1 x 14 plus double / family room
- **Booking** - Book ahead if possible by phone or email.
- **Price per night** - Adults £17. Under 14 £8. Double/family room £38/ £8 per child.
- **Public Transport** - Direct from Exeter Bus 359, indirect 178. From Okehampton or Newton Abbot Bus 173 or 179. Enquires Tel 0870 6082608.
- **Directions** - From Exeter, take the B3212 signposted on the one-way system at Exe Bridges. From Plymouth head towards Yelverton and then B3212. The hostel is on Ford Street (A382) 100 metres from tourist office.

CONTACT: Alison
45 Ford Street, Moretonhampstead, Dartmoor, Devon, TQ13 8LN
Tel: 01647 440318 - 07870 513570
ali@sparrowhawkbackpackers.co.uk www.sparrowhawkbackpackers.co.uk

Blytheswood Hostel is a detached wooden chalet in secluded woodland overlooking the Teign Valley on the eastern edge of Dartmoor. It is an ideal base for exploring rugged high Dartmoor and the delightful lower slopes rich in wild flowers, butterflies and birds. The surrounding native woodland and nature reserve are home to badgers, deer and otters. There are walks straight from the door (come and see the daffodils in spring) and fishing, golf and cycling nearby. Local attractions include Castle Drogo, The Miniature Pony Centre, Canonteign Falls and picturesque thatched villages. The cathedral city of Exeter is 8 miles away and the beaches of South Devon are 40 minutes drive. Blytheswood Hostel provides flexible accommodation in cosy rooms sleeping between 2 and 8 people in bunks. It is ideal for use by families and groups who can book sole use of the whole hostel. There is a fully equipped self catering kitchen, lounge/ dining room, drying room and picnic areas. Duvets and linen provided.

DETAILS

- **Open** - All year, reception open 8-10.30am and 5-8pm (hostel is closed between 10.30am and 5pm, unless arranged).
- **Number of beds** - 24: 1x2, 2x4,1x6,1x8
- **Booking** - Booking is essential. Deposit required.
- **Price per night** - £14pp. Children under 18 £8. Whole hostel £200 per night.
- **Public Transport** - Trains Exeter. Bus 359 from Exeter + 82 on summer wknds
- **Directions** - On the B3212 between Exeter and Moretonhampstead, 1mile outside Dunsford. Approx 100m from Steps Bridge, opposite car park. Please use car park when staying at the hostel.

CONTACT: Patrick and Tracey
Steps Bridge, Dunsford, Exeter, Devon, EX6 7EQ
Tel: 01647 252435
blytheswood@blueyonder.co.uk www.blytheswood.co.uk

EXETER
GLOBE BACKPACKERS

A city centre hostel within easy walk of the beautiful old port, Cathedral, shopping district and a wonderful mix of pubs, clubs, live music, restaurants and café scene. Great for the young and "young at heart" who enjoy a vibrant city centre. Twenty minutes drive to Exmouth with its 2 mile sandy beach for all sail sports, and the same to Dartmoor National Park for walking, climbing, cycling and horse riding. Exeter is also an excellent place to find work and just 2½ hours by train to London. The Globe has some new private rooms. In addition to male, female and mixed dorms there are three large double rooms with additional bunks, sitting area, tea/coffee making facilities, hairdryer and towels. One of these can be used as a twin room and another has a four poster bed. Free WiFi to all guests with laptops. Not suitable for hen and stag groups, DSS, unaccompanied under 18s and families. ID required from everyone.

DETAILS

- **Open** - All year. , Check in 3.30 -11pm only, closed 12 - 3.30pm, check out 8.30 -11am, earlier by arrangement
- **Number of beds** - 42:dorms: 1x10, 1x8, 2x6, private rms 3x4- can use as dbl/twin.
- **Booking** - To secure booking phone ahead.
- **Price per night** - From £17.50pp, Weekly rates from £75pp. Private rooms from £42 (2 sharing), £75 (4 sharing) 50p charge for cards.
- **Public Transport** - National Express, local bus companies and rail networks.
- **Directions** - Bus Station: Cross road, take side turning Southernhay East. Stay on LH side until Southgate Hotel. We are diagonally opposite on other side of junction. From Central Station go down Queen St to High St, turn right and at 1st lights turn left onto South St. Continue to junct. at bottom of hill. Cross at lights, we are on right.

CONTACT:
71 Holloway Street, Exeter, EX2 4JD
Tel: 01392 215521, Fax:
info@exeterbackpackers.co.uk www.exeterbackpackers.co.uk

A relaxed place with a variety of bedrooms and large garden.

Close to town, beaches and South West Coastal Path.

No stag groups please. An ideal base to see the South West's attractions: The Eden Project, Tintagel Castle, The Tamar Lakes, Dartmoor and Bodmin Moor. There are competition standard surfing beaches nearby. Families with children aged over 5 welcome. Meet old friends or make new ones, on the deck, in the lounge or around the dining room table after cooking up a storm in the fully fitted kitchen. You can make your stay whatever you want it to be.

DETAILS

- **Open** - All year except Christmas week, 8.30am to 1pm and 4.30pm to 10.30pm
- **Number of beds** - 39: 2x6 : 4x4 : 1x3 : 1x2 : 3xdbl
- **Booking** - Advisable, credit card secures booking. Photo ID at check in. (Groups 6 or more by prior booking) No stag groups . At least one Adult (18+)per booking.
- **Price per night** - From £14pp dorm rooms (single night supplement)
- **Public Transport** - To Bude: From Exeter Via Okehampton X9. From Plymouth X8. From Newquay X10 (changing at Okehampton). From Bideford 85. All buses- First Bus Company. There are train and bus links from London to Exeter.
- **Directions** - From A39, head into Bude down Stratton Rd past Morrisons on your right, follow the road down past Esso garage. Take the second road on the right, Killerton Road (before the Bencollen Pub). Continue up to the top of the road and Northshorebude is on the corner on your left. Turn into Redwood Grove and parking is the first on the left.

CONTACT: Sean or Janine
57 Killerton Road, Bude, Cornwall, EX23 8EW
Tel: 01288 354256 or 07970 149486
info@northshorebude.com www.northshorebude.com

HARTLAND
CAMPING BARN

Located in an area of outstanding beauty and renovated in 2009, this 200 year old barn offers a full spec self-catering kitchen with dining area in the porch and two hot showers. Hartland Camping Barn has three bedrooms with mattresses for 15 people (bring your own sleeping bag and pillow). There is a mobility shower/WC adjacent to a ground floor sleeping room for disabled people. Ideal for walkers and surfers, the barn is conveniently situated near the South West Coast Path and only 14 miles from the popular seaside town of Bude. This unspoilt part of Devon is rich in rugged coastlines, local shops, museums, RHS gardens, pubs, restaurants and historic sites. For the more active there is a range of local activities such as rock climbing, surfing, golfing and sailing all within a 15 mile radius of the barn. Facilities include: Shared indoor swimming pool, games room, sauna, laundry room, TV lounge, BBQ and picnic benches, on site car parking and WiFi.

DETAILS

- **Open** - All Year,
- **Number of beds** - 15
- **Booking** - Please phone or email
- **Price per night** - £15 pp. £70 p/week. Room for single group - £75 (£350 p/week). Total barn hire - £225 (Fri - Sun) £200 (Mon - Thurs) £1000 p/week.
- **Public Transport** - Local bus (319) running from Barnstable to Hartland. Hourly trains to Barnstable from Exeter.
- **Directions** - From A39 take B3248 and follow signs for Hartland & Stoke, bear left at junction for Lighthouse (still on B3248), 0.5 miles on left is Mettaford Farm drive.

CONTACT: Steve & Sue Hilsdon
Hartland Camping Barn, Mettaford Farm, Hartland, North Devon, EX39 6AL
Tel: 01237 441249
hartlandcampingbarn@hotmail.com www.hartlandcampingbarn.co.uk

ELMSCOTT
HOSTEL

Elmscott, a former victorian school, offers a next-to-nature retreat, surrounded by unspoilt coastline with sea views of Lundy Island.

Great for walking, cycling, surfing and bird watching, there are amazing rock formations and many quiet lanes to explore. The famous fishing village of Clovelly is a few miles away with its cobbled streets and pretty harbour. Also nearby is Hartland Abbey where Sense and Sensibility was filmed. Elmscott is a few minutes walk from the South West Coast Path which passes many spectacular coves and river mouths. The accommodation is in one unit of 20 beds and another of 12. It has mixed dorms, single sex dorms and private rooms. In winter accommodation is only available for groups (up to 35 people). There is a kitchen, a well stocked shop in summer and a games room close by.

DETAILS

- **Open** - All year (winter for groups only), 24 hours
- **Number of beds** - 32 (35 in winter): 1 unit of 20: 2x6, 2x4; 1 unit of 12: 1x6, 1x4, 1x2. Extra 3 bed room available for sole use bookings in winter.
- **Booking** - In summer book direct with the hostel by phone or email. In winter book via the YHA website, or for last minute sole use bookings call the owners.
- **Price per night** - Adult £16 to £20, under 16s £12.50 to £15.50 (discounts for YHA members). Enquire for special prices for groups or longer stays.
- **Public Transport** - Nearest trains Barnstaple (25 miles). Buses from Barnstaple to Hartland (4 miles from hostel). Phone hostel for taxi service.
- **Directions** - The hostel is in the small hamlet of Elmscott 4 miles from the village of Hartland. Grid Ref 231 217.

CONTACT: John & Thirza Goaman
Elmscott, Hartland, Bideford, Devon, EX39 6ES
Tel: 01237 441276, Hostel 01237 441367
john.goa@virgin.net www.elmscott.org.uk

OCEAN
BACKPACKERS

Ocean Backpackers is a clean, homely hostel with a relaxed atmosphere and no curfews. It's situated in a quaint North Devon town built around an ancient fishing harbour. Central to the harbour itself, the bus station, high street, pubs, restaurants and many surfer's favourites; Woolacombe, Croyde and Saunton. Surf's down? Don't despair! Try other local activities such as quad biking, paint balling, kayaking, coasteering, horse riding and mountain biking. Adrenalin not your thing? Then take a trip to Lundy Island (a national marine reserve) and spot rare birds, seals, dolphins and basking sharks. It's wonderful walking country! The coastal path between Woolacombe and Lynton is breathtaking and Exmoor has an abundance of walks through Britain's most spectacular scenery. Hostel facilities include lounge, free internet access, self-catering kitchen, surf board storage and a car park. Ilfracombe has plenty of summer work so why not come and hang out here for a while.

DETAILS

- **Open** - All year, reception 9am-10pm. No curfew.
- **Number of beds** - 44:- 1x8, 5x6, 1 x double, 1 x double & bunk.
- **Booking** - Booking advised but not essential.
- **Price per night** - From £11-£15 in dorm. Double/Twin £30 - £38 per room.
- **Public Transport** - Direct coaches from London Victoria/Heathrow/Plymouth/Exeter. By train take the Tarka line to Barnstaple then bus to Ilfracombe.
- **Directions** - From M5 take A361. From Cornwall take A39 to Barnstaple then follow the signs to Ilfracombe. Ocean Backpackers is by the harbour opposite the bus station. For more detailed directions go to our website and click on directions.

CONTACT: Chris and Abby
29 St James Place, Ilfracombe, Devon, EX34 9BJ
Tel: 01271 867835
info@oceanbackpackers.co.uk www.oceanbackpackers.co.uk

MANORVILLE HOSTEL
YHA WESTWARD HO!

Manorville is situated on the beautiful North Devon coast only three minutes walk from the golden sandy beach in Westward Ho! Here you will receive a genuine and friendly welcome. There is a mixture of 2-7 bed rooms, many en suite and with sea views. The lounge area is in a sun-drenched, light filled conservatory with comfy settees, leading out on to a decked area, where you gaze out to the shimmering bay and Lundy Island. The ultra modern kitchen has brilliant facilities, ideal for cooking for groups, and a dishwasher. The dining room can seat up to 20. Westward Ho! has shops, pubs, fish and chips, locally made ice creams and mouth watering Devonian cream teas. It is on the South West Coastal Path and only four miles from the Tarka Trail bike path. The local beaches are great for learning how to surf / kite surf and the countryside ideal for hiking. Only four miles from Bideford where boats go out to Lundy Island.

DETAILS

- **Open** - 1st April to 31st October, all day
- **Number of beds** - 27: 2x 6/7,1x 4/5, 1x4, 2x2
- **Booking** - Book online, by phone or by email
- **Price per night** - Dorms from £20 adult. Double en suite from £52 per room. £3 discount for YHA members. Reduced rates for children. Special deals from £9.99pp.
- **Public Transport** - Bus stop 200m away with direct buses to Barnstaple and Bideford which have connections on to Exeter for trains.
- **Directions** - From A39 take turn to Westward Ho! Follow until you enter the town one-way route, take the first left (Kingsley Road) and follow this until you turn right. Manorville is situated on the right next to Culloden Guest House.

CONTACT:
1 Manorville, Fosketh Hill, Westward Ho!, Devon, EX39 1UL
Tel: 01237 479766
manorville@talktalk.net www.manorvillehostel.com

YARDE ORCHARD
CAFÉ AND BUNKHOUSE ENGLAND

At the highest point on the popular Tarka Trail off-road cycling and walking route, Yarde Orchard also offers a convivial stopover on the Sustrans Devon Coast to Coast and West Country Way routes. The bunkhouse offers accommodation for up to 14 in two bunk rooms (4 and 6) and a self contained double+2 with shower and toilet, a small self-catering kitchen/dining area, 2 hot showers, 2 toilets and communal seating areas. There are three yurts (2x12ft, 1x20ft) with woodburning stoves as well as camping options – own tents (small backpacking/cycletouring tents only) or our own 2 person ridge tents (4). There is a fire pit and barbecue. Yarde Café offers a hearty menu with an emphasis on local produce and a bar providing Devon ales and ciders. The café is available for breakfast, lunch and supper through the summer and Easter holidays, weekends and half-terms, and can be opened at other times for group bookings.

DETAILS

- **Open** - All year, cafe every day April - October. Weekends November-March
- **Number of beds** - 14: 1x6, 1x4, 1x4 (family)
- **Booking** - Book by phone or email
- **Price per night** - Bunk/sleeping bag £13.50 per night (£9 under 18). Double+2 £48. Exclusive use (max.14 people) £150 1st night, £130 subsequent nights. 12ft yurt £35, 20ft yurt £70, Tent for 2 £15, own tent £6pp.
- **Public Transport** - 118 bus (Barnstaple-Tavistock), alight at Gribble Inn. Trains: Barnstaple station (with cycle hire) then 18 miles along Tarka Trail to Yarde.
- **Directions** - By car: from Great Torrington take A386 towards Hatherleigh. After 2 miles at Gribble (118 bus stops here), take minor right turn signed Petersmarland, Petrockstowe. By bike: Yarde Orchard is located on NCN routes 3 & 27 at East Yarde

CONTACT: David Job
Yarde Orchard, East Yarde, Petersmarland, Torrington, Devon, EX38 8QA
Tel: Cafe: 01805 601778 Evenings: 01805 624007
info@yarde-orchard.co.uk www.yarde-orchard.co.uk

YENWORTHY
LODGE

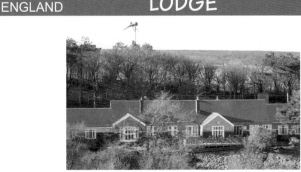

Yenworthy Lodge is situated within Exmoor National Park. It is an ideal location for a variety of sports and leisure activities including walking on Exmoor and the Coast Path, surfing on the region's world famous beaches, mountain biking, riding and fishing, or just relaxing away from it all in the peace of Exmoor with its wonderful wildlife and nature. The centre has excellent facilities: clean and spacious dormitory style bedrooms, a well equipped kitchen, a lovely dining room and eating terrace overlooking the sea, a comfortable lounge, showers and drying rooms. It is ideally suited to large groups. All the accommodation is on one level, with two bedrooms and one bathroom being equipped for special needs. It is surrounded by 6 acres of its own private grounds with woodland, a decked pond area, tepee and yurt (also available for accommodation). Plenty of on site parking is available. We can offer self catering, half board or even full board activity holidays led by our experienced qualified instructors.

DETAILS

- **Open** - Weekends and school holidays, 24 hours
- **Number of beds** - 42: 11 rooms of 2 to 6 beds, plus camping in Yurt and Tepee
- **Booking** - Booking essential. Contact centre for availability.
- **Price per night** - Sole Use. Term time weekends £600 per night. Holiday periods £1750 for Mon-Fri £1950 and Sat-Fri £2500 .VAT and catering extra.
- **Public Transport** - Trains to Tiverton, Barnstaple and Taunton. A local bus runs from Minehead to Yenworthy, and Barnstaple to Lynton and then on to Yenworthy. However we are fairly rural so travel by public transport needs to be well planned.
- **Directions** - Just off to the north of the A39 halfway between Porlock & Lynmouth

CONTACT: Head of Centre
Yenworthy Lodge OEC, Oare, Lynton, EX35 6NY
Tel: 01598 741266, Fax: 01598 741919
admin@yenworthylodge.co.uk   www.yenworthylodge.co.uk

Exmoor Bunkhouse is a converted barn giving comfortable, high standard accommodation. There are 2 large dormitories each sleeping 8 in bunkbeds and a 2 bedded leaders' room. There are excellent hot showers, drying room, lounge/eating area, fully equipped kitchen plus a barbecue and outdoor seating. Environmental awareness is practiced with recycling and composting facilities, and hot water and heating provided by solar energy (with a back-up boiler for those less than sunny days). The Bunkhouse is situated at Countisbury on the North Devon coast. The surrounding countryside includes the dramatic Watersmeet Valleys, moors of Exmoor and coastal paths. Lynton and Lynmouth are the nearest villages and the Atlantic surf beaches are within easy reach. Other local activities include walking, horse riding, boat trips, fishing and cycling. However you spend your time the bunkhouse is ideal for getting away from it all with friends, family or as an organised group.

DETAILS

- **Open** - All year, 24 hours
- **Number of beds** - 18: 2x8, 1x2
- **Booking** - Booking essential with deposit
- **Price per night** - £120 midweek nights, £180 Fri/Sat/Sun nights. £50 for day access after departure. 10% discount for 4+ nights (except Easter, Christmas & New Year). Earn a free nights stay in exchange for a days work with the NT Rangers.
- **Public Transport** - The nearest train and coach stations are in Barnstaple (approx. 20 miles), from there take a local bus to Lynton. Buses to Countisbury are very limited and summer only. Taxis from Lynton approx £5.
- **Directions** - Grid Ref SS 746 495. On the A39, car park opposite.

CONTACT: Karen
Countisbury, Lynton, Devon, EX35 6NE
Tel: 01598 741101 / 07974 829171
karen.birch@nationaltrust.org.uk   www.nationaltrust.org.uk/basecamps

BASE
LODGE

Base Lodge is ideally situated for exploring Exmoor, the Quantocks and the North Devon coast by mountain bike or foot. Excellent off and on road mountain biking for all levels. Guided mountain biking and secure lock up facilities. Exmoor affords excellent scenic moor and coastal views and the 600+ mile long South West Coastal Path starts here in Minehead. Other activities can be arranged including mountain biking, navigational training, climbing, surfing, pony-trekking and natural history walks and talks.

Base Lodge is clean, comfortable and friendly, providing a shared fully equipped kitchen and dining room. Local pubs and restaurants are all within walking distance.

DETAILS

- **Open** - All year, all day access once booked (reception open from 3pm).
- **Number of beds** - 22: 2x2, 1x7, 1x6, 1x5
- **Booking** - Booking advisable, bookings taken by phone or email or take a chance and call in. Deposit required for groups or exclusive use.
- **Price per night** - Dorms £15, private single £5 supplement, twin/ double £34. exclusive use of Base Lodge from £250. Family room discount.
- **Public Transport** - Coach station 5 min walk. Buses from Taunton, Exeter and Tiverton. Train station: Taunton (26 miles). Steam railway from Taunton to Minehead.
- **Directions** - With the sea behind you, drive/walk up The Parade until you reach Park Street, continue straight on until you reach a fork. Take the right fork into The Parks (Baptist Church on your right). Only limited parking is available.

CONTACT: Wendy or Graham
16 The Parks, Minehead, Somerset, TA24 8BS
Tel: 01643 703520 or 0773 1651536
togooutdoors@hotmail.com www.basesurflodge.com

The Campbell Room offers self-catering group accommodation for Scouts and other youth organisations, schools and universities, training courses, and groups of walkers, cyclists and others. Sheltered at the mouth of a rural valley on the edge of the Quantock Hills Area of Outstanding Natural Beauty, the building offers a main activity hall which can also sleep 18 on comfortable mattresses, 2 bedrooms each sleeping 3, a multi-use cabin, fully equipped kitchen, washrooms, showers, drying room, campfire area and space for 1 or 2 tents. Many walking, hiking and mountain biking routes pass close to the centre, a swimming pool is nearby and the forest is within 10 minutes walk. Other attractions and activities in the area include horse riding, high ropes, water sports, beaches with rock pools and fossils, the coastal resort of Minehead, the West Somerset Railway, Wells Cathedral, Glastonbury Tor, Wookey Hole, Cheddar Gorge, Dunster Castle, Tropiquaria Animal and Adventure Park, Exmoor, and the county town of Taunton.

DETAILS

- **Open** - All year,, by arrangement. Check current availability on our web site.
- **Number of beds** - 24 recommended (see website). 2 x 3, 1 x 18 max, 1 x 8 max
- **Booking** - Booking essential, one month in advance with deposit.
- **Price per night** - £4.50 pp (2 leaders free for groups over 12), min £54 per night.
- **Public Transport** - Buses Mon to Sat from Bridgwater. Details on website.
- **Directions** - 10 miles from the M5 (junction 23 or 24). Centre is at T junction west of Aley, 1.5 miles south of Nether Stowey (on the A39 Bridgwater to Minehead road). GR ST187381. TA5 1HB / TA5 1HN. Full directions on our website.

CONTACT: Pat Briggs
36 Old Rd, North Petherton, Bridgwater, Somerset, TA6 6TG
Tel: 01278 662537
info@campbellroom.org.uk www.campbellroom.org.uk

MENDIP
BUNKHOUSE

Larkshall (Mendip Bunkhouse) is the Cerberus Spelaeological Society's headquarters and offers excellent modern facilities. As well as for members it is available for use by guest individuals or groups wanting accommodation on Mendip. It makes an ideal base for caving as well as many other outdoor activities including walking, cycling, climbing etc. It is also a good base for anyone wanting to explore the Somerset countryside and within very easy reach are the famous tourist attractions of Wells, Wookey Hole, Cheddar Gorge and Caves, and the city of Bath. The accommodation provides all the home comforts with a kitchen/dining room, large lounge, showers and changing facilities. For anyone so inclined the central corridor can be traversed using the climbing holds fitted along the wall. There are two guest communal bunkrooms sleeping 12 and 19 respectively, with ample space to sleep large groups in comfort. For those that prefer, it is possible to camp. There is a large car park

DETAILS

- **Open** - All year, 24 hours. Key available by prior arrangement.
- **Number of beds** - 31 (1 x 12 + 1 x 19). Unlimited camping available.
- **Booking** - Advisable. Email preferred, Deposit required. Availability on website.
- **Price per night** - £5 per person. Sole use of bunkrooms £60 and £95. Minimum charge £10 per person per stay.
- **Public Transport** - There is a bus stop near the crossroads in Oakhill on the A367. Taxis are available in Shepton Mallet, Wells and Frome
- **Directions** - Larkshall is 4 miles north of Shepton Mallet and 15 miles south of Bath off the A367. At the crossroads in Oakhill take road to Stoke St Michael. Larkshall is about one mile from Oakhill on the right (ST 6505 4720).

CONTACT:
Cerberus Spelaeological, Larkshall, Fosse Road, Oakhill, Somerset, BA3 5HY
Tel: 0845 475 0954
hostelbookings@cerberusspeleo.org.uk www.cerberusspeleo.org.uk

Just 10 miles outside Bristol, Goblin Combe Lodge is set in 8 acres of its own grounds with stunning views across the Severn Estuary and beyond. The 130 acre semi ancient woodlands are rich in history and geology and with 50 acres designated as a site of special scientific interest, it offers something for everyone. The timber framed building is clad in larch and has a biomass central heating system, rainwater harvesting and a sewage treatment plant. Groups of up to 38 can be accommodated in 10 bedrooms sleeping 2, 4 & 6 people. The cottage alongside the Lodge provides a lounge, dining and catering facilities for up to 38 people and is the ideal place to relax and warm yourself after a long day of activities or to prepare for an exciting night walk where you might meet the resident owls and other creatures of the night. The 18ft Mongolian yurt is a great place for a drumming workshop, a day of meditation or just a get-together for any occasion. Fire pits and a BBQ area are included in the price. Smaller groups may be accommodated - please contact for information

DETAILS

- **Open** - All year, please contact for opening times.
- **Number of beds** - 38
- **Booking** - Book by phone or email.
- **Price per night** - £425. No minimum stay. The price may vary - please contact.
- **Public Transport** - The bus X1 between Bristol & Weston Super Mare stops at the end of Cleeve Hill Road on the A370. Nearest Train Stain - Yatton - 3 mile.
- **Directions** - Twelve miles south west of Bristol. The A370 runs almost past the doorstep and Goblin Combe is sandwiched between the A38 airport road and the M5.

CONTACT: Louise Ferguson
Goblin Combe, Plunder Street, Cleeve, North Somerset, BS49 4PQ
Tel: 01934 833723
enquiries@goblincombe.org.uk www.goblincombe.org.uk

BATH
YMCA

Bath YMCA offers a warm welcome and the best value accommodation. From its central location all the sights of this World Heritage City are easily reached on foot. Bath is also an ideal base for the explorer. Staying longer brings Stonehenge, Wookey Hole Caves, Cheddar Gorge, the southern reaches of the Cotswolds, and more exciting destinations all within reach. With a total of 210 beds, Bath YMCA has a great deal of experience in making guests feel comfortable. There is a fully air conditioned lounge area, colour TV and restaurant which offers a varied lunch menu at special YMCA subsidised prices. Laundry, lockers, pool and football table, telephone, fax and internet facilities are available. The Health and Fitness suite provides a steam and sauna room and new equipment with qualified staff who work hard to provide 'Fitness with Fun'. Couples, families, groups and backpackers are all welcome. All these facilities and the YMCA's traditional sense of community will make your stay a truly memorable one. Awarded 3 stars by VisitBritain.

DETAILS

- **Open** - All year, 24-hour reception
- **Number of beds** - 210: 2x14, 1x12, 3x10, 7 x 4, 6 x 3, 40 x 2, 11 x 1
- **Booking** - Credit card guarantees.
- **Price per night** - From £20pp (dorm), Single £31, Twin £27, Triple £22, Quad £21 pp pn including light breakfast.
- **Public Transport** - Bath has a train station and is served by National Express.
- **Directions** - Located approximately ½ mile from rail and bus station. Broad Street is located near the Podium Shopping Centre off Walcott Street.

CONTACT: Reception
International House, Broad Street Place, Bath, BA1 5LH
Tel: 01225 325900, Fax: 01225 462065
stay@bathymca.co.uk www.bathymca.co.uk

BRISTOL
BACKPACKERS HOSTEL ENGLAND

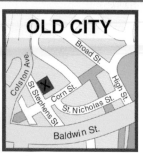

City Centre hostel - clean & comfy beds - free linen & hot showers - big kitchen - free tea, coffee & hot choc - indoor bicycle storage.

Late night basement bar - piano & guitar room - dvd lounge - cheap internet machines - free laptop wireless access - luggage storage room - laundrette.

Run by backpackers for backpackers - mixed/single sex dorms - private rooms - no curfew after check in.

DETAILS

- **Open** - All year, reception hours 9am -11.30pm (No curfew)
- **Number of beds** - 90: Bunk bed accommodation in private twin, private triple or 6, 8 and 10 bed dorms.
- **Booking** - Most cards, phone or walk in.
- **Price per night** - £16pp. Private rooms from £36. See website for discounts.
- **Public Transport** - See below.
- **Directions** - Located in 'Old City', the historic centre of Bristol. From Bristol Central Bus Station (Marlborough St) 7 mins walk. Follow pedestrian signs to 'Old City' then see map above. From Bristol Temple Meads train station 12 mins walk. Follow pedestrian signs to 'Old City' then see map above. Or take bus number 8 or 9 to the 'Centre Promenade'. Disembark at The Bristol Hippodrome. From Airport take the 'Shuttle' to the Central Bus Station. By road follow signs for Baldwin Street in the city centre.

CONTACT:
17 St Stephen's Street, Bristol, BS1 1EQ
Tel: 0117 9257900
info@bristolbackpackers.co.uk www.bristolbackpackers.co.uk

CHOLDERTON
(STONEHENGE)

Situated on a delightful family owned farm, this four star Youth Hostel provides family/child friendly accommodation suitable for groups or singles who enjoy the countryside. The hostel is located 8 miles from historic Salisbury with its Cathedral, and only 5 miles from Stonehenge World Heritage Site. As a welcome they provide a cup of tea on arrival, fresh bed linen and a cereal breakfast. Cholderton also offers cooked breakfasts for a small additional fee if preferred. Entrance to the adjoining Cholderton Charlie's rare breeds farm is free of charge to guests, and you are invited to explore it at your leisure during your stay. It offers a range of daily activities including the famous pig racing and large indoor play barn. There is a fully licensed bar, a comfortable lounge to relax and unwind, and a well equipped self catering kitchen. If booked in advance they can offer a range of delicious home cooked meals, freshly prepared by their own chef.

DETAILS

- **Open** - All Year, Reception open 4-8pm
- **Number of beds** - 70
- **Booking** - Booking in advance is advisable.
- **Price per night** - From £17.45 Adult or £13.45 Child including free entry to Cholderton Charlies rare breeds farm and a cereal and toast breakfast. Discounts available for large groups.
- **Public Transport** - Buses from Salisbury, stop 1 mile away (no Sunday service). Grateley (3.5 miles) has a frequent train service from Waterloo.
- **Directions** - From A303/A338 junction follow brown road signs to Rare Breeds Farm. From M4 Junction 15 follow A346 to Marlborough then follow A338.

CONTACT: Ben Cooper
Beacon House, Amesbury Road, Cholderton, Salisbury, Wiltshire, SP4 0EW
Tel: 01980 629438
choldertonstonehenge@yha.org.uk   www.choldertonyouthhostel.co.uk

Briantspuddle Small Hostel welcomes walkers and cyclists. This traditional car-free hostel is situated by the picturesque Dorset villages of Affpuddle and Briantspuddle. The hostel is close to five long distance tracks and cycle ways: Jubilee Trail, Hardy Way, Purbeck Cycle Way (within 800m), Frome Valley Way and NCR2 (within 2.5mls), making it an ideal stop over on a long distance route. Bike and walker courier is available from Moreton village. The area is popular for day walks with a number of forest, circular and linear routes. DH Lawrence's cottage, Thomas Hardy's birthplace and the Labour Martyrs' museum are all within walking distance along the low Dorset hills. The Purbeck coastline is a short cycling distance, mainly off road. Bring a map to plan your days out. Families, couples and individuals are all welcome provided they arrive on foot, by bike or bus. Gareth welcomes you into his home where you will have private bedrooms with freshly made up beds and shared kitchen, bathroom and living room. Small garden and safe bike store. Pub 2 miles, shop 4 miles. NO CARS

DETAILS

■ **Open** - Opening May. Closed some periods, check in by 7pm, check out by 10am
■ **Number of beds** - 5: 1x twin, 1x double, 1x1
■ **Booking** - Book by phone. Prebooking is essential.
■ **Price per night** - £14 per person.
■ **Public Transport** - 387 bus from Poole or Dorchester stops outside hostel. Trains on the Weymouth line stop at Wool and Moreton which can be reached by bike.
■ **Directions** - Last house on the right out of Briantspuddle opposite the Beehive cottage, on the corner of the B3390.

CONTACT: Gareth
Appletrees, 23 Affpuddle, Dorset, DT2 7HH
Tel: 07848007771
garethhowell@phonecoop.coop www.readytowalk.co.uk

HARROW HOUSE

RESIDENTIAL FACILITY

Harrow House is located in the centre of Swanage, gateway to the Jurassic Coast. It is the perfect base for any group (e.g. school, scientific interest, outdoor activities, youth and walking groups) to access the wealth of learning and leisure opportunities on the Isle of Purbeck. It is large capacity centre sleeping 150+ which provides high quality, full-board accommodation in spacious dormitories sleeping 2-6. Bed linen is provided and beds are made up for arrival. Rooms are cleaned daily and laundry facilities are available on site. En suite rooms can be booked for a supplement subject to availability. Hot meals are served from the cafeteria or you can choose a packed meal. Please see the website for a sample menu. There is a licensed bar, games room with WiFi access, two large meeting rooms, presentation rooms with projectors, classrooms and 2 ICT suites. The excellent on-site sports facilities include tennis, volleyball and squash courts, a heated indoor swimming pool, free pool tables, multipurpose Astroturf and more. Harrow House can offer sports, adventure or geography courses, please see the website for details.

DETAILS

- **Open** - Mid Sept - Mid June,
- **Number of beds** - 150+
- **Booking** - Booking is essential. 25% deposit required.
- **Price per night** - Full-board accommodation from £35+VAT per night
- **Public Transport** - Wareham rail station 10 miles, regular bus service from Poole or Bournemouth, National Express direct from Victoria.
- **Directions** - Coordinates: 50.615244, -1.965137

CONTACT: Dawn Ramsden
Harrow Drive, Swanage, Dorset, BH19 1PE
Tel: 01929 475081
schools@harrowhouse.co.uk www.harrowhouse.net

Swanage Auberge, the bunkhouse that cares, is a refuge for climbers, walkers and divers. Situated at the eastern end of the Jurassic Coast with excellent walking, diving and rock climbing on the doorstep. The bunkhouse is in the centre of Swanage town, a stone's throw from the South West Coast Path and all local amenities - pubs, shops, restaurants etc. Swanage Auberge is family run and self-contained with central heating, fully equipped self-catering kitchen, drying and laundry facilities and a meals service if required. There are two bunk rooms, one with 4 standard bunks and the other with 6 alpine style places (3 and 3).There is also a 4 bed dorm in the adjoining house. Towel, plus pillows are provided and bedding is available for hire. There are three showers, loos and washrooms and an area to hang and wash wet-suits. Once booked in, the Auberge is available 24 hours a day. Parking is available for 2 vehicles and is allocated on a first come, first served basis. Price includes cereal breakfast and beverages. Packed lunches available (see website for further details).

DETAILS

- **Open** - All year, opens 5.30pm (all day once booked in)
- **Number of beds** - 17: 1x6, 2x4, family room (dbl + single)
- **Booking** - Book by phone or email. Booking form online. 20% deposit required.
- **Price per night** - £18 pp including cereal breakfast and free tea or coffee. Group rates available. Hire of duvet with sheets £2.00. Credit cards not accepted.
- **Public Transport** - Bus from Poole or Wareham. Train service to Wareham.
- **Directions** - At the end of the first left hand alley off Mount Pleasant Lane.

CONTACT: Pete or Pam
45 High Street, Swanage, Dorset, BH19 2LX
Tel: 01929 424368, mobile 07711 117668
bookings@swanageauberge.co.uk www.swanageauberge.co.uk

DAVID DONALD
FIELD STUDIES BASE

The David Donald Field Studies Base offers accommodation for educational, family and other groups in a converted 1940 RAF radar station, renovated with central heating and double glazing. It sleeps 24 but up to 40 if some wish to camp and share the indoor facilities. There is a well equipped kitchen, a spacious community room, a drying room, picnic area, BBQ / campsite area, a games area and lots of parking. There are ramps to the main building and adapted toilets for wheelchair users, but for these the drive to the centre is very difficult without a car. This is an outstanding area for environmental studies and is also popular with groups or families enjoying a relaxing break, reunions, walking, outdoor actvities and other social events. It is within an SSSI, and has Lulworth Cove, Durdle Door, The Arne Nature Reserve, Purbeck Marine Reserve, Corfe Castle, Poole Harbour and lots of other interesting sites nearby.

DETAILS

■ **Open** - All year
■ **Number of beds** - 24: 1x2, 1x2 en suite, 1x9, 1x11 plus camping
■ **Booking** - Booking required with £200 deposit. Phone for availability. Forms can be downloaded from website and returned to P&D Adv Centre, Recreation Road, Parkstone, Poole, BH12 2EA.
■ **Price per night** - Prices for 2012: whole centre from £300 per night. £5 per person for numbers exceeding 24, up to a maximum of 30. Bed linen £5 per person.
■ **Public Transport** - Train to Wareham. Wilts & Dorset Buses to Worth Matravers.
■ **Directions** - Arriving in Worth Matravers from Kingston bear right by duck pond into Pikes Lane. After Renscombe Farm road turns sharp right then left onto Renscombe Rd. 200m further the driveway to the base is on the right. OS SY967777

CONTACT: David Donald Field Studies Base
Off Renscombe Rd, Worth Matravers, Isle of Purbeck, Dorset BH19 3LL
Tel: 01202 710701
enquiries@dorsetadventure.co.uk www.dorsetadventure.co.uk

Gumber Bothy is a converted traditional Sussex barn on the National Trust's Slindon Estate in the heart of the South Downs. It provides simple overnight accommodation or camping for walkers, riders and cyclists, just off the South Downs Way.

The bothy forms part of Gumber Farm and is 5 minutes walk from Stane Street, the Roman Road that crosses the South Downs Way at Bignor Hill. Facilities include sleeping platforms in 3 dorms sleeping up to 25, good hot showers and basins, kitchen/diner with gas hob and washing up facilities. A few pots and pans are provided. There is a paddock for friendly horses and racks for bikes. Wheelchair accessible (please phone for details). Sorry, but as we're a sheep farm, no dogs and most definitely NO CARS. Not suitable for under fives.

DETAILS

■ **Open** - March to October (inclusive), flexible opening hours
■ **Number of beds** - 25: 1 x 16, 1 x 5, 1 x 4 plus overflow area
■ **Booking** - Booking by phone or email. Booking required for groups with 50% deposit.
■ **Price per night** - £10 (adults), £5 (under 16s).
■ **Public Transport** - Train stations, Arundel (urban) 5 miles, Amberley (rural) 5 miles, Chichester (8 miles). National Express stop at Chichester. Buses 84 and 85 from Chichester, stop at Fontwell and then it is a 3 mile walk to the Bothy. Taxi fare from Arundel to Northwood Farm is approx £10, followed by a 2 mile country walk.
■ **Directions** - OS Map LR197 or E121 GR 961 119. Nearest car park GR 973 129. No vehicular access. One mile off South Downs Way on Stane Street bridleway

CONTACT: Bothy Warden
Slindon Estate Yard, Slindon, Arundel, West Sussex, BN18 0RG
Tel: 01243 814484
katie.archer@nationaltrust.org.uk

PUTTENHAM
ECO CAMPING BARN

Puttenham Eco Camping Barn offers simple overnight accommodation and a warm welcome for walkers and cyclists - individuals, families or groups - in the Surrey Hills Area of Outstanding Natural Beauty.

Located on the North Downs Way and Sustrans NCN22 cycle route, the Barn has a fully equipped self-catering kitchen, a shower, toilets and foam covered sleeping platforms, as well as a garden with picnic benches. Electricity and hot water included but bring your own towel and sleeping bag (or hire one - £3 a stay). Evening meals are available in the village. The Barn has many sustainable features including solar panels and rainwater collection for flushing toilets. NO CARS ON SITE. Excellent cycle shed. Young people are welcome but must be accompanied by a responsible adult. The Barn is wardened.

DETAILS

- **Open** - Easter to October, 1700 to 1000
- **Number of beds** - sleeping platforms for 11
- **Booking** - booking is essential
- **Price per night** - £14 adults; £11 under 18 (accompanied by adult). Sole use by arrangement. £4 `green` discount if arriving by foot, bicycle or public transport.
- **Public Transport** - Trains (08457 484950) at Wanborough (3.5 km), Guildford (7 km) and Farnham (9 km). The X65 Stagecoach bus (0845 1210180) from Guildford and Farnham drops you within 1 km of the barn. Alight at Puttenham Hogs Back and walk south to village (see our website).
- **Directions** - GR SU 933 479. In Puttenham village (halfway between Farnham and Guildford) the Camping Barn is on 'The Street' - opposite the church.

CONTACT: Bookings
The Street, Puttenham, Nr Guildford, Surrey, GU3 1AR
Tel: 01629 592 700 or 0800 0191 700, Fax: 01629 592627
bookings@puttenhamcampingbarn.co.uk   www.puttenhamcampingbarn.co.uk

KIPPS
BRIGHTON

Kipps Brighton is in the centre of Brighton, with views of the Royal Pavilion, close to the attractions, the pier and beach. Guests can relax on the roof terrace or in the lounge area and enjoy a continental breakfast in the dining room or a drink at the bar. Kipps Brighton has eight quality, well equipped private bedrooms all featuring TV, clock radio, CD player and wash basin. There are also two en suite dormitory rooms for groups or individuals. The hostel has a self catering kitchen and offers nightly events and friendly knowledgable staff.

Kipps also have a hostel in Canterbury, a short walk from the town centre and historic attractions. See page 66 for details.

DETAILS

- **Open** - All year, reception 8am-11pm – No Curfew
- **Number of beds** - 36: 1x1, 6x dbl, 1x twin, 1x3, 1x8, 1x10
- **Booking** - Please book by phone, email or online.
- **Price per night** - From £15 per person per night
- **Public Transport** - We are close to Brighton train station and bus station. From train station: exit and walk ahead down the main street for a few minutes, turn into Church Street (on your left) and walk along Church Street until the end, the hotel is opposite. From bus station: exit onto Old Steine Road and turn left towards the Royal Pavilion. At the far end of the Pavilion and opposite is the hostel.
- **Directions** - Take the M23, then A23 towards Brighton Town Centre. The hostel is opposite the Royal Pavilion on Grand Parade.

CONTACT: Reception
76 Grand Parade, Brighton, BN2 9JA
Tel: 01273 604182
kippshostelbrighton@gmail.com   www.kipps-brighton.com

PALACE FARM
HOSTEL

Palace Farm Hostel is a relaxing and flexible hostel on a family run arable and fruit farm. It is situated in the village of Doddington, which has a pub, in the North Kent Downs Area of Outstanding Natural Beauty. The area is great for walking, cycling (cycle hire available £5 a day) and wildlife. The location is central for exploring Canterbury, Rochester, Chatham, Leeds Castle and the many other historic towns, villages and castles in Kent. The accommodation, in converted farm buildings, consists of ten fully heated en-suite rooms sleeping up to 38 guests. The rooms surround an attractive courtyard garden with lawns, patio and barbecue area, ideal for families and groups. The en suite rooms cater for all age groups and those with disabilities. There are quality double beds & 3ft bunk beds. Duvets, linen and continental breakfast included. Small tent only campsite. Green Tourism Business Scheme GOLD Award winner.

DETAILS

- **Open** - All year, 8am to 10pm flexible, please ask
- **Number of beds** - 39: 1x8, 1x6, 2x5, 1x4, 1x3 and 4x2
- **Booking** - Advised.
- **Price per night** -   From £15 to £26 (all private en suite rooms). Reduction for groups, see website.
- **Public Transport** - Trains: Sittingbourne (London Victoria to Dover). Buses from Sittingbourne station to Doddington two hourly (Mon-Sat), last buses 16.30 & 17.30.
- **Directions** - From A2 between Sittingbourne and Faversham turn south at Teynham, signed to Lynsted. Go through Lynsted and over M2 bridge, take 2nd turning right into Down Court Rd. Farm is 90 metres on left.

CONTACT: Graham and Liz Cuthbert
Down Court Road, Doddington, Sittingbourne / Faversham, Kent, ME9 0AU
Tel: 01795 886200
info@palacefarm.com www.palacefarm.com

KIPPS
CANTERBURY

Kipps is an ideal home-from-home for backpackers, visitors or small groups looking for self-catering budget accommodation in Canterbury. It is a short walk to the town centre and the historic attractions including the renowned Canterbury Cathedral. Canterbury also makes an ideal base for day trips to Dover, Leeds Castle and the many local beaches.

Facilities include dining room, TV lounge with digital TV, a garden, a fully equipped kitchen, a small shop offering breakfast and other food items, bicycle hire. Free WiFi & broadband access. Rooms include single/double/twin/family & dorms of up to 8 beds (most en suite). Camping available in summer. Free on-street parking. Kipps also have a hostel / hotel in Brighton, opposite the Royal Pavilion and close to town. See page 62.

DETAILS

- **Open** - All year, , no curfew, reception 7.30am to 11pm
- **Number of beds** - 51:- 2 x 1, 2 x 2, 1 x 3, 1 x 5, 1 x 6, 1 x 7, 2 x 8, 1 x 9
- **Booking** - Advance booking recommended. Book online.
- **Price per night** - Dorms £16pp, Singles £22pp, Doubles £37, Quads £50. Weekly and winter rates available. Credit cards accepted.
- **Public Transport** - Canterbury East train station on London Victoria to Dover line, is ½ mile by footpath (phone hostel for directions). The local C4 bus stops by the door of the hostel. Taxi from coach/rail stations is £3.
- **Directions** - By car :- Take B2068 to Hythe from City Ring Road (A28). Turn right at first traffic lights by church. Kipps is 300 yds on left.

CONTACT: Reception
40 Nunnery Fields, Canterbury, Kent, CT1 3JT
Tel: 01227 786121
kippshostel@googlemail.com www.kipps-hostel.com

Situated mid-way between Alton and Petersfield in glorious Hampshire countryside, the Privett Centre offers lowest cost, comfortable short-stay accommodation in a unique rural setting. The centre is a picturesque converted victorian school and schoolhouse located next to the church in a farming hamlet which lies within the East Hampshire 'Area of Outstanding Natural Beauty'. Sleeping a maximum of 18 dormitory style with 2 single bedrooms (one with disabled access en suite), the centre is designed to accommodate small to medium-sized groups who prefer the freedom of hiring a small centre all to themselves.

The centre provides the basics – a self-catering kitchen, bunk beds mainly in bedrooms, a large common room, games room and shower rooms all under one roof. Outside a large paddock and asphalt playground provide secure and spacious recreational and parking space. Available for weekday, weekend and day use all year, the Privett Centre is an ideal residential setting.

DETAILS

- **Open** - All year,
- **Number of beds** - 20
- **Booking** - Phone or email
- **Price per night** - From £120 per night, sole use only.
- **Public Transport** - Nearest train station - Petersfield, approx 6 miles from centre.
- **Directions** - From the A272 follow signs to Petersfield. Go straight across crossroads, centre is signposted on left after approx 2 miles.

CONTACT: Angela Grigsby
Church Lane, Privett, Hampshire, GU34 3PE
Tel: 01730 828238
info@privettcentre.org.uk www.privettcentre.org.uk

WETHERDOWN
LODGE AND CAMPSITE ENGLAND

Wetherdown Lodge is part of The Sustainability Centre which promotes environmental awareness and low impact living. It is at the heart of the South Downs National Park and is an award-winning example of an eco-renovation, just a few steps from the South Downs Way national trail. It is ideal for walkers, cyclists, business away-days and family get-togethers. The hostel has a fully equipped self catering kitchen, a communal area, comfortable bedrooms with linen provided, and separate bathrooms/toilets. A 'help yourself' breakfast is included in the price. Packed lunches are available by order. The centre has large grounds with woodland trails and a cafe open Wed-Sun. The Campsite has teepees and yurts for hire, as well as fire pits, secluded woodland pitches and hot solar showers, offering a peaceful real camping experience. Within 2 miles of the hostel are 4 country pubs, local shops, and chinese and indian takeaways who can deliver to the Lodge

DETAILS

- **Open** - All year, all day
- **Number of beds** - 39: 11 x 3, 3 x 2
- **Booking** - Book by telephone / email.
- **Price per night** - Twin/triple £23pp. Single room £30. 5-15 year olds £18. Exclusive use available. All prices include linen & breakfast.
- **Public Transport** - Trains at Petersfield, 6 miles (£16 by taxi). 38 bus to Clanfield from Petersfield or the 67 to East Meon from Petersfield/Winchester. 41 bus to Clanfield from Portsmouth Harbour .
- **Directions** - GR 676 189. From A3 take Clanfield turn (brown sign). Turn right after Rising Sun in Clanfield. At top of hill, turn left signed Droxford.

CONTACT: Jonathan, Ashley or Angie
The Sustainability Centre, Droxford Road, East Meon, Hampshire, GU32 1HR
Tel: 01730 823549, Mob: 07884 258713, Fax: 01730 823168
accommodation@sustainability-centre.org www.sustainability-centre.org

THE GLADE
AT BLACKBOYS

The Glade is a quiet retreat in the heart of rural East Sussex, just over an hour's drive from South London and 45 minutes from Brighton and the south coast. This former YHA hostel is set in an acre of its own grounds, close to the intersection of the Weald and Vanguard Ways and a short drive from the climbing crags at Harrisons Rocks and Bewl outdoor centre.

The small dorms and private location make it ideal for sole use, for family re-unions, parties or corporate team-building groups. When the hostel is open to all, the pleasant lounge/dining room, with its wood burning stove and relaxed atmosphere, makes a great place to socialise. The kitchen is fully equipped for self-catering, with cookers, ovens, fridges, toasters, microwaves and a small freezer. All bedding is provided, but all guests have to bring their own towels. Outside there is a secure bike shed and picnic benches which are great for al-fresco eating. There is also woodland parking space for several cars.

DETAILS

- **Open** - All year, closed between 10am and 5pm (when not in sole use)
- **Number of beds** - 30:1x6,1x5, 2x4,3x3, 2x1
- **Booking** - Please enquire by phone or email.
- **Price per night** -   Sole use £400 per night. At all other times, £15 per adult and £10 for under 16s.
- **Public Transport** - Stagecoach Bus 32 stops at Blackboys village 0.5 miles from hostel. Trains at Buxted 2.5 miles away. National Express at Uckfield 4 miles away.
- **Directions** - From Blackboys village take Gun Road and look for signs.

CONTACT: Alan
The Glade, YHABlackboys, Gun Road, Blackboys, Uckfield, Sussex, TN22 5HU
Tel: 01825 890607
blackboys@yha.org.uk www.the-glade.co.uk

Harlow International Hostel is situated in the centre of a landscaped park and is one of the oldest buildings in Harlow. The town of Harlow is the ideal base from which to explore London, Cambridge and the best of South East England. The journey time to central London is only 35 minutes from the hostel door and it is the closest hostel to Stansted Airport. National Cycle Route 1 passes the front door. There is a range of room sizes from single to eight bedded including two rooms with double beds. Self-catering facilities, refreshments and a small shop are all available. During your visit you can relax with a book or game from our large collection. A children's zoo, orienteering course and outdoor pursuit centre are available in the park as well as pleasant river walks.

Meals can be provided for groups. Airport parking available.

DETAILS

- **Open** - All year, , 8am-12pm (check in 4-10.30pm)
- **Number of beds** - 29: 2x1 : 5x2 : 1x4 : 1x6 :1 x 7
- **Booking** - Advance booking (can be taken 18 months in advance) is recommended. Deposit of £2pppn of stay.
- **Price per night** - £17 per adult. Family rooms £65 (sleeps 4), £75 (sleep 5), £85 (sleep 6). Please check our website for latest prices and discounts.
- **Public Transport** - The rail station is only 800m from hostel with links to London, Cambridge & Stansted Airport. Buses connect to London and airports.
- **Directions** - J7 of M11 take A414 into Harlow. At the 4th roundabout take 1st exit (First Ave). Drive to 4th set of traffic lights. Immediately after lights turn right (School Lane). Hostel is on left opposite Greyhound Pub.

CONTACT: Richard or Iku
13 School Lane, Harlow, Essex, CM20 2QD
Tel: 01279 421702
mail@h-i-h.co.uk www.h-i-h.co.uk

EQUITY POINT

The new Equity Point hotel is located in the high-end Paddington neighbourhood. Close to Paddington train station where the Heathrow Express connects to the main London airport, and just 15 minutes to the city centre.

Enjoy nearby Hyde Park, the green heart of the city, just minutes away, or the magic of nearby Notting Hill. The Georgian building with its white columns and iconic Georgian windows, has 68 en suite rooms spread over 7 floors. It offers guests the choice of many types of accommodation from doubles to 8-bed rooms, all completely renovated. Community areas with TV and WiFi, internet technology, a bar for guests to use, wheelchair access and lockers for each bed are some of the facilities. Under 18s must stay in private rooms or dorms booked for sole use of one family or group.

DETAILS

- **Open** - All year, 24 hours
- **Number of beds** - Twin, double and family rooms, 4, 5, 6, and 8 bed dorms.
- **Booking** - Book online or by phone. Credit card payments £1 extra pp per night.
- **Price per night** - 8 bed dorms £15pp (Mon-Wed), £18 (Thurs-Sun) off peak. £17pp (Mon-Wed), £20 pp(Thurs-Sun) at peak times. Double/twin rooms from £45 to £53pp. Breakfast and linen included.
- **Public Transport** - Underground: Take Circle, District or Hammersmith/City lines to Paddington Staion, or Central Line to Lancaster gate Station. From Heathrow the Heathrow Express takes 18 mins to Paddington Station.
- **Directions** - From Paddington Station turn right out of station along Praed St, continue along Craven Rd then turn right into Westbourne Terrace.

CONTACT: Reception
100-102 Westbourne Terrace, Paddington, London, W2 6QE
Tel: 0207 0878001
infolondon@equity-point.com www.equity-point.com

ALL STAR
HOSTEL

All Star Hostel is a new hostel very close to Kilburn tube station (only 15 mins from Central London) and the 24 hour bus routes. Completely refurbished with brand new facilities including pressure showers, fully fitted kitchens, wooden floors, lounge room with Sky TV, free internet, laundry facilities (free soap powder), and security lockers in all the rooms. Choose from 6 bed dorms, female only rooms, double rooms with TV/DVD, or private studio apartments.

FREE tea and coffee, FREE toast and jam breakfast, FREE WiFi. The All Star Hostel will offer you a comfortable homely stay with a friendly atmosphere at great prices for your trip to London. Accommodation London also operates over 300 STUDIO apartments and shared antipodean houses in North West London, with secure private rooms. Providing a great atmosphere with other working holidaymakers to give you that feel for London living.

DETAILS

- **Open** - All year, office hours 8am 6pm Mon-Sat. Sundays 9am-5pm .
- **Number of beds** - 100+ beds plus apartments and houses.
- **Booking** - Book online.
- **Price per night** - Minimum of 4 nights' stay. Dorms from £15, private rooms from £20pp. Long term from £10 a night. £15 check-in fee on Sundays.
- **Public Transport** - Close to Kilburn tube station on the Jubliee Line (zone 2). Free pick up from tube station (office hours only). Frequent bus services including a night bus from the city .
- **Directions** - Located a short distance from the main arterial roads through the city.

CONTACT: Reception
39 Chatsworth Road, London, NW2 4BL
Tel: 0208 459 6203 , Fax: 0208 451 3258
info@accommodationlondon.net www.accommodationlondon.net

PICCADILLY
BACKPACKERS HOSTEL ENGLAND

Only a heartbeat from London's most popular attractions including the famous nightspot Leicester Square, the trendy area of Soho, the bustling shopping area of Oxford Street and London's renowned central Theatre Land. Trafalgar Square, Big Ben and the London Eye are also all within 10 minutes walk.

Piccadilly Backpackers Hostel offers an unbeatable blend of value for money, comfort and security, and is undeniably the greatest portal for visitors looking for budget accommodation in London.

With 700 beds, spread over 6 colourful floors in the heart of Piccadilly Circus, Piccadilly Backpackers can prove to be an exciting and eventful experience in itself! Odds are you are guaranteed to meet interesting people from different cultures and backgrounds.

DETAILS

■ **Open** - All year, 24 hours
■ **Number of beds** - 700
■ **Booking** - Advisable, groups require deposit
■ **Price per night** - From £12
■ **Public Transport** - One minutes walk from Piccadilly Circus tube station.
■ **Directions** - Take exit 1 from Piccadilly Circus tube station, head down Sherwood Street, Piccadilly Backpackers is on your right just after Piccadilly Theatre. By car follow signs for central London, then to Piccadilly Circus, then follow signs to nearby NCP car park.

CONTACT: Reception
12 Sherwood Street, Piccadilly, London, W1F 7BR
Tel: 0207 434 9009, Fax: 0207 434 9010
bookings@piccadillybackpackers.com www.piccadillybackpackers.com

MEININGER HOTEL
LONDON

Meininger Hostel, The urban traveller's home in West Kensington makes a great base for visitors to London. Just 150m from the nearest tube station, making all central London's attractions easy to reach, and just a stone's throw from the Science, Natural History and Victoria and Albert Museums.

Meininger Hotel offers 48 comfortable rooms over 6 floors, all with their own shower/WC, air conditioning and TV. Rooms are accessed by a key-card. Bed linen is included. There is a free luggage room and safe deposit boxes are available. Other facilities (with charges applicable) include internet stations, washing machine and dryer, and a large car park in the basement.

4-star classified (Visit Britain Hostel Award 2007).

DETAILS

- **Open** - All year, 24 hour reception. Check in from 3pm, check out 10am.
- **Number of beds** - 48 rooms over 6 floors. Dorms have max 12 people. Mixed dorms over 18s only.
- **Booking** - Booking advised. Online or phone. Groups of 12 or more email groups@meininger-hotels.com
- **Price per night** - Online booking prices: dorms £19pp, twin rooms £47pp, multiple bed rooms £35pp, single rooms £70pp. Breakfast £4.50pp
- **Public Transport** - Gloucester Road is the nearest underground station (on District, Piccadilly and Circle lines).
- **Directions** - From Gloucester Rd tube Station head north for 50m, turn right into Cromwell Rd, then find hotel on left after 100m

CONTACT: Reception
65-67 Queen's Gate, London ,SW7 5JS
Tel: 020 331 81 407
welcome@meininger-hotels.com www.meininger-hotels.com

DOVER CASTLE
ENGLAND HOSTEL AND FLATSHARES

Dover Castle Hostel and Flatshares, located close to London Bridge in Central London (Zone 1), offers backpackers great value, short and long stay accommodation. Located in the centre of the city it is walking distance to sights such as Tower Bridge, St Paul's Cathedral, London Dungeon, Shakespeare's Globe, Tate Modern and the London Eye. Prices include free breakfast and free WiFi. The hostel has a guest kitchen and common room, free luggage room, a laundry service as well as a late guest bar with pool table and super drink offers. Guests wanting to stay in London for longer can rent rooms in Dover Castle house / flatshares. These furnished houses and flats are a short bus ride to London Bridge in Zone 2 (South East London). Single occupancy double rooms cost £130 per week and twin rooms cost £80 per week per person inclusive of bills and WiFi for a 6 week minimum stay. See www.london99.com for more info on the flatshares. Short or long term guests can find their home in London with Dover Castle!

DETAILS

- **Open** - All year, 24 hours. No Curfew
- **Number of beds** - 68: 1x4, 2x5, 1x8, 2x10, 2x12
- **Booking** - Booking advisable. Credit card secures bed.
- **Price per night** - £14-£22 pp incl. breakfast. Discounted weekly rates available
- **Public Transport** - Nearest main line station is London Bridge. Take underground Northern Line to Borough. The hostel is opposite Borough underground station between London Bridge and Elephant and Castle. 10 mins from Waterloo Station.
- **Directions** - From Borough tube, cross to Great Dover Street, 1 min walk on right.

CONTACT: Sam Davidson
6 Great Dover Street, Borough, London, SE1 4XW
Tel: 020 74037773, Fax: 020 77878654
info@dovercastlehostel.com www.dovercastlehostel.com

GENERATOR
LONDON

Generator
HOSTEL LONDON

The Generator is London's largest, liveliest and funkiest hostel with over 800 beds and is famous for its party atmosphere. We are open 24 hours a day, 365 days a year with friendly staff who are always on hand to help. Just minutes from Covent Garden and Leicester Square, The Generator is located in the heart of Bloomsbury. There is a late bar (open 6pm to 2am) which provides the perfect environment to meet young travellers from all over the world. Other facilities include a laundry, chill out room, games room with pool tables and satellite TV, internet café, safety deposit boxes and free luggage storage on departure. Continental breakfast is free for everyone, as are bed sheets & 24hour hot showers and a walking tour of London. Accommodation is available in singles, twins, triples, quads plus both small and large dorms. The hostel is generally suitable for 18-35s. It is a must-stay hostel for all backpackers if you want to meet loads of people from all over the world and party the night away.

DETAILS

- **Open** - All year, 24 hours
- **Number of beds** - 840
- **Booking** - With credit card- 48 hr cancellation.
- **Price per night** - From £15 per person in a dorm room.
- **Public Transport** - King's Cross/Euston Station are both approx 5 minutes walk from the hostel. The nearest National Express station is Victoria and the closest tube station is Russell Square.
- **Directions** - From Russell Square tube cross onto Marchmont Street, walk to traffic lights and turn right onto Tavistock Place - the hostel is at number 37.

CONTACT:
Compton Place, (off 37 Tavistock Place), Russell Square London, WC1H 9SE
Tel: 0207 388 7666
london@generatorhostels.com   www.generatorhostels.com

CLINK78

Clink78 is a hip, modern backpackers hostel in the cool soul of London King's Cross. Set in a 200-year-old magistrates courthouse where Charles Dickens was inspired to write Oliver Twist and where The Clash stood trial. Restored to create a unique backpackers' bolt hole, it combines history with edgy and cool design. It's not a generic hostel! Facilities are modern, beds clean and cosy and the international staff friendly and fun! The atmosphere is lively with a mix of young travellers meeting in our famous clashbar for happy hour music and fun; sharing food and tales in our modern self-catering kitchen; playing pool in our games area; and chilling in front of the TV. Try innovative pod beds in dorms of varying sizes or book a private room, some en suite. Our authentic Prison Cells and Deluxe Female dorms are recently refurbished with warmth and humour. So while visiting London, come and get locked-in at Clink and judge for yourself!

DETAILS

- **Open** - All year, 24 hours - no curfew or lockouts
- **Number of beds** - 600: 4-16 bedded, triple, twin, single, ensuite, cell rooms(for 2).
- **Booking** - Book online, by email or by phone.
- **Price per night** - From £10pp incl FREE breakfast, FREE bed linen and FREE London walking tour. Group discounts.
- **Public Transport** - Just round the corner from King's Cross / St Pancras Station with direct links to Heathrow, Luton, Gatwick, Victoria, Eurostar, and one change to Stansted.
- **Directions** - King's Cross station is 10 mins away by foot. Exit the station, walk down King's Cross Road for 500m and you'll find us on your left.

CONTACT: Reception
78 Kings Cross Road, King's Cross, London, WC1X 9QG
Tel: 020 7183 9400, Fax: 020 7713 0735
info78@clinkhostels.com www.clinkhostels.com

CLINK261

Clink261 is one of London's best established independent backpacker youth hostels. We offer brand new, trendy and stylish accommodation in the very centre of London. Recently refurbished, this rather glamorous boutique hostel offers a very cosy and intimate atmosphere, combined with a personalised service. Our hostel attracts a diverse mix of individual and group travellers of all ages from around the world. You'll also find yourself a stone's throw from the British Museum, Covent Garden, Bloomsbury and Camden Market or just minutes away from the bright lights of Piccadilly Circus and Leicester Square. Our improved security system gives you key card access to the building and your room and our self catering kitchen and tour desk will ensure you have everything you need for a great and unforgettable stay in London!

DETAILS

- **Open** - All year (except for Christmas), 24 hours - no curfew or lockouts
- **Number of beds** - 3 large dorms, 6 dorms, 12 small dorms and 4 private rooms
- **Booking** - Advanced booking recommended.
- **Price per night** - From £10pp including FREE breakfast. Group discounts.
- **Public Transport** - Just beside King's Cross / St.Pancras which houses the Eurostar Station and has UK mainline trains, underground, local buses and direct links with all major airports - Heathrow, Gatwick, Luton and Stansted. .
- **Directions** - Only 2 mins walk away from Kings Cross / St Pancras. From the station take the exit for Gray's Inn Road, departing the exit McDonald's will be on right. Keep McDonald's right, walk straight ahead, passing an exchange bureau, the police station and KFC. The road curves to the right - this is Grays Inn Road - the hostel is 200 metres up the road on the right, opposite the hospital.

CONTACT:
261-265 Gray's Inn Road, King's Cross, London, WC1X 8QT
Tel: 020 7833 9400, Fax: 020 7833 9677
info261@clinkhostels.com www.clinkhostels.com

SMART RUSSELL SQ
HOSTEL
ENGLAND

Smart Russell Square Hostel is perfectly located in the heart of London to provide a great experience, created with backpackers and budget travellers in mind. Located just off London's and Europe's most popular shopping area, Oxford Street, it is less than 400 metres from the British Museum, a short walk from many of the iconic and famous sites of London and in an ideal area for any type of trip. The hostel has 24 hour reception, FREE WiFi and internet cafe, TV common room, self service laundry facilities, FREE breakfast, guest kitchen facilities, currency exchange, travel shop and much more. It also offer transfers, sightseeing tours, walking tours, pub tours, discounted theatre tickets and fast track attraction tickets including Madame Tussauds, London Eye, Tower of London and many more.

The Smart Space Group also has other hostels located in Bayswater, Camden, and Brighton. Check website for more details.

DETAILS

- **Open** - All year, 24 hours. Check in, with photo ID, from 11am, check out 10am.
- **Number of beds** - 460: private rooms and dorms from 6 to 24 beds
- **Booking** - Book online, by email or by phone.
- **Price per night** - From £10.99 includes breakfast and taxes. Group discounts.
- **Public Transport** - Very close to Russell Square underground station. London buses stop near the hostel. King's Cross, Euston and St. Pancras short walk away.
- **Directions** - Just behind Russell Square tube station. Just turn left out of the station then 2nd left into Guildford Street. Walk down Guildford Street 20m to No 71.

CONTACT: Receptionist
70-72 Guildford Street, London, WC1N 1DF
Tel: 020 7833 8818, Fax: 020 7278 7309
srsbookings@smartbackpackers.com   www.smartbackpackers.com

TRAVEL JOY
HOSTEL
ENGLAND

Travel Joy Hostel is a chilled-out and relaxed hostel, centrally located between Chelsea and Westminster and run by two Irish fellas - ideal for travellers looking for budget accommodation, central location and a great atmosphere. It's located on Grosvenor Road in Pimlico, a little south of Victoria, with views onto Battersea Power Station. Top rated in London on Hostelworld! We are famous for the friendly family feel in our hostel and we really believe in personalized customer service. We look forward to meeting new people with different backgrounds, stories and experiences. Reception is in the bar downstairs. Bar facilities include 3 large TVs with Sky and sports, large cinema screen for special events, pool table, table football, vending machines, restaurant / breakfast area, lounge area, internet / PC corner, library shelf, terrace with outside seating, barbecue on sunny days, stage for music events with LIVE MUSIC on Saturdays.

DETAILS

■ **Open** - All year, reception open 8am - 11pm. Contact in advance if arriving later.
■ **Number of beds** - 65:
■ **Booking** - Booking recommended. By email, phone or online.
■ **Price per night** - Dorm beds from £17. Includes free breakfast, bed linen, towel and parking.
■ **Public Transport** - Pimlico tube station (Victoria Line) is 5-7 minutes walk away. Victoria Station 10-15 minutes walk. Bus 24 runs into central London 24 hours a day.
■ **Directions** - From Pimlico tube station take Bessborough St South exit, follow Lupus St for 300m, turn left onto Claverton St and after 300m turn right onto Grosvenor Rd. Hostel is with the King William IV bar on the right.

CONTACT: Reception
111 Grosvenor Rd. London SW1V 3LG
Tel: 0207 834 9689, Fax: 0207 834 0747
info@traveljoyhostels.com   www.traveljoyhostels.com

STOUR VALLEY
BUNKHOUSE

Opened in 2007, and fitted with a wide range of modern facilities, Stour Valley Bunkhouse is set in peaceful surroundings on an historic 1000 acre working farm, an ideal base for exploring Constable Country. Close to the Stour Estuary, there are excellent opportunities for bird watching, walking and cycling on the doorstep. Alton Water is only 3 miles away for sailing and windsurfing. Ipswich is 6 miles away. For children of all ages there is a huge choice of local attractions, such as Jimmy's Farm or Colchester Castle. Colchester Zoo and Sutton Hoo are good options for a wet day, and there are excellent beaches at Dovercourt, Frinton and Walton. The bunkhouse sleeps up to 20 in 5 rooms. It is self catering, with a shop and pub within a mile. The bunkhouse is unsuitable for stag parties or groups that are likely to be very noisy or drink heavily.

DETAILS

- **Open** - All year round (sole use groups only), Arrivals 4pm-10pm, depart by 10 am.
- **Number of beds** - 20 beds : 2 x 6, 1 x 4, 2 x 2
- **Booking** - Advance booking essential. Group bookings only.
- **Price per night** - From £115 for up to 12 beds, £165 for whole bunkhouse. Only available to groups. Not open to individuals at present.
- **Public Transport** - Manningtree Station 2.4 miles (less using bridle path) with regular service to London Liverpool St (1hr), Harwich Port and Ipswich. Taxis from Manningtree Station about £4. National Express coaches at Ipswich and Colchester.
- **Directions** - Grid Reference: TM120340. Six miles south of Ipswich on A137. Look out for The Bull pub, then cross the railway bridge and turn left after 200 yards, between white railings. Follow the drive to the crossroads, turn left and the bunkhouse is on the right hand side.

CONTACT: Caroline
Brantham Hall, Brantham. nr Manningtree, Suffolk, CO11 1PT
Tel: 01473 327090 / 07857 630692
stourvalley@yha.org.uk www.yha.org.uk

COURT HILL
CENTRE

Just 2 miles south of Wantage, and only a few steps from the historic Ridgeway National Trail, The Court Hill Centre enjoys breathtaking views over the Vale of the White Horse.

Reclaimed barns surround a pretty courtyard garden, on the site of a disused rubbish dump! Offering accommodation to families, groups and individuals, a popular year-round destination. The centre offers evening meals, breakfasts, and picnic lunches, all prepared using as much local produce as possible. Meals are served in the beautiful high-roofed dining room which retains the impressive proportions and atmosphere of the old barn. Before and after your meal relax in the cosy sunken lounge with a log fire when it's chilly. Pitches for small tents are available and the centre and can accommodate small groups by arrangement. A meeting/classroom is also available.

DETAILS

- **Open** - Open all year round, to check availability please call 01235 760253.,
- **Number of beds** - 59: 1x15, 1x9, 1x6, 1x5, 6x4, 1x2
- **Booking** - Essential 24 hours in advance.
- **Price per night** - Adult £17.50, Under 18 £13.50
- **Public Transport** - Train, Didcot Parkway 10 Miles. Stagecoach, 32/A, X35,36 from Didcot Parkway to Wantage 2 Miles. There is no direct connection to the centre.
- **Directions** - From the M4 Jct 14, follow signs to Wantage. From Oxford A420 and A338 through Wantage. The Courthill Ridgeway Centre is accessed from the A338 close to Letcombe Regis

CONTACT: Reception
Courthill, Letcombe Regis, Wantage, OX12 9NE
Tel: 01235 760253
info@Courthill.org.uk www.Courthill.org.uk

WOODSIDE LODGES
BUNKHOUSE
ENGLAND

Woodside Lodges is a landscaped park with lakes, grass and woodland managed to encourage wildlife. In addition to the Scandinavian pine wood lodges and campsite there is a modern barn converted into 5 self catering units for walkers and cyclists. 4 units sleep 2 and 1 sleeps 4 (additional camp beds are available). Each unit has a cooking area with kettle, toaster, microwave, 2 electric rings, fridge and basic utensils. Electricity is by coin meter and bedding can be provided for an extra charge (or bring your own sleeping bag). The bunkhouse has a small common room, the toilets and showers are shared with the campsite. Close to the Herefordshire Trail, the Malvern Hills and the Forest of Dean the area is ideal for walkers. Nature lovers will enjoy the site with its backcloth of mixed woodland, wild flowers, pools and waterfalls where fishing, wild swimming and picnics can be enjoyed. The nearby town of Ledbury is famous for its black and white buildings, cobbled streets and Poetry Festival.

DETAILS

- **Open** - All year, All day
- **Number of beds** - 12 : 4x2, 1x4
- **Booking** - Booking in advance advised.
- **Price per night** - Telephone for prices
- **Public Transport** - Public transport is available within 1/2 mile.
- **Directions** - From Junction 2, M50 take the A417 to Ledbury. At the first roundabout turn left following Leadon Way (the by-pass). At the third roundabout turn left into Little Marcle Road. Go past the factory and take the right turn signposted Falcon Lane & Baregains Lane. Woodside Lodges is the sixth entrance on the right.

CONTACT: Woodside Lodges Country Park
Woodside Lodges, Falcon Lane, Ledbury, Herefordshire, HR8 2JN
Tel: 01531 670269, Fax: 0560 1153922
info@woodsidelodges.co.uk www.woodsidelodges.co.uk

BERROW HOUSE
BUNKHOUSE & CAMP SITE

Berrow House is situated in Hollybush between Rugged Stone Hill and Midsummer Hill in the Malvern Range. It is ideally suited for families, groups and individuals (including those with special needs) who want easy access to the countryside. The Forest of Dean, the Welsh border and the start of the Worcestershire Way Walk are near, with the towns of Malvern, Ledbury, Tewkesbury, Worcester, and Gloucester, all within a half hour drive. The Bunkhouse has sleeping accommodation for 5 in the main room and 3 more beds on the upper floor. The main room has heating and easy chairs. The adjacent kitchen/dining room has hot water, cooker, cutlery, crockery and cooking utensils. Toilets, dryer and shower are adjacent. The Fold is a separate building which has sleeping accommodation for 4 in two rooms, a fully equipped kitchen, heating, toilet, shower and a cloakroom. The Nook (caravan) has a double and single bed and uses the bunkhouse facilities. Camping, picnic area, water garden and car park are also available.

DETAILS

- **Open** - All year, 24 hours
- **Number of beds** - 8 (Bunkhouse), 4 (The Fold), 3 (The Nook) and 8 tents.
- **Booking** - Not required for individuals
- **Price per night** - £12 per person.
- **Public Transport** - Nearest train station and National Express service are in Ledbury, which is 3 miles from the hostel and would cost approx. £5 in a taxi.
- **Directions** - Take A449 from Ledbury towards Malvern. Turn right on to A438 through Eastnor. Berrow House is behind phone box in Hollybush (yellow sign).

CONTACT: Bill or Mary Cole
Hollybush, Ledbury, Herefordshire, HR8 1ET
Tel: 01531 635845, Fax: 01531 635845
berrowhouse@tiscali.co.uk www.berrowhouse.co.uk

BERROW HOUSE

CAMPING

CARAVANS

BUNKHOUSE

YE OLD FERRIE INN
BUNKHOUSE

This beautiful riverside pub has been standing on the banks of the River Wye since the 15th Century. With charming traditional features, warming open fires and stunning views across the valley, Ye Old Ferrie Inn is the ideal base for your explortion of the Wye Valley.

Ye Old Ferrie Inn bunkhouse, adjoining the Inn, is the perfect place for you to hang up your rucksack, kick off your walking boots and relax. There are two bunkrooms, sleeping 6 and 12, which are cosy, practical and affordable. You can watch the world float by on the two riverside terraces and meals are available in the Inn which serves traditional pub food using locally sourced ingredients. The Inn also has double B&B rooms with riverside views.

The area is ideal for canoeing, walking and rock climbing.

DETAILS

- **Open** - All year, all day
- **Number of beds** - 18: 1x12, 1x6 plus double B&B rooms
- **Booking** - Book by phone or email.
- **Price per night** - From £15 per person. For sole use please ring to enquire.
- **Public Transport** -   Train stations at Newport, Lydney, Hereford or Gloucester. Regular buses from Monmouth or Ross-on-Wye.
- **Directions** - From A40 Ross-on-Wye to Abergavenny road take junction signed Whitchurch/Symonds Yat West (B4164). Stay on B4164 and take slight left at Ferrie Lane and continue onto Washings Lane.

CONTACT: Jamie
Ferrie Lane, Symonds Yat West, Herefordshire HR9 6BL
Tel: 01600 890 232
hello@yeoldferrieinn.com www.yeoldferrieinn.com

This small hostel, once the old village school, is tucked away in the Shropshire hills with the Long Mynd to the east and Stiperstones to the west. It is an ideal spot for ramblers with the Shropshire Way passing close by and a great network of uncrowded paths to explore. Ideally situated for the End to End cycle route and plenty of mountain biking opportunities. The nearby small towns of Ludlow, Much Wenlock, Bishops Castle and sleepy Montgomery are all worth a visit. There's also the Acton Scott working farm museum and Snailbeach former lead mines close by. The hostel has a good kitchen, lounge with wood fire, books and games, a drying room, a food shop and a large garden. One ensuite room has some facilities for the disabled, phone to discuss your requirements. Meals are available, camping is allowed and there is a pub nearby.

DETAILS

- **Open** - All year, Reception 8-10 am, 5-10 pm. Hostel closes at 11pm.
- **Number of beds** - 38: 2x4 en suite, 1x6 or 8, 1x10, 1x12
- **Booking** - Telephone to book. No credit or debit cards accepted. Cheques must be made payable to Bridges Youth Hostel not YHA.
- **Price per night** - Adults £16, plus £3 for non YHA members. Under 18's £11.50 plus £1.50 for non YHA members. Camping £8.
- **Public Transport** - Trains at Church Stretton (5 miles) with a shuttle bus to Bridges at weekends from April to September.
- **Directions** - From Church Stretton, take 'The Burway' road uphill. Take right fork at top of Long Mynd. From Shrewsbury take road via Longden and Pulverbatch, then left by Horseshoe Inn. Access from Church Stretton over the Long Mynd Hill is not advisable in bad weather during winter

CONTACT: Bridges Youth Hostel
Ratlinghope, Shrewsbury, Shropshire, SY5 0SP
Tel: 01588 650656, Fax: 01588 650531

ALL STRETTON
BUNKHOUSE

All Stretton Bunkhouse offers comfortable self-catering accommodation with underfloor heating for individuals and small groups of up to 10 people. It has easy access to the Long Mynd which offers walks and bike rides for all levels of fitness. It is within easy reach of the busy town of Church Stretton and all its facilities, and just 10 minutes walk from the local pub (but please always book meals as it is not very big). Takeaway food is available in Church Stretton.

There are three bedrooms in the bunkhouse: Synalds and Cardoc have two bunks (sleeping 4) and Novers has two singles. A cot is also available. The well-equipped kitchen has cooker, microwave, toaster, kettle and fridge. There is a shower, two toilets and a tumble dryer. The track up to the property is steep and rough so wheelchair access is difficult.

DETAILS

- **Open** - All year, 5pm to 10.30pm. Reception 5pm to 9pm.
- **Number of beds** - 10 plus 1 cot.
- **Booking** - Book by phone, post or online.
- **Price per night** - Starting from £15.50 until February 2012.
- **Public Transport** - Trains to Church Stretton from Shrewsbury, Hereford and Cardiff. Station 1.2 miles walk (or taxi) from Bunkhouse. National Express buses to Shrewsbury, hourly local buses from Shrewsbury to Church Stretton via All Stretton.
- **Directions** - 300m on right going up Batch Valley bridleway (off the B5477, a mile north of Church Stretton).

CONTACT:
Meadow Green, Batch Valley, All Stretton, Shrops, SY6 6JW
Tel: 01694 722593   Mob: 0781 5517482
info@allstrettonbunkhouse.co.uk   www.allstrettonbunkhouse.co.uk

BIG MOSE BASECAMP
& MOSE COTTAGE

ENGLAND

Situated on the Dudmaston Estate, a National Trust property 4 miles east of Bridgnorth, Big Mose Basecamp accommodates groups of up to 20 people in 4 bunkrooms of varying sizes. The converted Tudor Farmhouse offers a large living area with a TV/DVD and lots of games for those rainy days, a dining area where everyone can sit together and enjoy reflecting on the days adventures and a fully equipped kitchen area. Sleeping bags required. Joined to the farm house is Mose Cottage, a recently converted Forester's Cottage which sleeps 10 people in two twin-bedded rooms and one six bed bunkroom. Mose Cottage (graded as 3 star hostel) is a half-way house between the luxury of a holiday cottage and the more basic bunkhouse offering self catering facilities and an open fire for those cold winter nights. Both properties can be opened for groups larger than 20.

DETAILS

- **Open** - All year except New year and Xmas.
- **Number of beds** - Basecamp 20:1x2, 1x4, 1x6, 1x8, Mose cottage 10: 1x6, 2x2
- **Booking** - Recommended
- **Price per night** - £320.00 per week (Mon - Fri 4 nights) £180.00 per weekend (Friday to Sunday 2 nights) £ 90.00 per night.
- **Public Transport** - Train stations at Telford, Wolverhampton or Kidderminster.
- **Directions** - From Bridgnorth take A458 towards Stourbridge. Travel 3 miles and after a small pine wood on right, take right hand turning to Mose. Approx 1/4 mile along take a left down a track with a small National Trust sign leading to the basecamp.

CONTACT: Nicola Hook
Big Mose Cottage, Quatford, Bridgnorth, Shropshire, WV15 6QR
Tel: 01746 780838
Nicola.Hook@nationaltrust.org.uk www.nationaltrust.org.uk/dudmaston

STOKES BARN
BUNKHOUSES

Stokes Barn is located on top of Wenlock Edge, an Area of Outstanding Natural Beauty, in the heart of Shropshire countryside. Two bunkhouses are available; the Threshing Barn (sleeping 28) and the Granary (sleeping 16).

These offer comfortable, centrally heated, dormitory accommodation for a wide range of groups and provide an ideal base for corporate groups, field study groups, universities, schools, stag and hen parties, walkers or just a relaxing reunion with friends or family. The Ironbridge World Heritage Site is only 6 miles away and is a great attraction. Walk to the historic town of Much Wenlock to visit shops, pubs and sports facilities. Situated only a few miles from Church Stretton and the Long Mynd the barn is in a walking / cycling haven. Many activities available. Have a relaxing and enjoyable stay.

DETAILS

- **Open** - All year, all day
- **Number of beds** - Threshing Barn 28: 1x12,1x10,1x6 Granary 16:1x10,1x4,1x2
- **Booking** - Deposit required. Minimum stay 2 nights.
- **Price per night** - Minimum of two nights. Barn £540 two nights mid week, £800 two nights weekend. Granary: £384 two nights mid week, £550 two nights weekend.
- **Public Transport** - Trains at Telford (10 miles) and Shrewsbury (10 miles). National Express coaches call at Shrewsbury from London, call 0839 142348 for information. Midland Red buses stop in Much Wenlock, enquires 01952 223766.
- **Directions** - GR 609 999. From the M6 take M54 Telford following Ironbridge Gorge signs. A4169 to Much Wenlock, joining A458 for Shrewsbury. The Barn is signed at Newton House Farm (TF13 6DB) on the Much Wenlock to Shrewsbury Rd.

CONTACT:
Stokes Barn, Newtown Farm, Much Wenlock, Shropshire, TF13 6DB
Tel: 01952 727491 ext 2
info@stokesbarn.co.uk www.stokesbarn.co.uk

SPRINGHILL FARM
BUNKHOUSE

Springhill Farm Bunkhouse is on a hill farm at 1475ft above sea level, near the Welsh/Shropshire border with beautiful views over the Ceiriog Valley and Berwyn Mountains. Great for walking and activity breaks or just to relax.

The main bunkhouse sleeps around 21 and the 2 smaller self catering cottages can sleep up to 12 more. There is also a separate large room with its own kitchen which can be used for meetings or as a camping barn. The bunkhouse has under-floor heating, entrance hall with w/c and drying room, large kitchen, dining room and sitting room. There are 5 bedrooms sleeping 1-8 people. Outside is a large patio and lawn, BBQ and hot tub. Available onsite are cycle hire, archery and horse riding. Your own horse and pets welcome on request.

DETAILS

- **Open** - All year, all day (please don't phone after 9pm)
- **Number of beds** - 30+: 20 (bunkhouse) + two cottages + camping barn
- **Booking** - Advisable, deposit required
- **Price per night** - £18pp (including bedding but not towels)
- **Public Transport** - Nearest train station Chirk (8 miles). Nearest bus service is in the village Glyn Ceiriog (2.5 miles). Transfer can be arranged.
- **Directions** - GR SJ 210 346. On the A483 from Wrexham, take the third exit on the first roundabout (McDonalds). At the next roundabout take the first exit, continue into Chirk, and then turn right for Glyn Ceiriog. After 6 miles you will arrive at Glyn Ceiriog. At the mini roundabout turn left, go over the bridge, and then straight away turn right into a small lane. Continue up the hill for about two miles, do not turn off.

CONTACT: Sue Benbow
Springhill Farm, Selattyn, Oswestry, Shropshire, SY10 7NZ
Tel: 01691 718406
sue@springhillfarm.co.uk www.atspringhill.co.uk

Womerton Farm Bunkhouse is situated right next to the Long Mynd, an Area of National Beauty in the heart of the Shropshire Hills. It offers small select accommodation to sleep eight, six in bunks downstairs and two in a double sofa bed upstairs. There is a fully equipped kitchen and living area upstairs.

The bunkhouse is 3 miles from Church Stretton, 12 miles from historic Shrewsbury and 15 miles from Ludlow, food capital of Shropshire. There are many local attractions such as Acton Scott Working Farm Museum, Stokesay Castle, Museum of Lost Content and Discovery Centre. The Long Mynd is fantastic for walking, mountain biking and horse riding. Horses can be field-accommodated if arranged in advance. Well behaved dogs that are not moulting allowed. For photo gallery, directions and details please visit website.

DETAILS

- **Open** - All year, all day. Closed from 11 am to 4pm on change over days.
- **Number of beds** - 9: 1x6, 1x1 + double sofa bed in living area
- **Booking** - Booking recommended to guarantee a place.
- **Price per night** - £80 Christmas / New Year, £80 Easter to Sept, £60 off peak. Stay 3 nights get next 1 to 3 nights half price. Phone or email for midweek offers.
- **Public Transport** - Nearest train and bus station is Church Stretton (3 miles). Taxi fare is about £10.
- **Directions** - From Church Stretton follow A49 north. Past coffee shop and craft centre take a left turn signed Lower Wood. From Shrewsbury on A49 south, pass though Leebotwood then take the right turn signed Lower Wood. Follow this road for 1 mile, cross a cattle grid onto the Long Mynd and we are the first farm on the right.

CONTACT: Ruth or Tony
Womerton Farm, All Stretton, Church Stretton, Shropshire, SY6 6LJ
Tel: 01694 751260
ruth@womerton-farm.co.uk www.womerton-farm.co.uk

FOXHOLES CASTLE
BUNKHOUSE

Foxholes Castle Bunkhouse at Bishops Castle is situated within a relaxed, family-run campsite, surrounded by glorious views of South West Shropshire's beautiful hill country. Within a few minutes walk of the Shropshire Way, Offa's Dyke Path, the Sustrans cycle network and the lively town of Bishop's Castle it is ideal for families, couples, walkers, cyclists and photographers. The bunkhouse is a 8m x 3m heated area, divided in half by a partition with an open doorway. There is a single bed and one set of bunks in each section (no bedding is provided). In heated buildings next to the bunkhouse (shared with the campsite) you will find a wet room, showers, fridge, freezer and washing-up sink. A second set of showers and toilets are 30 seconds walk away. There is good accessibily for wheelchair users. There is an outside table, seating and space for a BBQ. There are no cooking facilities but there are lots of pubs, restaurants, cafes and takeaways 5 minutes walk away in Bishops Castle.

DETAILS

- **Open** - All year, 24 hours
- **Number of beds** - 6: 2 x 3
- **Booking** - Bookings by phone or send an email.
- **Price per night** - £10 per person or £40 for whole bunkhouse (sleeps 6).
- **Public Transport** - Trains at Craven Arms (12 miles). Buses from Shrewsbury to Bishops Castle (5 mins walk from bunkhouse) every 2 hours.
- **Directions** - Bishops Castle is on the A488 about 20 miles south of Shrewsbury, and 35 miles from the M54. Foxholes is on the B4385 Montgomery Road just north of the town. Look for our sign, and follow our driveway for half a mile. GR SO 324 897

CONTACT: Chris or Wendy Jones
Foxholes Camping, Montgomery Rd, Bishops Castle, Shropshire, SY9 5HA
Tel: 01588 638924, mobile 07890 231351
foxholes.castle@googlemail.com www.foxholes-castle.co.uk

Your ideal choice for city central accommodation, Hatters Birmingham has combined hotel quality en suite rooms with the social atmosphere of an international travellers' hostel. Catering for groups of all sizes and independent travellers, you can enjoy the comforts of FREE WiFi, breakfast, en suite rooms, large communal areas and enthusiastic, informative staff. Full board or half board options are available for groups of over 15 people. Conveniently located for all city centre attractions and transport links, ask our reception staff about discounts to Cadbury World, Warwick Castle, Sealife Centre, and many other FREE adventures, including our FREE City Walking Tours and Quiz nights. If you are into the outdoors we have the largest bouldering complex just around the corner, or try out your mountain biking skills at Cannock Chase (30mins drive). So come and stay with us and we'll show you what's fun in Brum.

DETAILS

- **Open** - All year. Reception available 24 hours. Check in 2pm. check out 11am.
- **Number of beds** - 100: single, double, twin, triple, 4, 6, 8 and 12 bed rooms.
- **Booking** - Booking not essential but recommended, especially at weekends.Photo ID (ie passport, ID card or driving license) required at check in.
- **Price per night** - From £14.50 dorms, from £35 private rooms, inc b/fast & linen. For group prices and bookings contact groups@hattersgroup.com
- **Public Transport** -   Easy walking distance from all public transport hubs: New Street Station 15mins, Snow Hill Station 5mins, Digbeth Coach Station 20mins. Local taxi service @ £5.00 for all city centre travel.Taxi Service: BB's Taxi 0121 693 3333
- **Directions** - Please contact the hostel reception for directions.

CONTACT: Reception
92-95 Livery Street, Birmingham, B3 1RJ
Tel: 0121 236 4031, Fax: 0121 2366694
birmingham@hattersgroup.com www.hattersgroup.com/#bham

Birmingham Central Backpackers is Birmingham's first and best independent backpackers hostel and THE place to stay while exploring the brilliance of Birmingham. Located a minute's walk from the National Express coach station, 1 minute from the buses to the NEC and Airport and a mere 7 minute walk to New Street train station, our location can't be beaten for convenience. Rooms include 4-8 person dorms, a pod dorm and singles and privates. Friendly international staff, two cosy common rooms for relaxation, guest kitchen, free breakfast and nightly snack buffet, free WiFi and budget computer stations, gigantic cinema screen (with over 600 movies to choose from), Playstation 3, Nintendo Wii, pool, travel information centre, outdoor patio and guest-only bar. So when in Birmingham make us your place to stay, you won't regret it!

DETAILS

- **Open** - All year, check-in from 2pm-11pm. Common area open 8am-12am.
- **Number of beds** - 80: 11 rooms of 4-8 beds 1x3, 3x2, 2x1 + pod dorm
- **Booking** - Book by phone, email or online. 2% credit card fee, 40p debit card fee for bookings of £50 or more.
- **Price per night** - From £16 weekdays, £17 Fri and Sat, inc. linen, light breakfast and nightly snack buffet.
- **Public Transport** - Digbeth coach station and New Street train station near by.
- **Directions** - From Digbeth coach station take Milk Street (Big Bulls Head on corner). Hostel located above Billy's Bar, one block down. From New Street Station, walk down New Street through the Bull Ring and down the steps to the markets. Take a left at the markets and go to the traffic lights. Cross over the lights to the Digbeth High Street. Walk 4 blocks, and turn left onto Milk Street.

CONTACT: Mike
58 Coventry Street, Digbeth, Birmingham, B5 5NH
Tel: 0121 6430033 Mobile: 07756 829970
info@birminghamcentralbackpackers.com www.birminghamcentralbackpackers.com

Only 2 miles from the centre of Birmingham lies Ackers Adventure, a centre for adventurous activities. Set in 70 acres of semi-rural land the centre has a 100m dry ski slope, climbing walls, archery course and canoeing on the Grand Union Canal, which runs straight though the site. Ackers Residential Centre (ARC) and Ackers Adventure are run by a charitable organisation that offers subsidised rates to schools and youth groups but also welcomes family groups, corporate groups and clubs. All groups get sole use of the centre.

The purpose-built centre, opened in 2008, has 9 sleeping rooms, a fully equipped kitchen, refectory area with chairs and tables and a recreation room with a TV & DVD player and games. Facilities include ample secluded parking, showers and changing rooms, disability lift, self catering kitchen, function room, picnic and BBQ area. A stay at Ackers Adventure could be combined with a visit to The Sea Life Centre, Cadbury World, Thinktank, The Bull Ring shopping centre, National Motorcycle Museum, the NEC as well as art galleries, museums and theatres. Instructor led activities and lessons are available.

DETAILS

- **Open** - All year, 24 hours. Office staffed 10am -5pm (9pm on weekdays).
- **Number of beds** - 26: 4x4, 5x2
- **Booking** - Please book by phone.
- **Price per night** - From £195 for sole use of centre.
- **Public Transport** - A few minutes walk from Small Heath rail station.
- **Directions** - Entrance off the Small Heath Highway (dual carriageway), see signs

CONTACT:
Ackers (ARC), Waverley Canal Basin, Small Heath, Birmingham, B10 0DQ
Tel: 0121 772 5111 , Fax: 0121 766 7870
info@ackers-adventure.co.uk   www.ackers-adventure.co.uk

THE IGLOO
BACKPACKERS HOSTEL

Located within an easy walk of the city centre the Igloo is Nottingham's most popular choice for budget-minded travellers. It offers a clean, safe and warm overnight stay in a large, listed Victorian house from just £15 per night, with many homely comforts: bunk bed dorms, hot power showers, lounge with TV, films, internet stations and WiFi, games room with pool table, fully-equipped kitchen, free tea & coffee, laundry facilities and good company. It is the ideal home-from-home for resting while enjoying all that this lively university city has to offer. Private rooms now also available in the brand new 'Igloo Annexe' located over the road, with double, triple and family rooms, freeview TV, WiFi and memory foam mattresses in all rooms. Check out our website.

DETAILS

■ **Open** - All year, all day
■ **Number of beds** - 36:1x6; 1x8; 1x10;1x12, plus doubles, triples and family rooms.
■ **Booking** - Essential during summer months. Groups must confirm by email or by phone with deposit.
■ **Price per night** - Dorms: £16pp. £60 per week after 10 nights stay. Private rooms from £20 pp. Seasonal discounts.
■ **Public Transport** - Direct, regular trains from London etc. National Express to Broadmarsh bus station. From bus/train stations 20mins walk, £4 taxi ride or catch tram to Trent Uni (4th stop), take next right (Peel St), follow to Golden Fleece pub.
■ **Directions** - From the Tourist Information Centre (Market Square) turn right out of TIC, take next left onto Cumber Street, keep walking straight on for ten mins, past the Victoria Shopping centre, untill you reach the Golden Fleece Pub. The Igloo is directly opposite. Entry is on the side of the buidling.

CONTACT: Igloo Backpackers Hostel
110 Mansfield Road, Nottingham, NG1 3HL
Tel: 0115 9475250
reception@igloohostel.co.uk www.igloohostel.co.uk

If you enjoy walking, cycling, bird watching or fun on the beach, Hunstanton Hostel provides an ideal affordable family break or activity getaway. The nearby Norfolk Coast Path and Pedlars Way are great for wildlife spotting, or you can take a boat trip to Seal Island - a hit with all the family. The sleeping accommodation is in bunks in rooms of various sizes with one family room which has a double and bunks. You can book private rooms for your sole use or a bed in a dorm. The whole hostel is available for sole use for groups, friends reunions and family get togethers. Meals can be provided and there is a self catering kitchen, a large lounge and a conservatory dining area. The classroom / training area is ideal for courses and the hostel can provide all meals and drink requirements. The compact garden has sea air and a five minutes walk will take you to the sea front and town centre shopping area with a Sealife sanctuary, fantastic local beaches and cliff top walks. You will receive a friendly welcome at Hunstanton Hostel a great home-from-home on the east coast.

DETAILS

- **Open** - All year (group bookings only Oct - March), Reception 8-10am 5-10pm
- **Number of beds** - 40: 1x2, 1x3, 3x4, 1x4(family), 1x5, 1x6, 1x8.
- **Booking** - Book online, by phone or email
- **Price per night** - Adults from £20.40 low season to £22.40 high season and school holidays. Enquire for prices for family rooms and sole use of hostel.
- **Public Transport** - Coast Hopper. Trains at Kings Lynn with bus to Hunstanton.
- **Directions** - Follow the coast road to Hunstanton, then signs for South Beach (Southend Rd). Turn right into Park Road, then first left, hostel is 20 yds on the left.

CONTACT: Neal or Alison Sanderson
15-17 Avenue Road, Hunstanton, Norfolk, PE36 5BW
Tel: 01485 532061 Mob: 07737 642828
hunstantonhostel@talktalk.net www.yha.org.uk

OLD RED LION

Visitors to Castle Acre are entranced by the special atmosphere of this medieval walled town which lies within the outer bailey of an 11th-century castle. Castle Acre is on the Peddars Way, an ancient track now a long distance path. The Old Red Lion, a former pub, is centrally situated and carries on the tradition of serving travellers who seek refreshment and repose. Guests can stay in private rooms or dormitories, where bedding and linen are provided free of charge. There are quiet areas (with wood burning stoves) for reading, meeting other guests and playing. There are two large areas: the flint and timber walled converted pub cellar, suitable for yoga; and The Garden Room with kitchen and toilet adjacent, ideal for group use: celebrations, classes, courses, workshops and retreats. There is a ground floor room with double bed, sofa bed and disabled toilet. Drying facilities. Local shops and pubs. No smoking.

DETAILS

■ **Open** - All year, all day access. Arrival times by arrangement.
■ **Number of beds** - 24: 1x10, 1x6, 1x double, 1x double+sofa bed(en suite), 2xtwin
■ **Booking** - Useful but not essential
■ **Price per night** - Prices include: self-service wholefood breakfast, all-day access, parking. For one night stays: dormitory £22.50, double en suite £35. Reductions possible for longer stays. Single supplement may apply
■ **Public Transport** - Train stations at King's Lynn & Downham Market (14 miles). Buses from King's Lynn to Swaffham. Daily National Express coach between Victoria Coach Station & Swaffham. Norfolk Bus info 0500 626116. Taxi from Swaffham £7.
■ **Directions** - GR 818151. Castle Acre is 3.5 miles north of Swaffham (A47) on the A1065. The hostel is on left, 75yds down from Bailey Gate in village centre.

CONTACT: Alison Loughlin
Old Red Lion, Bailey Street, Castle Acre, Norfolk, PE32 2AG
Tel: 01760 755557
oldredlion@yahoo.co.uk www.oldredlion.org.uk

DEEPDALE GRANARY
GROUP HOSTEL
ENGLAND

A perfect base for groups to stay, explore and absorb the stunning North Norfolk coast. Deepdale Granary is a self-contained 17th century building sleeping 18 in four bedrooms with a fully fitted kitchen and dining/sitting room. Part of the award winning Deepdale Farm, right on the coast in the heart of an Area of Outstanding Natural Beauty. There are excellent pubs nearby, both traditional and chic, great restaurants and miles of unspoilt beaches and dunes. The Norfolk coast is perfect for walking and cycling with miles of coast path and picturesque villages. Take time to discover our heritage sites including the Sandringham and Holkham estates or enjoy birdwatching in the tranquil beauty of the unique saltmarsh. The Granary is fully heated, has showers, a drying room and solar water heating. Next door Dalegate Market has shops, a supermarket, and a brilliant café serving locally sourced food.
Camping and Teepees also available.

DETAILS
- **Open** - All year, all day. Collect key from Deepdale Information.
- **Number of beds** - 19: 2 x 6 : 1 x 4 : 1 x 3.
- **Booking** - Essential, 20% deposit, balance in advance. See website for details
- **Price per night** - From £150 per night, for up to 19 people.
- **Public Transport** - Trains / coaches at King's Lynn (25 miles) then excellent Coastal Hopper bus to Burnham Deepdale. Coastal Hopper services the coast from King's Lynn to Cromer, including Sandringham. Traveline 0870 608 2 608.
- **Directions** - GR 803443. On A149 coast road, halfway between Hunstanton and Wells-next-the-Sea. Beside Deepdale Garage & opposite Deepdale Church.

CONTACT:
Deepdale Information Centre, Burnham Deepdale, Norfolk, PE31 8DD
Tel: 01485 210256
info@deepdalebackpackers.co.uk www.deepdalebackpackers.co.uk

Eco-friendly award-winning backpackers' hostel on the beautiful north Norfolk coast. Escape the smog of the cities to this stunning part of the world. Deepdale Backpackers offers private en suite rooms (double, twin, triple, quad and family), single sex and mixed dorms. There's so much to do here, adrenaline sports, great pubs and restaurants, miles of sandy beaches. Deepdale is a perfect base for walking and cycling with miles of coast path, the famous big skies and quaint fishing harbours. Or just come and chill. The facilities are second to none, all rooms are en suite, there is a fully equipped farmhouse kitchen and a really cosy lounge with a TV and a wood burner for cooler nights. There's a lovely courtyard with barbeques for summer evenings. Deepdale is a working farm and eco-friendly with recycling, underfloor heating and solar water. Next door Dalegate Market has shops, a supermarket, and a brilliant café serving locally sourced food. Camping and Teepees also available.

DETAILS

- **Open** - All day every day, collect key from Deepdale Information.
- **Number of beds** - 50: 5xdbl, 1twin, 1triple, 1quad, 2 family rms up to 6, + dorms
- **Booking** - Pre-booking recommended. Max group size 12. See website.
- **Price per night** - From £10 (£63 per week) dorm room. £30 twin/double room.
- **Public Transport** - Train and coaches at King's Lynn (25 Miles). Coast Hopper bus to Burnham Deepdale on the coast road from King's Lynn to Cromer, stops at Sandringham, Holkham and Titchwell Bird Reserve. Traveline 0870 6082608
- **Directions** - GR 803443 On A149 coast road halfway between Hunstanton and Wells-next-the-Sea. Beside Dalegate Market, opposite Deepdale Church.

CONTACT:
Deepdale Information Centre, Burnham Deepdale, Norfolk, PE31 8DD
Tel: 01485 210256
info@deepdalebackpackers.co.uk www.deepdalebackpackers.co.uk

SHINING CLIFF
HOSTEL

With its own crags, streams, lakes and over 100-acres of mature woodland, the hidden Shining Cliff Hostel has nature on its doorstep. Completely refurbished in 2009, the hostel is ideal for schools, clubs and groups of families and friends wishing to enjoy time away in a peaceful woodland setting.

The entrance porch, with space for hanging coats and boots, leads into the open plan kitchen, dining and lounge area. In the well equipped kitchen, there is a 6 ring gas hob, electric oven, microwave, fridge, freezer, dishwasher and water boiler. The dining area comfortably seats 20 people whilst the lounge provides seating and space to relax. The hostel offers a full range of activities, some are on-site such as bushcraft, abseiling, ecology and environmental art, while climbing, caving or canoeing can be enjoyed a little further a field. The hostel is nestled within woodland a five minute walk from the nearest parking area. Other paths lead through the woods to the A6 at Ambergate (20 mins walk). Ambergate has a food shop, pubs, buses to Derby and a train station with connections to Derby, Nottingham and London (in less than 3 hours).

DETAILS

- **Open** - All Year,
- **Number of beds** - 20: 1x4, 2x6, 2x2
- **Booking** - Phone or email
- **Price per night** - £180 (Apr-Oct), £150 (Nov-Mar).
- **Public Transport** - Ambergate station (1 mile). Transpeak bus service on A6.
- **Directions** - See website or ask for directions. Sat Navs not recommended.

CONTACT:
Jackass Lane, Alderwasley Belper, DE56 2RE
Tel: 01433 620 377
ShiningCliff@hollowford.org www.shiningcliff.org

The Glenorchy Centre is situated in the heart of the Derbyshire countryside on the edge of the Peak District National Park. Suitable for self-catering groups wishing to explore this attractive area. A few minutes walk in any direction will find you in the rolling Derbyshire countryside. Within walking distance of the High Peak Trail for walking, pony trekking and cycling, and Black Rocks - great for bouldering and climbing. Nearby Cromford has Arkwright's mills and Cromford Canal to explore. The fully heated accommodation comprises 8 and 12 bed dormitories, one 4 bed and one 2 bed room, all with showers and toilets. Sheets and duvets provided, but not towels. There is a fitted kitchen with dining area and a large multi-purpose room with a large stage, ideal for recreation, conferences etc. There is a TV, table tennis and a snooker table. Disabled access is possible to the main hall and dining area.
All groups must include at least 4 adults.

DETAILS

- **Open** - Mid Feb to Early Dec., 24 hours
- **Number of beds** - 26: 1x12, 1x8, 1x4, 1x2
- **Booking** - Book with 25% deposit. Booking form on website or ring 01629 824323. WDURC, Coldwell Street, Wirksworth, Derbyshire, DE4 4FB
- **Price per night** - Mon 12am - Fri 12am £795; Fri 4pm - Sun 4pm £495; Sat 2pm - Sat 10am £1195. Smaller groups £15pp, minimum £260 per night. Incl. 9hrs heating per day, extra heating £5 per hour.
- **Public Transport** - Frequent local buses run to Belper and Matlock. Nearest trains at Cromford (2 miles).
- **Directions** - From the town centre go down past Red Lion pub then take next left.

CONTACT: The Secretary
Chapel Lane, Wirksworth, Derbyshire, DE4 4FF
Tel: 01629 824323
secretary@glenorchycentre.org.uk www.glenorchycentre.org.uk

The Reckoning House camping barn has been renovated to a high standard including double glazing and insulation. It is situated on the edge of Lathkill Dale, 3 miles from Bakewell. Lathkill Dale is a nature reserve managed by English Nature to protect a variety of flora and fauna as well as some outstanding geological features. Horse riding, fishing, golf and cycle hire are all available locally. There are also many local walks including the Limestone Way.

It has a cooking area, 4 calor gas rings (gas supplied) a washing up sink with hot water, a toilet, wash basin, storage heaters in all rooms and shower inside the barn. Upstairs there are two separate rooms with bunkbeds.

DETAILS

- **Open** - All year, by arrangement
- **Number of beds** - 12
- **Booking** - Sole use bookings only, in advance (min 2 nights at weekends). 10% deposit, balance 4 weeks before arrival.
- **Price per night** - £10.50 per person. Sole use £95 per night, Reduction for sole use on Sun (excluding bank holidays), Mon, Tue, Wed or Thurs nights.
- **Public Transport** - Train stations at Buxton (10 miles) and Matlock (13 miles). National Express drop at Bakewell. Local buses (enquiries 01332 292200) go to Bakewell from Monyash, Over Haddon, Matlock and Buxton.
- **Directions** - GR 184 666. Take the B5055 out of Bakewell towards Monyash. Continue for 3 miles. After passing Haddon Grove holiday cottages (the second set of cottages on right), take the first turn left at the signpost to Haddon Grove. Bear left at the bottom of the lane. The camping barn is the first on the left in a half mile.

CONTACT: Julia Finney
Mandale Farm, Haddon Grove, Bakewell, Derbyshire, DE45 1JF
Tel: 01629 812416
julia.finney@virgin.net www.mandalehouse.co.uk

BARN FARM
BARNS AND CAMPSITE

Barn Farm is a working farm in the village of Birchover with fine views over the Derwent valley. Nearby are Stanton Moor with Victorian stone carvings and Nine Ladies stone circle, Robin Hood's Stride and other bouldering and climbing areas, the Limestone Way, a village shop and two pubs serving food.

Four camping barns are available: Sabine Hay has 15 bunkbeds arranged around a communal space with fully fitted kitchen, Hill Carr and Warren Carr have a similar arrangement with 15 and 12 single beds. Stables Barn has 6 bunkbeds. All bunkhouses have self-catering facilities, are heated and have private bathroom and shower facilities in adjacent barns. Also available: two en suite double-bed units, the Garden Room and the Gatehouse Barn. There's also space for camping (no single sex groups), caravans and camper vans with good showers, toilets and laundry facilities, games room and childrens play area.

Indoor or outdoor storage for caravans and camper vans available.

DETAILS

- **Open** - All year, accommodation available all day.
- **Number of beds** - 52: 1x15, 1x15, 1x12, 1x6, 1x2, 1x2 plus camping.
- **Booking** - Booking advisable 50% deposit.
- **Price per night** - Hill Carr £150, Sabine Hay £140, Warren Carr £240, Stables Barn £100, Garden Room £45, Gatehouse Barn £85/night (min.2 nights) Weekly rates available. Camping £7.50pp (£5pp D of E groups).
- **Public Transport** - The 172 bus from Bakewell to Matlock runs approx. hourly.
- **Directions** - From the A6 between Matlock and Bakewell take the B5056. Follow signs for Birchover, continue past the Druid Inn to farm sign at the top of the village.

CONTACT:
Birchover, Matlock, Derbyshire, DE4 2BL
Tel: 01629 650245
gilberthh@msn.com www.barnfarmcamping.com

SHEEN
BUNKHOUSE

Sheen Bunkhouse is a newly converted barn in a quiet corner of the Peak District, close to the beautiful Dove and Manifold valleys. Comprehensively equipped, it offers a large TV lounge, well-equipped self-catering facilities and two bunkrooms with wash basins. Toilets and showers are conveniently located for both rooms.

Passing close by the barn, the Manifold Valley Track, Tissington Trail and High Peak Trail provide easy access to beautiful countryside, ideal for families and cyclists. Dovedale, the Upper Dove Valley and the remote and mysterious moorlands around Flash and Longnor offer stunning scenery for walkers. Visit the markets and parks at Buxton (8 miles), Leek (10 miles) and Bakewell (12 miles) for a great day out. Other attractions include Alton Towers (20 mins by car) and the famous Opera House and show caves at Buxton.

DETAILS

- **Open** - All year, 24 hours access, reception 8am - 9pm
- **Number of beds** - 14: 1x8, 1x6
- **Booking** - Book by phone or email
- **Price per night** - From: Adults £16, Under 16s £11.
- **Public Transport** - Train station at Buxton. Daily bus operated by Bowers from Buxton to Hartington passes close to bunkhouse.
- **Directions** - On the B5054 between Hartington and Hulme End take the turning to Sheen (also signposted for 'Staffordshire Knott'). The bunkhouse is on the right 200yds after the pub.

CONTACT: Graham Belfield
Peakstones, Sheen, Derbyshire, SK17 0ES
Tel: 01298 84501, Fax: 01298 84501
grahambelfield@fsmail.net

THORPE FARM
BUNKHOUSES

Thorpe Farm Bunkhouses are situated a mile northwest of Hathersage, on a family-run mixed dairy farm which makes its own ice cream.

The bunkhouses are 2 miles west of Stanage Edge. Other popular climbing and walking areas are nearby. Castleton is 6 miles up the Hope Valley and Eyam is 6 miles southwest. Each bunkhouse has dormitories with individual bunks each with mattress and pillow. There is some sleeping space in the sitting rooms and room for camping outside. The bunkhouses have heating, drying facilities, hot showers, toilets, electric / gas cooking, fridges, freezers, electric kettles, toasters etc. The Byre is all on one level with disabled facilities.

DETAILS

- **Open** - All year, no restrictions
- **Number of beds** - Old Shippon 32: 2x12, 2x4. Byre 14: 1x6, 2x4. Old Stables 14: 1x8, 1x6. Pondside 14: 1x8, 1x6
- **Booking** - Essential for weekends.
- **Price per night** - See own website.
- **Public Transport** -   Train station at Hathersage, 10 mins walk from bunkhouse. Bus service 272 operates from Sheffield to Hathersage. . Details phone Busline 01298 230980 or 01246 250450.
- **Directions** - GR 223 824. If walking from A6187/A625 in Hathersage turn right (just past the George Hotel) up Jaggers Lane, turn second right up Coggers Lane and fifth turning on left (signed Thorpe Farm). If driving follow the road from Hathersage towards Hope for ¾ mile, then turn right into private drive (signposted Thorpe Farm).

CONTACT: Jane Marsden
Thorpe Farm, Hathersage, Peak District, Via Sheffield, S32 1B
Tel: 01433 650659
jane@hope-valley.co.uk www.thorpe-bunk.co.uk

PINDALE FARM
OUTDOOR CENTRE

Pindale Farm Outdoor Centre is a mile from Castleton in the heart of the Peak District. It comprises a farmhouse pre-dating 1340 and lead mine buildings from the 1850s, which have been completely rebuilt from a near derelict condition. The Centre offers 5 different kinds of accommodation. The farmhouse offers traditional bed and (an AGA cooked) breakfast. The Barn has 6 independent self-catering units, 3 of these can accommodate people with certain physical disabilities. The Old Lead Mine Engine House is a self-catering unit sleeping 8. The Powder House, originally the mine's explosive store, is a small camping barn with basic facilities for up to 4 people. A campsite, adjacent to the Centre, has showers, hot water, and toilet facilities. Many rooms have Freesat TV and WiFi is available in the barn and most of the camping areas (cost £2 a day). The Centre is the ideal base for walking, climbing, caving, horse riding etc. Instruction is available if required. Well behaved pets welcome.

DETAILS

- **Open** - All year (Camping March-October), 24 hours
- **Number of beds** - 64 bunkbeds plus camping and B&B
- **Booking** - Early booking (deposit) is best.
- **Price per night** - Camping £6 pp (£4 for hook up), Barns £12 pp plus £1 extra for one night stays. B&B with four poster bed and AGA breakfast enquire for prices.
- **Public Transport** - Train station in Hope. On local buses ask for Hope. Hope is 15 minutes walk from the hostel. National Express Sheffield (taxi fare £15-£20).
- **Directions** - GR 163 825 From Hope follow cement works signs, turn off main road between church and Woodroffe Arms.

CONTACT: Alan Medhurst
Pindale Lane, Hope, Hope Valley, Derbyshire, S33 6RN
Tel: 01433 620111, Fax: 01433 620729
pindalefarm@btconnect.com www.pindalefarm.co.uk

HOMESTEAD
AND CHEESEHOUSE

These two bunkhouses are situated on a small mixed farm in the middle of Bamford, just 3 miles from Stanage Edge. The Derwent Dams are between 1.5 and 7 miles further up the valley. Castleton is 5 miles to the north, Chatsworth House and Park 10 miles to the southwest.

Both bunkhouses have individual bunks each with mattress, fitted sheets and pillow, gas central heating and drying facilities. Homestead has 22 beds in 3 rooms, and 2 bathrooms with 2 toilets and showers in each, a large dayroom with oak seating and a fully equipped kitchen with gas cooker. Cheesehouse is a self-contained bunkhouse with four bunks, ideal for a small family or group. It has a shower and toilet and is equipped with a kitchen having cooking rings, a microwave oven, toaster and kettle. The bunkhouses are 2 minutes walk from two pubs. Sorry, no dogs (working dogs on site).

DETAILS

- **Open** - All year, no restriction
- **Number of beds** - Homestead 22: 1x10, 2x6. Cheesehouse 4: 1x4.
- **Booking** - Recommended for weekends.
- **Price per night** -   From £12 per person. Sole use: Homestead £175, Cheesehouse £40.
- **Public Transport** - Nearest train station Bamford, 10 mins walk. Bus 274 & 275 operates Sundays Bamford to Sheffield or Castleton. Bus 272 Bamford to Sheffield and Castleton. Bus 241 Bamford to Bakewell.
- **Directions** - The farm is in the centre of Bamford on South View Lane (turn off A6013 at the 'Country Stores').

CONTACT: Helena Platts
The Farm, Bamford, Hope Valley, S33 0BL
Tel: 01433 651298

DALEHEAD
BUNKHOUSE

Recently refurbished, Dalehead Bunkhouse is a renovated gritstone farmhouse on a working hill-farm at the remote head of Edale. It provides basic but comfortable accommodation heated by log burner. There is a cooking area with fridge, a lounge and plenty of parking. Visitors will need to bring their own sleeping bags, pillows and towels. Edale is a very popular destination for walkers, climbers, mountain bikers, hang-gliders or for just enjoying the magnificent scenery. It lies between the gritstone of the peat-topped Kinder moors to the north and the cave-riddled limestone of the White Peak to the south. Despite its proximity to major cities and the straightforward rail service to Sheffield and Manchester, the Dark Peak remains unspoilt, with many places where it is possible to enjoy a sense of remoteness. Dogs are welcome on the ground floor of the bunkhouse for an extra charge of £15 per stay.

DETAILS

- **Open** - Open all year round, 24 hours
- **Number of beds** - 20: 1x6, 1x8, 1x6
- **Booking** - Telephone, fax, email or complete enquiry form on our website. Contact Postal Address: National Trust, Dark Peak Area Office, Edale End, Edale Road, Hope Valley, Derbyshire, S33 6RF.
- **Price per night** - Weekdays (Monday to Thursday) £180 per night. Weekends (Friday to Sunday) £250 per night. £150 booking, damage and cleaning deposit.
- **Public Transport** - Trains at Edale (2 miles) to Sheffield and Manchester. Taxi service only available from Hope Station. Nearest bus station at Castleton (3 miles).
- **Directions** - SK101841 (OS map no. 110). At the western end of the dale 2 miles from Edale church .

CONTACT: Lucy Chadburn (Administrator)
Dalehead Bunkhouse, Upper Booth, Edale, Hope Valley, S33 7ZJ
Tel: 01433 670 368 , Fax: 01433 670 397
peakdistrict@nationaltrust.org.uk www.nationaltrust.org.uk/peakdistrict

PUBLIC FOOTPATH
CHAPEL GATE

JOHN HUNT BASE

ENGLAND

The John Hunt Base, part of Hagg Farm Outdoor Education Centre, offers comfortable accommodation in a converted 19th century hill farm in the Upper Derwent Valley, with unparalleled views across the open moors of the Dark Peak. Walks from the door lead onto the high moors of Kinder and Bleaklow and around the Ladybower reservoirs and dams.

The Base has a lounge, TV/DVD/video, payphone, showers and toilets, drying room and kitchen, with good wheelchair access throughout. In the grounds are a wildlife garden, field, artificial climbing boulder, jacobs ladder, climbing tower and access to woodland. The site also lends itself to quiet pursuits such as art retreats. Groups have sole use during their stay, and all bedding is provided.

Instructional support for various outdoor activities can be booked for a group of up to 12 people for £198 per day.

DETAILS

- **Open** - All year, 24 hours
- **Number of beds** - 16: Rooms with 2 to 8 beds.
- **Booking** - Advance booking essential.
- **Price per night** - £216 per night including bedding. Minimum hire 2 nights. Please enquire for Xmas & New Year prices. Prices current at time of going to print.
- **Public Transport** - Trains Bamford 7 miles, with trains to Sheffield & Manchester.
- **Directions** - From Ladybower Reservoir junction take A57 3 miles to west - look for sign to Hagg Farm on the right.

CONTACT:
Hagg Farm OEC, Snake Rd, Bamford, Hope Valley, S33 0BJ
Tel: 01433 651594, Fax: 01433 651525
haggfarm@nottscc.gov.uk www.nottinghamshire.gov.uk/haggfarm

BACK TOR

Back Tor is part of the Hollowford Centre site at Castleton and is open all year round. This self-contained group accommodation offers en suite bedrooms for up to 29 people, a self-catering kitchen and a comfortable lounge for relaxing. For those who don't want to cook the Hollowford centre can provide a range of meal options using Fair Trade and locally purchased fresh food with all dietary needs catered for.

Back Tor is set in beautiful countryside within the pretty village of Castleton. Stepping outside the Centre, the ridge from Losehill to Mam Tor will tempt you to put on your walking boots and head for the hills. With a wealth of countryside on your doorstep, Back Tor provides an excellent base from where you can access caves, crags, rivers, moors and limestone dales.

The Hollowford Centre offers a full range of activities, some are on-site at Hollowford, others, such as climbing, caving or canoeing, a little further a field.

DETAILS

- **Open** - All Year,
- **Number of beds** - 29 (3 x 6, 1 x 5, 2 x 3)
- **Booking** - Phone or email.
- **Price per night** - £20 pp. Min charge of £400 per night. Min stay 2 nights.
- **Public Transport** - Buses to Castleton from Hope and Sheffield. Nearest train station - Hope.
- **Directions** - See website or ask for directions. Sat Navs not recommended.

CONTACT:
Lindley Educational Trust, Hollowford Centre, Castleton, Hope Valley S33 8WB
Tel: 01433 620 377
enquiries@hollowford.org www.hollowford.org

Moorside Farm is a 300-year-old farmhouse set 1200 feet up in the beautiful Peak District National Park on the Derbyshire / Staffordshire border and approximately five miles from the historic town of Buxton. Sleeping accommodation is provided in two areas, one for 14 - this is alpine style with pine clad ceiling and a pine floor with bunk beds. The second area has 6 beds, also in bunks and is an ideal room for a small group or family. Downstairs there are showers, toilets and a large dining / general room. The farmhouse has full central heating and drying facilities are available. Provided at the bunkhouse is a three course breakfast, packed lunch and a substantial dinner in the evening, vegetarians are catered for. A small kitchen is available for making tea and coffee. Ample parking space is provided. All bookings have sole use of the accommodation.

DETAILS

- **Open** - All year, 24 hours
- **Number of beds** - 20: 1 x 14 : 1 x 6
- **Booking** - Deposit required with minimum two weeks notice.
- **Price per night** - £30.00 per person per night, includes bed, breakfast, packed lunch and evening meal. Bed and breakfast only £20.00 per person per night. Minimum booking 4 persons
- **Public Transport** - Nearest train station Buxton. Take bus to Longnor or Travellers Rest. Bus enquiries 01332 292200.
- **Directions** - GR SK 055 670. Leave A53, Buxton to Leek road, at Travellers Rest, take 4th lane on left, down to T junction, take first left, Moorside Farm is first right entrance.

CONTACT: Charlie
Hollinsclough, Longnor, Buxton, Derbyshire, SK17 0RF
Tel: 01298 83406
charliefutcher@aol.com   www.moorsidefarm.com

BUSHEY HEATH
FARM

Bushey Heath Farm is a family-run smallholding in the heart of the Peak District, central to all the popular visitor centres, but just off the beaten track. Offering a summer campsite and 'top of the range' bunkbarns for up to 28 people in three self contained units.

The farm has been developed in an environmentally sensitive way with ground source heating, a wind turbine for electricity and rainwater harvesting for wc flushing, so visitors can experience practical sustainable ideas. The Hen House Bunk Barn has two bedrooms with bunks for 4 in each. The Little Barn has a large single bedroom with bunks for 6 people. Hadfield Barn sleeps 14 in two rooms of 6 and 8. All have luxury shower rooms and a combined fully equipped kitchen/diner open area. Sleeping bags/duvets required. Good dogs accepted.

DETAILS

- **Open** - All year. Campsite May till October, opening hours by arrangement
- **Number of beds** - 8: Hen House, 6: Little Barn, 14: Hadfield Barn. 30 pitches.
- **Booking** - Camping at bank hols only. Bunkhouse: early with deposit advisable.
- **Price per night** - Camping Adult £6, Child £2, Vehicle £2. Bunkbarns prices per night for sole use. Hen House : £140. Little Barn : £105. Hadfield Barn : £245.
- **Public Transport** - Nearest trains at Hope (4 miles). Nearest buses in Tideswell (2 miles). Bus numbers 65, 66, x67, 173, 177, 197, 202.
- **Directions** - GR SK 146 785. From Tideswell take Manchester Road past Star Pub and cross over A623, road stops at farm. Going west along A623, 1.5 miles past the Anchor Pub turn right at crossroads in 's' bends..

CONTACT: Rod Baraona or Lisa Thomas
Tideswell Moor, Tideswell, Buxton, Derbyshire, SK17 8JE
Tel: 01298 873007, Mobile: 07710 163376
rod@baraona.freeserve.co.uk www.busheyheathfarm.co.uk

Eat, drink, be merry and stay in a refurbished stone barn with a traditional award winning Peak District country pub on site. The Royal Oak serves fantastic pub grub and local cask ales (Winner of 'Derbyshire Pub of the Year Awards' in 2010 and runner up in 2011). The Royal Oak has direct access to the High Peak and Tissington Cycle Trials which use disused railways providing easy off road cycling. The area is also ideal for climbing and walking with stone circles and limestone gorges to explore. The bunkbarn is perfect for any number from 1 to 42 (small and large groups welcome) wanting comfortable, clean, dormitory style accommodation. There are six separate bunk rooms all heated and lockable. All the bunk beds have comfortable mattresses, a pillow and fresh linen, just bring a duvet or sleeping bag. There is a small communal kitchen with fridge, oven and kettle and seating for 5/6 people. Separate ladies and gents toilets and hot showers are included in the simple per person tariff. Campsite and holiday cottages (some sleeping large groups) available.

DETAILS

- **Open** - All year, all day
- **Number of beds** - 42: 4 x 8, 1 x 6, 1 x 4
- **Booking** - Booking in advance by phone or email
- **Price per night** - April to Sept £15pp, Oct to March - £13pp.
- **Public Transport** - Nearest trains Buxton (8 miles). Local bus no.42 (Buxton to Ashbourne) drops off 15 minutes walk away on A515
- **Directions** - From the A515 Buxton to Ashbourne road take road to Hurdlow oposite to B5055 road to Bakewell.

CONTACT:
The Royal Oak, Hurdlow, Nr Buxton, SK17 9QJ
Tel: 01298 83288, Fax: 01298 83696
hello@peakpub.co.uk www.peakpub.co.uk

CHESTER
BACKPACKERS

Chester Backpackers is a small, friendly, cosy hostel near the heart of Chester (formerly the Waterloo Pub). This self-catering hostel has 5 private rooms which are all en suite. They have 2 dormitories, an 8 bed en suite dormitory and an 18 bed dormitory with 2 toilets and 3 showers on the lower floor. In total they can accommodate 35 people. There is an outside terrace garden, lounge area with DVD/video library, digital television, free book exchange and free WiFi. Chester is a great social arena with a large number of pubs dating back to the 11th Century with great food and excellent ales. Chester Backpackers exercises a strict no smoking policy in the building and smoking is only allowed in the outside designated smoking area. Chester Backpackers is located only 5 mins walking distance from the city centre and train station. North Wales, Liverpool and Manchester are less than an hour from Chester.

DETAILS

- **Open** - All year, 24 hours; no curfew
- **Number of beds** - 35: 1 x 18 : 1 x 8 : 4 x 2 : 2 x 1
- **Booking** - Book by phone or email. Strongly recommended at weekends.
- **Price per night** - Dorm £15.95pp (£17 at weekend), Single £25pp (£30 at weekend). Dbl/ twin £40 per room (£45 at weekend). Long term rates available. Prices may vary for Chester Events.
- **Public Transport** - Hostel is 10 mins walk from train station and National Express coach station. Liverpool and Manchester airports are 30 mins drive away.
- **Directions** - From train walk up City Rd. At ring road (nr Last Orders) bear left into Boughton (A41). Hostel 100 metres on left. From National Express walk up Union St with park on right, turn right at major junction. Hostel 100m on left. Car park at rear.

CONTACT: Alastair King
67 Boughton, Chester, CH3 5AF
Tel: 01244 400185
sales@chesterbackpackers.co.uk   www.chesterbackpackers.co.uk

CHESTER
BUNKROOM

The Bunkroom in Chester is a small independent hostel located only 2 minutes walk from the train station and 4 minutes from Chester city centre. Beautifully presented in a 120 year old Georgian town house with a mix of old world charm and very modern facilities, The Bunkroom hostel provides a friendly, relaxed atmosphere in a safe and clean environment. Facilities include en suite bathrooms, quality linen and duvets, excellent self catering facilities, spacious lounge for chilling with TV / DVD and games, a great bar for meeting like minded travellers, outdoor walled garden with BBQ, drying room for wet gear, free WiFi broadband with Skype headsets and secure storage facilities for bikes and bags. Group meal service available. Full English breakfast (£4), washing and drying machines (£3), towel hire (£2), safe lockers (£3). Pub crawl tour every week (free). Hugs (free). Being next to Chester city centre, the hostel is surrounded by cafes, pubs and shops, making this the perfect location for backpackers, groups and families to explore this vibrant city.

DETAILS

- **Open** - Open all year, 24 hours
- **Number of beds** - 28: 2,4 and 6 bed rooms
- **Booking** - Bookings over phone or email. Debit / Credit cards accepted.
- **Price per night** -   £17.00 per person per night regardless of room.
- **Public Transport** - 300m from Chester train station.
- **Directions** - From train station, turn right and follow the road around to the left for 300 meters, you will see the hostel on the left. By car head for city centre and then the train station, follow the road around to the left for 300 meters, hostel on the left..

CONTACT:
The Bunkroom,106 Brook Street, Chester, CH1 3DU
Tel: 01244 324524
admin@thebunkroom.co.uk   www.thebunkroom.co.uk

The Old Smithy is a camping barn or 'stone-tent' situated in the village of Burwardsley, which is mid-way along the Sandstone Trail in Cheshire. The central section of the Sandstone Trail takes in Beeston and Peckforton castles. The barn is also on NCR45 Mercian Way cycle route.

The Old Smithy offers basic accommodation to groups of walkers, cyclists and others visiting this part of Cheshire. It is on Burwardsley Road, on the outskirts of the village, close to the Post Office. The Old Smithy provides space for up to eight people, with an area for cooking, washing up, a toilet and sleeping platform. There is no electricity or hot water. You will need to bring your own sleeping bag and roll mat, a cooker, food and matches. Lighting is via lanterns (provided) but you will need a torch. You can buy food and pre-book food parcels at the Burwardsley Village Post Office . The nearest pub is The Pheasant Inn (it has its own website).

DETAILS

- **Open** - All year, 24 hours. Pre-arrange arrival times.
- **Number of beds** - 8: 1 x 8
- **Booking** - Bookings by phone or email.
- **Price per night** - £5 per person per night.
- **Public Transport** - The nearest train station is Chester (10 miles) with an hourly bus service to Tattenhall (2 miles).
- **Directions** - The Barn is on Burwardsley Road, on the outskirts of the village, close to the Post Office. Grid reference: 513 569 OS Landranger No.117

CONTACT: Mandy Geall
Burwardsley Village Store, Harthill Road, Burwardsley, Cheshire CH3 9NU
Tel: 01829 770359
mandy_geall@hotmail.com

EMBASSIE
LIVERPOOL BACKPACKERS

The Embassie is a terraced house in an unspoilt Georgian square used in the filming of 'In the Name of the Father'. The house was built in 1820 and until 1986 it was the Consulate of Venezuela. It is only 15 minutes walk from the city centre.   Liverpool is known for its nightlife, a student population of 70,000 ensures a lively scene, bands start playing at 11pm and bars are regularly open till 2am. The hostel has been refurbished and there are new kitchen facilities, a brand new shower suite and an all new games room and relax area with Sky Sports and HD Television. Hostellers have a key to come and go, the hostel is clean, safe and staffed 24 hours. Bedding is provided (including sheets) and free coffee, tea, toast and jam are available 24 hours, eat as much as you want.

International, or UK regional travellers only, NO LOCALS.

DETAILS

- **Open** - All year, 24 hr access with key.
- **Number of beds** - 40
- **Booking** - Booking is not essential for individuals.   Groups larger than 6 should book (20% deposit).
- **Price per night** - £16 (Sunday to Thursday), £21 (Friday and Saturday).
- **Public Transport** - Liverpool has a train station and is served by National Express Coaches.   A £3.50 taxi fare will bring you from the train or bus station to the hostel door, (good idea if you have a heavy rucksack).
- **Directions** - From the Anglican Cathedral (the third largest in the world) continue uphill along Canning Street away from the city centre. This will bring you into Falkner Square (15-20 mins). The hostel has a red door and is by a phone box.

CONTACT: Kevin
1 Falkner Square, Liverpool, L8 7NU
Tel: 0151 7071089
embassie@gmail.com www.embassie.com

INTERNATIONAL INN

ENGLAND

The International Inn is a multi award-winning hostel in a converted Victorian warehouse, located in the heart of Liverpool city centre's cultural quarter. Liverpool has a wealth of attractions for visitors and you will find theatres, heritage, two Cathedrals as well as the City's renowned nightlife venues just a stone's throw away. The Hostel is also ideally located for visiting students, being opposite the University.

The International Inn provides fully heated accommodation in en suite dormitories of 2, 4, 6, 8 and 10 beds. Private fully furnished apartments also available and newly opened cocoon pod hotel rooms. Facilities include a café, fully equipped kitchen, TV/DVD/games lounge, laundry, baggage store, internet access and information desk. There are no curfews to curtail your evening's fun.

DETAILS

- **Open** - All year, all day
- **Number of beds** - 103: 4x2, 5x4, 2x5, 1x6, 1x7, 4x8, 2x10 plus apartments
- **Booking** - Advisable at the weekend
- **Price per night** - From £15 (dorm) or £18 per person in twin room. Price includes tea, coffee, toast'n'jam 24hrs.
- **Public Transport** - Liverpool Lime Street Station 10 minutes walk away. National Express Station 10-15 minutes walk.
- **Directions** - From Lime St Station take the Skelhorn St exit. Turn left up hill and continue along Copperas Hill. At Main Road jnct. turn right along Russell St, continuing along Clarence St then Rodney St. At jnct. of Hardman St (HSBC bank on corner) turn left. South Hunter St is 2nd on left. The hostel is 20m up on the right.

CONTACT:
South Hunter Street, (off Hardman Street), Liverpool, L1 9JG
Tel: 0151 709 8135
info@internationalinn.co.uk www.internationalinn.co.uk

HATTERS
LIVERPOOL

Your ideal choice for city central accommodation, Hatters Liverpool has combined hotel quality en-suite rooms with the social atmosphere of an international travellers' hostel. Catering for groups of all sizes and independent travellers, you can enjoy the comforts of WiFi, continental breakfast, en suite rooms, large communal areas and enthusiastic, informative staff. We also offer full board or half board options for groups of over 15. Conveniently located for all city centre attractions and transport links, ask the reception staff about discounts to Alton Towers, Beatles tours, Football Stadium tours, Albert Docks, or many other FREE adventures....The perfect base for day trips to the historic city of Chester, Chester Zoo, or the majestic Lake District. Come and stay and enjoy what is making Liverpool one of the UK's top tourist destinations!.

Three star graded by Quality in Tourism.

DETAILS

- **Open** - All year, 24 hour reception. Check in after 2pm, check out 11am.
- **Number of beds** - 300 beds; single, double, twin, triple, 4, 6, 8 and 12 bed rooms.
- **Booking** - Booking not essential but recommended, especially at weekends.We require photo I.D (passport/ Drivers' Licence) and credit/ debit card. For all group bookings please contact groups@hattersgroup.com
- **Price per night** - From £15.00 for dorms and from £39.00 for privates. Prices include en suite, linen and breakfast. Please email for group rates.
- **Public Transport** - Within walking distance of all public transport hubs.Liverpool Lime Street Station – 5mins, Northern Street Coach Station – 15mins
- **Directions** - Please contact the hostel reception for directions

CONTACT: Reception
56-60 Mount Pleasant, Liverpool, L3 5SH
Tel: 0151 709 5570, Fax: 0151 703 9283
liverpool@hattersgroup.com www.hattersgroup.com/#lpool

HATTERS
ON HILTON STREET
ENGLAND

Hatters on Hilton Street brings new meaning to 'flash packing'! Your ideal choice for city centre accommodation in the heart of the bohemian Northern Quarter, with a combination of hotel quality en suite rooms with the social atmosphere of an international travellers' hostel. Catering for groups of all sizes and independent travellers, you can enjoy the benefits of WiFi, breakfast, en suite and standard rooms, large communal and outdoor areas, and enthusiastic, informative staff. Full board or half board options for groups of over 15. Convenient for all city centre attractions and transport links. Ask about discounts to Alton Towers, and about Man Utd and City football stadium tours. Lest we forget all that is FREE to do in Manchester...We are more than happy to help. Also a great base for day trips to the Peak District.

Come and enjoy our hospitality and explore all that Manchester has to offer!

DETAILS

■ **Open** - All year, 24 hour reception. Check in 2pm, check out 11am
■ **Number of beds** - 155; single, twin, double, triple, 4, 6, 8, and 12 bed rooms
■ **Booking** - Booking not essential but recommended especially at weekends, with credit/debit card. Photo ID (eg. passport, driving license,) required on check in. For group bookings please contact groups@hattersgroup.com
■ **Price per night** - From £15.50 dorms, from £35 private rooms. All rooms include en suite, linen and breakfast. For group prices email groups@hattersgroup.com
■ **Public Transport** - Only 5 minutes walk from Picadilly train and bus stations and Shudehill bus station, and 10 minutes walk from Victoria train station.
■ **Directions** - Please contact the hostel reception for details.

CONTACT: Reception
15 Hilton Street, Manchester, M1 1JJ
Tel: 0161 236 4414 , Fax: 0161 236 5740
hilton@hattersgroup.com   www.hattersgroup.com/#mcr

BROOK HOUSE
BARN

Brook House Barn provides comfortable, self-catering accommodation ideally suited for families, groups or individuals. This high standard, boutique barn conversion has a fully equipped kitchen/dining area, drying room, utility, and a large lounge with panoramic views over the Wolds countryside. There are 2 bedrooms on the ground floor and 3 bedrooms and a small lounge on the first floor. The bedrooms have a mix of beds and bunks, bed linen is provided and all have en suite shower rooms. A two bedroom (4/5 person) cottage converted to a similar standard (graded Visit Britain 4*) is also available. The village of Scamblesby, at the heart of the Lincolnshire Wolds and on the Viking Way, has footpaths, bridle ways and meandering country lanes. The historic market towns of Louth and Horncastle are 10 mins drive, Lincoln, Boston and the coastal beaches are 1/2 hour away. Cadwell Park racing circuit, Market Rasen racecourse and the Battle of Britain and Aviation Heritage centres are nearby.

DETAILS

- **Open** - All year, flexible accesss.
- **Number of beds** - 22
- **Booking** - Booking advisable, 20% deposit, balance 1 month prior to visit.
- **Price per night** - From £20pp, family and group rates available. Whole barn hire Fri Sat Sun, 2 nights £350 per night, 3rd night at £270. Mon to Thurs, 2 nights £250 per night, 3 or 4 nights £220 per night. Whole barn £1500 per week.
- **Public Transport** - Trains: Lincoln, Grimsby. Coaches: Louth, Horncastle. Interconnect 6 (0845 234 3344) calls at Scamblesby and other villages in the Wolds.
- **Directions** - Scamblesby village is just off the A153 Horncastle to Louth road.

CONTACT: The Strawsons
Watery Lane, Scamblesby, Nr Louth, Lincolnshire, LN11 9XL
Tel: 01507 343266
enquiry@brookhousefarm.com www.barnbreaks.co.uk

Naburn Station is a converted railway station situated on the Trans Pennine Trail and Sustrans cycle route 65. It offers accommodation ideal for cyclists and walkers. It also provides the perfect base for exploring the many delights of York and North Yorkshire with easy access to the city, the moors, the dales and the coast. The local village pub provides basic groceries and good food and there are other pubs and shops within easy walking and cycling distance.

Cycle and boat hire are available locally and there are riding stables in the village. Facilities include a well equipped kitchen, drink making facilities in each room, washing machine, off road parking, secure bike storage and internet access. Bedding and towels provided. No smoking. Pets and children welcome.

DETAILS

- **Open** - All year, 24 hours
- **Number of beds** - Singles / twins / doubles
- **Booking** - Advised.
- **Price per night** - £18pp, under 14s £10. Including bedding, towels, tea and coffee. Camping £5 per person. 10% discount for cyclists.
- **Public Transport** - Trains at York (5 miles) and Selby (10 miles). Arriva bus 42 between Selby and York stops at bottom of the drive. Collection can be arranged from either station and local bike hire is available.
- **Directions** - On A19 from York turn right at sign to Naburn just before A64 ring road junction. From A64 Selby junction follow A19 towards York. Take first left signed Naburn. Just before the village go under the old railway bridge and turn immediately left. On Sustrans cycle route 65, 5mins walk from Naburn village centre.

CONTACT: Ann
Station House, Naburn, York, YO19 4RW
Tel: 01904 647528 mob: 07834 324 431
Saturn65@btinternet.com www.naburnstation.co.uk

free Wireless internet
access at all times

ACE HOSTEL
YORK

Ace York is a city centre boutique hostel situated on Micklegate, one of the oldest parts of York. This grand Grade 1 Georgian building was built in 1752 as a 'Town House' for the very wealthy John Bourchier of Benningbrough Hall. The Hostel has many impressive features including a stone flagged entrance hall leading to a grand carved sweeping staircase. With its panelled rooms, vaulted cellar and fabulous Rococo ceiling depicting Shakespeare's & Newton's heads, the hostel holds a wealth of history and architecture. The ground floor has a great bar with a pool table, internet lounge, guest kitchen and spacious dining room.The oak beamed basement has a TV/games lounge, cinema room & sauna which leads onto a private courtyard. The rooms & dormitories are all en suite (except the 4 bed dorm) and have exquisite views. Ace York is the top end of budget accommodation, less than 5 minutes from the main train & bus station. It offers fantastic views of York, including the huge Gothic Cathedral (the Minster) and the medieval city walls.

DETAILS

- **Open** - All year, 24 hours
- **Number of beds** - 136: 1x14,4x10,3x8,1x7,5x6,1x4,1x3,4x2,1xfamily(4),1xdouble.
- **Booking** - Credit card guarantees bed, Groups (10+) 50% deposit.
- **Price per night** - From £16 per person. Weekly rates available.
- **Public Transport** - 5 mins walk from rail and bus stations.
- **Directions** - Car: Take A1036 into York.Continue past racecourse into Micklegate. We're 100m along on the left opposite the church. By rail or bus: turn right out of station for 300m. Take the first left through the medieval gate into Micklegate.

CONTACT: Reception
Micklegate House, 88-90 Micklegate, York, YO1 6JX
Tel: 01904 627720, Fax: 01904 339350
reception@ace-hotelyork.co.uk www.ace-hotelyork.co.uk

YORK
RACECOURSE CENTRE

York Racecourse Centre is just a few minutes drive from the centre of York, in one of the quietest parts of the city, overlooking the historical Knavesmire. The modern buildings provide quality budget accommodation for student & adult groups. The Centre has 4 Star Hostel rating by the English Tourism Council. The two-storey building contains 21 twin bed rooms with en suite toilets, that can be converted into four bed rooms by unfolding bunk beds from the wall. The single storey annexe contains single, twin and family rooms, each with washbasin. This building has separate toilet and shower facilities. There's a spacious dining room with cafeteria style seating up to 100 and a large lounge on the first floor of the main building suitable for conferences etc. A very large sports field adjoins the complex and the centre lies on the National Cycle Network Route 65 which gives traffic free access into the centre of town. B&B (full English breakfast), D,B&B and Full Board packages available. There is plenty of secure, free parking for coaches and cars and secure bike storage.

DETAILS

■ **Open** - All year (except during race meetings), all day
■ **Number of beds** - 133: 1x10, 1x7, 21x4, 12x twin, 8 x single.
■ **Booking** - Booking essential, by phone or email
■ **Price per night** - B&B(Full English Breakfast):1 night:£36pp, 2+nights £31.50pp. Based on twin occupancy. Towels included. Enquire for school group rates.
■ **Public Transport** - Trains: 20 min walk. City centre buses every 10 mins.
■ **Directions** - Situated on the right hand side of the A1036 Tadcaster Road as you head towards York City Centre, opposite the Fox & Roman pub.

CONTACT: Stuart or Amanda
York Racecourse Centre, York Racing Stables, York, YO24 1QG
Tel: 01904 620 911 ext. 284, Fax: 01904 611 301
info@racecoursecentre.co.uk www.racecoursecentre.co.uk

HIGH MILL HOUSE
ENGLAND GROUP ACCOMMODATION

Adjacent to the North York Moors Railway and below Pickering Castle, High Mill House has been extensively renovated to modern day 4-star standards. It comprises 4 en suite bedrooms with bedding and towels provided, a well-equipped kitchen/diner, a lounge with log fire and a ground floor wet-room and laundry area. Within the grounds is Lime Cottage, a bungalow with twin/double bedroom, kitchen and lounge dinner. All heating and electricity is included in the price, so no need to be cold (you have full control of the heating).
Popular for family get-togethers, walkers, cyclists, stag and hen dos. Pickering has 9 local pubs and a wealth of restaurants to choose from. Good walking and world-renowned cycling routes close by in Dalby Forest and Moors area. 30 minutes from the coast and from York. Advance booking essential.

DETAILS

■ **Open** - All year, 24 hours. New arrivals after 3.30, depart before 10am on last day.
■ **Number of beds** - House 12: 4x3;   Lime Cottage: 2:1x2
■ **Booking** - Booking essential, online or by phone.
■ **Price per night** - From £882 to £1470 per week (£10.50 to £17.50 pppn) based on 12 sharing. Weekends £588 to £980. Contact for prices for smaller groups.
■ **Public Transport** - Mainline train station at Malton 9 miles. A taxi or bus available opposite station. Nearest bus stop outside Tourist Information Centre (Scarborough and District), or Eastgate for Coastliner.
■ **Directions** - North of the A170 Pickering traffic lights, on the left 200 metres beyond Pickering railway station. Pass the Mill and take the first left, signposted for NYMR car park. Our entrance is immediately left after crossing the bridge.

CONTACT: Cheryl
High Mill, Undercliffe, Pickering, YO18 7BB
Tel: 01751 477113
cheryl@highmillpickering.co.uk www.highmillpickering.co.uk

BANK HOUSE FARM
HOSTEL

ENGLAND

This is a new barn conversion (2011) on a working organic farm, set in the beautiful dale of Glaisdale in the North York Moors. The views are stunning and the accommodation homely. Under-floor heating, drying room, 2 showers, 3 private toilets and one large dorm sleeping 14. Beds have sheet, pillow & slip. Large comfy kitchen/dining/living room with sofas. Picnic/BBQ area and garden with panoramic views. There are some facilities for the disabled but steps are unavoidable. You need to bring sleeping bag/duvet, toiletries, towel and food. Farm's own organic beef & lamb available for sale. Public footpaths/bridleways on the doorstep, Wainwright's Coast to Coast route 1m, Whitby & Jurassic coast 12 miles, Grosmont steam trains 3m, Esk Valley walk 3m. Sole use policy - we don't mix groups and individuals.

DETAILS

- **Open** - All year, 9 am – 9 pm for phone calls
- **Number of beds** - 1 x 14
- **Booking** - Booking preferred. Deposit £50 with booking, balance 4 weeks before.
- **Price per night** - Weekdays Adults £20,Children 6-16 £10. Wkends £400 for up to 10 persons (+£10/ch or +£20/ad per night for over 10), Bank Hols: £550 (Fr, Sa, Su).
- **Public Transport** - Glaisdale train station 3miles. 'M&D Transport' minibus from Castleton to Whitby in Glaisdale village (2.5 miles). Nat. Express coaches at Whitby.
- **Directions** - From Glaisdale station go uphill through village and turn left at T junction 'Glaisdale Dale Only'. After 1 mile turn left by Witchpost Cottage. Pass New House Farm & Sheds then turn left over cattle grid. Follow farm track 1/3 mile to farmyard. Hostel is attached to farmhouse. Call at farmhouse for keys

CONTACT: Chris or Emma Padmore
Bank House Farm, Glaisdale, Whitby YO21 2QA
Tel: 01947 897297
info@bankhousefarmhostel.co.uk www.bankhousefarmhostel.co.uk

Harbour Grange is Whitby's long established, friendly backpackers hostel. It is beautifully situated on the River Esk, in Whitby itself, and only 5 minutes walk from train and bus stations. The hostel is all on the ground floor and has good facilities for self-catering with a dining area and a separate lounge area, both big enough to seat 24 people. There are 5 dormitories and family rooms are available on request. The hostel is open all day but so that everyone can have a chance of a good night's sleep there is a curfew at 11.30 (quiet at midnight). The premises are non-smoking.

Whitby is a beautiful little fishing town surrounded by beaches and moorland. Here you can find stunning views from cliff walks and visit lovely villages like Grosmont where steam trains run from Whitby to Pickering and Goathland where Heartbeat is filmed. Take a look at where Captain Cook lived and the Abbey that has stood as a landmark for 800 years.

DETAILS

■ **Open** - 1st April - 31st Oct. Open all year for groups booked in advance, hostel open all day. Check in 5pm-9pm.
■ **Number of beds** - 24: 1 x 2 : 2 x 4 : 1 x 6 : 1 x 8.
■ **Booking** - Booking advised for weekends and for groups, 10% deposit.
■ **Price per night** - From £17 per person. Sole use £290 a night.
■ **Public Transport** - Whitby has a train station and a bus station.
■ **Directions** - From Whitby train and bus stations: cross the bridge and turn right. Follow the river. First right after the junction Churchstreet and Green Lane.

CONTACT: Birgitta Ward-Foxton
Spital Bridge, Whitby, North Yorkshire, YO22 4EF
Tel: 01947 600817, Mobile 0777 9798611
backpackers@harbourgrange.co.uk www.whitbybackpackers.co.uk

HEBDEN BRIDGE
HOSTEL

Hebden Bridge Hostel (aka Mama Weirdigan's) is located in a former concert hall adjacent to a Grade II listed Baptist Chapel. The Hostel provides accommodation in 4-bed dorms, a 6-bed bunk-room and in private rooms for 2-4 people. Nestled into woodland and yet only a short walk from the town centre, river and canal, the hostel makes a good base for hiking, sight-seeing, shopping or experiencing Hebden Bridge's vibrant music and arts scene. Close to the Pennine Way, Calderdale Way and Hebden-Haworth walks. 10am-5pm access to the lobby only. No evening curfew (but please respect other guests). Bed linen is provided in the dorms & private rooms. Bring sleeping bag and pillow if staying in the bunk-room. Free internet. Self-catering vegetarian-only kitchen. Light breakfast included in the price.

DETAILS

- **Open** - Open Easter to November. Whole-hostel bookings possible in closed season., Check-in 5-8pm, checkout 9-10am.
- **Number of beds** - 36 : 7x4, 1x6, 1x2
- **Booking** - Booking recommended but not essential (full payment on booking).
- **Price per night** - Bunk-room £12.50pp. Small dorm £18.50pp. Twin/double room £55. Private 4-bed room £70. Sole use available.
- **Public Transport** - 15 mins walk from Hebden Bridge train station (frequent, quick service to Leeds and Manchester). Buses from the station stop outside the Birchcliffe Centre (Dodd Naze Circular). The closest coach station is in Bradford.
- **Directions** - From station follow road to T-junction, turn left (Burnley Rd), take next right (Keighley), right again (Birchcliffe Rd). Hostel is behind Birchcliffe Centre.

CONTACT: Em or Dave
The Birchcliffe Centre, Hebden Bridge, W Yorks, HX7 8DG
Tel: 01422 843183
mama@hebdenbridgehostel.co.uk www.hebdenbridgehostel.co.uk

The Friends of Nature (FoN) invite you to stay in this beautiful historic cottage in the peaceful village of Earby, Lancashire. Earby FoN House is a cosy cottage with a picturesque garden, stream and waterfall close to the Pennine Way. An ideal stop for the Pennine Way walker, as a base for local day hikes and for cyclists and those interested in the countryside and local heritage. Particularly suited to individuals, families and small groups. There are 2 comfortable lounges, a well equipped kitchen and seating for 18 in the dining areas. Real ale pub and meals nearby. Breakfast café in village and late stop Co-op. Secure bike storage. On-line booking. Visit Britain 3* Hostel, 'Walkers Welcome', and 'Cyclists Welcome'. FoN is one of Europe's oldest environmental groups with 600k members and 800 houses across Europe. Under 16s must be accompanied by adult aged 18 or over and of same sex if in shared dormitory.

DETAILS

■ **Open** - From 2 weeks before Easter until 1st November (during winter open for sole-use bookings by arrangement), 7am to 10am and from 5pm to 11pm
■ **Number of beds** - 22 beds in 1x2, 2x6 and 1x8 bed rooms.
■ **Booking** - Real-time live web bookings up until 5pm daily. Verbal bookings can only be held until 6pm daily. Book via website, email or phone.
■ **Price per night** - Adults from £16 and under 18's from £12. Members of Friends of Nature, IFN and YHA pay discounted members rates
■ **Public Transport** - Skipton-Burnley bus (hourly) drops ½ mile from Hostel. Skipton rail station for Leeds and Settle–Carlisle line, and Colne for Manchester
■ **Directions** - Grid Ref SD915469. Geo-Coords 53.918065, -2.13064. 7 miles west of Skipton. In Earby village off the A56 Skipton-Colne road, 300m past Red Lion pub.

CONTACT: Manager
9-11 Birch Hall Lane, Earby, Lancashire, BB18 6JX
Tel: 01282 842349
earby@thefriendsofnature.org.uk www.thefriendsofnature.org.uk

WEST END
OUTDOOR CENTRE

Situated in the Yorkshire Dales amidst stunning landscape overlooking Thruscross Reservoir in a designated Area of Outstanding Natural Beauty on the edge of the Dales National Park, this self-catering accommodation centre offers excellent facilities for up to 30 people in 9 bedrooms with bunk beds. The centre is fully centrally heated. Accommodation is in small dorms of 2 to 6 beds and the leaders' en suite accommodation has private catering, dining and lounge facilities. The main kitchen is well-equipped with a 4-oven Aga cooker, two fridges and a freezer, together with all the cooking utensils and equipment. There are 4 showers, 4 hand basins and 4 toilets. There are no extra charges for heating, lighting and hot water. Ideal for team building courses, schools, Scouts, Guides and family parties etc. Located only 12 miles from Harrogate and Skipton, 30 miles from the City of York. Tourist Board inspected (3 star) and managed by the owners. All groups must be accompanied by an adult (25+).

DETAILS

- **Open** - All year, flexible
- **Number of beds** - 30 :- 4 x 2 : 3 x 4 : 1 x 6 : 1 x 4 en suite
- **Booking** - Advisable at weekends
- **Price per night** - £15pp. Sole use £280 (Sat/Sun/Bank Hol), £200 any other night (minimum stay 2 nights), £650 for 4 nights midweek. Sunday night, if staying for 2+ nights £150.
- **Public Transport** - Nearest train stations are at Harrogate and Skipton, both 12 miles from the hostel. Taxi fare from either station would be approximately £22.
- **Directions** - GR 146 575. Leave A59 at Blubberhouses, signed West End 2.5 miles. Do not turn off, centre is on left side.

CONTACT:
West End, Summerbridge, Harrogate, HG3 4BA
Tel: 01943 880207
m.verity@virgin.net www.westendoutdoorcentre.co.uk

Situated in a medieval deer-park, Whitefields Cottage offers self-catering accommodation within Fountains Abbey and Studley Royal Estate. Cared for by the National Trust and awarded World Heritage Site status in 1986, the estate contains a beautiful water garden, Elizabethan mansion and a Cistercian abbey. Whitefields is a 19th century cottage on the edge of Studley Royal Deer Park, home to around 500 Red, Fallow and Sika deer. Whether you want to explore the water gardens and impressive abbey, or walk around the North York moors (1hr drive) or Yorkshire Dales, Whitefields is ideal.

It offers groups of up to 16 people inexpensive but comfortable accommodation.

DETAILS

- **Open** - All year, except Christmas and New Year, no restrictions
- **Number of beds** - I6: 1 x 6 : 1 x 8 : 1 x 2.
- **Booking** - Bookings required 2 weeks in advance, non refundable deposit £60
- **Price per night** - Mid week £120, Weekend (Fri/Sat) £160. Whole week £840.

- **Public Transport** - Train station and National Express coaches at Harrogate (15 miles). Regular bus service between Harrogate and Ripon. Taxis Ripon to Whitefields £5 - Harrogate to Whitefields £20.
- **Directions** - From B6265 turn to Studley Roger. Drive through village, bear sharp right, before the National Trust sign, into deer park. Half a mile up main avenue turn right sign-posted 'estate vehicles only'. Turn right up the track at the end of this road, Whitefields is at top of track.

CONTACT: Andrew Moss
Fountains Abbey and Studley Royal Park, Fountains, Ripon, HG4 3DY
Tel: 01765 643172
andrew.moss@nationaltrust.org.uk www.fountainsabbey.org.uk

Dalesbridge is located on the A65 at Austwick, on the edge of the Yorkshire Dales National Park, just five miles from both Ingleton and Settle. It is a comfortable venue for those visiting the Yorkshire Dales, whether you are a family, a group or an individual. The six bed units have a kitchen area with a cooker, fridge, washing up sink, shower and toilet. Crockery, cutlery and cooking pots are provided and there is a seating area in the middle of the room. The four bed units have a shower and toilet, small seating area with kettle, toaster, microwave, crockery and cutlery. These rooms are ideal for the smaller group not requiring full self-catering facilities. Utilising all the units provides group accommodation for up to 40. You will need to bring your own sleeping bag and pillow, alternatively bedding is available to hire. We have a great deal to offer: bar, drying room, functions, B&B, and campsite.

DETAILS

- **Open** - All year, reception open 9am - 5pm
- **Number of beds** - 40
- **Booking** - Advance booking with deposit
- **Price per night** - £16 per person. £90 for 6 bed unit; £60 for 4 bed unit. Less out of season check www.dalesbridge.co.uk.
- **Public Transport** - Settle railway station is 5 miles away and Clapham station 1.5 miles. There are infrequent buses but if you would like collection from either railway station please give us a call.
- **Directions** - GR 762 676. The hostel is on the main A65. When travelling from Settle towards Ingleton we are situated on the left hand side between the two turnings into Austwick.

CONTACT: Jon
Austwick, Nr Settle, LA2 8AZ
Tel: 015242 51021
info@dalesbridge.co.uk www.dalesbridge.co.uk

Clapham Bunk, within the grade II listed Old Manor House, offers self-catering facilities for up to 23 people in three dormitories (2x10 and 1x3 beds). The bunkhouse is situated in the North Yorkshire village of Clapham in the Yorkshire Dales National Park, ideal for walkers, cyclists, cavers and other outdoor enthusiasts. There are numerous walks (notably the Three Peaks), cycle ways (NCN Route 68/69), The Way of the Roses) and other attractions directly on the doorstep including Gaping Gill, Ingleborough and White Scar show caves, and the Ingleton Waterfall Walk. The Reading Room Café and Bar is available to both residents and non-residents who can enjoy the open fires, real ales and ciders, hot meals and homemade cakes . The bar operates limited hours and this cosy room with its magnificent 13 foot inglenook fireplace becomes available exclusively to residents outside licenced hours.

Breakfast, lunches, packed lunches and evening meals can be provided on site. There is also a range of restaurants, pubs, cafes and tea rooms in the local area. Dogs and children welcome.

DETAILS

- **Open** - All Year,
- **Number of beds** - 23: 2x10, 1x3
- **Booking** - Please phone or email.
- **Price per night** - From £13.50 pppn
- **Public Transport** - Bus 100yds away. Clapham train station1.25 miles away.
- **Directions** - Head for Clapham Village. Phone for more details.

CONTACT: Brenda
The Old Manor House, Church Avenue, Clapham, North Yorkshire, LA2 8EQ.
Tel: 015242 51144
info@claphambunk.com www.claphambunk.com

Situated 4.5 miles from Ingleton in Yorkshire Dales limestone country, between Ingleborough and Whernside with superb views of both, the bunkhouse makes an ideal base for sporting or nature holidays.

The area is well known for its scenery including the Three Peaks walk, (Ingleborough, Pen-y-ghent and Whernside), the Waterfalls walk and some of the best caves and potholes in the country including the famous Gaping Ghyll system and the White Scar show cave. This is a stone property, which has been converted from an old school, with much of the character remaining. It provides self-catering accommodation for up to 30 people and has a lounge, drying room, 4 shower rooms with hand basins and toilets, well equipped kitchen / dining room with industrial cooker, toaster, fridge, freezer, dishwasher, microwave, and payphone. No pets allowed. Nearest pub 100 yds.

DETAILS

- **Open** - All year, 24 hours
- **Number of beds** - 30 (5 x 6)
- **Booking** - Early booking advised for popular times. £100 deposit for 2 nights. 25% for 3 nights or over.
- **Price per night** - £240 per night (sole use) with an extra £12 per person for groups over 20 people. Minimum of 2 nights at weekends.
- **Public Transport** - Ribblehead station 1 mile. No buses.
- **Directions** - 4.5 miles on the B6255 Ingleton to Hawes Road, just after Chapel-Le-Dale village on left hand side. 11 miles from Hawes on B6255.

CONTACT: Clare and Peter Fox
Chapel-le-Dale, Ingleton, Carnforth, Lancs, LA6 3AR
Tel: 01729 823835
pfox119@btinternet.com www.oldschoolbunkhouse.co.uk

HARRIS
HOUSE

Harris House is the outdoor pursuits centre of the William Hulme's Grammar School (Manchester). The centre occupies an old village school, with attached headmaster's house, on the edge of the hamlet of Hardraw. It is a grade II listed building built in 1875 in attractive Dales stone. Ample parking is available in the old playground and the large schoolroom is used for communal activities. The well appointed and practical accommodation is centrally heated throughout and can accommodate groups of up to 34. Hardraw has a camp site, a café and the Green Dragon Inn (adjacent to Hardraw Force waterfall). Many groups use these facilities to complement their visit. The café offers good value, substantial home cooking for groups. In the locality are opportunities for caving, rock climbing, fell walking and cycling (secure storage). The Pennine Way passes the centre. The local town of Hawes has a full range of shops. Harris House is an ideal base for Duke of Edinburgh's award expedition training or educational visits.

DETAILS

- **Open** - All year, 24 hours
- **Number of beds** - 32: 3x8, 2x3, 1x2
- **Booking** - Essential (20% deposit) but short notice bookings are often available.
- **Price per night** - £15 per person, min £150.
- **Public Transport** - Garsdale Station is 8 miles away, connected by infrequent buses. Hawes, a pleasant one and a half mile walk away, has more frequent buses.
- **Directions** - Turn north off A684 1 mile to the west of Hawes and proceed for ½ mile. Harris House is at the west end of the hamlet of Hardraw.

CONTACT: Warden
The Old School, Hardraw, near Hawes, Wensleydale, North Yorkshire, DL8 3LZ
Tel: 0161 226 2054
Harris.house@whgs-academy.org www.whgs-academy.org

Marsett Barn is a back to nature experience, an old barn in an old landscape.

The barn is basic but full of character and has been sympathetically restored to retain its special place in this Dales setting.

On the ground floor there is an entrance area with living and dining space, a wood burning stove, a kitchen area and a downstairs toilet.

Upstairs there are two sleeping areas, each with platform, to sleep 20 people. Also toilets with handbasins and showers with a limited hot water supply.

Contact the centre for more details.

DETAILS

- **Open** - All year
- **Number of beds** - Sleeps approx 20 people
- **Booking** - Booking is essential
- **Price per night** - £9 per person (minimum of £36 per night) includes gas.
- **Public Transport** - The nearest bus stop is Bainbridge (4 miles) and nearest train station Garsdale (11 miles).
- **Directions** - Parking is on Marsett Green and access is on foot. From the green, follow the track on the left signposted Stalling Busk. The Barn is in a field on the right, approximately ½ kilometre from the green

CONTACT:
Marsett Barn, Marsett, North Yorkshire, DL8 3DG
Tel: 01969 650432
info@lowmill.com www.lowmill.com

LONGRIGG
RESIDENTIAL CENTRE

Longrigg Residential Centre is within walking distance of Sedbergh, only 10 miles from Kendal and less than 10 minutes from the M6, an ideal location for exploring the Lakes and the Yorkshire Dales. The centre stands in its own grounds and overlooks the unspoilt splendour of the Howgill Fells. Perfect for mixed groups or families. Walking, cycling, canoeing and caving are nearby. The centre has recently been refurbished. It has two dormitories each sleeping 6 in the main building and a larger separate building sleeping 20 in dormitories of 2,4,6 and 8. There are ample shower and toilet facilities. Sleeping bags and pillowcase are required. The large kitchen is equipped for group catering. The lounge has easy chairs and gives access to the patio area. A separate games room has pool table, TV and table football. There is a drying room and tumble dryer. The Centre holds an Adventure Activity Licence and can offer instruction and equipment. Entry is by a touch lock system. The centre is owned by an Education Authority and complies with relevant Health and Safety requirements.

DETAILS

- **Open** - All year, all day
- **Number of beds** - 32: 1x8, 3x6, 1x4, 1x2
- **Booking** - Book by phone or email
- **Price per night** - £15.00 minimum of 10 people.
- **Public Transport** - Trains at Oxenholme on the West Coast Line.
- **Directions** - Longrigg Centre is located near the village of Sedbergh which lies on the edge of the Yorkshire Dales and is just 30 minutes from the Lake District. Easy access via M6 junction 37.

CONTACT: Rob Gregory
Frostrow Lane, Sedbergh, Cumbria, LA10 5SW
Tel: 01539 621161
longrigg.centre@kencomp.net   www.longrigg.org.uk

DALES
BIKE CENTRE

The Dales Bike Centre is the perfect venue for cycling and walking in the Yorkshire Dales, and is right on Wainwright's famous Coast-to-Coast walk, the infamous Woodcocks off-road Coast-to-Coast mountain bike trip and the Yorkshire Dales Cycle Way. Four Star rated Hostel accommodation, café, bike shop, bike workshop, bike hire, secure bike store, drying room and a wealth of advice about the Dales. Cycle Friendly, and Walker Friendly awards. The centre has 14 beds, in smart 2 and 4 bedded rooms, warmly decorated and with amazing views across the dale. Bedding is provided, and there is access to a kitchenette with free tea and coffee. After 5pm, the café lounge can be used, with magazines, free WiFi internet, internet radio and 24 hour cake access! A hearty breakfast is included. Evening meals are available in pubs and restaurants in Reeth, a five-minute stroll away. Based in the tiny village of Fremington, in Swaledale, surrounded by the best biking in Yorkshire with a stunning landscape, crisscrossed by ancient lanes, moorland tracks and roads.

DETAILS

- **Open** - All year, 24 hours
- **Number of beds** - 14. Old barn 1x4, 1x2; New barn 1x4, 2x2,
- **Booking** - Book by phone or email.
- **Price per night** - Bunk bed and breakfast £28. Single occupancy £38.
- **Public Transport** - Trains Darlington (25 miles). Buses X26 & X27 every 15 mins from Darlington to Richmond. Bus 30 from Richmond to Reeth (7 per day till 6.15pm).
- **Directions** - 20 mins from A1M: from Richmond take A6108 then B6270 signed to Reeth. Once through Grinton, DBC is on left at end of a row of tall trees.

CONTACT:
Parks Barn, Fremington, Richmond DL11 6AW
Tel: 01748 884908
enquiries@dalesbikecentre.co.uk   www.dalesbikecentre.co.uk

Richmond Camping Barn is converted from 3 former byres which are part of a listed traditional dales longhouse. It is situated at East Applegarth Farm, 3 miles west of the town of Richmond on the Coast to Coast walk. Grid ref NZ135017 OS Map 92. The farm borders the Yorkshire Dales National Park, with panoramic views over the lower valley of Swaledale and the River Swale.

The Barn is a great base for exploring the historic town of Richmond and The Yorkshire Dales National Park with all it has to offer. Sleeping accommodation is in two rooms on raised platforms with mattresses, pillows and lightweight sleeping bags. Heating and cooking facilities are available on a meter. Lighting is not metered and is included in the price. The shower is available on a seperate meter. Cutlery, crockery and pans are provided.

DETAILS

- **Open** - 1st March to 30th November, access after 4pm and departure by 10.30am unless otherwise arranged.
- **Number of beds** - 12: 1 x 8, 1 x 4
- **Booking** - Book by phone or email
- **Price per night** - £7.50 per person. £90 sole use of barn.
- **Public Transport** - Nearest railway 15 miles away at Darlington. Bus service 3 miles away at Richmond. Local taxi service is available.
- **Directions** - On the A6108 in Richmond at the Total petrol station (Victoria Road) turn right into Hurgill Road. Continue for 3miles. Farm entrance is on the left in a dip in the road 200 yds past the 2 radio masts on the right. The barn is at the end of the tarmac road ignoring the T-junction.

CONTACT: Mrs J Atkinson
East Applegarth Farm, Westfields, Richmond, North Yorkshire DL10 4SD
Tel: 01748 822940
rebekah.atkinson@virgin.net

FELL END
BUNKHOUSE

Fell End, overlooking the unspoilt Howgill Fells, consists of two 18th century buildings providing comfortable bunkhouse accommodation for people wishing to explore this beautiful area. Perfect for mixed groups, families and people with special needs or mobility difficulties. Walking, cycling, canoeing and caving nearby and the Lake District only 1 hour away. The Schoolhouse (white building) sleeps 8 people in bunks in the central area with an extra bed in an adjoining room. There is a fully equipped kitchen with a fridge, freezer, microwave and cooker. The bathroom has two toilets, one shower and 4 wash basins. The living room has a multi-fuel stove, which also heats the radiators. Greenslack has a further 2 bunks and 1 single bed plus a bathroom for people with mobility problems. Get in touch if your group has fewer than 8 people but you require Greenslack for these facilities. Entry into both buildings is by a touch lock system. Dogs allowed under strict supervision. Fell End is owned by the Bendrigg Trust, a charity offering outdoor activities for disabled people.

DETAILS

- **Open** - All year, 24 hours
- **Number of beds** - 14: 1 x 8 : 1 x 5 : 1 x 1.
- **Booking** - 20% deposit to Bendrigg Trust, Old Hutton, Kendal, Cumbria, LA8 0NR.
- **Price per night** - £10 + VAT. Minimum booking: 6 for Schoolhouse only, 8 for both buildings. 12 people if booking for 1 night only.
- **Public Transport** - Trains at Kirkby Stephen (6 miles) on the Carlisle/Settle/Leeds line. Then take bus 564 Mon to Sat (4 per day). Tel 0871 200 2233 for times.
- **Directions** - GR:723983 (postcode CA17 4LN). Directions given on booking.

CONTACT: Lynne Irish
Ravenstonedale, Kirkby Stephen, Cumbria, CA17 4LN
Tel: 01539 723766, Fax: 01539 722446
Lynne@bendrigg.org.uk www.fellend-bunkhouse.org.uk

Bents Camping Barn was formerly a shepherds' cottage in the 1600s. There are 2 sleeping rooms on the first floor with bunk beds. On the ground floor there is a kitchen with cooking area, a dining area with tables and benches and a WC with washbasins. Other facilities include electric lighting and power points throughout (£1 coin meter), crockery, cutlery, toaster, microwave, 3 electric cooking rings, 2 electric kettles, 2 electric convector heaters and parking. You will need sleeping bags, walking boots and warm clothes.

The barn is accessible from the Coast to Coast path and there is good fell walking in the Howgill Fells, Wild Boar Fell and Crosby Garrett Common. Smardale Gill Nature Reserve and Sunbiggin Tarn are nearby. The area is ideal for mountain biking and the Settle to Carlisle Railway is five miles away at Kirkby Stephen. There is a shop 2 miles away.

DETAILS

- **Open** - All year, all day
- **Number of beds** - 12 to 14: 1x10, 1x6
- **Booking** - Booking is essential for groups in advance with full payment. Individuals are advised to phone first.
- **Price per night** - £8.50 per person.
Full barn £119 per night.
- **Public Transport** - Train station at Kirkby Stephen (5 miles). Local buses to village of Newbiggin-on-Lune.
- **Directions** - GR MY 708 065 OS map 91. From Junction 38 of the M6 take the A685 to Newbiggin-on-Lune. Take Great Asby Road on left then first right through tall gate. Follow tarmac road past Tower House and follow signs to Bents Farm up track.

CONTACT: Dorothy Ousby
Newbiggin-on-Lune, Kirkby Stephen, Cumbria, CA17 4NX
Tel: Booking 017687 74301   Dorothy 01768 371760
www.bentscampingbarn.co.uk

KIRKBY STEPHEN
HOSTEL

Kirkby Stephen Hostel, a Methodist church converted by the YHA to Kirkby Stephen Youth Hostel, has been independent since 2010. The old chapel has a range of accommodation for individuals, families and groups amongst beautiful authentic features; stained glass windows, arches, oak panels and stone covings. The chapel houses a large dining room and kitchen, with a lounge/reading room in the gallery. The bedrooms and dormitories are in a building at the rear, with ample lavatories and showers.

Kirkby Stephen is a pleasant market town in the upper Eden valley, situated 15 miles from Kendal, 15 miles from Hawes and on Wainwright's coast to coast path and the W2W cycle path. It enjoys easy access to Lady Anne's Walk, the Howgill Hills, the Dales National Park and the Lake District. The hostel stands prominently on the main street, with a range of restaurants, cafes, pubs, fish and chip shops and food shops on the doorstep. Paragliding is also available.

DETAILS

- **Open** - All year, please arrive after 5pm
- **Number of beds** - 40: 1x8, 3x6, 2x4, 1x2, 1x2 en suite
- **Booking** - Book by phone. Booking advised but not essential.
- **Price per night** - £18pp. Reductions for groups.
- **Public Transport** - One mile from Kirkby Stephen train station on the Leeds-Carlisle line. Regular buses from Penrith, Kendal and Appleby stop outside hostel.
- **Directions** - In the centre of town on main road. From M6 leave at junction 38 and follow signs towards Appleby.

CONTACT: Denise
Market Street, Kirkby Stephen, Yorkshire, CA17 4QQ
Tel: 01768 371793 or 07812 558525
info@kirkbystephenhostel.co.uk www.kirkbystephenhostel.co.uk

ORMSIDE MILL
RESIDENTIAL CENTRE ENGLAND

Ormside Mill sits on the banks of Helm Beck in Cumbria's beautiful Eden Valley, just three miles from the lovely market town of Appleby-in-Westmorland. Within easy reach of both the Lake District and the Pennines, the Mill is a great base to enjoy the stunning scenery and beautiful landscape of this picturesque region. Sitting in its own wooded grounds, the Mill provides comfortable, self-catering accommodation for up to eighteen people.

The Mill is centrally heated throughout and has a log-burning stove in the lounge. There is also a communal dining area, fully-equipped self-catering kitchen and utility room. Upstairs there are a range of bedrooms (all bedding provided) and shower facilities. The converted barn opposite provides a large indoor space as well as a drying room, a classroom and additional showers. Outside there is a large grass paddock with views of the Pennines, a relaxing decking area, barbecue facilities and a small orchard.

DETAILS

- **Open** - All year (except Christmas period), all day (key supplied)
- **Number of beds** - 18: 3x4, 2x2, 2x1
- **Booking** - Book in advance by phone or email.
- **Price per night** - From £195 per night. Exclusive use.
- **Public Transport** - Bus and train station Appleby-in-Westmorland (3 miles).
- **Directions** - Grid Ref: NY 703166, village postcode: CA16 6EJ. Turn off B6260 at Burrells, take first left towards Ormside village, then first right and continue past the caravan park entrance. Cross the ford to reach the Mill.

CONTACT:
Ormside Mill, Ormside, Appleby-in-Westmorland, Cumbria, CA16 6EJ
Tel: 01768 351131 or 07713 624236
ormside@ormsidemill.org.uk www.ormsidemill.org.uk

DUDDON SANDS
HOSTEL

The purpose built, self catering Duddon Sands Hostel, overlooking the Duddon Estuary, stands in the grounds of The Ship, a cosy village inn built in 1691 and known for its friendly atmosphere, good ales and ghost story. The pub beer garden has wonderful views of the estuary and fells, it also has a brazier which guests can use and an all-weather barbecue hut which seats 16 comfortably. The pub is open Tue to Sun, with a fun quiz on Thursdays. It does not serve food, but with notice a meal for a large group can be arranged. There are two other pubs in the village which do food and several excellent take-aways nearby which will deliver. All bedding is provided (not towels) and a cot or cot sides are available. Bike wash / storage is available by prior request. The hostel is easily accessible being on the Cumbrian Coastal Railway & the Cumbria Coastal Path. Extra accommodation is available nearby for larger parties if required. Celebrate an event, reunions, staff trips, a big birthday or just Friday again!

DETAILS

- **Open** - All year, all day (phone to arrange arrival)
- **Number of beds** - 19 : 2x4, 1x8 + cot + 2-3 air beds (half price)
- **Booking** - Recommended, especially for large groups. A deposit required.
- **Price per night** - From £14 per person. Special rates 4 nights sole use Mon to Thurs £550, 3 nights sole use Fri to Sun £550.
- **Public Transport** - Train: request stop at Kirkby. Bus: Take 7 or 7a (Barrow-in-Furness to Millom) get off at Moorland Stores Kirkby, follow signs for hostel & trains.
- **Directions** - At Moorland Stores crossroads on A595 in centre of Kirkby take turn for Sandside and Train Station. Hostel is at bottom of hill.

CONTACT: Tony
The Ship Inn, Askewgate Brow, Kirkby-in-Furness, Cumbria, LA17 7TE
Tel: 01229 889454
theship1691@googlemail.com www.theship1691.co.uk

ROOKHOW
CENTRE

Perhaps the best situated small hostel in the Lake District. Peaceful, in 12 acres of its own woodland, but close to the heart of the Lakes, ten minutes from Coniston Water and Windermere, and on the edge of the famous Grizedale Forest Park with its trails and sculptures. Superb area for walking, cycling and all outdoor activities. Also for quiet retreat, relaxation, study and artistic pursuits. The Rookhow Centre is within the former stables of the nearby historic Quaker meeting house which is also available for conferences and group sessions. Guests find the centre warm, comfortable and well equipped, with electric heating and a wood burning stove. There are three cosy sleeping areas (often let as private or family rooms), a kitchen/dining area and picnic tables and barbecue. There is a bonfire area within the centre's private woodland.

DETAILS

- **Open** - All year, all day
- **Number of beds** - 20: 1x9 : 1x8 : plus extra on bed settees. Also camping.
- **Booking** - Booking is essential (deposit).
- **Price per night** - From :- Adult £15.00, £7.50 for under 16's. Sole use from £180 (minimum) per night. Camping rate half the above. Duvet Hire £5 pp.
- **Public Transport** - Trains at Grange-over-Sands and Ulverston. (11 miles, approx £25 by taxi). A seasonal bus service sometimes operates - check with the warden.
- **Directions** - GR 332896. From M6, Junction 36, follow A590, signs for Barrow. Leave A590 at Greenodd (A5092) junction and follow sign for Workington for ¼ mile. Take minor road to right signed Colton / Oxen Park. Continue through Oxen Park for 2 miles. Centre on left. From Ambleside : to Hawkshead, then to Grizedale. Continue beyond Grizedale for 3.5 miles (Satterthwaite - Ulverston Road). Centre on the right.

CONTACT: Warden
Rusland Valley, nr Grizedale, Ulverston, Cumbria, South Lakeland, LA12 8LA
Tel: 01229 860231 Mob: 0794 350 8100
straughton@btinternet.com www.rookhowcentre.co.uk

NEW ING
LODGE

A friendly, self catering B&B and Hostel directly on the Wainwright's Coast to Coast and the Westmorland Way. The Lodge has two mixed dormitory rooms that sleep 6 & 8 people along with 7 private B&B rooms. Recently awarded a Silver in Green Tourism and Gold within Cumbria Green Enterprises. Ideal for individuals, families & groups, within three miles of Junction 39 on the M6 and on the A6 making it great for a break in a journey. It has a wild location on the edge of the Lake District National Park, the Howgill Fells and the Pennines. There are 4 pubs within walking distance and the Lodge recently got their alcohol license and serve quality local ales and evening meals from £7. Camping, secure bikes storage, dog friendly & laundry facilities available. Dormitory and campers have the option of breakfast, cereal, toast, tea, coffee and fresh orange juice for £4 or £8 for a full English/vegetarian breakfast.

DETAILS

- **Open** - All year, every day.
- **Number of beds** - 30:1x8,1x6,1x3,2x2(twin),2x2(dbl),1x1,1x4(family) + camping
- **Booking** - Advisable - deposit 25%. WorldPay via our website or card payment.
- **Price per night** - £15pp (dorm) plus £2 for bedding, B&B rooms (doubles, twins, singles and family Room) from £25pp, including full english breakfast. Home cooked evening meals from £7. Discounts available for larger groups and longer stays.
- **Public Transport** - Bus from Penrith or Kendal station. Pick-up from stn possible. No buses on Sunday.
- **Directions** - North end of Shap Village, opposite the Bampton and Haweswater junction. Fifth building on the left hand side if travelling from the North.

CONTACT: Scott or Jamie
New Ing Lodge, Shap, Penrith, Cumbria, CA10 3LX
Tel: 01931 716719 or 07792 222881
info@newinglodge.co.uk www.newinglodge.co.uk

Situated in the heart of South Lakeland in secluded woodland, 4 miles from the village of Ambleside, High Wray Basecamp provides an ideal base for groups wishing to explore and take part in activities in the Lake District area. Local attractions include rambling, fell walking, climbing and water sports, with the Basecamp ranger being happy to assist with information on local walks and activities. The Longland Block has two separate fully centrally heated dormitories each sleeping 8, with a separate washing and living area/kitchen block. The comfortable living area is heated by a central wood burning stove and the kitchen has a commercial gas cooker, fridge freezer, microwave and utensils. The Acland block has two separate centrally heated dormitories sleeping 10 each, with toilet and shower room attached. The kitchen / lounge area is fitted with commercial gas cooker, fridges, microwave and utensils.

DETAILS

- **Open** - All year, 24 hours
- **Number of beds** - 16 + 22
- **Booking** - Booking with deposit of £50
- **Price per night** - Longland £10.00pp (Mon-Thur), £13.00pp (Fri-Sun). Acland £10.50pp (Mon-Thur), £14.00pp (Fri-Sun).
- **Public Transport** - Nearest train station Windermere 8 miles. Local bus (505 'Coniston Rambler' Windermere - Hawkshead) stops 2 miles away at turning to Wray Castle (Cumbria travel-line 0870 6082608)
- **Directions** - GR: 373 995 Take A593 from Ambleside towards Coniston, bear left onto the B5286 signed Hawkshead, fork left for High Wray village, signed Wray Castle. Basecamp is ¼ mile up dirt road on the left at the end of High Wray village.

CONTACT: Jamie Preston
High Wray, Ambleside, Cumbria, LA22 0JE
Tel: 015394 34633
jamie.preston@nationaltrust.org.uk

WYTHMOOR FARM
CAMPING BARN

Wythmoor Camping Barn is on the Walney to Wear coast to coast cycle route and a few hundred metres from the Dales Way long distance footpath. It enjoys great views of the Howgill fells and the distant mountains of the Central Lakes. Being only 4.5 miles from Kendal and less than 10 mins from the M6 this is an ideal location for exploring the Lake District and the Yorkshire Dales. The 19th century barn has hot water provided by solar panels, underfloor heating powered by ground source heat pump and mains electricity supplemented by wind turbine. The barn is generously sized for twelve people and includes facilities for wheelchair users, two separate heated shower rooms and a food preparation area with sinks and cooking slabs (bring your own camping stove). Kettle and microwave are provided. Local taxis available for transport to Kendal and Sedburgh. Holmescales Farm Outdoor Centre is close by.

DETAILS

- **Open** - All year, all day
- **Number of beds** - 12: 1x12 (10 single beds, 1 double)
- **Booking** - Book online, by phone or email. Booking not always required
- **Price per night** - £8.50 per person.
- **Public Transport** - Oxenholme (6.5 miles) and Kendal (4.5 miles) have stations.
- **Directions** - Take Appleby Road (A685) from Kendal. After 2.5 miles turn right signed 'Docker' (single track). Opposite Docker Hall Farm, take left fork signed Lambrigg. Continue for 2 miles, barn is on left next to white farmhouse. From M6 Junction 37 take A684 towards Sedbergh; then direct left signed Lambrigg/Beck Foot. After 1.5 miles take left signed Lambrigg and Docker (single track). Barn is on right in half a mile next to white farmhouse. Sat Navs will direct you to a private drive.

CONTACT: Bruce Withington
Wythmoor Farm, Lambrigg, Kendal, LA8 0DH
Tel: Booking office 017687 74301, Farm mobile 07971 018567
info@lakelandcampingbarns.co.uk www.lakelandcampingbarns.co.uk

FELL END
CAMPING BARN

Fell End is a traditional 18th Century Lakeland stone barn, located within its own grass courtyard approximately ½ mile from the farm. It is in the centre of a 500 acre estate in the western fells with easy access to some spectacular scenery, ideal for walkers, cyclists and wildlife enthusiasts. It is a short drive from Coniston (6 miles) and the Duddon Valley (5 miles). There are magnificent views, star-filled skies (a truly breathtaking sight) and the tranquil 'sound of silence'. Fell End Barn is lit by chandeliers and tea lights (provided) and heated by woodburing stove (a gas heater is also available for hire). There is no electricity and you will need to bring your own cooking and lighting equipment and bedding with mat. There are 2 picnic style tables, a wash basin and WC. Ideal for campfires or BBQs. Wood is available from the farm. Check the website www.lakelandcampingbarns.co.uk and book online.

DETAILS

- **Open** - All year, all day
- **Number of beds** - 12: 1x12
- **Booking** - Book online. Booking in advance is essential.
- **Price per night** - £8.50 per person.
- **Public Transport** - Trains: Foxfield (3 miles). Buses: Grizebeck (3 miles).
- **Directions** - Leave M6 at J36, follow the A590 towards Barrow. Near Greenodd Estuary take A5092 signed to Broughton-in-Furness. Follow this road until you reach Grizebeck. Just before Grizebeck garage take lane on right signposted 'Woodland'. Follow for 2 miles, over a cattle grid, until road becomes level. Take lane on left signed 'Woodland Hall' and follow for 1 mile.

CONTACT: Booking office / Jean
Thornthwaite Farm, Woodland, Broughton in Furness, Cumbria, LA20 6DF
Tel: Booking Office 017687 74301, Farm 01229 716 340
info@lakelandcampingbarns.co.uk www.lakelandcampingbarns.co.uk

SHEPHERD'S CROOK BUNKHOUSE

Noran Bank Farm is situated at the south end of Lake Ullswater just through Patterdale Village and only 5 minutes walk away from the Coast to Coast route. Shepherd's Crook Bunkhouse is a barn conversion adjacent to the 17th Century farm house. It has been converted to a very high standard and has a fully equipped kitchen, seating area in which to relax, loo and wet room with 2 showers on the ground floor. Duvets, linen and towels are provided. DIY breakfast and packed lunches are available if pre-booked. The Bunkhouse has wonderful views of the Lake District fells and is Ideally situated for numerous walks for all levels including High Street, Angle Tarn, St. Sunday Crag, Fairfield and of course Helvellyn. There are lots of water sports on Lake Ullswater, canoeing, rowing and motor boats, there's also Ullswater Yachting Club or even the steamers running daily from Glenridding to Howtown and Pooley Bridge. The Bunkhouse has proved immensely popular as an overnight stay on the Coast to Coast route. A well behaved dog considered at owners' discretion.

DETAILS

- **Open** - All year,
- **Number of beds** - 8: 1x6, 1x2
- **Booking** - Please book by phone or email.
- **Price per night** - £13pp(6 bed room), £18pp (double room) plus £5 for single occupancy. Sole use: £100 per night, D.I.Y breakfast £6, B&B in farmhouse £29pp. Dogs £4 per dog per night. Packed Lunch £5.
- **Public Transport** - Trains at Penrith (14 miles). Buses at Patterdale (half a mile).
- **Directions** - Take A592 from Patterdale south, farm is on right in half a mile.

CONTACT: Mrs Heather Jackson
Noran Bank Farm, Patterdale, Penrith, Cumbria, CA11 0NR
Tel: 017684 82327 Mob: 07833 981504, Fax: 017684 82327
heathernoranbank@fsmail.net www.patterdale.org/Noranbank.htm

AMBLESIDE
BACKPACKERS

Get away to The English Lakes National Park, one of the most beautiful scenic areas in the UK. The hostel is in a marvellous location with fell and mountain walks, boating, scenic drives, cycle touring, mountain biking and outdoor activities practically from the doorstep. Set just 4 minutes walking from the centre of Ambleside it is also a great centre for visiting places made famous by Wordsworth, Ruskin and Beatrix Potter. Ambleside is excellent for shopping and eating out with many outdoor equipment shops, restaurants and pubs. With 60 beds Ambleside Backpackers can accommodate groups and individuals in either single sex or mixed dorms. A large, traditional Lakeland cottage featuring a great lounge with a fire and piano, dining room, large well equipped kitchen for your use - not to mention central heating, showers and washing/drying facilities. Free light breakfast, tea/coffee and internet access. Good bus links to most fell walk starting places and lakes makes this hostel an ideal base for exploring.

DETAILS

■ **Open** - Open most of the year except Christmas, opening hours 4.30pm - 10.30am
■ **Number of beds** - 60: 1x12, 1x10, 4x6, 3x4, 1x2
■ **Booking** - Recommended, essential for groups, deposit required.
■ **Price per night** - Prices: £20pp inc. £17pp for three or more nights. Special winter breaks. All prices include light breakfast, tea, coffee, internet access(not at night).
■ **Public Transport** - Windermere train station 4 miles then 555 bus to Ambleside.
■ **Directions** - From Ambleside bus stop: up hill to T junction, across road to Old Lake Rd, 200m up on left. By road : A591 Windermere to Ambleside. At 2nd Hayes Garden Ctr. sign. turn right into Old Lake Rd. 300m on right.

CONTACT: David
Ambleside BPs, Iveing Cottage, Old Lake Rd, Ambleside Cumbria, LA22 0DJ
Tel: 015394 32340
bookings@amblesidebackpackers.com www.amblesidebackpackers.com

THORNEY HOW
INDEPENDENT HOSTEL

Thorney How Independent Hostel, formerly YHA Grasmere, offers clean and comfortable holiday accommodation in Grasmere, the heart of the Lake District. Family-run and welcoming it provides bed and breakfast and self catering accommodation for individuals, families and groups. With the backdrop of magnificent fells, adjacent to the Coast to Coast path, local village amenities and lake, the tranquil location provides the perfect place from which to explore all the Lake District has to offer. The main house, a 350 year old Gentlemen's farmhouse, is charming with well proportioned rooms and fabulous views. The separate annexe sitting underneath Helm Crag creates an independent 20 bed unit suitable for groups. Discounts are available for large or charitable groups. Private parking, cycle store, drying room, licensed bar and spacious grounds complete the experience.

DETAILS

- **Open** - Open all year, 24 hours - check in 3.30pm to 10pm
- **Number of beds** -   50: bunk beds in 12 rooms, from 2 beds to 6 beds per room.
- **Booking** - Booking online recommended, by phone or email. First nights accommodation non-refundable payment required to secure booking,
- **Price per night** - Per bed with continental breakfast £20 to £26.50, full english breakfast upgrade for an additional £2.50 per person. Per bed, annexe only, from £16.50 to £23.00. Discounts are available for large group bookings and charity groups. Sole use room booking prices are also available .
- **Public Transport** - National Express Coaches stop in Grasmere. Local bus 555 to / from Windermere & Keswick. Train station at Windermere.
- **Directions** - Grid ref: 332084. Half a mile NW of Grasmere Village.

CONTACT:
Thorney How, Grasmere, Cumbria LA22 9QW
Tel: 015394 35597
enquiries@thorneyhow.co.uk   www.thorneyhow.co.uk

GRASMERE
INDEPENDENT HOSTEL

This small deluxe hostel is situated on a farm right at the heart of the Lakes. See the best of Lakeland right from our doorstep. Give the car a holiday. Take the Wordsworth walk around Grasmere and Rydal Lake, or do a mountain classic, climb Helvellyn or Fairfield from our door. The Coast to Coast footpath goes right through the farm. Over 101 other local attractions and activities, including a good pub with fine bar meals just 300 yds down the road. Our English Tourism Council 4 star graded hostel has en suite bedrooms with made up beds (sheets & duvets), lockers, bedside lights, a coin operated sauna, commercial laundry, drying room, dining room, 2 self-catering kitchens with microwaves, fridges, toasters etc. A stunning common room with large TV, a lockable bike / luggage store and private parking. We are resident proprietors. Cleanliness and friendliness assured. Totally non-smoking. Individuals, families and groups all welcome. Please always check availability by phone.

DETAILS

- **Open** - All year (winter, subject to minimum numbers), 8am to 10pm,(keys issued)
- **Number of beds** - 24: 1 x 3 : 1 x 4 : 1 x 5 : 2 x 6.
- **Booking** - Advisable, credit card confirms bed.
- **Price per night** - From £20.50 pp. Sole use £415 to £550 per night.
- **Public Transport** - Train to Windermere (11 miles from hostel), catch 555 bus from Windermere or Keswick, ask for Traveller's Rest pub. There is also a National Express coach that runs between London and Grasmere daily.
- **Directions** - GR 336 094 1.25 miles north of the village. Stay on the A591 right to our drive, 400m north of Traveller's Rest pub on the right hand side.

CONTACT: Mr Bev Dennison
Broadrayne Farm, Keswick Road, Grasmere, Cumbria, LA22 9RU
Tel: 015394 35055
Bev@grasmerehostel.co.uk www.grasmerehostel.co.uk

DERWENTWATER
YOUTH HOSTEL

Derwentwater Youth Hostel is a 220 year old Georgian mansion in 17 acres of grounds. Its glorious setting, with views of the lake and surrounding mountains, is just 2 miles from Keswick, the main town in the Northern Lakes.   A great base for individuals, families, groups and conferences the hostel has plenty of lounges and games rooms. It is licensed and offers a full meal service with a good reputation for home made food and the ability to cater for special diets. The rooms are spacious with period features and the bedrooms range in size from 4 to10 bunks with one magnificent 22 bed room. The grounds are teaming with wildlife, with plenty of space for children to play, football goals, picnic tables and ample parking. Borrowdale has something for everyone, walks along the lake shore, challenging mountains, water sports, mountain biking, climbing, gorge scrambling and tourist attractions. The C2C route passes close by. Friendly staff will advise and welcome you to this family run hostel.

DETAILS

- **Open** - All year, 7.00 am - 11.00 pm
- **Number of beds** - 88: 1x4, 2x5, 3x6, 3x8,1x10,1x22
- **Booking** - Advance booking recommended - especially for groups
- **Price per night** - From £18.40 (adult), £14.50 (child), Family rooms from £60.
- **Public Transport** - Train to Penrith then X4 bus to Keswick. From Keswick take the Launch to the jetty 100 metres from hostel or bus no 78 to hostel drive.
- **Directions** - Two miles south of Keswick on the B5289 Borrowdale road. Hostel entrance is directly off the main road, 150m after the turning to Watendlath.

CONTACT:
Derwentwater Youth Hostel, Barrow House, Borrowdale, Keswick, Cumbria,
CA12 5UR
Tel: 017687 77246
contact@derwentwater.org www.derwentwater.org

FISHER-GILL
CAMPING BARN

Situated in Thirlmere at the foot of the Helvellyn range of mountains, close to Sticks Pass and spectacular Fisher-gill waterfall, with numerous walks, hill and rock climbing from the barn, it's an ideal place for touring the Lake District being just off the A591 road, with local and national bus stops at the end of the lane.

Accommodation consists of two rooms: a kitchen/diner with fridge, 4 ring calor gas stove, kettle, toaster, tables and chairs, and all pots, pans etc and a sleeping area consisting of 10 bunk beds with mattresses, pillows, blankets and duvets (sleeping bags/liners are required). Both rooms have a wood-burning stove with a daily allowance of wood included (extra is available from the farm).

There's also a shower cubicle (metered), toilet, wash basin and a small seating area. Outside there is ample parking with a small patio area with barbeque, tables and chairs. A pub serving meals is nearby (approx a quarter of a mile). Keswick is 5 miles, Grasmere 7 miles. Open all year. Pets by arrangement.

DETAILS

- **Open** - All year, all day
- **Number of beds** - 10
- **Booking** - Advanced booking recommended.
- **Price per night** - £13pp. £130 sole occupancy.
- **Public Transport** - Local and national buses stop at the end of the lane on A591.
- **Directions** - Travelling on the A591 SE from Keswick, after about 5 miles take 1st lane on left after junction with B5322. Barn is after about 100m.

CONTACT: Mrs Jean Hodgson
Stybeck Farm, Thirlmere, Keswick, Cumbria CA12 4TN
Tel: 017687 73232 or 017687 74391
stybeckfarm@farming.co.uk www.stybeckfarm.co.uk

ST JOHN'S-IN-THE-VALE
CAMPING BARN

St John's-in-the-Vale Camping Barn is adapted from an 18th Century stable and hayloft, in an idyllic setting. Overlooking St John's Beck, the peaceful hill farm has stunning views to Blencathra, Helvellyn and Castle Rock.

The Barn has a sleeping area upstairs (mattress provided) with a sitting and dining area below. Separate toilet, shower and cooking area (bring your own stove, cooking and eating equipment) are within the building. A wood-burning stove provides a focal point and warmth!

There is a BBQ and seating area outside and, as there is no light pollution, this is magical on a star-filled night.

Low Bridge End Farm has a tea garden - all home baking.
To see more and book online go to: www.lakelandcampingbarns.co.uk

DETAILS

- **Open** - All year, 24 hours
- **Number of beds** - 8 : 1x8
- **Booking** - Advised in advance. Credit card booking available on 017687 74301
- **Price per night** - £8.50 per person.
- **Public Transport** - Trains terminate at Windermere. From there take a 555 bus towards Keswick. Get off at Thirlmere Dam Road End (Smaithwaite). Climb over ladder stile and we are ½ mile north along a footpath.
- **Directions** - Leave M6 at junction 40. Take A66 towards Keswick for 14 miles. Turn left onto B5322 St Johns in the Vale Road. 3 miles along the road on the right.

CONTACT: Graham or Sarah
Low Bridge End Farm, St John's-in-the-Vale, Keswick, CA12 4TS
Tel: 017687 79242 (Bookings 017687 74301)
info@campingbarn.com www.campingbarn.com

LAKE DISTRICT
BACKPACKERS

Situated in the heart of Windermere and central Lakeland, you will find our cosy, friendly hostel ideally situated for exploring the surrounding area. We can advise you on routes for walks and cycle rides and provide you with maps. We are often asked to help organise abseiling, canoeing, sailing, windsurfing, even caving! There is easy access to the lake and fells from our door and we are adjacent to the main 555 bus route through Lakeland.

The hostel with its small dormitories provides you with every comfort but at a budget price. We are right next to a number of pubs, restaurants and take-aways and only minutes away from the rail and bus stations. Lockers are available and internet access, with WiFi and Sky TV keep you in touch! A well equipped kitchen and comfortable common room make your stay one to remember.

DETAILS

- **Open** - All year, 24 hours
- **Number of beds** - 20:- 1x7, 2 x 4, 1x 3, 1 x2
- **Booking** - Essential, 24 hours in advance.
- **Price per night** - £15 dorms/ £17.50pp private rooms. £2 discount per night for stays of 3+ nights. Includes self service continental breakfast and free tea/coffee.
- **Public Transport** - Windermere train station is 2 minutes walk. National Express coach stop 2 minutes walk.
- **Directions** - Turn left out of station, walk to information centre, hostel is opposite, next to Simpson and Parsons Insurance Company.

CONTACT: Paul
High Street, Windermere, Cumbria, LA23 1AF
Tel: 015394 46374, Fax: 015394 88611
fletcher_recruitment@yahoo.co.uk www.lakedistrictbackpackers.co.uk

SWIRRAL
CAMPING BARN

Swirral Barn is one of a group of mine buildings situated at 1,000ft on the flank of the Helvellyn Mountain Range. It offers the basic necessities: hot water, toilet, tables, benches and a sleeping platform with mattresses. You will need to bring a stove and utensils if you wish to cook, a torch and a sleeping bag. The location is perfect for walking over the fells. Popular routes to Striding Edge and Swirral Edge pass the door, and there is quick access to Ullswater and the Eastern Fells. Enjoy a hike up Helvellyn and the surrounding peaks or, for less strenuous walking, try the scenic lake shore paths around Ullswater. Rowing, sailing and steam boat trips are available on Ullswater, where you can relax by the waterside. There are so many thing to do in this beautiful area.   The barn's facilities are: sleeping platform on the first floor, slate cooking area, hot & cold water in barn and toilet, plus electric lighting. Nearest pub is only 1 mile away, with the nearest village store only 1.5 miles away.

DETAILS

- **Open** - All year, all day
- **Number of beds** - 8: 1x8
- **Booking** - Book online. Booking in advance is essential.
- **Price per night** - £8.50 per person.
- **Public Transport** - Buses run every 2 hours from Penrith to Glenridding. It is just over 1 mile walk from bus stop to barn.
- **Directions** - From Pooley Bridge take A592 to Glenridding then to main car park. Follow the sign post to Helvellyn Youth Hostel. Swirrel Barn is 100 metres past the hostel on the left.

CONTACT: Jeanette
Striding Edge, Glenridding, Cumbria, CA11 0NR
Tel: Booking office 017687 74301, Farm mobile 07775 561512
info@lakelandcampingbarns.co.uk www.lakelandcampingbarns.co.uk

MAGGS HOWE
CAMPING BARN

Kentmere is a quiet, unspoilt valley within the Lake District National Park. It's a ramblers' paradise with woods, fields, lanes, a scattering of traditional lakeland farms and dwellings, and of course the fells with their walks so favoured by Wainwright. The Lakeland to Lindisfarne long distance path passes this way as well as the mountain bikers' and horse riders' Coast to Coast. Kentmere offers plenty of activities which include biking, riding and fishing, but most of all quiet enjoyment. A pleasant day's visit can be found at the market town of Kendal and Lake Windermere which are only 20 minutes away. The converted barn has two sleeping areas, kitchen, two showers and toilets. All you need is your sleeping bag, mattresses are provided. Breakfasts and suppers are available next door at the B&B with notice.

DETAILS

- **Open** - All year, 24 hours
- **Number of beds** - 14: 1 x 6   1 x 8
- **Booking** - Recommended with 50% deposit for groups. Individuals can book but not essential
- **Price per night** - £10 per person or £100 sole use. Friday and Saturday night must be on a sole use booking at £100 per night or a surcharge of £50 added if only 1 night taken.
- **Public Transport** - Staveley 4 miles with train and bus service. Oxenholme train station is 10 miles. Kendal / Windermere National Express 8 miles.
- **Directions** - GR 462 041, MAP OS English Lakes South East. Green Quarter. Leave the A591 and come into Staveley, proceed to Kentmere for 4 miles, then take right fork to Green Quarter keeping right until you reach Maggs Howe.

CONTACT: Christine Hevey
Maggs Howe, Kentmere, Kendal, Cumbria, LA8 9JP
Tel: 01539 821689
enquiry@maggshowe.co.uk   www.maggshowe.co.uk

Refurbished recently, Rydal Hall Youth Centre is situated in the centre of Rydal Hall estate, sheltered on three sides by the Fairfield Horseshoe and offering access to the best of Lakeland's activities. Facilities inside provide accommodation for groups of up to 28. There are 2 dormitories sleeping 10 in each and 2 leader rooms each sleeping 4. There is a large common room which can be used for dining or recreation. A drying room on the ground floor. A welcoming log burner provides additional warmth to the ample heating powered by our nearby water turbine. The kitchen is fully equipped for cooking. Guests need to bring sleeping bags, pillow cases and extra blankets during winter.

Rydal Hall also offers camping to groups and families and there is residential accommodation for up to 56 at the Hall in single, twin, double and family rooms with private facilities.

DETAILS

- **Open** - All year, 24 hours
- **Number of beds** - Dormitories 28: 2x10 , 2x4.
- **Booking** - Required with deposit. No bookings by email please.
- **Price per night** - Nov-Mar £205, Apr-Oct and Christmas & New Year £305, sole use. 10% discount for youth groups + midweek. Individual bookings by arrangement.
- **Public Transport** - Trains at Windermere. National Express at Ambleside. Local Stagecoach service (555) from Lancaster to Keswick stops 200 yards from Hall.
- **Directions** - GR 366 064. Take the A561 from Ambleside to Grasmere, Rydal is reached after 2 miles. By the church turn right and go up lane for 200m.

CONTACT:
Rydal Hall, Ambleside, Cumbria, LA22 9LX
Tel: 01539 432050, Fax: 01539 434887
mail@rydalhall.org   www.rydalhall.org

DENTON
HOUSE

Denton House is a purpose built hostel and outdoor centre in the heart of the Lake District. The hostel is designed for group use so has plenty of hot water for showers, central heating throughout, a commercial kitchen, a large dining room and solid bunkbeds! Denton House welcomes individuals too with facilities designed to be homely as well as functional. Denton House Outdoor Centre can provide traditional activities for groups of all ages. The centre is particularly suitable for those wanting to explore the great outdoors; we have storage for kayaks and bikes and there's access / egress to the River Greta just across the road. Qualified instructors are available to provide advice as well as to run trips and help organise expeditions. Denton House is primarily an adult hostel; under 16s are welcome in supervised groups or in exclusive use dorms with parents. Dogs welcome in some rooms if pre-booked. Due to the large number of school, youth and military groups, corporate teambuilds and celebration weekends, early booking is advised.
Under new management as of Jan 2012.

DETAILS

- **Open** - All year, all day.
- **Number of beds** - 56: 1x4 : 2x6 : 1x8 : 2x10 : 1x12.
- **Booking** - Preferred (25% deposit for groups)
- **Price per night** - £15 midweek, £16 weekends
- **Public Transport** - Nearest train station Penrith, buses hourly to Keswick.
- **Directions** - From centre go out of town towards Windermere, keep the river on your left (approx 10mins). We are on the right after post sorting office.

CONTACT:
Penrith Road, Keswick, Cumbria, CA12 4JW
Tel: 017687 75351
keswickhostel@hotmail.co.uk www.keswickhostel.com

At 1550 feet, Skiddaw House is the highest YHA affiliated hostel in Britain. A former shooting lodge and shepherd's bothy on the Cumbria Way, it is an ideal base for exploring the little used and quiet northern fells. This is a remote and isolated place in which to reflect on the wilderness, with no sign of the 21st Century in any direction. With no electricity, phones ringing or TV to distract from the vista of a clear unpolluted starry night, this is simple accommodation with log and coal fires the only heating. No noise pollution from traffic as the nearest road is 3½ miles away, yet only an hour or so's walk from civilisation. Walkers and cyclists are advised to bring a map and torch. Campers welcome.

DETAILS

- **Open** - 1st March (to be confirmed) to 31st Oct (groups only Nov-Dec), opening hours are mornings untill 10am and 5pm to 11pm
- **Number of beds** - 22 : 1 x 8, 2 x 5, 1 x 4
- **Booking** - Book in advance for groups of 5 or more, by email, text, phone or post (postal service is slow). 50% deposit required for advance bookings.
- **Price per night** - £17 (over 21), £12.50 (16-21), £8.50 (under 16). YHA members £1.50 - £3 discount. Camping £8.50. Credit / debit cards not accepted.
- **Public Transport** - Nearest trains and National Express coaches at Penrith. From Penrith take X4 or X5 bus towards Keswick and Workington. Alight at the Horse and Farrier (Threlkeld). From Carlisle take 554 bus to Keswick (only 3 per day). Alight at Castle Inn (Bassenthwaite) and then walk 6 miles.
- **Directions** - No access for cars, nearest tarmac road 3½ miles. Vehicles can be left at Fell Car Park by Blencathra Centre above Threlkeld, at Lattrigg Car Park (end of Gale Rd near Applethwaite) or at Whitewater Dash Falls south of Bassenthwaite.

CONTACT: Martin or Marie
Bassenthwaite, Keswick, Cumbria, CA12 4QX
Tel: 07747 174293
skiddawhouse@yahoo.co.uk www.skiddawhouse.co.uk

HUDSCALES
CAMPING BARN

Hudscales Camping Barn is part of a group of traditional farm buildings, situated at 1000ft on the northern-most flank of the Lakeland Fells. It overlooks the villages of Caldbeck and Hesket Newmarket and is in an ideal position for exploring the northern fells. It is situated right on the Cumbria Way.

Sleeping accommodation is on the ground floor along with a separate cooking and eating area. You will need to bring sleeping bags and mats. If you wish to cook bring a camping stove and all utensils / crockery. There is a separate toilet and washbasin and a metered shower. A wood-burning stove is provided for added comfort (logs extra) and there is electric lighting plus metered power points. There's also a games room with pool table and dart board - new for 2011

Check the website www.lakelandcampingbarns.co.uk and book online.

DETAILS

■ **Open** - All year, all day
■ **Number of beds** - 12: 1x12
■ **Booking** - Book online. Bookings preferred but not essential.
■ **Price per night** - £8.50 per person.
■ **Public Transport** - Penrith station 12 miles. Carlisle station 15 miles. No buses from Penrith. Limited service from Carlisle. Taxi fare from Carlisle approx £20.
■ **Directions** - Leave M6 at J41 and take B5305 for Wigton. After approx 9 miles take left turn for Hesket Newmarket. Drive to top end of village and take left turn for Fellside. Hudscales Camping Barn is approx 1 mile on left up a lane.

CONTACT: Booking office / William or Judith
Hudscales, Hesket Newmarket, Wigton, Cumbria, CA7 8JZ
Tel: Booking office 017687 74301, Farm 016974 78637
wr.cowx@btconnect.com www.lakelandcampingbarns.co.uk

Catbells Camping Barn is part of a traditional set of farm buildings dating back to the 14th Century. The barn is on the slopes of Catbells in the tranquil Newlands Valley, with magnificent views over the Lake District. The Cumberland Way passes through the farmyard. Keswick is only 4 miles away and both Borrowdale and Buttermere are within walking distance. The camping barn is on the ground floor and has sleeping accommodation for 12, with mattresses provided. Bring your own sleeping bags. The barn is heated with a multi-fuel stove (not suitable for cooking) and coal can be bought at the farm. In the adjacent building is a toilet and a cooking area suitable for a camping stove. Bring your own stove, cutlery, crockery and cooking utensils. It is possible to walk to a pub which serves food. Breakfast can be provided with notice.

DETAILS

- **Open** - All year, 24 hours
- **Number of beds** - 12: 1x12
- **Booking** - Advisable, groups require deposit.
- **Price per night** - £8.50 per person.
- **Public Transport** - Trains at Penrith (20 miles). Regular buses (meet the trains) from Penrith to Keswick. Summer bus from Keswick to Buttermere stops ½ mile from Barn. Summer ferry from Keswick to Hawes End (¾ mile from barn).
- **Directions** - GR 245211. Leave the M6 at Junction 40 and follow the A66 past Keswick. At Portinscale turn left, follow the Buttermere road for 3 miles. Turn sharp left at Stair, follow the sign for Skelgill, up the road for ½ mile and right into farmyard. Please follow these directions and not those from 'sat-nav'.

CONTACT: Mrs Grave
Low Skelgill, Newlands, Keswick, Cumbria, CA12 5UE
Tel: 017687 74301 or 0709 2031363
info@lakelandcampingbarns.co.uk www.lakelandcampingbarns.co.uk

HAWSE END
CENTRE

Hawse End Centre, at the head of the magnificent Borrowdale Valley and directly across Derwentwater from Keswick, has stunning views and access to lakeside, mountains and Keswick (via launch or lakeside walk). Hawse End House is a large, comfortable, country mansion, ideal for groups. It has 50 beds, large dining room, lounge, games room, classroom and extensive grounds leading down to the lake shore. Hawse End Cottage has 24 beds for individuals, families and groups in a cosy, homely environment. It has a basic self-catering kitchen, a living room and a patio with picnic tables and views of the lake. Two large Yurts (sleeping up to 12 each) with stunning views and transparent domes for star gazing, are on a wooden platform close to the house. These felt and wood structures have electric, tables and chairs (optional) and mats for sleeping on. On the platform are picnic tables seating up to 24, a gas barbeque and water. Toilets are close by and showers a short walk away. A catering service, including buffets and barbecues may be available in the accommodation, by prior arrangement. Outdoor activities may be available.

DETAILS

- **Open** - All year, all day
- **Number of beds** - House 50: Cottage 20: 3x4, 1x2 and 1x6 Yurts: 2 x 12
- **Booking** - Please book by phone or email. Deposit required.
- **Price per night** - Price on application, subject to availability and season.
- **Public Transport** - Trains at Penrith (18 miles). Keswick Launch passenger ferry from Keswick to Hawse End. Service buses within walking distance in high season.
- **Directions** - 4 miles outside of Keswick.

CONTACT:
Hawse End Centre, Portinscale, Keswick, CA12 5UE
Tel: 01768 812280 , Fax: 01768 775108
cumbriaoutdoors.enquiries@cumbria.gov.uk www.cumbriaoutdoors.com

High House in Seathwaite, at the head of the popular valley of Borrowdale, offers comfortable bunkhouse / hostel self-catering accommodation in a converted 16/17C farmhouse set within its own grounds. It is popular with walking and climbing clubs and is regularly used by outdoor education and corporate groups. Early booking is advised, especially for weekends. The building is let to one group at a time. Two dorms are available each with toilet, washbasin and shower. There is a third dorm reserved for K Fellfarers members and on some occasions club members may use this room during your stay. There's a common room with stove, easy chairs, library and dining area, a recently upgraded kitchen and car parking. You will need to bring sleeping bags or duvets plus sheets, pillows, tea towels, firelighters and food. Basic food (eg. milk) is available from the cafe in Rosthwaite and the nearest supermarket is in Keswick. Eco friendly washing up liquid is provided to aid the septic tank.

DETAILS

- **Open** - All year, 24 hours
- **Number of beds** - 25: 1 x18, 1 x7
- **Booking** - Early booking essential. Minimum 2 nights at weekends. £65pn deposit. Send to Briarcliffe, Carr Bank Rd, Carr Bank, Milnthorpe, Cumbria, LA7 7LE.
- **Price per night** - £130 for 2012 irrespective of numbers. Midweek rates negotiable. Includes electricity and fuel for heating. £20 key deposit required.
- **Public Transport** - The nearest train station is in Penrith which is 26 miles away. Buses run from Penrith to Keswick, and from Keswick to Seatoller (which is 1 mile from High House).
- **Directions** - OS Grid Ref NY235119

CONTACT: Hugh Taylor
High House, Seathwaite , Borrowdale , Keswick.
Tel: 01524 762 067
jhugh.taylor@btinternet.com k-fellfarers.homecall.co.uk/ff.htm

LOW GILLERTHWAITE
FIELD CENTRE
ENGLAND

Towards the head of Ennerdale valley, one of the most beautiful, least spoilt and quietest valleys in the Lake District, at the foot of Pillar and Red Pike sits Low Gillerthwaite Field Centre. An ideal base for fell walking, classic rock climbs, bird and wildlife watching, mountain biking, orienteering, canoeing (instruction available for groups) and environmental studies.

Originally a 15th Century farmhouse, the Centre has group self-catering facilities, drying room, a library of environmental books, a group lecture room and two lounges with log burning fires. Due to its remoteness the Centre generates its own electricity via a hydroelectric scheme. Vehicle access is by forest track and a BT payphone is on site (most mobiles do not work here). Low Gillerthwaite is an ideal base for clubs, extended family groups, school and youth groups.

DETAILS

- **Open** - All year (except Christmas and Boxing Day), 24 hours
- **Number of beds** - 40: 2x4 : 1x8 : 1x10 : 1x14
- **Booking** - See booking link. Always phone to check availability
- **Price per night** - From £10 per person (children and students), £13.50 (adults), camping is £5 per person.
- **Public Transport** - Whitehaven Station 12 miles. Buses to Ennerdale Bridge from Cleator Moor or Cockermouth (5 miles).
- **Directions** - GR NY 139 141. From Ennerdale Bridge take road east, via Croasdale, 3.5 miles to Ennerdale Forest. Continue on forest track 3 miles. Hostel is the first building below the RH road, 200m before the YHA.

CONTACT:
Ennerdale, Cleator, CA23 3AX
Tel: 01946 861229
Warden@lgfc.org.uk www.lgfc.org.uk

CRAGG BARN
CAMPING BARN

Cragg Barn Camping Barn is a traditional stone-built barn with stunning views of Buttermere fells. It has a kitchen and seating area with electric heater and socket on a meter, a sink and cold running water. There is a hot shower on a meter and a toilet and washbasin with hot and cold water. The sleeping area has 8 mattresses, bring your own sleeping bag. You need a stove and eating utensils if you wish to self cater. Well behaved dogs welcome - sole occupancy only. Cragg Barn is a great base for walkers of all abilities. It is also ideal for climbing, fishing and wildlife/bird-watching. There are many local tourist attractions within a short drive. Cragg House Farm also has a holiday cottage sleeping two. Check the websites www.buttermerecottage.co.uk or www.lakelandcampingbarns.co.uk and book on line.

DETAILS

- **Open** - All year, all day, late arrivals by arrangement.
- **Number of beds** - 8: 1 x 8
- **Booking** - Booking essential at least 24 hrs in advance. Book online.
- **Price per night** - £8.50 per person.
- **Public Transport** - Train stations at Penrith / Workington. Bus links from Penrith station and Workington town centre to Keswick. Bus runs seasonally from Keswick.
- **Directions** - GR NY 173 171. From Keswick follow signs to Borrowdale, continue through Rosthwaite, Seatoller and over Honister Pass. Continue past Buttermere lake into Buttermere village. Keep on main road. Cragg House Farm is on the left on the brow of the hill before you get to NT car park. In icy conditions approach from Cockermouth town centre and continue through Lorton. Turn left to Buttermere following road signs. Cragg Farm is 1st on the right past the Buttermere village sign.

CONTACT: John and Vicki Temple
Cragg House Farm, Buttermere, Cockermouth, Cumbria, CA13 9XA
Tel: Camping Barn 017687 74301. Holiday Cottage 017687 70204
info@lakelandcampingbarns.co.uk www.buttermerecottage.co.uk

Lying in the picturesque Loweswater Valley, Swallow Barn is part of a traditional set of buildings dating back to 1670 on a working beef and sheep farm. The barn accommodates 18 people on mattresses in 4 sleeping areas.

There is a cooking and eating area with tables and chairs, 2 coin-operated showers and 2 toilets. The barn is an excellent base for exploring the western fells with both high and low level walks and spectacular views, or you can enjoy the peace and tranquillity of the valley. Boat hire and fishing permits are available from the farm. The coast to coast cycle route is right on the doorstep. The Kirkstyle pub provides excellent food, just over a mile away and the market town of Cockermouth is only 8 miles.

Check the website www.lakelandcampingbarns.co.uk and book online.

DETAILS

- **Open** - All year, all day
- **Number of beds** - 18: 1x9, 3x3
- **Booking** - Book online in advance, especially for school and bank holidays.
- **Price per night** - £8.50 per person.
- **Public Transport** - The nearest train station is Penrith with a bus to Cockermouth, then a taxi costing approximately £25.
- **Directions** - Leave the M6 at junct. 40 and follow the A66 to the Egremont turn off at Cockermouth. Follow the A5086, Egremont road for 6 miles. Turn left at Mockerkin and follow road to Loweswater. The farm is just past the Grange Hotel on the left .

CONTACT: Kath Leck
Waterend Farm, Loweswater, Cockermouth, Cumbria, CA13 0SU
Tel: Booking office 017687 74301, Farm 01946 861465
info@lakelandcampingbarns.co.uk www.lakelandcampingbarns.co.uk

FELLDYKE
BUNKHOUSE

Felldyke Bunkhouse is set in an idyllic location against the stunning backdrop of the Lake District mountains. Located near Loweswater and 5 minutes walk from Cogra Moss, the bunkhouse is just 100m from the SUSTRANS 71 (C-2-C) cycle route. Able to cater for groups of up to 23 in two bunkrooms, the accommodation includes a downstairs disabled access room for 3 people, which is ideal for leaders and teachers should a separate room be required. The upstairs room sleeps 20 and is sub-divided for privacy into sections of between four and six. Five high quality single occupancy shower rooms are provided, including heated towel rails. The right level of equipment has been invested in to allow a large number of people to be easily catered for, which includes: a drying cupboard; a range cooker; two dishwashers; plenty of fridge and freezer space; lots of food storage, large pans and sharp knives. This will hopefully keeping your beer cold, your food hot and your fingers intact.

DETAILS

- **Open** - All year
- **Number of beds** - 23
- **Booking** - Phone or email.
- **Price per night** - Circa £500 per weekend, see website for tariff and deposits.
- **Public Transport** - Local bus service runs within 10 minute walk, nearest train station in Whitehaven.
- **Directions** - From Cockermouth follow the A5086 for approx 6 miles past signs for Mockerkin. At Crossgates turn left. Go straight over staggered crossroads past Inglenook caravan park. Entering Felldyke turn immediately left into car park.

CONTACT: Phil and Rachel Gerrard
Felldyke Bunkhouse, Felldyke, Lamplugh, Workington, Cumbria, CA14 4SH
Tel: 01900 826698 or 07884 476708
felldyke.bunkhouse@gmail.com www.felldyke-bunkhouse.co.uk

Tarn Flatt Camping Barn is a traditional sandstone barn on St Bees Head overlooking the Scottish coastline and the Isle of Man. It is on a working farm which also includes a lighthouse, RSPB bird reserve on 100 metre cliffs and access to Fleswick Bay - a secluded shingle cove. There is canoeing and fishing in the area and the rock climbing and boulders at the base of the cliff are superb. There are several local circular walks with panoramic views of the coast and the fells and there is easy access to the quieter western Lakeland fells and lakes. The award-winning historic Georgian town and harbour of Whitehaven is only 3 miles away and St Bees (the starting point of the Coast to Coast walk) is 2 miles via the coastal path. The barn has a raised wooden sleeping area on the ground floor. There is electric light, a cooking slab (please bring your own stove and utensils) and an open fire (wood available from the farm). Toilets, wash-basin and showers are in adjacent buildings. Meals are available by arrangement. Children welcome. Dogs are accepted in sole use only.

DETAILS

- **Open** - All year, 24 hours
- **Number of beds** - 12 bed spaces.
- **Booking** - Booking in advance is advised.
- **Price per night** - £8.50 per person.
- **Public Transport** - Trains at Whitehaven (4 miles) and St Bees (3 miles). Buses also at Whitehaven.
- **Directions** - GR 947 146. With Sandwith village green on right, pass row of houses and turn right, at phone box take private road for 1 mile.

CONTACT: Janice Telfer
Tarn Flatt Hall, Sandwith, Whitehaven, Cumbria, CA28 9UX
Tel: Detail 01946 692162, Booking 017687 74301
stay@tarnflattfarm.co.uk www.tarnflattfarm.co.uk

HILLSIDE FARM
BUNKBARN

Hillside Farm is a Georgian farmstead in a conservation area just steps away from Hadrian's Wall. It is located in the small village of Boustead Hill, near the Solway Coast Area of Outstanding Natural Beauty and RSPB nature reserve. The farm has stunning views over the Solway Firth marshes towards Scotland. Hadrian's Wall National Trail and Hadrian's Cycleway pass right by. Hillside farm is a working farm and the 4th generation of a farmers welcome you to stay in the bunkbarn or the B&B rooms in the farmhouse. The bunkbarn is a conversion of a Georgian stable block. It has cooking slabs, cutlery and crockery and a 2 ring gas stove, microwave and small electric oven. There are hot showers and towels and sleeping bags can be hired if required. There is heating downstairs in the barn. You can arrange delivery of shopping via the farmhouse and with notice you can have breakfast or bacon sandwiches. Walking, cycling and family groups are most welcome. Visit England Approved.

DETAILS

- **Open** - All year, all day
- **Number of beds** - 12
- **Booking** - Book by phone or email.
- **Price per night** - £10 per person including shower. £4 full English breakfast, £2 bacon/sausage sandwiches.
- **Public Transport** - Nearest train station Carlisle. Bus: Stagecoach 93.
- **Directions** - From M6 junction 43 follow signs for A595 past the castle, turn at small roundabout onto B5307. After 1 mile turn right following signs for Burgh-by-Sands. Pass through town and cross the cattle grid onto Marsh Road. Take next left into village of Boustead Hill, then 2nd turning on left under arches into farmyard.

CONTACT: Mrs Sandra Rudd
Hillside Farm, Boustead Hill, Burgh-by-Sands, Carlisle, Cumbria, CA5 6AA
Tel: 01228 576398
ruddshillside1@btinternet.com www.hadrianswalkbnb.co.uk

Eden Valley Bunkhouse, in the heart of undiscovered walking and cycling countryside, has been sympathetically converted from sandstone farm buildings with rustic old beams. It is well away from main roads and the busy Lake District, yet within easy reach of Ullswater, Hadrian's Wall and the Scottish Borders. Situated around a courtyard are four spacious bedrooms, three sleeping 4 in bunk beds (with space for a camp bed) and one sleeping 6 in an old smithy. The kitchen, converted from the old dairy, contains cooking and eating utensils, stove, mircowave and fridge. The showers and toilets are of a high standard. The farm has beautiful views, woodland picnic area, riverside walks and salmon and trout river fishing. An easy walk away is Kirkoswald village, which has a shop, post office and two inns. A mile and a half's walk over a picturesque sandstone bridge is the village of Lazonby with a heated out-door pool, supermarket and station. The bunkhouse is half a mile off the C2C cycle route and surrounded by quiet and serene public footpaths. The farm also has a small caravan/camp site and operates the "C2C Hassle Free" service.

DETAILS

- **Open** - All year, all day
- **Number of beds** - 18: 1x6,3x4 (plus extra camp bed if required)
- **Booking** - Book by phone or email. £5 per person deposit to secure.
- **Price per night** - £14 per person. £50 per room.
- **Public Transport** - Trains: Penrith (8 miles), Lazonby (1 mile) collection possible.
- **Directions** - Between the village of Glassonby and Kirkoswald. Look for Mains Farm Campsite and Bunkhouse sign opposite a wood.

CONTACT:
Mains Farm, Kirkoswald, Penrith, Cumbria CA10 1DH
Tel: 01768 898342
pickthalls@themains-kirkoswald.co.uk www.edenvalleybunkhouse.co.uk

GREENHEAD
HOSTEL

Greenhead Hostel is a converted Methodist Chapel in the village of Greenhead on Hadrian's Wall. It is ideal for those walking the Pennine Way or The Wall and is in a great location for those exploring the nearby Roman heritage sites. The church was built in 1886 to serve the village miners and gave its last service in 1972. It has been a YHA hostel since 1978. Greenhead Hostel has a self catering kitchen and guest lounge. There are 40 beds in four rooms of six beds and two rooms of eight beds. These can be booked as family rooms, by groups or by individuals by the bed. Evening meals, breakfast and packed lunches available. The hostel is operated by Greenhead Hotel (over the road) with a welcoming hotel bar and restaurant. VisitEngland approved.

DETAILS

- **Open** - All year, hostel is open all day.
- **Number of beds** - 40: 2x8, 2x6 + family rooms
- **Booking** - Book by phone or email.
- **Price per night** - Adult: £15, Under 18 £10.   Reductions for large groups or full rooms. Sole use of hostel £400.
- **Public Transport** - Trains: Haltwhistle 3 miles, Carlisle 19 miles, Newcastle 45 miles. Bus: May to Sept service Stagecoach AD 122 from Newcastle to Bowness-on-Solway. Arriva 685 Carlisle-Newcastle passes Haltwhistle station and runs hourly all year.
- **Directions** - From Carlisle take the A69 to Newcastle, turn off for Greenhead (19 miles), turn right at the T- junction and the hostel is on the left opposite the Greenhead Hotel. From Newcastle take the A69 to Carlisle, turn right at the sign for Greenhead, follow instructions above.

CONTACT: Sue and Dave
Greenhead Hotel, Greenhead, Brampton, Cumbria, CA8 7HG
Tel: 01697 747411
daveandsuegreenhead@btconnect.com Greenhead-hotel.co.uk

Gibbs Hill Farm Hostel is a new conversion of a barn on a traditional working hill farm near Once Brewed on Hadrian's Wall. The hostel is designed to reduce energy consumption and is centrally heated throughout. There are 3 bunkrooms, 2 shower rooms, 2 toilets, a well equipped kitchen, comfortable sitting and dining area and a large deck where you can enjoy the evening sun.

The hostel has a drying room, lockers, laundry facilities and safe cycle storage. Ideal for families who may take a whole room with private facilities. Study groups welcome. Situated near Hadrian's Wall it is an excellent base for exploring the Roman sites, Hadrian's Wall Trail and Northumberland National Park. Basic items of food may be purchased and evening meals can be ordered the day before. Continental breakfast £5 packed lunches £6.

DETAILS

- **Open** - All year, hours flexible but no check in after 9pm.
- **Number of beds** - 18: 3x6
- **Booking** - Advisable, groups require full payment 4 weeks before arrival.
- **Price per night** - £16 adult, £12 child (under 12), including bedding.
- **Public Transport** - Trains at Haltwhistle 6 miles. Regular bus service along A69 between Newcastle and Carlisle, and in summer the Hadrian's Wall Bus runs between Newcastle and Carlisle. Alight at Once Brewed Information Centre and walk north to farm. Last bus 5.30pm from Haltwhistle.
- **Directions** - From the A69, turn north at Bardon Mill, signed 'Once Brewed'. Follow the signs towards 'Housesteads'. At the B6318, turn right and then immediately left towards 'Steel Rigg'. Follow for 1 mile, turn right to 'Gibbs Hill'.

CONTACT: Valerie Gibson
Gibbs Hill Farm, Bardon Mill, Nr Hexham, Northumberland, NE47 7AP
Tel: 01434 344030, Fax: 01434 344030
val@gibbshillfarm.co.uk www.gibbshillfarm.co.uk

LOW LUCKENS
ORGANIC CENTRE

Set on an organic farm in rural North Cumbria, close to the Scottish Borders and Hadrian's Wall, Low Luckens provides an ideal base for walking or cycling along peaceful country lanes or travelling wider afield. The Centre provides simple, clean and inexpensive self-catering accommodation for groups and individuals who enjoy the countryside, or want to be involved in farm or conservation work. Children of all ages are welcome. The ground floor has a large resource room with wood burning stove; a self-catering kitchen equipped for 12, a shower, toilet, linen cupboard and single / disabled sleeping accommodation. The first floor has two four-bed rooms, one with en suite shower and toilet. Organic vegetables can be purchased from the farm in advance and there is a local pub within walking distance serving excellent traditional dishes. Bedding, bed linen, heating & hot water included in price. Dogs are welcome by prior arrangement.

DETAILS

- **Open** - All year, 24 hours
- **Number of beds** - 9: 1x4, 1x4 en suite; 1x1 for a disabled person. 3 extra temporary beds available for larger groups.
- **Booking** - Booking necessary. A non-returnable deposit of 25% is required at the time of booking.
- **Price per night** - £20 (1 night), £35 (2 nights), £15 per night (3-6 nights), £90 (7 nights). Children half price. Whole centre: Weekend (2 nights) £300 (9 beds) + £20/person for extra mattresses. 7 nights £500 (9 beds) + £40/extra person.
- **Public Transport** - Public transport available to Brampton. Taxi from Brampton.
- **Directions** - See location page of website for directions.

CONTACT: Jill Jones
Low Luckens, Roweltown, Carlisle, Cumbria, CA6 6LJ
Tel: 016977 48186
lowluckensorc@hotmail.com www.lowluckensfarm.co.uk

Barrington Bunkhouse is situated in Rookhope in the stunning surroundings of Weardale. Rookhope is a pleasant sleepy little village with a shop and a primary school, and is situated in an AONB. Next door is The Rookhope Inn for a welcome pint and a very substantial meal. The Bunkhouse provides clean, comfortable accommodation with a self service continental breakfast ready for your day's activities ahead. There are kettles, toasters and a microwave. Eggs are supplied which can be scrambled or poached. A microwave poacher is supplied. Anyone is welcome, especially cyclists on the Coast 2 Coast (C2C), walkers on the Weardale Way and groups visiting the area. There are 12 bunk beds with an additional fold-up bed if needed. All bunks have a personal reading light. It has a fully fitted disabled wet-room with toilet, basin and shower, plus one able bodied shower and separate toilet. There is a large cast iron multi-fuel stove used from October to March and oil-filled radiators to provide extra warmth. There is a tumble dryer, and a hair dryer is available on request. Visitors can also camp on the lawns - some camping equipment is available.

DETAILS

- **Open** - All year, all day
- **Number of beds** - 12 (+1): 1 x 12 plus 1 fold up bed
- **Booking** - Booking recommended, by phone or email. 50% deposit is required.
- **Price per night** - £22pp incl. continental breakfast. Camping £14 with breakfast, £10 without. Sole use rates negotiable depending on group size and time of year.
- **Public Transport** - Trains Stanhope(6 miles). Bus to Durham & Bishop Auckland
- **Directions** - Next door to the Rookhope Inn in Rookhope.

CONTACT: Valerie Livingston
Barrington Cottage, Rookhope, Weardale, Co. Durham, DL13 2BG
Tel: 01388 517656
barrington_bunkhouse@hotmail.co.uk www.barrington-bunkhouse-rookhope.com

SWALLOW'S REST

ENGLAND

Popular with cyclists on the Coast to Coast cycle route, and in ideal walking country, Swallow's Rest is located outside of Rookhope, a village in an area of outstanding beauty in the North Pennines. Swallow's Rest offers a secluded self-contained, one bedroom cottage that can sleep up to 8 adults situated on the owner's land so you are guaranteed a restful night's sleep. The cottage consists of a fully equipped kitchen, living room with TV, DVD player, secure lock up for cycles, drying facilities and space to sleep 4 adults, a single bedroom with bunk beds for sleeping 4 and a shower room with hand basin, all decorated to a high standard. A full English or continental breakfast is provided as a self-catering hamper and evening meals and packed lunches can be provided with notice. Swallow's Rest is located 0.5 miles from the C2C route and is within easy reach of Hexham, Alston, Durham City and Teesdale. Located only a short walk from Rookhope Village where you can enjoy real ales and home cooked meals at the Rookhope Inn, a comfortable and friendly watering hole. Midweek deals are often available at Swallow's Rest

DETAILS

- **Open** - All year,
- **Number of beds** - 8 in total. 2 bunk beds sleeping 4 and 2 sofa beds sleeping 4.
- **Booking** - Recommended
- **Price per night** - £35 pppn
- **Public Transport** - Buses available to Rookhope Village
- **Directions** - Approx 200 metres up the hill you will come to an upside down white SLOW sign painted on road, turn right onto dirt track. Follow down to gate.

CONTACT: Stephen or Helen
Swallow's Rest, Redburn House, Rookhope, Weardale, Co Durham, DL132DE
Tel: 01388517589 or 01388443145
stephen.foster24@yahoo.co.uk

HOUGHTON NORTH
FARM ACCOMMODATION

Houghton North Farm, partly built with stones from Hadrian's Wall, has been in the Laws Family for five generations. It is situated in the beautiful Northumberland countryside right on the Heritage Trail and 15 miles from the start of the Hadrian's Wall Trail. Within the region walkers can enjoy marked woodland trails, rugged moorland and hills, and some of the most beautiful deserted beaches in the UK. The newly built spacious accommodation can take a group of up to 23 and is also ideal for individuals and families. It is a 4 Star Hostel with Visit Britain. The bunk style rooms (some en suite) are located around the central courtyard and include the use of a self-catering kitchen where a light breakfast is served. There is also a well appointed TV lounge with log fire and internet access, barbecue, secure cycle storage and parking. Long-term parking, baggage transfer and packed lunches are available on request. Within 10 mins walk are pubs, a restaurant and shops in Heddon-on-the-Wall.

DETAILS

- **Open** - All year (except Christmas and New Year), all day
- **Number of beds** - 22: 1x5, 3x4, 1x3, 1x2
- **Booking** - Book with a non-refundable deposit of £10 per person per night
- **Price per night** - From £25 (adult), £15 (under 12) inc breakfast. Group discounts.
- **Public Transport** - Trains at Wylam (2 miles) and Newcastle (7 miles). The 685 Newcastle-Carlisle bus stops right outside the farm. Baggage transfer is available.
- **Directions** - From Newcastle take the Heddon turn off the A69 to the B6528. Farm is 1/4 mile outside of the village of Heddon. From Carlisle take Horsley junction and continue approx 3 miles beyond Horsley. Farm is on the left at the top of a hill.

CONTACT: Mrs Paula Laws
Houghton North Farm, Heddon-on-the-Wall, Northumberland, NE15 0EZ
Tel: 01661 854364
wjlaws@btconnect.com www.houghtonnorthfarm.co.uk

HOWNSGILL
BUNKHOUSE & TEAROOM ENGLAND

Hownsgill Bunkhouse and Tearoom is in a great location for walkers and cyclists, situated close to the Coast 2 Coast route at Lydgetts Junction. An ideal base to explore NCN routes 7 and 14 or the Waskerley Way over the fabulous Hownsgill Viaduct with breath-taking views over valleys and moorland.

The accommodation is converted from a milking parlour on a working farm. It has 4 bedrooms, a well equipped kitchen, drying facilities, seating for 12 in the dining area, secure storage for bikes, and a wet area with WC and showers, with access for the less able. The beds are made up with fresh linen and towels are provided. A free help-yourself breakfast of toast, cereal and fruit juice is included. Also on site is the Hownsgill Tearooms for a friendly atmosphere, good quality food at reasonable prices, and superb views. Static caravans and touring caravan pitches are also available to rent on site.

DETAILS

- **Open** - All year, 24 hours
- **Number of beds** - 12: 2x4 bunk rooms, 1x2 bunk room, 1x double.
- **Booking** - Booking advisable. Phone or email.
- **Price per night** - High season (Mar- Oct incl.) £20 pp/£16 under 18s, £17/£14 pppn for 4+ nights. Low season £18pp/£14 under 18s, £15/£12 pppn for 4+ nights. Sole use £500 per week high season, £400 low season.
- **Public Transport** - Nearest train station is Durham (12 miles). Local buses from Durham stop half a mile from the bunkhouse.
- **Directions** - Down a track on left of A692 midway from Templetown to Castleside.

CONTACT: John & Stephen Shaw
Hownsgill Farm, Consett, Co. Durham, DH8 9AA
Tel: 01207 503597 / 07946 797278
hownsgill_bunkhouse@hotmail.co.uk www.c2cstopoff.co.uk

GREENWELL HILL
FARM ACCOMMODATION

Greenwell Hill Farm lies in Weardale on the edge of the North Pennines, an Area of Outstanding Natural Beauty known as England's Last Wilderness. Sandstone farm buildings have been sensitively converted to provide three high standard self catering barns. These are comfortable and nicely furnished and have central heating, double glazing, honey pined furniture, fitted carpets, natural beams, TVs, DVDs, spring water, modern kitchens and en suite bathrooms. Bed linen, towels and heating are included in the price. The Barn (13) has 6 en suite rooms, two kitchens, courtyard with BBQ and a lounge on each floor, one of which is a very large circular living area 'The Gin Gan' with plenty of space for large groups to dine together. The Stable (6) has an upstairs open-plan lounge/kitchen with stunning views of Weardale. The Byre (4) has a mezzanine loft balcony above the lounge/kitchen. All cottages are available for short breaks: 3 nights weekend or 4 nights midweek. You are welcome to explore the farm, follow the nature trail or feed the chickens. Lambing time is in April. Local activities include pony trekking, trout fishing, mountain biking in Hamsterley forest or walking in the Durham Dales. B&B also available.

DETAILS

- **Open** - All year, all day 4pm arrival time unless otherwise arranged
- **Number of beds** - Barn: 13: 5x2,1x3   Stables: 6: 1x2,1x4   Byre 4: 2x2
- **Booking** - Booking essential. £10 deposit per person.
- **Price per night** - From £16.50pp (min 3 nights). Weekly rates from £295 - £1300.
- **Public Transport** - Nearest buses are in the villages of Wolsingham or Tow Law.
- **Directions** - From Tow Law take Wolsingham Rd. Turn L after 1.5 miles then nxt R

CONTACT: Mrs A. Turnbull
Greenwell Hill Farm, Wolsingham, County Durham, DL13 4PH
Tel: 01388 710350
enquiries@greenwellhill.co.uk   www.greenwellfarm.co.uk

Now you can "budget stay – your way" in Newcastle at the brand new, city centre Euro Hostel! Euro Hostel Newcastle is the perfect base to enjoy this fabulous city. On the doorstep of all the city's attractions, just 2 blocks from Grey Street, a short stroll to the famous Quayside, Bigg Market and Gate areas and all they have to offer. Perfect for everyone, solo travellers, couples, business travellers, families and large groups.

Facilities include a guest kitchen, guest laundry, WiFi access throughout (free in the bar!), internet terminals, secure luggage storage, a meeting room with phone, and specially built female-only rooms and dorms with all the trimmings. Also on site is the Ware Rooms Bar for a relaxing meal or a great night out with great tunes, cheap drinks and cocktail specials!

DETILS

- **Open** - All year, 24 hours
- **Number of beds** - 260. All rooms en suite ranging from single/double to 10 beds
- **Booking** - Booking advised, by phone or online.
- **Price per night** - From just £16 per person per night in 10 bed room, £29 pp in private rooms, inc. a fabulous continental breakfast..
- **Public Transport** - Just a 10 minute walk from Central Station or 3 minutes from Manors or Monument metro stations
- **Directions** - From Central Station turn right onto Neville Street. Cross the road and walk along Mosley Street, past the Cathedral until you come to 55' North (a large roundabout with a block of flats above). Turn left up Pilgrim Street then take next right (Worswick Street). Cross the road at the bottom of the hill and see hostel on the right.

CONTACT: Steve Mackenzie
17 Carliol Square, Newcastle Upon Tyne, NE1 6UQ
Tel: 08454 900371
stevem@euro-hostels.co.uk www.euro-hostels.co.uk

ALBATROSS
BACKPACKERS IN!

Fly high with the award winning "Albatross"! . This clean and modern backpackers hostel is located in Newcastle's City Centre. All in walking distance from sporting, musical and conference venues, art galleries, historical attractions, food markets and public transport facilities. We are open all year round. The Albatross – www.albatrossnewcastle.com - is primarily designed to provide affordable accommodation in the city centre for the international travellers, walkers, cyclists and bikers, exchange student groups, sports teams, choirs etc. We provide rooms from 2 beds to 12 beds and anything in between for as little as £ 16.50 and £ 24.50. The overnight price includes; linen, 24hr reception, fully fitted self-catering kitchen with free tea, coffee and toast, free WiFi access and computer terminals, pool table, satellite TV, outside sitting/barbeque area, free baggage storage and laundry facilities. A young dedicated international team is looking forward to welcome you.

DETAILS

- **Open** - All yea, r24 hours
- **Number of beds** - 177
- **Booking** - Recommended. Photo ID at check-in (passport or driving licence).
- **Price per night** - From £16.50pp (dorm) to £22.50pp (2 bed room)
- **Public Transport** - Five minutes walk from central train, bus and metro stations.
- **Directions** - Central Station/Megabus drop off point: from main entrance, head right, take the first street on your left (Grainger St), you'll find us on your left 200m uphill. From National Express coach station: head down Scotswood Rd to Central Station. From Airport: take Metro to Central Station (20 mins travel). From port (ferry): buses travel between the port and Central Station and take 20 mins.

CONTACT: Reception
51 Grainger Street, Newcastle upon Tyne, NE1 5JE
Tel: 0191 2331330, Fax: 0191 2603389
info@albatrossnewcastle.co.uk   www.albatrossnewcastle.com

DEMESNE FARM
BUNKHOUSE

Demesne Farm Bunkhouse is a self-catering unit which was converted in 2004 from a barn on a working hill farm. The farm is situated on the Pennine Way, Route 68 cycle route, Reivers cycle route and is within 100 metres of the centre of the North Tyne village of Bellingham on the edge of the Northumberland National Park. The bunkhouse provides an ideal base for exploring Northumberland, Hadrian's Wall, Kielder Water and many climbing crags. It accommodates 15 and is perfect for smaller groups, individuals and families. The bedrooms are fitted with hand crafted oak man-sized bunk beds, high quality mattresses, pillows and curtains, and cushion flooring. The communal living area with potbelly stove and fitted kitchen includes cooker, microwave, fridge, kettle, toaster, crockery, cutlery, cooking utensils, farmhouse tables, chairs and easy chairs. It has 2 bathrooms with hot showers, basins, toilets and under floor heating. In the courtyard there is ample parking, bike lock up, drying room and a gravelled area with picnic tables. Complete bed linen is included.

DETAILS

- **Open** - All year, flexible, but no check in after 9pm
- **Number of beds** - 15: 1 x 8, 1 x 4, 1 x 3
- **Booking** - Please book in advance.
- **Price per night** - £17 per person (including linen).
- **Public Transport** - Trains at Hexham (17 miles), regular bus service from Hexham to Bellingham. Bellingham bus stop 100 metres from bunkhouse. By car: Newcastle 45 mins, Scottish Border 20 mins, Kielder Water 10 mins.
- **Directions** - 100 metres from centre of village, located next to Northern Garage.

CONTACT: Robert Telfer
Demesne Farm, Bellingham, Hexham, Northumberland, NE48 2BS
Tel: 01434 220258 Mobile 07967 396345
stay@demesnefarmcampsite.co.uk www.demesnefarmcampsite.co.uk

Located in a former schoolhouse in the historic town of Rothbury overlooking the River Coquet, Tomlinson's is a one-stop shop for low-cost accommodation, wholesome meals and cycle hire. Ideal for families, groups and independent travellers, there are five flexible rooms most with en suite showers. Guests can mix in the communal TV lounge, enjoy the views on the covered roof terrace or enjoy a homemade meal in the cafe. Big windows give big views overlooking the river and countryside and there are laundry facilities, a wash down area for bikes and boots, secure bike storage and drying room. For celebrations and meetings there is a 30 capacity function room for hire. Rothbury is being developed as Northumberland National Park's cycling hub and the bunkhouse is just metres from a string of off-road cycle tracks and public footpaths. The bunkhouse has a fleet of mountain bikes available to hire and instructors to lead cycle groups of all ages. The Cheviot Hills and the golden sands of the Northumberland Coast are within a 30 minute drive and the area is awash with castles including Alnwick which was Hogwarts in the Harry Potter films.

DETAILS

■ **Open** - All year, all day
■ **Number of beds** - 28: 1x7, 1x6 (+ 3 more rooms)
■ **Booking** - Book by phone or email.
■ **Price per night** - From £20 per person, £525 for the whole bunkhouse.
■ **Public Transport** - Trains at Morpeth (15 miles) and Alnmouth. Buses to Newcastle and Morpeth bus station run most days.
■ **Directions** - Overlooking river, near junction at Haw Hill off the B6342 in Rothbury.

CONTACT:
Bridge Street, Rothbury, Northumberland, NE65 7SF
Tel: 01669 621 979
jackie@tomlinsonsrothbury.co.uk   www.tomlinsonsrothbury.co.uk

FOREST VIEW
WALKERS HOSTEL

Forest View is set in the hamlet of Byrness on the edge of Keilder Forest and Northumberland National Park. An ideal stopover on the A68 England to Scotland route. Byrness is the penultimate stop on the Pennine way. Relax after a hard day's walking in the residents' bar/lounge at Forest View Inn.

A Visit Britain accredited accommodation with walker friendly awards, offering quality furnished single, twin, double and triple rooms and clean modern bathrooms. New for 2012 Foresters' Bar & Restaurant serving quality home cooked meals & hand pulled local craft ales along with weekly guest ales. Forest View also has a well stocked shop and free to use laundry and drying facilities. Camping is also available. A recent national feedback survey rated Forest View at 99.5% for cleanliness, service and facilities.

DETAILS

- **Open** - All year, check in from 4pm - check out by 10.30 am.
- **Number of beds** - 23: 2 x single, 2 x double, 3 x triple, 4 x twin (some en suite)
- **Booking** - Booking is recommended
- **Price per night** - Adult from £20. Under 16s £18
- **Public Transport** - Nearest rail station Newcastle upon Tyne (40 miles) then National Express to lay-by 200yds from hostel.
- **Directions** - Forest View is just off the A68, 4 miles from the Scottish Border, 16 miles south of Jedburgh and 10 miles north of Otterburn. The National Express bus drops off 200yds from the hostel.

CONTACT: Colin or Joyce
7 Otterburn Green, Byrness Village, Northumberland, NE19 1TS
Tel: 01830 520425
joycetaylor1703@hotmail.co.uk www.forestviewbyrness.co.uk

THE LOOKOUT
BUNKHOUSE

Springhill's Bunkhouse & Wigwams is ideal for groups, families or independent travellers looking for great value comfortable accommodation which can be booked as a whole or on a per bed per night basis. Superbly located on the Northumberland heritage coastline and AONB coastal path with stunning views towards the Farne Islands and Cheviot Hills, only 1 mile from Seahouses and 3 miles from Bamburgh. The fully heated Lookout Bunkhouse has 8 rooms of 4 with en suite shower rooms, fully equipped kitchen, dining and sitting area with TV/DVD, internet, BBQ and outdoor seating. The five wigwams each sleep up to five have electric heating, platform beds with mattresses, table, fridge, kettle lighting, electric sockets, a communal kitchen and sitting area with WiFi, TV/DVD, separate toilet block, BBQs, fire pits and outdoor sitting area. Bunkhouse and wigwams have access to a drying room, cycle store and laundry

DETAILS

■ **Open** - All year round, arrivals 3pm - 6pm, departures before 10am. Cleaning 12am-4pm
■ **Number of beds** - Bunkhouse 32: 8x4; Wigwams 25: 5x5
■ **Booking** - Online, phone or email.
■ **Price per night** - Bunkhouse £14 adult, £11 child (under 14) all year round Wigwams £19.50 adult £14 child (under14) all year round
■ **Public Transport** - Closest railway stop with easy bus transfers is Berwick upon Tweed. Buses run daily to Seahouses with the nearest bus stop being in North Sunderland which is the top end of Seahouses half a mile from Springhill.
■ **Directions** - Springhill Farm is 0.75miles from the coast road, which runs between Seahouses 1mile and Bamburgh 3.5miles. Alnwick is 15 miles and Berwick 25 miles

CONTACT: Sarah or Julie
Springhill Farm, Seahouses, Northumberland NE68 7UR
Tel: 01665 721820
enquiries@springhill-farm.co.uk www.springhill-farm.co.uk/bunkhouse

ALNWICK
YOUTH HOSTEL

Once the Town's Court House, today the accommodation offered by the Alnwick Youth Hostel is somewhat less austere. Newly opened in 2011, this 4 star standard hostel is sure to meet the needs of every traveller, with a variety of en suite rooms, cosy lounge, games room and a bright and airy dining room. It's town centre location makes it ideal for a visit to historic Alnwick Castle, the medieval home of the Dukes of Northumberland which had a starring role in the early Harry Potter films, as well as the neighbouring Alnwick Garden, recently created by the Duchess. A 15 minute car journey takes you to the endless beaches which comprise the Northumberland coast, with glorious views of Dunstanburgh and Bamburgh Castles and wildlife havens such as Holy Island and the Farne Isles. Only a short trip inland brings you to the stunning heather clad Cheviot Hills and Border Riever country. Great for families, groups, cyclists and backpackers.

DETAILS

- **Open** - All year, Reception open 08:00 to 10:00hrs and 16:00 to 21:00hrs
- **Number of beds** - 57 = 1 x 1, 3 x 2, 1 x 3, 6 x 4,1 x 5, 3 x 6
- **Booking** - Booking advisable by phone or e-mail or book online via our website.
- **Price per night** - Adult dorm beds from £18.00, under 18 from £13.50. 2 bedded rooms from £38.00, Family 4 bedded rooms available from £67
- **Public Transport** - Bus passes door (518, Newcastle - Alnwick), nearest station (Alnmouth) 4 miles. National Express services stop at Alnwick (5 mins walk).
- **Directions** - You will find the hostel opposite Alnwick library. A public car park is available at Roxboro Place, to the rear of the Job Centre.

CONTACT: Andrew Clarkson
34 - 38 Green Batt, Alnwick, Northumberland, NE66 1TU
Tel: 01665 660800
info@alnwickyouthhostel.co.uk www.alnwickyouthhostel.co.uk

Wooler Youth Hostel is set in its own spacious grounds on the edge of the town. It has 46 beds, a huge dining and common room, excellent drying facilities and a large self catering kitchen, making it great for groups. There is also an excellent value restaurant, on site car parking and secure cycle storage. Wooler has inns, grocery stores and specialist shops, and is an ideal base for exploring the Northumberland National Park, the Cheviot hills (rich in archaeological sites), local castles and fine sandy beaches. For walkers there's St Cuthbert's Way and the Ravenber long-distance walks and many day walks. For cyclists there's the Wooler cycle hub routes, Pennine Cycleway and many quiet lanes to explore. Nearby there are bridleways perfect for mountain-biking, some of the best bouldering in the UK, riding centres and even a gliding school. Bird watchers can take a boat trip to the Farne Islands to see puffins, and visit the Cheviots where a golden eagle, and Bill Oddie, were spotted recently.

DETAILS

- **Open** - April until Oct (whole hostel rental Nov-March), 7am-11pm
- **Number of beds** - 46: 4x2, 8x4, 1x6
- **Booking** - Booking advised. Always call the hostel in advance of arriving.
- **Price per night** - From £14.50 adults, £10.50 children. Group booking discounts available, contact the hostel for further details.
- **Public Transport** - Market Place, 400 yards from the hostel. Arriva Northumbria/ Travelsure 464, Border Village 267 from Berwick. Travelsure 470/3 from Alnwick.
- **Directions** - From the Market Place at the bottom of the high street go up Cheviot Street past The Anchor pub. The hostel is 300 yards up the hill on the right.

CONTACT: Mick
30 Cheviot Street, Wooler, Northumberland, NE71 6LW
Tel: 01668 281365
wooler@yha.org.uk   www.wooler.org.uk/hostel

BLUEBELL FARM
BUNKBARN

Bluebell Farm caravan and camp site is in the centre of the village, within walking distance of shops and pubs. It is ideally located for exploring Nothumberland's Heritage Coast Route, the Cheviot Hills National Park and the historic Scottish Borders. The Bunkbarn sleeps 14, and there is also a wooden ark and five self-catering cottages. The bunkbarn has a family room for 6, an 8 bed dorm and a fully equipped self-catering kitchen. The Ark has a sleeping platform for 4 (but if you book for two you have sole use), fridge, TV, microwave, toaster and kettle, with a patio area outside where you can cook on your own camping stove. All the beds are equipped with pillows and duvets and you can hire linen and towels or bring your own sleeping bag. Shared toilets block and bike store. Hot showers, electricity and gas included in the prices. Activities include golf, climbing, canoeing, diving, horse riding, fishing, cycling and walking. Dogs welcome by arrangement. Duke of Edinburgh groups welcome.

DETAILS

- **Open** - All year, check in by 9 pm, departure by 10 am.
- **Number of beds** - Bunkhouse 14 : 1 x 8, 1 x 6 Ark: 4
- **Booking** - Not essential
- **Price per night** - Bunkbarn: £12.50, under 14s £6.25. Ark: £15.50, under 14's £7.75. Linen and towel hire £6.25 per person. Exclusive use available.
- **Public Transport** - Trains at Berwick upon Tweed. Buses from Berwick to Belford. National Express coaches stop in Belford. Local bus from Newcastle.
- **Directions** - From the A1 take B1342 into the village. Turn onto B6349 signposted for Wooler. Bluebell Farm is first main driveway on right, almost opposite the Co-op.

CONTACT: Phyl
Bluebell Farm Caravan Park, Belford, Northumberland, NE70 7QE
Tel: 01668 213362
corillas@tiscali.co.uk www.bluebellfarmbelford.com

THE HIDEAWAY
HOSTEL

Centuries old, The Hideaway is conveniently situated in the heart of picturesque Old Berwick. Admire the magnificent stone fireplace as you toast yourself by the multi-fuel stove. Enjoy a barbecue on the verandah or in the tiny but delightful courtyard garden as you relax in the cool summer night air, heavy with the scent of honeysuckle and jasmine. Shared facilities include a well equipped kitchen, sitting room with TV and dining room. WiFi available throughout the property for a small charge. Family friendly, but due to layout not recommended for toddlers. Small price rise for 2012 - but still excellent value!. Berwick is an ideal base for exploring Northumberland, Lindisfarne and the Scottish Borders. It is also close to an amazing number of cycle routes. We have excellent secure cycle storage and drying facilities. Well behaved dogs ONLY by prior arrangement. No smoking.

DETAILS

- **Open** - All year, all day. Check in 4 - 10pm.
- **Number of beds** - 11: 1x3, 4x2 (1 twin ensuite, 2 double, 1 double en suite)
- **Booking** - Booking advisable. 33% deposit.
- **Price per night** -   £23 - £28pp. Price includes continental breakfast and bedding! Single supplement £5. Towel hire £1
- **Public Transport** - 10 mins walk from Berwick station and long distance buses.
- **Directions** - Look for Church Street by the Guildhall. The Hideaway can be found between "The Sporran" giftshop and "Hair at XI". Look for the cycle logos in the passageway through the wrought iron gate! For a detailed location map, go to Google Maps, and type Hideaway plus our postcode (TD15 1EE).

CONTACT: J Morton
1 The Courtyard, Church Street, Berwick-upon-Tweed, TD15 1EE
Tel: 01289 308737, Mobile 07989 468008
patmosphere@yahoo.co.uk

CHATTON PARK
BUNKHOUSE

Chatton Park Bunkhouse started life as a Smithy and has been converted into self-catering accommodation. It is situated on a mixed working farm which nestles around the river Till, half a mile from Chatton village.

Eight miles from the coast and five miles from the Cheviot Hills, Chatton Park is an ideal base for exploring Northumberland's vast empty beaches, heather clad hills & historic castles. Walking, water sports, climbing, fishing, golf and cycling are all available nearby. Accommodating 12, the bunkhouse is perfect for smaller groups, families & individuals. The 2 bedrooms are fitted with large custom made bunks and can be rented separately as secure units. Bedding can be provided at a small extra fee. The living area has a fully equipped kitchen & seating around the original blacksmith's fire. Wash & drying room with hot showers. Secure storage, ample parking. Room for camping. DIY livery. Dog kennels provided.

DETAILS

- **Open** - All year, flexible but no check in after 9pm
- **Number of beds** - 12: 2x6
- **Booking** - Booking recommended but not essential
- **Price per night** - £12 - £15 pp. Group bookings negotiable
- **Public Transport** - Nearest train station Berwick upon Tweed. Buses to Chatton from Alnwick / Berwick.
- **Directions** - From A1 take B6348 to Chatton. 4 miles at bottom of hill on right is Chatton Park Farm

CONTACT: Jane or Duncan
Chatton Park Farm, Chatton, Alnwick, Northumberland, NE66 5RA
Tel: 01668 215247
ord@chattonpk.fsnet.co.uk www.chattonparkfarm.co.uk

TACKROOM
BUNKHOUSE

The Tackroom Bunkhouse is situated on a mixed working farm between the seaside villages of Beadnell and Seahouses, a stones' throw from beautiful sandy beaches on the spectacular Northumberland Coast. The area is ideal for walking, water sports, climbing, cycling, diving or just sightseeing. Accommodating 12, the bunkhouse is ideal for smaller groups, individuals and couples. The two bedrooms are each fitted with 6 man-sized bunkbeds and a locker for each visitor. Sleeping bags are essential. The communal area has a mini kitchen with hob, microwave, fridge, toaster etc, a dining table to seat 12 and colour TV.

All crockery, cutlery and cooking utensils are supplied but there is no oven. Adjoining the bunkhouse is the shower/toilet block complete with washing machines and tumble driers. Also available is a lock-up and off road parking. The Tackroom Bunkhouse is heated.

DETAILS

- **Open** - All year, flexible, but no check-in after 10pm.
- **Number of beds** - 12: 2 x 6.
- **Booking** - Recommended but not essential
- **Price per night** - £13 per person or £130 sole use.
- **Public Transport** - Train station at Berwick upon Tweed. There are intermittent local buses to Seahouses and Beadnell, passing ½ mile away from the hostel.
- **Directions** - From A1 take the B1340, follow road to Beadnell (signed Seahouses/Beadnell). Annstead farm is approx ½ mile past Beadnell on the left.

CONTACT: Sue Mellor
Annstead Farm, Beadnell, Northumberland, NE67 5BT
Tel: 01665 720387, Fax: 01665 721494
stay@annstead.co.uk www.annstead.co.uk

MAUGHOLD VENTURE CENTRE BUNKHOUSE

Maughold Venture Centre Bunkhouse is built of Manx stone, overlooking farmland with views in the distance to the sea. It offers self-catering facilities with the option of purchasing meals from the neighbouring adventure centre if required (subject to availability). All bedrooms are en suite with full central heating. Facilities include a basic but functional games room and kitchen. The number of beds in each room can be altered to suit your requirements.

The local beach of Port e Vullen, 10 mins walk away, is popular with our visitors and the Bunkhouse is adjacent to the Venture Centre where you may arrange sessions of kayaking, abseiling, air rifle shooting, archery, gorge walking, dinghy sailing, power boating and team events. We have our own stop, Lewaigue Halt, on the Manx Electric Railway giving access to Douglas, Ramsay and to mountain walks and tranquil glens. Ideal for groups, families and individuals.

DETAILS

- **Open** - February to November, 24 hours
- **Number of beds** - 52   2x2 : 1x6 : 4x8 : 1x10
- **Booking** - Telephone reservation essential
- **Price per night** - £10-£15 per person
- **Public Transport** - No 3 bus or Manx Electric Railway from Douglas or Ramsey. Get off bus at Dreemskerry (5 mins walk); get off railway at Lewaigue Halt (nearby). Taxi from Ramsey £5. Taxi from Douglas £25.
- **Directions** - GR 469922. From Douglas take the A2 coast road. When the road begins to descend into Ramsey the Venture Centre is signposted on the right hand side. Follow the signs - it is the first building on the left.

CONTACT: Simon Read
The Venture Centre, Maughold, Isle of Man, IM7 1AW
Tel: 01624 814240
Contact@adventure-centre.co.uk www.adventure-centre.co.uk

King William's College is the only independent school in the Isle of Man and is located on Castletown Bay in the south of the island. The Isle of Man has lots to offer, including an interesting transport system, great beaches, mountainous heathland, historic sites, charming villages and numerous walks.

Junior House, formerly used for junior boarding, is set in the expansive College grounds and provides a mix of accommodation options ranging from twin rooms to dormitories. There is a lounge, laundry room, TV room, drying room and a limited kitchen area.

Junior House is an ideal location for all the attractions in the south of the island and the facilities are well matched to those looking for outdoor activity holidays. Catering can be provided at most times although guests should check at the time of booking. Junior House is relaxed, clean and well maintained.

DETAILS

- **Open** - All year (except Christmas and New Year), all day
- **Number of beds** - 60: 1x14 : 2x12 : 1x 8: 7x2
- **Booking** - Groups, TT races book with deposit.
- **Price per night** - From £15.50 per person. Breakfast extra.
- **Public Transport** - The airport is located next to the College. Ferries dock at Douglas from Liverpool, Heysham, Dublin and Belfast.
- **Directions** - From Douglas follow signs to Castletown and the Airport. Bus stop is located adjacent to the entrance to King William's College.

CONTACT: Reception
King William's College, Castletown, Isle of Man, IM9 1TP
Tel: 01624 820400 , Fax: 01624 820402
rooms@kwc.sch.im www.kwc.sch.im

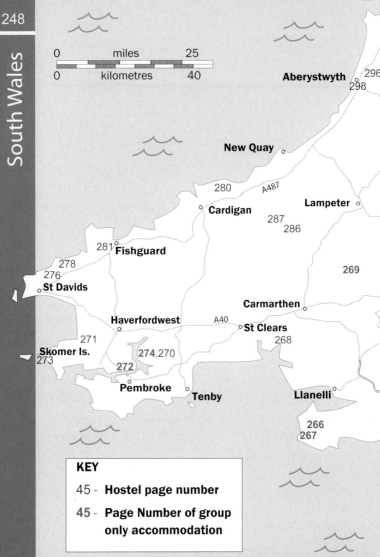

| 0 | miles | 25 |
| 0 | kilometres | 40 |

Aberystwyth 296
298

New Quay

280 A487

Cardigan Lampeter

287
286

281 Fishguard 269

278
276
St Davids

Carmarthen

Haverfordwest A40 St Clears

268

271
Skomer Is. 274,270
273 272

Pembroke Tenby Llanelli

266
267

KEY

45 - **Hostel page number**

45 - **Page Number of group only accommodation**

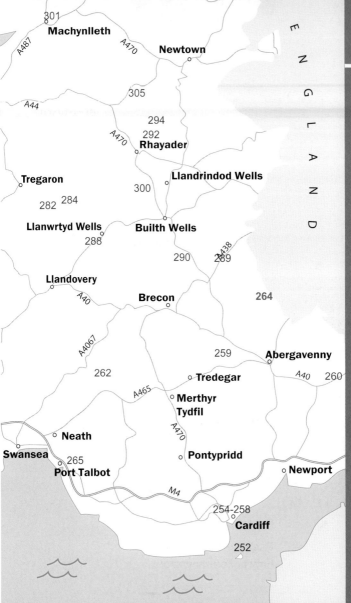

301 Machynlleth A470 Newtown

A487

A44 305

294
292
A470 Rhayader

Tregaron Llandrindod Wells

282 284 300

Llanwrtyd Wells Builth Wells
288

290 A438 289

Llandovery

A40 Brecon 264

A4067 259 Abergavenny

262 Tredegar A40 260

A465 Merthyr
Tydfil

A470

Neath

Swansea 265 Pontypridd

Port Talbot Newport

M4

254-258
Cardiff

252

ENGLAND

South Wales

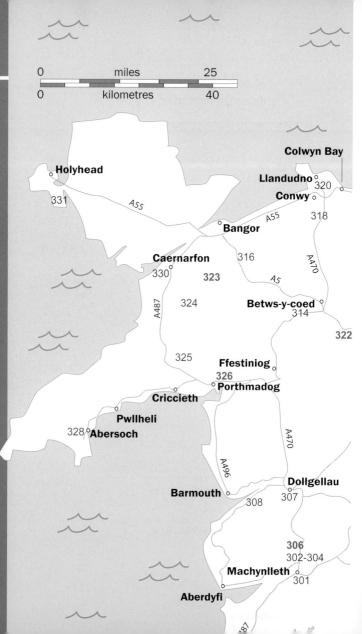

North Wales

0   miles   25
0   kilometres   40

Colwyn Bay

Holyhead

331   A55

Llandudno 320
Conwy

A55   318

Bangor

Caernarfon   316   A470

330   **323**

A5

324   **Betws-y-coed**
314

A487   **322**

325   **Ffestiniog**

326
Porthmadog

Criccieth

Pwllheli

328 **Abersoch**   A496

A470

Barmouth   **Dollgellau**

308   307

306
302-304

Machynlleth
301

Aberdyfi

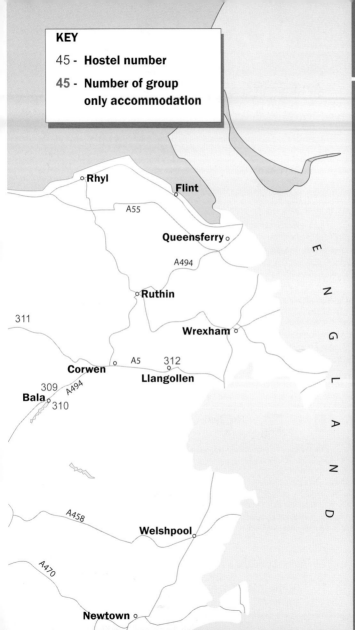

KEY

45 - **Hostel number**

45 - **Number of group only accommodation**

Rhyl

Flint

A55

Queensferry

A494

Ruthin

311

Wrexham

Corwen   A5   312

Llangollen

309   A494

Bala   310

A458

Welshpool

A470

Newtown

ENGLAND

North Wales

FLAT HOLM
FARMHOUSE

Travel to Flat Holm Island and stay in the most southerly hostel in Wales! The Flat Holm Farmhouse is located on the small Island just five miles from the Capital City of Cardiff, so why not visit and discover the magic of Island life? home to wardens and volunteers, you can enjoy a guided tour and experience its wealth of history and wildlife, take a shore walk and watch the sunset, or just sit back and relax in the cosy Island pub. An overnight visit includes a return boat trip from the Cardiff Bay Barrage, a guided tour of the Island and one night accommodation. Longer stays are available. The mixed dormitories, with bunkbeds, cater for up to 12 people in each room. Visitors have full use of the self-catering kitchen to prepare all their meals (snacks such as crisps and chocolate bars can be purchased in the Island gift shop). Please note: All trips to the Island are dependent on weather and may be cancelled due to strong winds, sometimes at short notice. If you cannot reschedule the ticket price will be refunded.

DETAILS

- **Open** - March to October.
- **Number of beds** - 24.
- **Booking** - Phone or Email.
- **Price per night** - Hostel £18 per night. Return Boat Trip £22.50.
- **Public Transport** - Boat - see website for details.
- **Directions** - The boat departs from the Cardiff Bay Barrage.
For directions visit their website.

CONTACT:
Cardiff Harbour Authority, Queen Alexandra House, Cargo Road, Cardiff Bay, CF10 4LY
Tel: 029 2087 7912 or 07929365077
flatholmproject@cardiff.gov.uk   www.flatholmisland.com

NOSDA STUDIO
HOSTEL

NosDa means "Good night" in Welsh and that is exactly what we promise. NosDa Studio Hostel is a hostel/hotel hybrid, a new concept of stylish budget accommodation. There's a choice of secure mixed and single sex dormitories and also a number of private rooms, each with their own pod style bathrooms, mini kitchens, TVs and even balconies. "NosDa is redefining the hostelling genre"- Lonely Planet. Uniquely situated along the banks of the river Taff, NosDa occupies a newly refurbished 19th century building with superb views of the iconic Millennium Stadium. Our lively bar has a selection of Welsh beers, ciders and spirits and the affordable menu lets you taste some delicious local produce. There is an in-house gym and nightclub, and if that wears you out why not chill in our new funky TV lounge. With the castle, stadium and train station all within sight, NosDa Studio Hostel is the most centrally located hostel with a view to die for and the facilities to match!

DETAILS

- **Open** - All year, 24 hours.
- **Number of beds** - 138: 3 x 4, 7 x 6, 3 x 8, 1 x 10 + 60 beds in private rooms.
- **Booking** - Essential for groups, advisable for individuals. Book online.
- **Price per night** - From £20.00, Double/twin from £44.
- **Public Transport** - Train, coach and bus stations 5 minutes walk from the hostel.
- **Directions** - By car: From the M4, take junction 32 and follow signs for city centre. Approaching the centre follow the road around the castle then straight ahead over the bridge crossing the River Taff. Take the next left into Lower Cathedral Road, then 1st left into Despenser Street. By foot from Cardiff Central Station turn left across the river and follow the embankment upstream, with the stadium opposite. Look ahead.

CONTACT: Reception
53-59, Despenser Street, Riverside, Cardiff, CF11 6AG
Tel: 029 2037 8866
info@nosda.co.uk www.nosda.co.uk

CARDIFF UNIVERSITY
ACCOMMODATION
WALES

Cardiff University provides single occupancy en-suite accommodation at a number of venues in the heart of the city close to all the tourist attractions. Single occupancy standard accommodation is also available for individuals and groups, approximately two and a half miles from the city centre. The accommodation is available during the summer holiday period (June – September inclusive). There are a range of options including self-catering and bed and breakfast. You will need to enquire about the availability of catering when you make your enquiry. All rooms are provided with bed linen and towels. Tea/coffee making facilities are available either in the bedroom or in the kitchen. Bedrooms are arranged in flats and these can vary in number of single occupancy bedrooms and all flats have a fully equipped kitchen. Cardiff University provides an ideal accommodation venue with comfortable and affordable accommodation.

DETAILS

■ **Open** - 22 June 2012 to 14 September 2012. , Reception open 8am-10pm.

■ **Number of beds** - 1200+ single occupancy en suite.

■ **Booking** - Telephone or email.

■ **Price per night** - GROUP PRICE (8 or more) Single en-suite bedrooms at £24.64 pppn, or single standard bedrooms at £20.44pppn. INDIVIDUAL RATES Single en-suite bedroom £29.23pppn. Single standard bedroom £25.04pppn.

■ **Public Transport** - Cardiff Central Station: trains, coaches, connections to airports. Buses from city centre.

■ **Directions** - Directions will be sent with your booking information as the en-suite and standard accommodation are in different locations.

CONTACT: Cardiff University Conference Office
Southgate House, PO Box 533, Cardiff, CF14 3UX
Tel: 029 2087 4702 / 4616 Fax: 029 2087 4990
Groupaccom@cardiff.ac.uk www.cardiff.ac.uk/CSERV/conferences

RIVER HOUSE
HOSTEL

This is an award-winning family run 4 star hostel in the heart of Cardiff, voted number 1 in the Hostelworld list of best hostels. Opened in 2007 to rave reviews, the brother and sister team have made sure this will be the best hostel experience you will come across on your travels. With fabulous views of the world famous Millennium Stadium and River Taff and with the central train and bus stations just 5 mins' walk away, what's stopping you?

Facilities include well equipped kitchen, cosy TV lounge, decked garden with barbecue, free lockers and free wireless broadband. Bikes, irons, and hairdryers available for hire. Linen, duvets and breakfast are included in the price and the beds are made up for you. Hostelworld awarded best Hostel in UK since 2008.

Treat yourself to a quality stay at budget prices.

DETAILS

- **Open** - All year, 24 hours.
- **Number of beds** - 50: 2 bed private rooms, 4 bed dorms and 6 bed dorms.
- **Booking** - Book by phone or online.
- **Price per night** - From £16pp. Private (twin) rooms from £40 for two people. All prices include breakfast.
- **Public Transport** - Cardiff Central coach and train stations, with regular services to UK cities and airports 5 minutes' walk away.
- **Directions** - From Central train station turn left and cross river on Tudor Street. Once over the river Fitzhamon Embankment is first turn on right.

CONTACT: Reception
59 Fitzhamon Embankment, Riverside, Cardiff, CF11 6AN
Tel: 02920 399 810
info@riverhousebackpackers.com www.riverhousebackpackers.com

Wern Watkin Bunkhouse is located in the Brecon Beacons National Park, high up on Mynnedd Llangattock. It is also known as YHA Llangattock Mountain. There is direct access on foot to the mountainside and a flat mountain road to a National Cycle Route. The Bunkhouse is a converted stone barn with bunks for 30 people in 7 mainly en-suite bedrooms. The massive dining room and seating area opens out onto ancient woodlands. It has under-floor heating throughout, excellent drying facilities and ample hot water. The location is ideal for caving, rock climbing, canoeing, abseiling, orienteering, pony trekking and mountain biking. Outdoor pursuit training can be arranged from local qualified instructors. The bunkhouse is within easy walking distance of Llangattock cave complex (one of Europe's most elaborate cave systems) as well as climbing crags and open moorland. A short drive away are the rest of Brecon Beacons, the scenic Wye and Usk river valleys and a wealth of industrial heritage at the World Heritage site of Blaenavon. Catering can be provided for groups.

DETAILS

- **Open** - All year, all day.
- **Number of beds** - 30: 4x6, 1x4, 2x2. All rooms except one en suite.
- **Booking** - Availability shown online. 10% deposit, balance two weeks in advance.
- **Price per night** - Sole use £450 week nights, £600 weekend nights. Smaller groups by negotiation £16pp weeknights, £18.50 pp weekend.
- **Public Transport** - Trains Abergavenny (8miles). Nearest buses Crickhowell.
- **Directions** - Access can be either from Crickhowell or Brynmawr on small mountain roads. Detailed instructions will be sent with your booking.

CONTACT: Andrew Fryer
Wern Watkin, Hillside, Llangattock, Crickhowell, NP8 1LG
Tel: 01873 812307
enquiries@wernwatkin.co.uk www.wernwatkin.co.uk

RICKYARD
BUNKHOUSE

Rickyard Bunkhouse is set amidst idyllic countryside and well away from the hustle and bustle. Offa's Dyke footpath passes the entrance and it is within 25 mins of Wye Valley, Symonds Yat, and the Forest of Dean. Many outdoor pursuits can be enjoyed - canoeing, rafting, potholing, quad biking, rock climbing and paint balling to name but a few. The River Trothy borders the land; kingfishers and otters enjoy the peace and tranquillity of the Trothy valley. Buzzards circle high above, easily recognised by their distinctive call. The Bunkhouse holds 20 easily, has an excellent, very well equipped kitchen, a separate dining/relaxing area with TV, and background heating. Sleeping accommodation is split into several areas. It is totally self-contained, and is ideal for reunions, groups and families. There is a large secure area for camping where children can safely play and ample parking with hard standing. Luggage transfer, breakfasts and packed lunches can be arranged. Bedding supplied, towels £1. Come and enjoy the tranquil surroundings (loud music or wild parties are not welcome). Exclusive use available, please enquire.

DETAILS

- **Open** - All year, all day.
- **Number of beds** - 20: + camping.
- **Booking** - Deposit required, no credit cards. Notice not always required.
- **Price per night** - £16.00pp. Prices include bedding, towels £1. Tents £5pp. Can be booked for sole use.
- **Public Transport** - Trains at Abergavenny (11m). Buses at Monmouth (3m).
- **Directions** - Next to the Hendre Farm House on the same side of the road.

CONTACT: Graham Edwards
Wonastow, Monmouth, NP25 4DJ
Tel: 01600 740128
rickyardbunkhouse@googlemail.com www.rickyardbunkhouse.co.uk

CLYNGWYN
BUNKHOUSE AND B&B

Clyngwyn Bunkhouse is situated in the Brecon Beacons, in the heart of waterfall country, very near to the caves and waterfalls of Ystradfellte and close to the famous Sgwd Yr Eira waterfalls. The terrain is ideal for mountain biking, gorge walking, canyoning, caving, abseiling, climbing, quad biking, photography and painting. Clyngwyn Bunkhouse is perfect for groups of friends or family. It sleeps up to 19 with camping available to larger groups and three double B&B rooms in the farm house. There is a fully equipped kitchen, central heating, lounge with TV-DVD, dining room for 20, four acres of land for ball games and a large decked out polytunnel acting as a marquee, lockable storage and drying area. Relax in the evenings and enjoy the mountain views by a fire or BBQ. The villages of Ystradfellte and Pontneddfechan (2½ miles by mini bus taxi) have pubs with restaurants. Four star graded by VisitWales. Dog friendly.

DETAILS

■ **Open** - All year, all day.
■ **Number of beds** - 19: 1x11, 2x4.
■ **Booking** - Booking essential. Only groups can book the bunkhouse at weekends. Credit/Debit cards not accepted
■ **Price per night** - Weekdays: sole use for up to 15 people £195,up to 19 people £247, £17pp for small groups. Weekends up to 15 people £225, or up to 19 £285. Small extra charge for bedding or bring your own. B&B in Farmhouse £25pp.
■ **Public Transport** - Trains Neath or Merthyr (11 miles). Minibus can be arranged.
■ **Directions** - From A465 leave at Glenneath drive-through and take signs for Pontneddfechan. Then 2.5 miles up Ystradfellte road, turn right down small track.

CONTACT: Julie Hurst
Clyngwyn Farm, Ystradfellte Rd, Pontneddfechan, Powys, SA11 5US
Tel: 01639 722930
enquiries@bunkhouse-south-wales.co.uk www.bunkhouse-south-wales.co.uk

THE WAIN HOUSE

WALES

This old stone barn continues the tradition of 900 years when Llanthony Priory provided shelter and accommodation. Surrounded by the Black Mountains in the Brecon Beacons National Park, this spectacular setting is a superb base for walking, riding, pony trekking and other mountain activities.

Sixteen bunks are split into three separate areas for sleeping. There is a fully equipped kitchen, hot water for showers, heating throughout and a wood burning stove in the eating area. Small or large groups are welcome, but there is a minimum charge at weekends. Two pubs offer real beer and bar food.

Just 50 minutes from the M4 Severn Bridge and one hour from the M5/M50 Junction, this must be one of the easiest bunkbarns to reach from the motorways - and yet you feel you are miles from anywhere.

DETAILS

- **Open** - All year, 24 hours, no restrictions
- **Number of beds** - 16: 1 x 8 ; 1 x 4 ; 1 x 6.
- **Booking** - Booking and deposit required.
- **Price per night** - £13 per person. Minimum charge of £280 at weekends (two nights).
- **Public Transport** - Abergavenny railway station 12 miles.
- **Directions** - GR SO 288 278 Map on website: Turn west off A465 Abergavenny to Hereford road at Llanvihangel Crucorney (5 miles' north of Abergavenny). Llanthony is 6 miles along country lane - follow signs to Priory. On cycle route 42.

CONTACT: Cordelia Passmore
Court Farm, Llanthony, Abergavenny, Monmouthshire, NP7 7NN
Tel: 01873 890359
courtfarm@llanthony.co.uk www.llanthony.co.uk

L&A Outdoor Centre is a friendly family-run destination offering quality affordable accommodation and activities in the Swansea Bay area. Tailor-made for family holidays, the 6 and 8 bed two-storey self-catering cabins have upstairs bedrooms sleeping 2-3 in each room and downstairs, the toilet and shower, lounge with TV, fully equipped kitchen and dining area, all overlooking a tree-lined mountain stream.   The bunkhouses, which sleep between 10 and 40, are clean and warm with access to self-catering. L&A facilities include a 10,000 sq.ft. activity hall, a large dining hall with professional catering, The Watering Hole bar/café, meeting rooms and over 50 acres of woodland and pasture with play area, open air swimming pool, campfire, pets corner, kennels, BBQs, bike wash and are dog friendly.   For any number up to 250, L&A is the perfect base for conferences, training courses, summer camps and retreats. Activity Packages can be arranged. The area is ideal for mountain biking with Afan Aergoed and Glyncorrwg Trails just 10 mins. away and the Millennium and Liberty Stadia within 30 mins.

DETAILS

- **Open** - All day.
- **Number of beds** - Cabin: 117: 6/8 bed units. Bunkhouse: 175:10,16,24,30,40 bed.
- **Booking** - Book or enquire by phone or email.
- **Price per night** - Bunkhouses: £12pp, £15 with bedding. Cabins: 6 bed £90 to £150, 8 bed £100 to £180, depending on length of stay. Groups please enquire.
- **Public Transport** - Nearest rain station is Port Talbot Parkway (two miles).
- **Directions** - One mile from Junction 40 of the M4

CONTACT: Nigel
Goytre, West Glamorgan SA13 2YP
Tel: 01639 885 509
info@landaoutdoorcentre.co.uk www.landaoutdoorcentre.co.uk

HARDINGSDOWN
BUNKHOUSE

Hardingsdown Bunkhouse provides comfortable accommodation for families or groups in a tastefully restored stone barn on an organic farm. The Gower has national nature reserves, outstanding coastal scenery, family beaches, castles and ancient monuments. Llangennith beach is one of the best surfing beaches in the south west, Mewslade Bay and Fall Bay are popular with climbers, while walkers and bikers can use the local network of footpaths and bridleways.

The ground floor consists of a fully equipped kitchen, 2 shower/toilet rooms, a living room with 2 single sofa-beds and comfy chairs. Off the living room is a bedroom with a bunkbed sleeping 2 people. A spiral staircase leads upstairs where there are 3 bedrooms sleeping 5, 3 and 2 in bunks and single beds. A separate drying room is available for outdoor gear and a lock-up for storing bikes, surfboards, canoes etc. There is ample parking and a patio area that catches the evening sun. Shops and pubs nearby.

DETAILS

- **Open** - All year, 24 hours.
- **Number of beds** - 14: 1x5, 1x3, 3x2.
- **Booking** - Non-returnable deposit of 30%, balance 1 month before arrival.
- **Price per night** - Sole use £200pn (weekends & bank holidays), £180pn (midweek). Whole week £1100. Smaller groups sharing the bunkhouse with other users, £15 per person.
- **Public Transport** - Regular bus (No116) from Swansea; 0870 6082608.
- **Directions** - Turn left off the B4295 ½ mile after Burry Green (by bus shelter and post box). Follow lane till it changes into a rough track and turn right into Lower Hardingsdown Farm. Bunkhouse is on left of farmyard.

CONTACT: Allison or Andrew Tyrrell
Lower Hardingsdown Farm, Llangennith, Gower, Swansea, SA3 1HT
Tel: 01792 386222
bunkhousegower@tiscali.co.uk www.bunkhousegower.co.uk

RHOSSILI
BUNKHOUSE

Situated at the end of the Gower Peninsula, in the UK's first Area of Outstanding Natural Beauty, Rhossili Bunkhouse is within easy walking distance of three glorious beaches, including Rhossili Bay (voted Britain's Best Beach 2010), and ideally located for a range of outdoor activities including walking, surfing, cycling, climbing and flying. The Gower Way starts nearby. Our 4 star Visit Wales bunkhouse is great for groups of friends or families. It is run by the trustees of Rhossili Village Hall for the benefit of the community. Duvets and pillows are provided. Please bring single bed linen or sleeping bags. Central heating throughout. Self-catering in fully equipped kitchen. Lounge/dining room opens onto patio and garden. Radio/CD player, games and books in lounge. Free WiFi in hall/foyer. Secure store for bikes and boards, with drying room for coats and boots. Outside area for rinsing and drying wet suits. Card locks on all doors. Hall and meeting room for hire. Car park. No pets. No smoking.

DETAILS

- **Open** - All year except January. Check-in 4-9pm; check-out by 10:30am.
- **Number of beds** - 18: 1x4, 2x3, 4x2. 4 sofa-beds in lounge (Sole use).
- **Booking** - Advance booking essential. Online form and virtual tour. Deposit 30%. Minimum booking: 2 people for 2 nights.
- **Price per night** - Shared (small groups) £15-£18 pp. Full (group of 18) £300. Sole (group of 22) £350.
- **Public Transport** - Regular buses (118, X18) from Swansea stop outside. Tel: 0871 2002233. www.swansea.gov.uk/index.cfm?articleid=6624.
- **Directions** - On the B4247 in Middleton, Rhossili. GR SS 421 878.

CONTACT: Josephine Higgins
Rhossili Bunkhouse, Rhossili, Swansea, SA3 1PL
Tel: 01792 391509
bookings@rhossili.org www.rhossilibunkhouse.com

PANTYRATHRO
INTERNATIONAL HOSTEL

Llansteffan is a beautiful, quaint village set at the tip of the Towi River and Carmarthen Bay. The sandy beaches nestled below the castle offer swimming and relaxation. The virtually traffic free country lanes make this area ideal for cycling. For the walker Carmarthenshire offers coastal walks and country walks. Carmarthen, Wales' oldest city and ancestral home to Merlin of King Arthur's legends, offers most social and cultural activities. The Pantyrathro International Hostel provides dorm and double room accommodation and also three new en suite units of 6, 8 and 12 beds. Facilities include self-catering kitchen, dining area, TV lounge and showers. Our two Mexican bars offer pool, darts, TV, weekly drink specials and food (eat-in or take-out). Horse riding, cycle hire and excursions for trekking, canoeing and surfing offered. Take a day trip or relax on the beaches or have a drink in our bars - something for everyone.

DETAILS

■ **Open** - Febuary to January, 24 hours.
■ **Number of beds** - 51: 1 x 12, 1 x 8, 2 x 6, 4 x 4, 1 x 3.
■ **Booking** - Booking recommended. 50% depost required in advance for groups.
■ **Price per night** - £14pp dorm, £15pp ensuite. Group discounts.
■ **Public Transport** - Carmarthen has both coach and train stations serving South Wales, SW England and London. Local bus runs six times a day to Llansteffan. Ask driver to let you off at Pantyrathro.
■ **Directions** - Pantyrathro is six miles from Carmarthen on the B4312, midway between Llangain and Llansteffan. Two miles from Llangain you will see the hostel signposted, turn right and follow signs to top of lane.

CONTACT: Ken Knuckles
Pantyrathro Country Inn, Llansteffan, Carmarthen, SA33 5AJ
Tel: 01267 241014, Fax: 01267 241014
kenknuckles@hotmail.com www.backpackershostelwales.co.uk

Gilfach Wen Barn has been converted to provide competitively priced self-catering accommodation for individuals, extended families or groups on a working farm adjacent to Brechfa Forest. Graded as a 4 star bunkhouse it sleeps up to 32 in 7 bedrooms and has a large kitchen/dining room, lounge and drying room. There is a downstairs bedroom and shower room for disabled. The facilities are walker, cyclist and equestrian friendly for guests enjoying being adjacent to Brechfa Forest, the Cothi Valley and Llanllwni Mountain. Gilfach Wen Barn is a perfect venue for a holiday or weekend away – if you do not want to drive you need never leave the valley. The barn is Wi-Fi enabled, fully equipped and the village is within walking distance (1 mile). This is a stunningly beautiful area close to Brecon Beacons National Park, in the foothills of the Cambrian Mountains but only a short drive to Cefn Sidan Sands - an award winning 7 mile long beach. 360 degree virtual tour available on their website.

DETAILS

- **Open** - Open all year, all day.
- **Number of beds** - 32: 3x6, 1x5, 1x4,1x3,1x2 in 10 double beds and 12 singles.
- **Booking** - Advance booking required.
- **Price per night** - £16 per person. Sole use £350 per night. Minimum weekend booking 2 nights sole use. Last minute and midweek special offers on website
- **Public Transport** - Trains and coaches at Carmarthen. Daily bus from Carmarthen to Brechfa passes gate. Bus is a request stop service. You can ask to be dropped of and can catch the bus at the bottom of the drive.
- **Directions** - GR SN 513 292 On the B4310 between Horeb and Brechfa.

CONTACT: Jillie
Gilfach Wen, Brechfa, Carmarthenshire, SA32 7QL
Tel: 07970 629726
GilfachWenBarn@aol.com www.brechfa-bunkhouse.com

LAWRENNY
MILLENNIUM HOSTEL

Set in a picturesque village, surrounded by organic farmland and ancient oak woodland, this relaxed and friendly hostel is a great base for launching into everything Pembrokeshire has to offer. The hostel is warm, clean and comfortable, with modern facilities. There are 24 beds in 5 rooms, all of which can be reserved as family rooms. There's a large open plan kitchen and living room, as well as a drying room, large car park and cycle shelter. Once a Victorian village school, the hostel is superbly placed for walking, boating, bird watching and kayaking, and is close to many top family attractions and the beautiful beaches of south Pembrokeshire. Groups are welcome and the whole hostel can be hired for holidays, training courses and events. Internet Wi-Fi is available. The adjoining village hall is available to rent. The hostel is run as a charitable trust and is a Friends of Nature hostel. The village has a community shop, pub and an award-winning tearoom.

DETAILS

- **Open** - All year, arrange check in with warden/all day access.
- **Number of beds** - 24: 2 x 4, 1 x 8, 2 x double + bunks.
- **Booking** - Online, email or telephone.
- **Price per night** - Adults £15, children (4-17) £10. Double rooms £35 (couple), £45 (with children). Sole use of hostel £250 per night.
- **Public Transport** -   Not easy.   Coach/train to Kilgetty (8m). Get the 381 bus (Tenby to Pembroke Dock) and from Cresswell Quay it's a 2.5 mile walk to the hostel.
- **Directions** - From A40 St Clears to Haverfordwest road take A4075 signed Tenby and Oakwood. Just past the turning to Oakwood, turn right and follow signs to Lawrenny. Bear right in front of church and follow the car park signs.

CONTACT: Laura Lort-Phillips
Lawrenny Millennium Hostel, Lawrenny, Pembrokeshire, SA68 0PW
Tel: 01646 651270
hostel@lawrennyvillage.co.uk www.lawrennyvillage.co.uk/hostel

Upper Neeston Lodges are environmentally sensitive barn conversions on a small family run sheep farm, close to the Milford Haven Waterway and in the Pembrokeshire Coast National Park. The Lodges are ideal for divers, climbers, walkers or for family and friends having a get-together. There are three independent units, all with access to garden/patio, laundry/drying room, wash-down area, secure storage and ample parking. THE COWSHED BUNKHOUSE is single storey with disabled access. It has a large sitting room and kitchen/dining area, and two bunkrooms sleeping 6 and 4, each with a large en-suite shower room. THE BARN BUNKHOUSE has two storeys with an upstairs sitting room and kitchen/dining area. The bunkrooms are downstairs and sleep 6 and 2, each with en-suite shower room. THE GRANARY BUNKHOUSE has two storeys with an upstairs sitting room/kitchen. The bedroom is downstairs and sleeps up to 3 people in 1 room with en-suite shower room. Each unit has a TV, CD player and wood burning stove. Graded 5 Star bunkhouse by Visit Wales.

DETAILS

■ **Open** - All year, check in from 4pm. Check out before 10.30am.
■ **Number of beds** - Cowshed 10: 1x6,1x4   Barn 8: 1x6,1x2, Granary 3: 3x1.
■ **Booking** - Provisional booking taken by phone/email and confirmed by deposit.
■ **Price per night** - £16pp (includes linen). Min of 6 people guarantees exclusive use of Barn, 8 for Cowshed. Min of 2 nights' stay weekends (3 nights on bank hols).
■ **Public Transport** - Puffin coastal shuttle passes farm www.traveline-cymru.org.uk
■ **Directions** - Follow A4076 through Milford Haven to roundabout by Docks. Take first exit (signed Hakin). Follow for 2 miles, look for first farm on left (next to layby).

CONTACT: Sean or Mandy Tilling
Upper Neeston Farm, Dale Road, Herbrandston, Milford Haven, SA73 3RY
Tel: 01646 690750
mail@upperneeston.co.uk www.upperneeston.co.uk

PEMBROKESHIRE
ADVENTURE CENTRE

Set in the heart of Britain's only Coastal National Park, the Pembrokeshire Adventure Centre is the perfect place to begin exploring this captivating edge of Wales. The modern and comfortable Bunkhouses overlook the stunning Cleddau Estuary and can sleep up to 80. Accommodation is in 4 blocks each with self-catering facilities, lounge area and 2/3 bathrooms. Guests have use of all on-site facilities including sports pitch, conference rooms and drying room.
Bedding is included and we can provide catering for larger groups. At the Adventure Centre you can try an array of land and water based activities from coasteering to rock climbing! We welcome all ages from 8-80 on a tailor made adventure – families, experts and beginners, no-one is left out! We also provide programmes for schools, youth groups, team building and adventure training.
Pembrokeshire's famous beaches like Barafundle Bay are under 30 minutes away. Alternatively try some local attractions like Oakwood or the Celtic Village at Castell Henllys! Feel free to ask us any questions, we are happy to help! The centre is situated in Pembroke Dock with excellent rail, road and ferry links.

DETAILS

- **Open** - All year, all day.
- **Number of beds** - 80: 2 houses of 6 x 4 beds; 2 blocks of 8 x 2 beds.
- **Booking** - Booking is essential.
- **Price per night** - From £15.60pp. Group discounts available.
- **Public Transport** - Pembroke Dock train station 1 mile, Irish ferry port 2 miles.
- **Directions** - From Pembroke head north on A4139, then onto A477. On A477 take 3rd right, just before the bridge. Turn right at roundabout, the Centre is after 1/2 mile.

CONTACT:
Cleddau Reach, Pembroke Dock, Pembrokeshire, SA72 6UJ
Tel: 01646 622013
adventure@princes-trust.org.uk www.princes-trust.org.uk/adventure

Skomer Island, just off the Pembrokeshire Coast, is surrounded by a Marine Nature Reserve and full of stunningly beautiful bird life and vistas. In April the bluebells start to flower and migrant birds begin to arrive on the island. From April until the end of September the haunting sound of Manx Shearwaters can be heard as they return to their burrows after dark. Seal pupping begins on the beaches and caves in August and continues through to the end of October. There are guided shearwater walks in August and September and the coastal path around the island makes a stunning half day walk. Staying overnight on Skomer you experience the tranquillity and spectacular sunsets after the day visitors go home. The bunkhouse is graded 3 star and has been developed sustainably. It provides simple, comfortable accommodation with electricity and hot water generated from the sun. There are private bedrooms and a shared kitchen, dining room and library. Pillows and duvets are available, bring sheets. Accommodation for 10 also available on Skokholm island, just south of Skomer.

DETAILS

- **Open** - 1 April until 31 October.
- **Number of beds** - 16: 1x5, 1x4 (with double), 1x3, 2x2.
- **Booking** - Availability online. View terms and conditions on our website.
- **Price per night** - Adults Low (April/Aug/Sept/Oct) £30, High (May/June/July) £50. Under 13s half price. Single occupancy Low £45, High £90.
- **Public Transport** - The boats runs 6 days (not Mon) from Martin's Haven (£10, child £7). Puffin bus operates from St Davids to boat www.pembrokeshire.gov.uk.
- **Directions** - Half mile walk from the boat. Luggage transported by tractor.

CONTACT: Booking office or Chris (after hours) on Mobile.
Welsh Wildlife Centre, Cilgerran, Cardigan, Pembrokeshire,SA43 3TB
Tel: 01239 621600, Mob:(outside office hours): 07971 114302
islands@welshwildlife.org www.welshwildlife.org

PENQUOIT
CENTRE

The Penquoit Centre is a welcoming courtyard of historic longhouses converted into hostel accommodation for groups of 10 to 25 people. The land on which the centre stands includes a range of fields, ancient woodland, direct access to the Cresswell river and the Pembrokeshire National Park. The land is rich in birdlife, river, sea and wildfowl and within easy reach of over 20 beautiful beaches, the Preselli Hills, castles, Tenby and Caldy, riding and canoeing.

The hostel consists of 2 dormitories (one on the ground floor), communal showers and toilets. There are 2 private rooms, a large dining room with wood burning stove and a long room ideal for group activities, workshops and creativity. The kitchen is fully equipped and the centre is centrally heated. The Centre is ideal for family and friend get-togethers, art, yoga, drama, healing and dancing.

DETAILS

- **Open** - All year, all day.
- **Number of beds** - 25+: 1 x 10, 1 x 15, plus 2 private rooms.
- **Booking** - Booking essential, deposit 25%.
- **Price per night** - £15 per person.
- **Public Transport** - Trains and National Express stop at Kilgetty or Tenby (7miles). Irish Ferry and Pembroke (6 miles). We can collect if necessary.
- **Directions** - M4 to Carmarthen, A40 towards Haverfordwest. At Canaston Bridge (just after Robeston Wathem) take A4075 for Pembroke. At Cresselly (6 miles) turn right, then right again at T junction. After small bridge turn left uphill towards Lawrenny, the Centre is on right (½ mile).

CONTACT: Joan Carlisle
Lawrenny, Kilgetty, Pembrokeshire, SA68 OPL
Tel: 01646 651666
joan@penquoit.plus.com

CAERHAFOD
LODGE

Ideally situated between the famous cathedral city of St Davids and the Irish ferry port of Fishguard, the Lodge overlooks the spectacular Pembrokeshire coastline. Within walking distance of the well known Sloop Inn at Porthgain and the internationally renowned Coastal Path. An ideal stopover for cyclists with The Celtic Trail cycle route passing the bottom of the drive. The Lodge is a great base for all outdoor activities: boat trips around Ramsey Island, coasteering, kayaking, surfing or just lazing on the beach. The lodge sleeps 23 in 5 separate rooms, all en-suite with great showers. There is a modern fully equipped kitchen/diner with sea view patio & picnic tables with a panoramic view from the Preseli mountains to Strumble Head and the North Bishop with glorious sunsets over the Irish sea. There is also a sitting room for cosy evenings, on-site washing/drying room and secure storage area. Dogs welcome by prior arrangement. Smoking outdoors. Visit Wales graded 4 star.

DETAILS

■ **Open** - All year, check in from 4pm, check out 10.30 am. All day access.
■ **Number of beds** - 23: 3x4 : 1x5 : 1x6.
■ **Booking** - Advised in high season. 50% deposit.
■ **Price per night** - Adult £17, Under 16 £13.50. Group rates available.
■ **Public Transport** - Trains at Fishguard (9m) and Haverfordwest (17m). Fishguard/Rosslare ferry. National Express: Haverfordwest. 413 Bus: St Davids-Fishguard 50yds from Lodge. Seasonal coastal shuttle service for walkers.
■ **Directions** - GR Landranger 157, SM 827 317. A40 from Haverfordwest, left at Letterston (B4331) to Mathry. Left onto A487 to St Davids, right in Croesgoch for Llanrhian, at crossroads right for Trefin. Lodge is on right after ½ mile.

CONTACT: Carolyn Rees
Llanrhian, St Davids, Haverfordwest, Pembrokeshire, SA62 5BD
Tel: 01348 837859
Caerhafod@aol.com www.caerhafod.co.uk

OLD SCHOOL HOSTEL
FORMERLY YHA TREFIN

Escape to this wonderful, wild and rugged corner of the Pembrokeshire Coast National Park. Stay in the centre of Trefin, an attractive village with a pub and cafe, just a quarter of a mile from the world famous coast path. The cathedral city of St Davids and the popular family and surfers' beach at Whitesands Bay are only 20 minutes away by car. Other stunning wild beaches and small harbour villages are close by and can be visited as part of a day's circular walk.
This friendly characterful 4 star hostel offers comfortable accommodation at prices that are hard to beat. There are singles, twins, doubles, family rooms and dorms and most have en-suite solar showers. Organic breakfast and packed lunches are available and there is free internet and Wi-Fi.
Affiliated to 'Friends of Nature', this hostel is powered by renewable energy, offers 'eco' discounts and plants a tree for every booking.
Help create a forest for the future – come and stay!

DETAILS

- **Open** - February-December, Check in from 5pm. All day access once checked in.
- **Number of beds** - 23 beds in 7 rooms: Singles,doubles,twins, private/family and small dorms.
- **Booking** - Advance booking recommended.
- **Price per night** - Dorms from £13, private rooms from £15 per person, singles from £18, family rooms from £38. Exclusive use of hostel from £225 per night.
- **Public Transport** - Train to Fishguard then bus 413 to Trefin or train/National Express coach to Haverfordwest then 2 x buses. Times on Traveline 0870 6082608.
- **Directions** - From the A40 turn left onto the B4331 at Letterston then left onto the A487. After 2.5 miles turn right just after the Square and Compass pub for Trefin.

CONTACT: Sue or Chris
Ffordd-yr-Afon, Trefin, Haverfordwest, Pembrokeshire, SA62 5AU
Tel: 01348 831800
oldschoolhostel@btconnect.com www.theoldschoolhostel.co.uk

PIGGERY POKE
4 STAR HOSTEL

Piggery Poke is on the public footpath that loops from the Ceredigion Coast Path between Mwnt and Aberporth. Local cycle routes link the road at the top of the entrance drive to long distance cycle routes Lôn Teifi (within 4 miles) and the Celtic Trail (see Sustrans Route 82). Piggery Poke is a new conversion of an old building and has 3 dormitories sleeping up to 8, 5 and 3, each with en-suite facilities. The dining room seats 16 at one sitting. There is a drying room on the ground floor and wireless broadband is available by arrangement. There is a large garden area with sea views and barbeque, and there is a secure cycle store. A courtesy collection and delivery service is usually available from points within 15 miles along the coast for walkers or cyclists and/or their cycles/luggage. Ample parking is provided. Four star graded by Visit Wales.

DETAILS

- **Open** - All year round. 4pm to 10pm and 7.30am to 10am.
- **Number of beds** - 16: 1 x 8, 1 x 5, 1 x 3.
- **Booking** - Book by phone or via website.
- **Price per night** - £18 per person.
- **Public Transport** - Trains at Aberystwyth and Carmarthen. From Aberystwyth station take the X50bus to Blaenannerch or 550 bus to Felinwynt, via Aberporth. From Carmarthen station take the 460 or 461 bus to Cardigan (Finch Square) then change to the 550 bus to Aberystwyth via Aberporth, alighting at Felinwynt.
- **Directions** - Piggery Poke hostel is part of Cardigan Coastal Cottages, which is at Ffrwdwenith Isaf, Felinwynt, half-way between Mwnt and Aberporth, 4 miles along the coast north of Cardigan. Lat: 52.13108, Long: -4.58939

CONTACT: Paul or Angela
Ffrwdwenith Isaf, Felinwynt, Cardigan, SA43 1RW
Tel: 01239 811777
hostel@piggerypoke.co.uk www.piggerypoke.co.uk

Hamilton Backpackers Lodge is an excellent overnight stop on the stunning Pembrokeshire Coast Path. It is also an ideal overnight stay five minutes from the ferries to Rosslare in Ireland. Pembrokeshire has a wealth of natural beauty and local history and many beautiful secluded beaches.

The Backpackers Lodge is a very comfortable and friendly hostel with small dormitories and a double room, all centrally heated. There is a dining room and TV lounge. The garden at the back of the hostel has a hammock, barbecue and picnic tables. Free tea, coffee and light breakfast are provided. There is parking close by and the hostel is in the centre of town near to a number of pubs serving good meals. There is no curfew. Smoking is permitted only in the garden patio. To find out more see website.

DETAILS

- **Open** - All year, 24 hours.
- **Number of beds** - 9: 1 x 4, 1 x 3 and 1 x 2.
- **Booking** - Booking advised to confirm beds. 50% deposit required from groups.
- **Price per night** - £17pp in dorms, £23pp in double ensuite.
- **Public Transport** - Fishguard ferry port has a train station and ferries to Rosslare in Ireland. The port is 1 mile from the hostel (approx taxi fare £7). National Express coaches call at Haverfordwest (15 miles). For local buses in Pembrokeshire phone Richard Bros 01239 613756.
- **Directions** - From Haverfordwest (A40) to Fishguard Square, across first right by tourist office, 50 yds on left. From Cardigan A487 (North Wales Road) up hill and first left. From harbour 1 mile to Fishguard Square, left, first right, 50 yards on left.

CONTACT: Steve Roberts
23 Hamilton Street, Fishguard, Pembrokeshire, SA65 9HL
Tel: 01348 874797 / 07813 687570
hamiltonbackpackers@yahoo.co.uk www.hamiltonbackpackers.co.uk

TY'N CORNEL
TYNCORNEL HOSTEL

Ty'n Cornel Hostel is an isolated old farmhouse in the hills, with a cosy open fire. Favoured by walkers, cyclists, bird watchers and lovers of solitude it is in the beautiful Doethie valley on the Cambrian Way long distance footpath. There are comfortable wooden bunk beds and good self-catering facilities.

You can enjoy the wild open moorlands of the Elenydd uplands. Other attractions include the Cors Caron National Nature Reserve, red kite feeding station, the Welsh Gold Centre at Tregaron, Teifi Pools, Llyn Brianne reservoir, Dolaucothi Roman gold mines, Strata Florida Abbey and Llanerchaeron country house (National Trust).

DETAILS

- **Open** - All year, 24 hours. Reception 5pm -11pm, 7am -10am.
- **Number of beds** - 16: 2x8.
- **Booking** - Booking advisable; essential mid November to mid March. Book online at www.yha.org.uk. or ring YHA booking office on 01629 592700. For bookings within a week of your stay, ring 01980 629259.
- **Price per night** - £12 per adult, £9 (under 18s). Block bookings negotiable.
- **Public Transport** - Trains: Aberystwyth 28m, Llanwrtyd Wells 16m, Cynghordy 12m. Coach: x40 (Cardiff – Aberystwyth) Lampeter 15m. Bus: 585 (Lampeter – Tregaron) Llanddewi-Brefi 7m.
- **Directions** - Road from Llanddewi-Brefi, near Tregaron: follow hostel signs SE 7m (last mile track). Bridle path S up Doethie valley on the Cambrian Way (Llandovery 15 m) or byway 2m NW from Soar y Mynydd chapel.

CONTACT: YHA booking office or www.yha.org.uk
Llanddewi Brefi, Tregaron, Ceredigion, SY25 6PH
Tel: YHA booking 01629 592700 or (within two days of stay) 01980 629259
Fax: 0870 7706081
tyncornel@yha.org.uk www.elenydd-hostels.co.uk

DOLGOCH
HOSTEL

Come and experience the peace of this unique location in the remote Tywi Valley. A stay in this 17th century farmhouse will take you into an era before electricity, with gas for lighting and a log burner for heat. Dolgoch is a traditional simple hostel now owned by the Elenydd Wilderness Trust. It has hot showers, a self-catering kitchen/dining room and 21 beds in 3 dormitories. It has been recently refurbished to include new toilets and showers and less able accommodation. Upgraded track. The Lôn Las Cymru (Welsh National Cycle Route) and the Cambrian Way pass nearby and there are many other mountain tracks to explore on foot, by mountain bike or pony. The hostel is ideal for bird-watchers and lovers of solitude and is close to an old drovers' track which leads over the scenic Cambrian mountains for five miles to the equally remote and simple Ty'n Cornel Hostel. Why not stay a night in each hostel and follow in the treads of the old drovers?

DETAILS

- **Open** - All year, 24 hours, Reception 5pm -11pm, 7am -10am.
- **Number of beds** - 21: (in 3 rooms).
- **Booking** - Booking information is available on the YHA website: yha.org.uk
- **Price per night** - £12 per adult, £9 (under 18). Campers £6.
- **Public Transport** - Train to Aberystwyth, Carmarthen or Llanwrtyd Wells. Bus X40: Cardiff/Carmarthen to Lampeter/Aberystwyth, Bus 585: Lampeter/Aberystwyth to Tregaron. Postbus 287: Llandovery to Rhandirmwyn.
- **Directions** - SN 806 562. You can walk to Dolgoch over the hills from Tregaron or take the winding Abergwesyn mountain road. The hostel is ¾ mile south of the bridge, along an unsurfaced track.

CONTACT: YHA Booking Office or Chris Mason
Dolgoch, Tregaron, Ceredigion, SY25 6NR
Tel: 0870 770 8868. For bookings within 5 days call 01782 253274
dolgoch@yha.org.uk www.elenydd-hostels.co.uk

THE LONG BARN

WALES

The Long Barn is a traditional stone barn providing comfortable and warm bunkhouse accommodation. It is situated on a working organic farm in beautiful countryside with views over the Teifi Valley. The stunning Ceredigion Coast and the Cambrian Mountains are both an easy drive away and the busy small town of Llandysul (1.5 miles) has all essential supplies.

The barn's location is ideal for exploring, studying or simply admiring the Welsh countryside. Activities enjoyed by guests in the surrounding area include fishing, swimming, climbing, abseiling, canoeing, farm walks and cycling.

The barn is open all year, having adequate heating with a lovely warm Rayburn, log fire, roof insulation and double glazing throughout.

DETAILS

- **Open** - All year, all day.
- **Number of beds** - 40.
- **Booking** - Essential, deposit required.
- **Price per night** - £10pp (adult). Discount of 10% for groups of 20 or more.
- **Public Transport** - Carmarthen (16 miles) has a train station and National Express service. Llandysul (1.5 miles away) has a local bus service, phone 0871 2002233 for details.
- **Directions** - OS map 146, GR 437 417. In Llandysul, at the top of the main street, take right hand lane. Turn sharp right down hill. After 100 yds turn sharp left. Another ½ mile turn first right. Continue for 1 mile and Long Barn is on your right.

CONTACT: Tom or Eva
Penrhiw, Capel Dewi, Llandysul, Ceredigion, SA44 4PG
Tel: 01559 363200 Fax: 01559 363200
cowcher@thelongbarn.co.uk www.thelongbarn.co.uk

Based on a small working farm in the hills near the West Wales coast, with Cardigan bay, one of only 2 places you can see Bottle nose Dolphins, and the closest beach about 7 miles away. Brechfa Forest, one of the seven top Welsh mountain bike areas, is nearby, as is one of the best rivers in the UK, the Teifi. Accommodation on the farm includes a basic cabin sleeping 15-20, and tents, some pre-erected of very nice standard with amazing views. What comforts there are run from solar, wind and wood. The cabin has comfortable camp beds, a fully equipped kitchen, log burning stove and an undercover outside area. As 'Adventure Beyond' we run various packages for families, stag and hen groups, schools, etc for team building or just a laugh. Activities include hill walking, canoeing, kayaking, raft building, climbing, fishing, farm fun, assault course, clay shooting, orienteering, coasteering, white water rafting and surfing.

DETAILS

- **Open** - All year, all day.
- **Number of beds** - 10: 2x8, 1x2 (family rooms on request).
- **Booking** - Booking is essential, deposit required if booking more then 1 week.
- **Price per night** - £10pp (bring your own bedding).
- **Public Transport** - Train and bus stations at Carmarthen. Bus stop at Croeslan.
- **Directions** - From Carmarthen follow the A485. At Windy Corner Garage take left turn A4459 to Pencader. After Pencader take the next left (at top of hill) to Llandysul. Follow the road over the river on the A486 to the village of Croeslan. Take the left turn to Maesllyn, a very small road. Follow the road down a large hill and up the other side. At the village of Coed-y-Bryn there will be a dead end road in front of you. Go down to the yard and you have arrived!

CONTACT: Jethro, Glenis or Stuart
Nant Y Pobty Farm, Coed Y Bryn, Llandysul, Ceradigion, SA44 5LQ
Tel: 01239 858852 Mob: 07787 123761
fun@AdventureBeyond.co.uk www.adventurebeyond.co.uk

STONECROFT
LODGE

Stonecroft Lodge self-catering guest house is situated in Llanwrtyd Wells, 'the Smallest Town in Britain'. Surrounded by the green fields, mountains and glorious countryside of mid Wales, Llanwrtyd is in renowned Red Kite country and is a great centre for mountain biking, walking, pony trekking, etc. The town hosts many annual events such as the Man v Horse Marathon, World Bog Snorkelling Championships and the mid-Wales Beer Festival.

The hostel offers a warm welcome and a comfortable stay. It is Wales Tourist Board Star Graded and has private and shared rooms with fully made-up beds. There is a fully equipped kitchen, a lounge with TV and video, free laundry and drying facilities, central heating, a large riverside garden and ample parking. The hostel adjoins our Good Beer Guide pub, Stonecroft Inn (where great food is available), and is truly your 'home away from home', offering the best of everything for your stay.

DETAILS

- **Open** - All year, all day - phone on arrival.
- **Number of beds** - 27: 1 x 1 : 3 x 4 : 1 x 6 : 4 x (dbl + 1 sgl).
- **Booking** - Welcome, 50% deposit.
- **Price per night** - £16. Discounts for 3+ nights. Phone for exclusive-use rates.
- **Public Transport** - Llanwrtyd Wells station on the Heart of Wales line is a few minutes walk from the hostel.
- **Directions** - GR 878 468. From Llanwrtyd town centre (A483) take Dolecoed Road towards Abergwesyn. Hostel is 100 yds on left. Check in at Stonecroft Inn.

CONTACT: Jane Brown
Dolecoed Road, Llanwrtyd Wells, Powys, LD5 4RA
Tel: 01591 610327 Fax: 01591 610304
party@stonecroft.co.uk www.stonecroft.co.uk

WOODLANDS
BUNKHOUSE

Woodlands Bunkhouse, renovated in 2010, is a converted stable in the grounds of Woodlands Centre, a late Regency building, set in 10 acres of grounds. Overlooking the River Wye and with wonderful views of the Black Mountains, Woodlands is within easy reach of the spectacular limestone area to the south. Nearby is the historic town of Hay on Wye, famous for its vast array of bookshops. With its modern facilities, the Bunkhouse provides comfortable accommodation for families and a variety of groups. With recent renovations increasing the capacity to 22, the ground floor has a new, well-equipped kitchen and dining room. There are 3 bedrooms on the ground floor, one with en-suite facilities and six first floor bedrooms and shared bathroom facilities on both floors. Camping is also available in the grounds. The bunkhouse can arrange courses in outdoor activities which are individually designed to suit groups of all ages and abilities run by their fully qualified instructors.

DETAILS

- **Open** - All year. 24 hours.
- **Number of beds** - 22 in rooms of 1 to 6 plus camping in the grounds.
- **Booking** - Booking Essential. Phone or email.
- **Price per night** - £16 pppn + VAT. Reduction for children and large group bookings.
- **Public Transport** - Trains to Hereford. A local bus then runs from Hereford to Glasbury on Wye, service 39.
- **Directions** - On the B4350 just through the village of Glasbury accessed via the A438 Brecon road.

CONTACT: Annie Clipson
Glasbury on Wye, Powys, HR3 5LP
Tel: 01497 847272
aclipson.woodlands@ocnmail.net www.woodlandsoec.org.uk

TRERICKET MILL
WALES RIVER CABIN & BUNKROOM

River Cabin (2 nights' minimum stay) is a traditional stone building in an old cider orchard overlooking the Sgithwen Brook. It sleeps up to 4 in a cosy bunkroom with a small kitchen/lounge, sun room and patio with plenty of outside space, picnic table, fire pit and BBQ. The price includes heating, hot water and shower, and use of the bike store. The small en-suite bunkroom (no minimum stay) overlooks the garden on the back of the Mill and is an ideal option for singles or 2 friends. Includes use of common room with hot drinks making facility. It can be booked on a bed only or bed and breakfast basis. There is also a small campsite. Located on the Wye Valley Walk and National Cycle Route 8. An ideal exploration base for walkers and cyclists and anyone wishing to relax and explore this beautiful part of Mid Wales. Canoeing, pony trekking and riding, gliding, cycle routes and bike hire, rope and climbing centre are all available locally.

DETAILS

- **Open** - All year, 24 hour access.
- **Number of beds** - 6 - 1 x 4, 1 x 2 en-suite, plus 6 veggie B&B beds and camping.
- **Booking** - River Cabin (sleeps 4) - minimum booking 2 people for 2 nights Bunkroom (sleeps 2) - singles welcome - no minimum stay.
- **Price per night** - From £16 per person
- **Public Transport** - Train stations at Builth Wells (10 miles), Hereford (30 miles), Merthyr Tydfil (30 miles). Daily bus service - ask to be dropped at Trericket Mill. For travel information: www.traveline-cymru.info
- **Directions** - GR SO 112 414. Set back from the A470 Brecon to Builth Wells road between the villages of Llyswen and Erwood.

CONTACT: Alistair / Nicky Legge
Erwood, Builth Wells, Powys, LD2 3TQ
Tel: 01982 560312
mail@trericket.co.uk www.trericket.co.uk

BEILI NEUADD
BUNKHOUSE

Beili Neuadd Bunkhouse is a converted 18th century stone barn beautifully positioned in quiet, secluded countryside with delightful views, its own paddocks, stream, pools and woodland. The centrally heated barn sleeps 16 in 3 en-suite bunkrooms and includes a fully equipped kitchen/dining room, drying room and facilities for wheelchair users. The bunks have a standard mattress, bed linen is included, towels can be hired. Accommodation for 4 is available in the adjacent Chalet, B&B with double rooms in the main house and there is space to camp in the paddock behind. There are picnic tables and BBQ in the paddock and ample parking in the yard. The barn is 2.5 miles from the small market town of Rhayader - the gateway to the Elan Valley reservoirs, 'the Lakeland of Wales'. A wide range of activities are possible including cycling, mountain biking, fishing, pony trekking, canoeing, bird watching and walking.

DETAILS

- **Open** - All year, all day access.
- **Number of beds** - 16: 2x6,1x4, Chalet: 1 double, 2 singles. B&B 3 double rooms
- **Booking** - Booking preferred (with deposit).
- **Price per night** - Bunkhouse: £17 per person, 4 bed room £65, 6 bed room £95, sole occupancy £245. Chalet £20pp or £80 full occupancy (4/5 people). B&B £35pp.
- **Public Transport** - Nearest trains at Llandrindod Wells -12 miles. Some buses from Rhayader. Taxi from Rhayader about £4. Assistance with transport available.
- **Directions** - OS Explorer 200/OS147 GR 994698. Take the A44 east bound from Rhayader town centre (clock). After 0.4 miles turn left on unclassified road signposted Abbey Cwm-hir with Beili Neuadd sign. Take 1st left after 1.5 miles. Beili Neuadd is 2nd farm on right after 0.4 miles.

CONTACT: David and Alison Parker
Beili Neuadd, Rhayader, Powys, LD6 5NS
Tel: 01597 810211
rhayaderbreaks@yahoo.co.uk www.midwalesfarmstay.co.uk

MID WALES
BUNKHOUSE

Mid Wales Bunkhouse at Woodhouse Farm provides affordable accommodation for groups of up to 20 or individuals. Set in the most wonderful countryside, midway between Rhayader and Llanidloes it is convenient for the Elan Valley, Wye Valley, Trans Cambrian Trail, Glyndwrs Way and Lon Las Cymru Cycle Routes 8 and 81. The area is ideal for walking, mountain biking, cycling, horse riding, bird watching, fishing and trekking. Grazing for horses available by arrangement. There is a kitchen for self-catering or we can prepare meals if arranged in advance. There is a garden area and where the River Marteg passes through the farm a private nature reserve is being established. Otters and many bird species have been spotted here. Camping and tipi available.

DETAILS

- **Open** - All year, 24 hours. Arrivals after 3pm (advise if after 7pm), depart by 11am.
- **Number of beds** - 20.
- **Booking** - Booking online, by email or phone with deposit, and full payment 8 weeks before arrival. If arriving at short notice please phone to check availability.
- **Price per night** - £14pp, £70 for private 6-bed room. Sole use of dormitory area (sleeps 14) £170 per night, sole use of entire bunkhouse (20 people) £220 per night.
- **Public Transport** - Trains at Llandrindod Wells/Newtown. Daily NE coach to Llanidloes. Buses from Llandrindod to Rhayader and limited service to St. Harmon and Pant Y Dwr. We can usually collect from Llandrindod, Llanidloes or Newtown.
- **Directions** - From the clock tower in Rhayader take A44/A470 towards Llangurig for about 100 metres then B4518 towards St Harmon. Follow for about 5 miles. At the Mid Wales Inn turn right, signed Bwylch-Y-Sarnau. After a mile turn right, just before a garage. Bunkhouse on right in half a mile. SatNav use is not advised. GR SN998750.

CONTACT: John or Steph
Woodhouse Farm, St Harmon, Rhayader, LD6 5LY
Tel: 01597 870081
john-steph@woodhouse-farm.org.uk www.bunkhousemidwales.co.uk

PLAS DOLAU
COUNTRY HOUSE HOSTEL

Plas Dolau is set in 25 acres of quiet countryside just 3 miles from the popular coastal town of Aberystwyth. Ideal for exploring West Wales, walking, cycling, riding, fishing and golf, etc. The holiday centre includes a warm country mansion (WTB 4 star hostel) with mainly dormitory style accommodation and an adjoining Scandinavian style farmhouse (WTB 3 star guest house).

Plas Dolau includes meeting rooms, dining rooms, games room, outdoor areas and walks. The centre can accommodate groups of up to 45 people. Various options for accommodation, provision of food, cooking facilities, etc are available. Ideally suited for youth groups, field courses, retreats, house parties and many other groups or individuals.
Please feel free to phone to discuss your requirements.

DETAILS

- **Open** - All year, 24 hours.
- **Number of beds** - 45: + cots etc. Plus 16 in farmhouse.
- **Booking** - Recommended.
- **Price per night** - Ranges from £18 (including basic breakfast) to £32 (private room, en-suite with full breakfast). From £650 per night for the whole mansion.
- **Public Transport** - Nearest train station is in Aberystwyth. Taxi from the station will cost around £5. National Express coaches and local buses (525 and 526) will set down at the end of the hostel drive.
- **Directions** - GR 623 813, OS map 135. On the A44, 3 miles from Aberystwyth, 1 mile from Llanbadarn railway bridge, 0.6 miles from turning to Bow Street. Sign on roadside says 'Y Gelli', B+B. Reception in 'Y Gelli'.

CONTACT:
Lovesgrove, Aberystwyth, Ceredigion, SY23 3HP
Tel: 01970 617834
enquiry@plasdolau.co.uk www.plasdolau.co.uk

MAES-Y-MOR

Maes-y-Mor offers superior accommodation at a budget price. Ideally situated near the town centre, 80m from the beach and 40m from the bus station. Accommodation at the hostel is room-only. There is a large kitchen diner with fridge-freezer, hob oven, microwave and toaster enabling guests to prepare their own food. Bedrooms have TV, tea/coffee making facilities and beds of a superior quality to ensure a good night's sleep. Towels are provided. Halls and landings are themed in Welsh history pictures. There is a car parking area at rear and secure shed for bikes. Free WiFi Internet.

Aberystwyth is an ideal base for north and south Wales. Visit Devil's Bridge with its dramatic waterfalls or Vale of Rheidol narrow gauge railway, the National Library of Wales, the castle and the harbour. Aberystwyth is a university town so there is plenty of night life. We offer a personal and helpful service.
Croeso Cymraeg Cynnes i bawb / a warm Welsh welcome to all!

DETAILS

- **Open** - All year, 8am to 10pm.
- **Number of beds** - 20: 8 x 2, 1 x 4 (en-suite).
- **Booking** - Booking advisable.
- **Price per night** - Twin and Double Room £22 per person; Single Room £28.
- **Public Transport** - Bus and train stations are within approximately 400 mts.
- **Directions** - From bus and train stations follow Terrace Road in a straight line towards beach. Turn right at Tourist Board Shop, then Maes-y-Mor is about 30 mts along next to the cinema.

CONTACT: Gordon or Mererid
25 Bath Street, Aberystwyth, Ceredigion, SY23 2NN
Tel: 01970 639270 or 07966 502715 Fax: 01970 623621
maesymor@hotmail.co.uk www.maesymor.co.uk

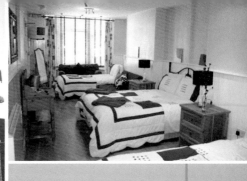

NEW INN
BUNKHOUSE

Stay at the 16th century New Inn on the River Wye and discover the forgotten countryside of mid Wales. The New Inn has a bunkhouse ideal for parties of walkers and cyclists as well as double, twin and family B&B rooms. The bunkhouse has its own entrance and a large lobby which can be used for boots and waterproofs. Secure storage is available for cycles and motor-cycles. The bunkhouse is self-contained with toilets and showers.

There are no self-catering facilities but the Inn specialises in serving imaginative home-cooked locally grown food. A Welsh breakfast of home-made sausages and dry cured bacon is available for £5. Explore the surrounding countryside, inhabited by red Kites, or relax in the secluded beer garden. There is plenty of parking and a large function room for parties.

DETAILS

- **Open** - All year, all day. Pub closed 3pm - 5pm some days.
- **Number of beds** - Bunkhouse 10: 1x6, 1x4; B&B 11: family rooms, double and twin.
- **Booking** - Book by phone or email.
- **Price per night** - £10 pp (Bunkhouse), £60 sole use of 6 bed room, £40 sole use of 4 bed room. Breakfast £5pp. Ensuite B&B in Inn £60 double/twin. Family rooms also available from £80.
- **Public Transport** - Trains at Llandrindod Wells (5 miless). Infrequent bus service.
- **Directions** - Newbridge-on-Wye is on the A470 between Builth Wells and Rhayader. Travelling north on the A470 take a right turn in Newbridge and the New Inn is on the right.

CONTACT: Debbie and Dave
New Inn, Newbridge-on-Wye, Llandrindod Wells, Powys, LD1 6HY
Tel: 01597 860211
dave@pigsfolly.orangehome.co.uk www.pigsfolly.co.uk/bunkhouse.htm

Toad Hall is a privately-owned family hostel in mid Wales, close to Snowdonia and in the beautiful Dovey Estuary (a designated biosphere including Yns Hir RSPB reserve and the long sandy beaches of Aberdovey). The influential Centre for Alternative Technology is 2 miles away, with around 100,000 visitors a year. Toad hall is very close to the railway station in the historical town of Machynlleth which was the seat of the first Welsh government in 1405. Nowadays it has a lively feel with a busy Wednesday market, and many residents with a progressive and alternative slant. The Corris and Tal y Llyn narrow gauge railways are nearby, Cader Idris mountain is 6 miles away. Toad Hall has 4 private bedrooms, a self-catering kitchen, a large games room (available until 9pm), a flat garden for bike/canoe storage and camping, and a workshop for bike repairs. Please phone to arrange use of any of these facilities. Under 18s and well behaved dogs are welcome with prior agreement.

DETAILS

- **Open** - All Year, 9am-9pm. Please vacate rooms from 12 till 3pm for cleaning. No arrivals after 11pm.
- **Number of beds** - 10: 1x4 (family), 1x2 (twin), 1x2 (dbl), 1x2.
- **Booking** - Advance booking not always essential- phone on the day if necessary. Payment in advance or a deposit of 1 night's fee.
- **Price per night** - £15 pp. Reductions possible for groups or long term bookings.
- **Public Transport** - 200m to train station (services to the Midlands, North Wales and Aberystwyth). Lloyds coaches and Arriva buses serve local area.
- **Directions** - Down a private lane opposite the turning to the train station.

CONTACT: Eva
Toad Hall, Doll St, Machynlleth, Powys, SY20 8BH
Tel: 01654 700597 Mob: 07807 849216 or 07866 362507
eva_edain@yahoo.co.uk

BRAICH GOCH
BUNKHOUSE & INN

The Braich Goch is a 16th century coaching inn situated 3 miles from Cadair Idris. There are stunning views of the Dulas Valley and Dyfi Forest. The Braich has been specifically set up with outdoor enthusiasts in mind. Facilities include drying room, secure bike storage and large well equipped self-catering kitchen. There are 6 bedrooms, 4 en-suite and a further two bathrooms. See a 360degree virtual tour on the website www.braichgoch.co.uk. The location is ideal for walking, mountain biking, cycling, climbing and canoeing at all levels as well as bird watching or simply chilling out. Dyfi Forest mountain bike trails are on the doorstep. The Braich is also a pub with pool table, darts and other games to keep you entertained in the evening! Also available are activity packages with qualified instructors suitable for all levels. In the area are King Arthur's Labyrinth and Corris Craft Centre, Centre for Alternative Technology, Coed-y-Brenin Forest Park and the coast. Wales Tourist Board 4 stars. Walkers & Cyclists Welcome Awards.

DETAILS

- **Open** - All year, all hours by arrangement.
- **Number of beds** - 26: 5 x 4 : 1 x 6.
- **Booking** - Essential for groups. 20% deposit, balance 4 weeks before arrival.
- **Price per night** - £17.50pp.
- **Public Transport** - Nearest train station to Corris is Machynlleth. Bus stop outside the 'Braich Goch' Inn. Taxis can be hired from Machynlleth.
- **Directions** - GR 754 075 On A487 between Machynlleth and Dolgellau at Corris turning. 2.5 miles north of Centre for Alternative Technology.

CONTACT: Ann or Andy
Corris, Machynlleth, Powys, SY20 9RD
Tel: 01654 761229 Mobile: 07881 626734
AnnBottrill@aol.com www.braichgoch.co.uk

CORRIS
HOSTEL

Nestled in the foothills of Cadair Idris, this award winning hostel enjoys splendid views over the Dyfi Valley. Corris Hostel is renowned as a spiritual haven with its caring, easy going atmosphere, friendly staff, meditation room, cosy wood fires and collection of books, games and artefacts. Outdoors the evolving landscaped gardens provide a serene, inspirational environment.

Environmental awareness is promoted through the hostel's vegetarian focus, recycling, composting, gardens and energy efficiency. Visitors can find more about Green lifestyle at the nearby Centre for Alternative Technology (celebrated worldwide as Europe's leading Eco-Centre). Down river are national Biosphere nature reserves and miles of golden beaches at Aberdyfi, while Cadair Idris nestles in the next valley. A range of environmental, and mind/body/spirit activities are available.

DETAILS

- **Open** - All year, all day access.
- **Number of beds** - 42/44.
- **Booking** - Phone to check.
- **Price per night** - Adult £15, child £12, Breakfast £4. Private rooms at extra cost.
- **Public Transport** - Buses 30, X32, 34 and Trawscambria pass Machynlleth train station on the Cambrian Coast line with connection to Aberystwyth and Birmingham.
- **Directions** - GR 753 080. We are in the mountain village of Corris 6 miles north of Machynlleth. At Braich Goch turn off A487 into Corris. At Slaters Arms pub turn left, hostel is 150m uphill beyond a small carpark.

CONTACT: Michael or Debbie
Old School, Corris, Machynlleth, Powys, SY20 9TQ
Tel: 01654 761686
mail@corrishostel.co.uk www.corrishostel.co.uk

Set in the beautiful mid Wales countryside on the Glyndwrs Way the Bunkhouse is an ideal location for exploring or unwinding. Built to the highest standards, newly opened in July 2008 and with 4 star tourist board rating it provides high quality accommodation for groups or individuals. It can also be booked for conferences and seminars. There is a well equipped kitchen and a large communal area with fabulous elevated views over the mid Wales countryside. The bunk beds are large with comfortable mattresses. Pillows and pillowcases are included, sheets and duvets can be hired for £3 per set. Attractions close by include sailing, golf course, outdoor pursuit centre, shooting range, motorbike school and the picturesque market town of LLanidloes (0.5 mile) with many places to eat and drink. You will need to bring your own soap and towels. Boots and dirty footwear must be kept in the drying room so please bring footwear for indoors. Bike hire, and taxis for walkers and cyclists to/from routes available.

DETAILS

- **Open** - All year, 24 hours. Arrival and departure times by arrangement.
- **Number of beds** - 23 in 2 dormitories and 1 family room.
- **Booking** - Booking is required (with non-refundable deposit) by phone, email or booking form on plasnewyddbunkhouse.co.uk.
- **Price per night** - Sole use £403 per night. Individuals £20 pp.
- **Public Transport** - Caersws train station (7 miles), Llanidloes bus station (0.5 mile). Pick ups can be arranged from these points if required.
- **Directions** - From Llanidloes take the Gorn Road and Plasnewydd is signposted on the left hand side after about half a mile.

CONTACT: Susan
Gorn Rd, Llanidloes, Powys, SY18 6LA
Tel: 01686 412431 or 07977 508 648 / 07975 913049
susanvaughan67@aol.co.uk www.plasnewyddbunkhouse.co.uk

TYN Y BERTH
MOUNTAIN CENTRE

Ty'n y Berth is a former school at the foot of Cadair Idris on the southern edge of the Snowdonia National Park. Surrounded by mountains, valleys and crystal clear rivers, yet only 12 miles from the coast, it's a great location for outdoor activities and family holidays. The spacious accommodation sleeps up to 43. The main room is divided into dining and lounge areas. There is a commercial kitchen, recently renovated, with large oven, hob and microwave; plenty of toilets and showers; drying room; pay phone; lockable storage for boats and bikes and parking for 10 cars. Corris is within walking distance and has two pubs: the Slaters Arms, which does bar meals, and the Braich Goch Inn, which regularly has live music. Courses are also available in climbing, mountain walking, abseiling, gorge scrambling, mine exploration, ropes courses, orienteering, and team building. Accommodation for a further 35 is available at the Bryn Coedwig Centre (also run by Wide Horizons), four miles from Tyn Y Berth in the village of Aberllefenni.

DETAILS

- **Open** - All year, all day.
- **Number of beds** - 43: 1x8, 4x6, 1x5, 1x3, 1xdbl, 2x1.
- **Booking** - Book by phone/fax or email.
- **Price per night** - £250.00 - £300.00 + VAT on a self-catering, sole use basis.
- **Public Transport** - Trains run from London to Machynlleth with a change at Birmingham New Street.
- **Directions** - On entering Corris Uchaf from north on A487 you will enter a 30 mph speed limit. Ty'n y Berth is the old school on the right, just inside the 30mph signs.

CONTACT: Jane or Dave
Corris Uchaf, Machynlleth, Powys, SY20 9RH
Tel: 01654 761678 Fax: 0872 115 3187
info@corris-bunkhouse.co.uk www.corris-bunkhouse.co.uk

HyB Bunkhouse is situated on Heol y Bont (Bridge St) in the old market town of Dolgellau, mid Wales, nestling at the foot of Cader Idris. It is centrally located above the design-led gift shop Medi, and has free private parking for up to six cars at the rear of the premises. Seconds from pubs and restaurants, launderette and bike repairers, it backs onto the Mawddach trail and the Marian playing fields, on the banks of the river Wnion and only 10 mins' drive to Coed y Brenin mountain biking centre. This quirky listed building has lovely original features such as oak floors, beams and panelling and consists of four bunk rooms, sleeping 16 in total. Each room has a mini-kitchen for basic self-catering with fridge, hob, toaster and kettle. One room is en-suite, and there are also two other lovely modern bathrooms. Communal lounge on the ground floor. Bring your own bedding. HyB has wireless internet connection for laptops.

DETAILS

■ **Open** - All year, all day.
■ **Number of beds** - 16: 4 x4.
■ **Booking** - Please phone or email.
■ **Price per night** - £18 per person.
■ **Public Transport** - Buses stop at Eldon square (1 minute walk) and links with main train stations at Machynlleth and Barmouth for connections to the Midlands and London.
■ **Directions** - HyB is above Medi - the last shop before the main bridge on the one way system out of Eldon square. By car turn into Y Marian car park and take a sharp left behind the public toilets into HyB car park through the double wooden gates.

CONTACT: Nia
2-3 Heol y Bont (Bridge St), Dolgellau, Gwynedd, LL40 1AU
Tel: 01341 421755
medi-hyb@tiscali.co.uk www.medi-gifts.com

CABAN CADER IDRIS
BUNKHOUSE

This self-catering bunkhouse is ideal for groups but also open to individuals. Caban Cader Idris is a listed building in a secluded wooded valley within walking distance of Cader Idris and the Mawddach Estuary in Eryri (Snowdonia National Park). It is in an ideal setting for field work and outdoor pursuits with wonderful unspoilt mountain, valley and estuary walks from the doorstep. Local activities include climbing, hill walking, pony trekking, biking, canoeing, rafting and fishing. The area is also ideal for the study of geology, geography, local history, industrial archaeology and ornithology (RSPB woods adjoin grounds). Nearby are slate mines, narrow gauge railways and beaches. There is a large kitchen/dining room, two dorms sleeping 6 and 10, a lounge (with 3 beds), toilets, hot showers and a drying room.
It is heated and open all seasons. Camping by arrangement.

DETAILS

■ **Open** - All year.
■ **Number of beds** - 19
■ **Booking** - Booking is essential. Always phone before arrival. £20 per night deposit. Last minute enquiries welcome from individuals or groups.
■ **Price per night** - Sole use: £100 midweek, £125 Fri, Sat, bank holidays and New Year. Reduced rates for whole week bookings. Individuals £10 pp when available.
■ **Public Transport** - Nearest train station is Morfa Mawddach (4 miles). Nearest bus stop is Abergwynant (¼ mile). For local bus info call 01341 422614.
■ **Directions** - GR 682169. From Dolgellau take the A493 to Fairbourne. 1 mile after Penmaenpool turn left just before Abergwynant Bridge. Bunkhouse 300yds on left.

CONTACT: Dafydd Ryhs
Islawrdref, Dolgellau, Gwynedd, LL40 1TS
Tel: 07887 954301 or 01766 762588
dafydd.rhys@virgin.net

BALA
BUNK HOUSE

The bunkhouse is a converted 200-year-old Welsh stone building. It carries WTB two star approval and is set back from the road in over an acre of picturesque grounds with a river and stream. Modernised to provide accommodation for outdoor activity groups, it is light, airy and comfortable with night storage heating and drying facilities. There is a large lounge/dining area and bunk rooms for 2, 4 and 8 plus annexe for 6. Separate ladies' and gentlemen's toilets have washing areas and hot showers. Fully equipped self-catering kitchen. The Little Cottage, a large converted self-contained bunkroom sleeping 6, with kitchenette, shower and toilet/washing area, is ideal for smaller groups and families. Sheets & pillowcases are provided - bring a sleeping bag.

There is a splendid view of the Berwyn Hills; together with the Aran and Arenig hills they provide superb walking. Bala Lake and the National White Water Centre are brilliant for water sports. Good pubs, restaurants and shops in Bala.

DETAILS

- **Open** - All year, no restrictions.
- **Number of beds** - 26 : 1x2 : 1x4 : 1x6 : 1x8.   1x6 self-contained.
- **Booking** - Book if possible, ring or write with 20% deposit. Weekends are busy.
- **Price per night** - Single night £16 pp, two or more nights £15 pp per night.
- **Public Transport** - Trains at Wrexham (30 miles). National Express at Corwen (10 miles). Local buses call at Bala (1.6 miles from hostel). Call hostel for a taxi.
- **Directions** - GR 950 372. From England take M6, M54, A5 through Llangollen then A494 for Bala. We are on the A494 1.5 miles before Bala.

CONTACT: Guy and Jane Williams
Tomen Y Castell, Llanfor, Bala, Gwynedd, LL23 7HD
Tel: 01678 520738 Fax: 01678 520738
thehappyunion@btinternet.com www.balabunkhouse.co.uk

BALA
BACKPACKERS

For Outdoor Adventures within the Snowdonia National Park, Bala Backpackers is Hostel-Style Good-Value Self-Catering Accommodation offering 30 Comfy SINGLE BEDS, 3 Private TWIN ROOMS and a Double Holiday-Let, in 1800's Character Buildings, located in a quiet, sunny chapel square, in the bustling market town of Bala, Mid North Wales. It is clean, safe and nice for the price with a careful, old, arty, homely atmosphere, with hints of Luxury, now called Posh-Packing! 4-Star Showers, Bedrooms, Wet-Room, Dining Facilities & Guest Kitchen. Catering is available. Bala boasts a five-mile-long Lake, a white-water river for raft rides, and nestles beneath three 900 metre Peaks.

The Lakeside, River and Leisure pursuits are 5 mins walk away. Plan your activities or just soak up the atmosphere by day or evening, in Town.

DETAILS

- **Open** - All year by arrangement, reception 5-10pm & 8am-10am.12.30am curfew.
- **Number of beds** - 33: 2x3, 3x4, 3x5 + 3 Twin Rooms + Double Holiday-Let.
- **Booking** - On-line or by phone or email.
- **Price per night** - Hostel: 1 Night £19.50, 2 Nights £35, 3 Nights £45, Weekly £90. Twin room: £47 or £55 ensuite. Holiday-Let: £220/4nights. All prices Include Bedding.
- **Public Transport** - Trains: Wrexham (30 miles) or Barmouth (30miles). Bus no 94 every 2 hours Daily from Wrexham and Barmouth.
- **Directions** - GR 926 358. Bala is on A494. Turn in the middle of Bala High Street, opposite the White Lion Royal Hotel, down Tegid Street to see HOSTEL Sign. Unload outside Hostel, but park round corner, in FREE overnight Pay & Display.

CONTACT: Stella Welch
32 Tegid Street, Bala, LL23 7EL
Tel: 01678 521700
info@Bala-Backpackers.co.uk www.Bala-Backpackers.co.uk

Tyddyn Bychan is an 18th century traditional Welsh farmhouse complex set in two and a half acres of private grounds surrounded on all sides by farmland. Situated in an excellent location for cycling, walking, climbing, fishing and numerous watersports including whitewater rafting.

The main bunkhouse sleeps 18 in two en-suite rooms. All the bunks are handmade and of a very high standard. The smaller bunkhouse sleeps 12 in two en-suite rooms and has its own kitchen and conservatory. All bedding, heating and electricity are included. Delicious homemade food in the farmhouse and packed lunches can be provided if pre-booked. The bunkhouses are very well equipped for self-catering with a well equipped kitchen/dining room. There is a large parking area well away from the road.

DETAILS

- **Open** - All year, all day.
- **Number of beds** - 30: 1x10; 1x8; 2x6.
- **Booking** - Booking is advisable
- **Price per night** - £13 pp including bedding.
- **Public Transport** - Nearest train station is at Betws-y-Coed. Nearest National Express service at Llandudno. Phone 01492 575412 for details.
- **Directions** - GR 931 504. Turn off A5 at Cerrigydrudion. Take B4501 out of village for Llyn Brenig, take the turning on left for Cefn Brith. After about 2 miles you will see a phone box on left, chapel on right and the road widens for a layby. The gate for Tyddyn is on the left directly opposite junction on the right.

CONTACT: Lynda
Cefn Brith, Cerrigydrudion, Conwy, LL21 9TS
Tel: 01490 420680 Mob: 07523 995741
lynda@tyddynbychan.co.uk www.tyddynbychan.co.uk

LLANGOLLEN
HOSTEL

Llangollen Hostel offers clean and comfortable twin and double rooms, en-suite family rooms, private four-bed and six-bed en-suite rooms, and a great value six-bed dorm. There is a fully-fitted kitchen and all prices include a complimentary breakfast. You can enjoy your meals in the dining room, then relax in the spacious lounge by the log fire. We have a book exchange, free WiFi, plenty of games, laundry facilities, a drying room, and bicycle/canoe storage. The location is perfect for walking, climbing, canoeing and mountain biking in the Vale of Llangollen. Families will love visiting the steam railway and Pontcysyllte Aqueduct - a World Heritage Site. The town offers a great choice of restaurants/pubs and is home to a fringe music and arts festival and the International Eisteddfod. Llandegla, Chester, Wrexham and Offa's Dyke Path are all nearby. At Llangollen Hostel you're assured of a happy and comfortable stay, freedom to come and go as you please, and above all, a warm welcome.

DETAILS

- **Open** - All year, all day.
- **Number of beds** - 32.
- **Booking** - Internet, email or phone.
- **Price per night** - From £18 dorm
- **Public Transport** - Daily National Express from London. Trains: Ruabon (5 miles). Buses all day (every 15 mins until 6pm).
- **Directions** - From the A5 heading west, the hostel is located 50 yards past the main set of traffic lights on the right. Parking is at the rear of the hostel on Market Street – at the main traffic lights, turn right then first left.

CONTACT: Arlo Dennis
Berwyn Street, Llangollen, LL20 8NB
Tel: 01978 861773, Mob: 07783 401894
info@llangollenhostel.co.uk www.llangollenhostel.co.uk

LLEDR
HOUSE

Nestled alongside the River Lledr in the heart of Snowdonia National Park, this former quarry manager's house is popular with bikers, walkers, schools, D of E groups and for family reunions. There is a large self-catering kitchen, dining room and TV lounge with Sky, all centrally heated and with laptop and free WiFi access. All bedding is provided in single, twin and family rooms plus a nine-bed dorm. With full double glazing, a private riverside garden, plenty of parking with a new extended car park, a patio and a BBQ area. Suitable for motorbike parking. There is also a luxury self-contained cedar log cabin, sleeping 5, in the grounds. A chicken run with bunnies is also in the forest! Lledr House is surrounded by woodland walks and cycle trails. Betws-y-Coed (4 miles) and stunning Llyn Elsi are popular tourist sites. Within walking distance of a pub and Spar shop, and 25 minutes' drive to Mount Snowdon. Walk from hostel to Moel Siabod. Tree Tops High Ropes Adventure Course 4 miles away.

DETAILS

- **Open** - All year (except Christmas week), check in from 5pm till 10.30pm.
- **Number of beds** - 31: 1x9, 2x4,1x6, 3x2, 2x1.
- **Booking** - Bookings by phone/email held till 6pm. First nights deposit for groups.
- **Price per night** - £13.50 adult, £11 for children under 16. Sole use of hostel £325.
- **Public Transport** - Pont-y-Pant station on the Conwy Valley Line is ¾ mile away. On Sunday there are 2 buses a day instead of the train.
- **Directions** - On the A5 from Llangollen to Bangor turn left just before Betws-y-Coed onto the A470 (signed Dolgellau). The hostel is 4 miles on right side of road. Walking from Pont-y-Pant station, turn left and left again after stone road bridge.

CONTACT: Brian or Melanie Quilter
Pont-y-Pant, Dolwyddelan, North Wales, LL25 0DQ
Tel: 01690 750202 Mobile: 07915 397705 or 07915 397660
Lledrhouse@aol.com www.ukyh.com

CABAN CYSGU
GERLAN BUNKHOUSE

Caban-Cysgu offers comfortable, purpose-built accommodation at the foot of the Carneddau in the Welsh-speaking village of Gerlan. Being a community-run bunkhouse, a warm welcome is guaranteed. This is an ideal location for walking in Snowdonia, and provides an obvious base for the 'Fourteen 3000ft Peaks' long-distance challenge. Cyclists are welcome too, the hostel being within a mile of Sustrans route 'Lôn Las Ogwen'. Rock-climbing at Idwal is close at hand, as well as the Carneddau crags. The nearby Afon Ogwen provides a popular venue for canoeists. For more leisurely pursuits, try visiting Coed Meurig, Penrhyn Castle or the Greenwood Centre.

Shops, pubs and cafés in Bethesda are within walking distance.

DETAILS

- **Open** - All year, all day.
- **Number of beds** - 16 : 1x5, 1x2, 1x1, 1x8.
- **Booking** - Not essential, but recommended (with 20% non-returnable deposit).
- **Price per night** - From £12.50 - £15 (with concessions for group bookings and children).
- **Public Transport** - Bangor train station is 6 miles. Catch a bus from Bangor bus station to Gerlan (66), or Bethesda (fare £1.40). Taxi from Bangor approx. £10.
- **Directions** - GR 632665. Travelling south on the A5, turn left in the centre of Bethesda just before Spar. Bear right, go up the hill over 2 cross-roads. Caban-Cysgu is the old school on the left, about ½ mile from the A5.

CONTACT: Dewi Emyln, Manager
Ffordd Gerlan, Gerlan, Bethesda, Bangor, LL5 3TL
Tel: 01248 605573 Mob: 07784760838
dewi@cabancysgu-gerlan.co.uk www.cabancysgu-gerlan.co.uk

CONWY VALLEY
BACKPACKERS BARN

Conwy Valley Backpackers is situated on a peaceful working farm with organic status in the heart of the beautiful Conwy Valley, with excellent access to Snowdonia. Centrally heated with fully equipped self-catering kitchen, log fires, hot showers and a fire alarm system. There are three separate dorms sleeping 4, 6 and 10, two of which have their own toilet facility. Secure bike/canoe storage, grazing for horses and tourist information are available.
Beside the barn is a small stream and guests may picnic and BBQ on the river bank. An ideal space for restoration, relaxation and retreat. Bring a sleeping bag or hire bed linen (£3). Continental breakfast (£3.50)/packed lunch (£5)/ and buffet suppers (£10) are available by arrangement. Local activities range from fishing and hiking to white water rafting and mountain biking, and there are some great pubs and eating places within walking distance.
Groups are welcome. No dogs.

DETAILS

- **Open** - All year, all day.
- **Number of beds** - 20: 1 x 4; 1 x 6; 1 x 10.
- **Booking** - Not essential but recommended
- **Price per night** - From £18pp. Sole use from £250. £2.50pp bed linen hire.
- **Public Transport** - Train stations and coaches at Llandudno Junction and Conwy. Local bus 19 or 19a runs every 20 minutes from Conwy and Llandudno Junction, ask driver to drop you at Pyllau Gloewon farm gate.
- **Directions** - GR 769 697. Six miles south of Conwy on the B5106, look for Backpackers sign just before entering Tal-y-Bont.

CONTACT: Claudia or Helen
Pyllau Gloewon Farm, Tal-y-Bont, Conwy, Gwynedd, LL32 8YX
Tel: 01492 660504
claudia.bryan@btconnect.com www.conwyvalleybarn.com

LLANDUDNO
HOSTEL

James and Melissa would like to invite you to their charming Victorian 4 star hostel. We are a friendly hostel where individuals, families and groups (including schools) are welcome all year. Some of the guests comments: "friendliest hostel we've ever stayed in", "Wow isn't it clean", "these bathrooms are fabulous, as good as any hotel". Come and try us, we love to meet new people and look forward to getting to know you. Set in the heart of the Victorian seaside resort town of Llandudno, an ideal place to shop or explore the many and varied local attractions. Excellent blue flag beaches, dry slope skiing, toboggan run, ten pin bowling, bronze age copper mine, traditional pier and many museums, fishing trips, etc. Llandudno is within easy travelling distance of Snowdon, Bodnant Gardens and local castles. We are able to book local attractions for groups and secure some discounts.

DETAILS

- **Open** - All year. Telephone in winter prior to arrival. All day.
- **Number of beds** - 46: 2x8 : 2x6 : 4x2 : 1x4 : 1 x family.
- **Booking** - Essential April to July.
- **Price per night** - From £20 per person, £48 per private twin room, £52 per private twin en-suite. Group and family rates on request.
- **Public Transport** - Trains at Llandudno. Turn right as you exit station, cross road, turn left down Vaughan Street (towards the beach), left into Charlton Street.
- **Directions** - From the A55 take A470 and follow signs to Llandudno town centre, straight through all roundabouts, after Asda turn 3rd left into Vaughan Street (signed train station), then 1st right into Charlton Street. Hostel is No 14.

CONTACT: James
14 Charlton Street, Llandudno, LL30 2AA
Tel: 01492 877430
info@llandudnohostel.co.uk www.llandudnohostel.co.uk

HENDRE ISAF
BASECAMP

Hendre Isaf is a 400-year-old converted farm building of stone and slate construction situated on the Ysbyty Estate. The 8,000 hectare estate takes in 51 hill farms, 31 cottages, forested valleys and high open moorland known as the Migneint. The Basecamp, set in a peaceful part of Snowdonia 6 miles from Betws-y-Coed, is available for private hire by groups and by negotiation is free for volunteers undertaking conservation work for the National Trust.

Local attractions include the dry ski slope and Plas y Brenin National Mountain Centre at Capel Curig, shops, leisure centre and swimming pool at Llanrwst, seaside resorts of Rhyl, Prestatyn and Llandudno. The centre may be able to accommodate one person with special mobility needs - telephone for details of access. No pets permitted.

DETAILS

- **Open** - All year, 24 hours.
- **Number of beds** - 17 in two dormitories on two floors.
- **Booking** - Early booking recommended (March to October is very busy). A non returnable deposit of £100 paid with booking (cheques payable to the National Trust).
- **Price per night** - £12pp (£15 bank holidays). Minimum of 8 people.
- **Public Transport** - Trains at Betws-y-Coed (6 miles), Llandudno Junction (20 miles) and Llanrwst (10 miles); National Express bus station at Llandudno. Some local buses to Betws-y-Coed, but we advise bringing your own transport.
- **Directions** - Situated 6 miles SE of Betws-y-Coed near the junction of the A5 and the B4407 (signposted Ysbyty Ifan and Ffestiniog). GR855511 (OS sheet 116).

CONTACT: Dilys Jones
National Trust Ysbyty Estate Office, Dinas, Betws-y-Coed, Conwy, LL24 0HF
Tel: 01690 713321 Fax: 01690 713301
dilysw.jones@nationaltrust.org.uk

Yr Helfa is a traditional bunkhouse situated in the heart of the Snowdonia National Park. This former farmhouse has been carefully restored and will sleep up to 18 people in 3 comfortable rooms. It has underfloor heating, 3 shower rooms with toilet and sink and a coal fire in lounge. All bedding is supplied. Winner of the Green Snowdonia Project Low Carbon Award, it has a wind turbine, solar panels and a wood pellet boiler. Yr Helfa nestles directly at the foot of Moel Gynghorion with panoramic views from the Llanberis path around to Bwlch Masgwn (Telegraph Pass). It is in a mountain environment with direct access to a number of routes up Snowdon and yet only 20 minutes' walk (1 mile) from Llanberis. The area is ideal for climbing, walking, fell running, horse riding and mountain biking. Award winning attractions include The Slate Museum, Electric Mountain, Dolbadarn Castle, Llanberis waterfall, Lake Railway and Snowdon Railway. Llanberis has several restaurants and plenty of pubs.

DETAILS

- **Open** - All year, all day.
- **Number of beds** - 18: 3x6.
- **Booking** - Availability and booking form on website. Book by post, 30% deposit.
- **Price per night** - Whole Bunkhouse - £150 per night, 7 nights £1,000. Smaller groups (6 or more) with shared occupancy £12 per person. Each room sleeps six.
- **Public Transport** - Trains at Bangor (10 miles). Buses from Llanberis to Caernarfon and Bangor every half hour.
- **Directions** - The bunkhouse is on the road to the beginning of the Llanberis Snowdon track. Carry on past the track and it is the first gate on your right. Park in the parking area then walk ten minutes down another track.

CONTACT: Jane ODonnell
Grove House, 18 High Street, Llanberis, Gwynedd, LL55 4EN
Tel: 0790 0087692
yrhelfa@hotmail.co.uk www.snowdonbunkhouse.co.uk

PENTRE BACH
BUNKHOUSE

Pentre Bach Bunkhouse provides alpine style bunkhouse accommodation, outdoor activities and a campsite. The Bunkhouse has two floors. The ground floor has tables with benches and a cooking area with gas burners, two microwaves, fridge and freezer. Heated via electric radiators upstairs and downstairs. Upstairs are alpine sleeping platforms with mattresses for 16. Drying room and toilets with washing facilities and showers, shared with the campsite, are just across the yard. Based between Waunfawr and Betws Garmon, Pentre Bach is surrounded by the superb scenery of Moel Eilio and Mynydd Mawr and has views towards Mount Snowdon. There are great walks from the bunkhouse or take a short car journey to the Nantlle ridge and the main footpaths up Snowdon (Ranger and Rhyd Ddu). Bach Ventures provide a variety of outdoor activities, whether you wish to be guided around the hills, try kayaking, climbing, or have an adventure gorge-scrambling.

DETAILS

- **Open** - All year, enquiries 9am until 10pm. Arrival after 4pm.
- **Number of beds** - 16: 1x16.
- **Booking** - One night's deposit required with balance payable before arrival. Short notice bookings accepted by phone or email with deposit/balance payable on arrival.
- **Price per night** - £10 per person (inc gas/electric/showers). Sole use bookings negotiable according to group size.
- **Public Transport** - Train station at Bangor. S4 bus from Caernarfon to Beddgelert stops at the bottom of the drive on request.
- **Directions** - GR 531 579. At Pentre Bach just south of Waunfawr on the Caernarfon to Beddgelert road (A4085). Look for Camping Barn sign.

CONTACT: Karen Neil
Pentre Bach, Waunfawr, Caernarfon, Gwynedd, LL54 7AJ
Tel: 01286 650643 or 07798733939
info@bachventures.co.uk www.bachventures.co.uk

Cwm Pennant Hostel is a 52 bed independent hostel offering relaxed accommodation for individuals, families and groups. It also offers residential adventure activities for groups provided by Outdoor UK Ltd. The hostel is set within stunning grounds in the Snowdonia National Park and has fantastic views of the Cwm Pennant valley and Moel Hebog. It is 5 miles from Porthmadog.

Cwm Pennant Hostel has a lounge, drying room and self-catering kitchen. Home cooked food is available on request. Guests have access to complimentary tea and coffee. A range of additional facilities are available including a power washer for mountain bikes, on-site parking and secure storage for bikes, kayaks and canoes. The area is ideal for hill walking, rock climbing and canoeing.

DETAILS

- **Open** - Open to advance bookings all year round, 7:30-12am; 5-10pm.
- **Number of beds** - 52: 5 x 4, 1 x 8, 1 x 10, 1 x 14.
- **Booking** - Advance booking is recommended and a deposit is required.
- **Price per night** - £17.50 (adult), £14 (under 18). B&B £20.50 (adult) and £17 (under 18). Full-board £34.50 (adult) and £28.50 (under 18).
- **Public Transport** - Porthmadog train station is 5 miles away. Take the number 1 bus towards Caernarfon and get off at the Cwm Pennant turning on the A487. From here follow the brown hostel signs - 1 mile walk to the hostel.
- **Directions** - From Porthmadog take the A487 towards Caernarfon. Take second turning on the right after passing through Penmorfa village and follow the brown hostel signs.

CONTACT:
Golan, Garndolbenmaen, Gwynedd, LL51 9AQ
Tel: 01766 530888
lindaharvey@cwm-pennant.info www.cwm-pennant.info

SNOWDON LODGE
GROUP HOSTEL

Stay in the birthplace of Lawrence of Arabia! Snowdon Lodge hostel provides comfortable self-catering style group accommodation in a large grade 2 listed character building. The property is located in the picturesque village of Tremadog. Snowdon Lodge is perfect for a family reunion or simply as a base for a group of friends to explore this beautiful part of Snowdonia and the nearby Lleyn Peninsula. The hostel has 10 rooms of different sizes (twins, doubles and small dormitories). Bathroom and shower facilities are shared. There is a large fully equipped self-catering kitchen, a dining room seating 36, 2 lounge/TV rooms with real log fires in winter, a drying room and a private car park leading to extensive woodland walks. Snowdon Lodge is ideally positioned just 6 miles from Mount Snowdon, yet only 2 miles from beautiful beaches such as Black Rock Sands. The famous Italianate village of Portmeirion is also only 4 miles away. Within a mile are the Ffestiniog and Welsh Highland railways and the famous Tremadog rocks for climbers. Sorry, no stag or hen parties.

DETAILS

- **Open** - January – December, all day access.
- **Number of beds** - 35: 2 x 6 (family), 1 x 5, 1 x 6 , 3 x twin, 3 x double.
- **Booking** - Essential.
- **Price per night** - Sole use £550 per night. Minimum 2 nights, Bank Holidays minimum 3 nights.
- **Public Transport** - Half mile from Porthmadog train station and 250 yards from National Express coach stop.
- **Directions** - Half a mile from Porthmadog on Caernarfon road (A487).

CONTACT: Carl or Anja
Lawrence House, Tremadog, Nr Porthmadog, Snowdonia, LL49 9PS
Tel: 01766 515354
info@snowdonlodge.co.uk www.snowdonlodge.co.uk

Croeso/Welcome! Sgubor Unnos provides luxury bunkhouse accommodation on a Welsh speaking, traditionally run, family farm in the village of Llangian, one mile from Abersoch, famous for its watersports and surfing beaches, Hell's Mouth and Porth Ceiriad. Centrally located, it is the ideal base for outdoor activities including walking the newly opened Llyn Coast Path, surfing, cycling, golf, fishing and sailing. Situated a few miles from Llangian, at the tip of the Peninsula lies Bardsey Island where 20,000 saints are buried! Why not pay them a visit? Trips around the island for its wildlife and heritage can be arranged. The modern bunkhouse offers three bedrooms ideal for individuals or groups. Fully equipped kitchen/lounge, disabled facilities, covered BBQ area, secure storage, private parking, traditional village shop and phone box 500m away. For details on area see www.abersoch-holiday.co.uk.
Photos taken by Tony Jones www.llynlight.co.uk

DETAILS

- **Open** - All year, all day.
- **Number of beds** - 14: 2 x 4 : 1 x 6.
- **Booking** - Not essential but recommended.
- **Price per night** - £18 (adult), £8 (under 10 years), including a light breakfast and bed linen. Discount for more than 2 nights.
- **Public Transport** - Nearest train station is Pwllheli (7 miles). Good local bus and taxi service to Llangian. Public transport details on web site.
- **Directions** - GR 296 288 On entering Abersoch from Pwllheli, take the right hand turning up the hill signed to Llangian (follow brown signs). On left on leaving village.

CONTACT: Phil or Meinir
Fferm Tanrallt Farm, Llangian, Abersoch, Gwynedd, LL53 7LN
Tel: 01758 713527
enquiries@tanrallt.com www.tanrallt.com

TOTTERS

Totters is situated in the heart of the historic castle town of Caernarfon. Sheltered by the castle town wall, it is only 30 metres from the shores of the Menai Straits and enjoys some fantastic sunsets. The town not only offers the visitor a huge selection of pubs and restaurants to choose from, but also acts as the perfect base for trips into the Snowdonia National Park. There is very good public transport in and out of the National Park.

The hostel is a 200-year-old, five floored town house, which is fully heated and with all the comforts of home. There is a common room with TV and games, book exchange, dining room and a secure left luggage facility. The bedrooms sleep either 4 or 6 and can be arranged as mixed or single sex dorms. Also available is the 'Penthouse', a huge double en-suite room with views over the Straits. This can be arranged as a family room.

DETAILS

- **Open** - All year, all day access. Book in by 10pm.
- **Number of beds** - 30 : 4 x 6, 1 x4, 1 x 2 (en suite).
- **Booking** - Booking is essential for groups in June, July, August and September.
- **Price per night** - £17pp. £47.50 for double en-suite. Discounts for groups.
- **Public Transport** - Bangor train station is 7 miles from the hostel. Catch a bus from outside the station to Caernarfon. National Express coaches drop off in Caernarfon 200m from the hostel.
- **Directions** - Coming by road: follow signs for town centre, turn right 200m after the big Celtic Royal hotel, keep going and Totters is the last house on the left.

CONTACT: Bob/Henryette
Plas Porth Yr Aur, 2 High Street, Caernarfon, Gwynedd, LL55 1RN
Tel: 01286 672963 Mob: 07979 830470
totters.hostel@googlemail.com www.totters.co.uk

Wonderfully situated at the south end of Holy Island, Anglesey, in a 7 acre Area of Outstanding Natural Beauty, and 300m from a beach. The centre is an excellent base for so much in the outdoors and is immediately adjacent to the Anglesey Coastal Path - good walking on a varied and accessible coast. All around there are prehistoric remains, spectacular geology, a wide range of habitats and species of marine life and plants, and excellent bird watching opportunities. For kayakers there are classic sea tours, overfalls, playwaves, surf and rockhopping. Climbers have Gogarth nearby and Rhoscolyn offering all grades in an attractive setting. Divers can beach launch for wrecks and fish.

The Centre has two self-contained units and camping with toilets and showers. Careful energy use is encouraged, with composting and recycling. Nearby Holyhead has rail links and ferries to Ireland. Walking distance to pub.

DETAILS

- **Open** - All year, 24 hour access.
- **Number of beds** - 20: 2x2, 1x4, 2x6. 16: 1x3, 2x4,1x5.
- **Booking** - Essential.
- **Price per night** - £295 for exclusive use, £18.60 per person.
- **Public Transport** - Trains at Holyhead (10km) (London direct 4.5 hrs) or Valley (5km). National Express at Valley (6km). Bus 23/25 Holyhead - Rhoscolyn (1km) or 4/44 Holyhead - Four Mile Bridge (3km). Ferry: Holyhead - Dublin or Dun Laoghaire.
- **Directions** - GR SH 278 752.   From A5 traffic lights at Y Fali/Valley take B4545 Trearddur. After 2km at Four Mile Bridge fork left at sign to Rhoscolyn 2miles. After 2km sharp left at camping symbols. After 800m fork right at large white gatepost.

CONTACT: Jacqui or Andy
Cerrig-yr-Adar, Rhoscolyn, Holyhead, Anglesey, LL65 2NQ
Tel: 01407 860469
enquiries@outdooralternative.co.uk www.outdooralternative.co.uk

425
424
423

Inverness o 401

SKYE

404

400

417

416

422
412

Aviemore

414 415

402,403

Newtonmore o 388

413

410

406

409

408

Mallaig o

386

EIGG

411

407

383-385

378-381

Fort William o

376 390

391

382

Kinlochleven o

375

355 360

TIREE
372

358

356

MULL 374

Oban o

354

366-370

IONA
373

353

Stirling o

371

346

COLONSAY

Glasgow o 349

350

Tarbert o

BUTE

352

ISLAY

ARRAN

351

o **Ayr**

0   miles   50

0   kilometres   80

**Castle
Douglas** o

Stranraer o

336

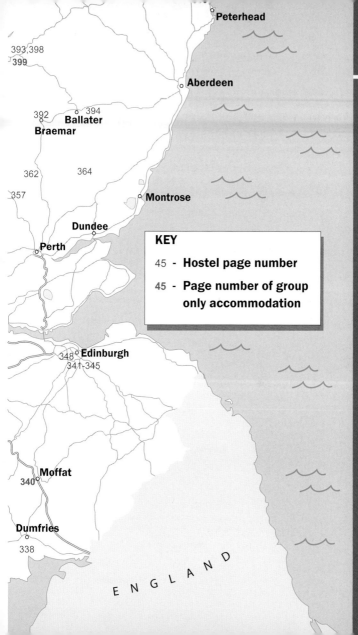

Peterhead

393, 398
399

Aberdeen

392 394
Ballater
Braemar

362 364

357

Montrose

Dundee

Perth

KEY

45 - **Hostel page number**

45 - **Page number of group only accommodation**

348 **Edinburgh**
341-345

Moffat
340

Dumfries
338

E N G L A N D

KEY

45 - **Hostel page number**

45 - **Page number of group only accommodation**

0   miles   50

0   kilometres   80

Durness 436

Stornoway
420,421

LEWIS

434

HARRIS 419

426

428

Ullapool

427

Gairloch

425

NORTH UIST

424

423

Portree

422
412

404

SKYE

417

416   415

414

402,403

SOUTH UIST

406

413

BARRA

410

418

Mallaig **408**

409

386

411

407

EIGG

383-385

376 390

Fort William 378-381

382

391

Kinlochleven

375

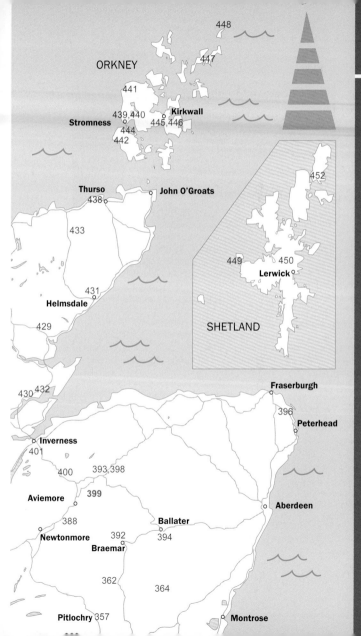

ORKNEY

448

447

441

Stromness 439,440 **Kirkwall**
444 445,446
442

Thurso John O'Groats
438

433

431
Helmsdale

429

430 432

Inverness
401

400 393,398

Aviemore **399**
388
Newtonmore 392 **Ballater**
Braemar 394

362 364

Pitlochry 357 **Montrose**

452

449 450
Lerwick

SHETLAND

Fraserburgh
396
Peterhead

Aberdeen

CASTLE CREAVIE
HAY BARN

Castle Creavie Haybarn has recently been converted to a comfortable family friendly Independent Hostel sleeping 4. Quietly set on a working farm it is surrounded by spectacularly beautiful Galloway countryside. Hugely spacious open plan design, oak floors, with 4 comfortable beds, dining area, woodburning stove, separate kitchen with basic cooking facilities, fridge, washroom and W.C. Also available on site are: hot showers, washing/drying facilities, bike wash and safe store, farmhouse breakfast (pre booked) £5 pp. Ideal base for walkers and cyclists with 7 Stanes and NCN Route 7 (3 miles away). Guests are welcome to enjoy the farm footpaths and observe the daily life on this working sheep farm. Available seasonally: fresh baked bread, cakes and honey, home reared pork and lamb, sausage, bacon and fresh farm eggs. Castle Creavie is named after two Iron Age forts, and is 4 miles from the popular harbour town of Kirkcudbright which has a good range of pubs, cafes, and restaurants. Galloway is famed for its many castles, abbeys, first class walking and long sandy beaches.

DETAILS

- **Open** - All year, all day.
- **Number of beds** - 4: 1x4
- **Booking** - Book by phone and online. Deposit required by post or PayPal.
- **Price per night** - £15pp with beds made up.
- **Public Transport** - 4 miles from Kirkcudbright citylink services.
- **Directions** - From the A75 take the A711 to Kirkcudbright. In the town centre turn left at the Royal Hotel onto the B727 (Gelston), pass the cemetery and at the next road junction go straight on (Auchencairn / Dundrennan). Follow for approx 4 miles.

CONTACT: Charlie and Elaine Wannop
Castle Creavie, Kirkcudbright, Dumfries and Galloway, DG6 4QE
Tel: 01557 500238 Fax: 01557 500238
castle.creavie@btinternet.com www.castlecreavie.co.uk

MARTHROWN
OF MABIE BUNKHOUSE

Marthrown is set in the heart of Mabie Forest, about 6 miles south of Dumfries. It has a traditional sauna, a wood burning spring water hot tub, a large BBQ, garden areas and plenty of room for groups. The forest has newly developed mountain bike routes, ranging in length and difficulty. Bike hire is available nearby and there is access to the 7 Stanes mountain bike trails. Although we are a self-catering hostel meals are available to order.

Marthrown is suitable for all age groups. Facilities include secure dry store for bikes and equipment and a large dining area suitable for meetings. For something a little different why not try staying in the Roundhouse or Yurt. For more info see website.

DETAILS

- **Open** - All year, 24 hours - late arrival by arrangement.
- **Number of beds** - 26: 1x8:1x7:1x6:1x5 + Roundhouse, Yurt and Tipi.
- **Booking** - Telephone a few days in advance.
- **Price per night** - £16 to £19.50.
- **Public Transport** - From Dumfries (White Sands) take the Stagecoach bus service 372 to Mabie Forest. It is best to arrive in daylight. 1.5 mile walk from road.
- **Directions** - From Dumfries take A710 (west) to Mabie Forest passing through the village of Islesteps. Turn right signposted Mabie Forest and Mabie House Hotel. Follow tarmac road over speed bumps to the end of the Hotel and Forest Rangers Office, through courtyard and onto forest track, Marthown is signposted and is exactly one mile into the forest.

CONTACT: Mike or Pam Hazlehurst
Mabie Forest, Dumfries, DG2 8HB
Tel: 01387 247900
mike@marthrown.com www.marthrownofmabie.com

WELL ROAD CENTRE
SCOTLAND GROUP ACCOMMODATION

The Well Road Centre is a large Victorian house set in its own grounds in the charming spa town of Moffat. The centre is ideal for youth groups, adult groups, conferences, residential workshops, sports events, multiple family gatherings and outdoor activity clubs. All rooms are fully carpeted and centrally heated. There are two spacious meeting rooms, a large bright self-catering kitchen fully equipped for 65, a games hall for indoor sports, a table tennis room and a snooker room. The are 13 bedrooms of various sizes, two of them with en-suite facilities. Two separate toilet/shower areas for mixed groups. Bring your own sleeping bags or duvets. Ample parking for cars, minibuses and equipment trailers and the nearby park can be used for football matches.

Moffat is in the Southern Uplands, an hour from Edinburgh and Glasgow. Ideal area for golfers, bird watchers, walkers and cyclists. All groups have sole use.

DETAILS

- **Open** - All year, all day/
- **Number of beds** - 70: in 13 rooms (2 en-suite).
- **Booking** - Check availability and send £100 deposit to secure booking.
- **Price per night** - From £660 for two nights for up to 30 people. £22 per person for 31 people or more.
- **Public Transport** - Trains at Lockerbie (16m). Citylink bus to Glasgow/Edinburgh.
- **Directions** - From A74 take Moffat turning and enter the High Street (town square). Turning to the right around the shops on the south side of the square, follow Holm St to the T-junction. Turn left into Burnside, following up and right into Well Rd.

CONTACT: Ben Larmour
Huntly Lodge, Well Road, Moffat, DG10 9BT
Tel: 01683 221040
Ben8363@aol.com   www.wellroadcentre.co.uk

CASTLE ROCK
HOSTEL
SCOTLAND

In a wonderful location, facing south with a sunny aspect and panoramic views over the city, Castle Rock Hostel is just steps away from the City Centre with the historic Royal Mile, the busy pubs and late-late nightlife of the Grassmarket and Cowgate, and of course the Castle. Most of the rooms have no traffic noise, there are loads of great facilities, 24 hour reception and no curfew.

With its beautiful and dramatic skyline Edinburgh is truly one of the world's great cities. The cobbled streets of the Old Town lead past mysterious gothic buildings up to the magnificent castle. Below the castle's rocky pinnacle lies the New Town's 200 year old Georgian splendour.

DETAILS

- **Open** - All year, 24 hours.
- **Number of beds** - 289.
- **Booking** - Booking not always essential. First night's payment needed to book.
- **Price per night** - From £14 per person. ID required for check in.
- **Public Transport** - 5/10 minute walk from Edinburgh Bus Stn and Waverley Train Stn. (taxis £3-£5). Airport bus goes to train station so it's easy to get to the hostel.
- **Directions** - 10 minutes walk from Waverley Train Station – turn left out of the station and continue to small roundabout. Cross over and continue up Cockburn Street to the top. Turn right onto the Royal Mile and follow uphill towards the Castle. Take the left fork at the Hub (church) and the hostel is situated 200 yards on the left side of Johnston Terrace next to two red telephone boxes. By Car – follow signs for City Centre towards the Castle turning onto Royal Mile uphill towards the castle then left fork at the Hub on to Johnston Terrace.

CONTACT: Receptionist
15 Johnston Terrace, Edinburgh, EH1 2PW
Tel: 0131 225 9666
castlerock@scotlandstophostels.com www.scotlandstophostels.com

HAGGIS
HOSTELS

Occupying a recently renovated Georgian building dating from 1862, Haggis Hostels is situated in the heart of Edinburgh just 50 metres from Princes Street. The hostel offers self-catering facilities and fully equipped rooms with privacy curtains and international sockets so there is no need for travel adaptors. There is adjustable heating in every room. The communal kitchen is of a high specification and features two of every appliance – ideal for groups of up to 34. Being so centralised in the Scottish capital, Haggis Hostels has everything on its doorstep whether you're heading to the theatre, concert hall, pub or club. There is something for everyone. Their staff will help you plan your day's excursion in and around Edinburgh and provide you with all the information you need to make your stay as enjoyable as possible. The hostel offers free breakfast, high speed WiFi internet access, luxury bedding and towels, a laundry service, secure storage and a communal kitchen with dining area.

DETAILS

- **Open** - All Year, 24 hour reception.
- **Number of beds** - 34.
- **Booking** - Phone or Email.
- **Price per night** - Standard mixed room - from £18. Male only room, female only room and family room from £22. Breakfast included in all prices.
- **Public Transport** - Buses to St Andrew Square Bus Station.
Air link shuttle service to Waverley Direct from Edinburgh Airport.
- **Directions** - At the east end of Princes Street, follow the road round to the left, and you will find us on the right.

CONTACT:
Haggis Hostels 5/3 West Register Street, EH2 2AA
Tel: 0131 557 0036
info@haggishostels.co.uk www.haggishostels.co.uk

HIGH STREET
HOSTEL

The High Street Hostel has become a hugely popular destination for world travellers since opening in 1985 and is one of Europe's best regarded and most atmospheric hostels.

Located just off the historic Royal Mile in a 400 year old building it is the perfect base for exploring all the city's attractions – and of course its wonderful nightlife.

Providing excellence in location, ambience and facilities, the hostel is highly recommended by more than ten of the world's top backpacker travel guides.

DETAILS

■ **Open** - All year, 24 hours.
■ **Number of beds** - 156.
■ **Booking** - Booking in advance not always crucial, 1 night's payment for booking.
■ **Price per night** - From £14 per person. ID required for check in.
■ **Public Transport** - Only a 5/10 minute walk from Edinburgh bus station or Waverley train station. Taxis cost between £3-£5 from each. The airport bus also stops outside the train station on the last stop so it is very easy to get to the hostel.
■ **Directions** - From the bus station (St Andrews Square) turn left onto Princes Street then first right onto Northbridge. At top turn left onto the High Street on the Royal Mile and hostel is on Blackfriars St. on right. From railway station main exit turn left onto Waverley Bridge then right at the mini rounbdaout and straight ahead up the Mound, at the junction go left, then at cross roads left again going down the Royal Mile. Cross at the traffic lights at Northbridge and Blackfriars St is second on the right. From airport take bus 100 to last stop, Waverley Bridge and follow as above.

CONTACT: Reception
8 Blackfriars Street, Edinburgh, EH1 1NE
Tel: 0131 557 3984
highstreet@scotlandstophostels.com www.scotlandstophostels.com

ROYAL MILE
BACKPACKERS
SCOTLAND

Royal Mile Backpackers is a small and lively hostel with its own special character! Perfectly located on the Royal Mile, the most famous street in Edinburgh, Royal Mile Backpackers is the ideal place to stay for the independent traveller.

Our comfortable beds and cosy common areas will make you feel at home and our friendly staff are always on hand to help you make the most of your time in Edinburgh.

DETAILS

- **Open** - All year, all day, Reception 7am – 3am (24hrs during August).
- **Number of beds** - 48.
- **Booking** - Booking not always essential, 1st night's payment required for booking.
- **Price per night** - From £14 per person. ID required for check in.
- **Public Transport** - Only a 5/10 minute walk from both Edinburgh bus station and Waverley train station. A taxi costs between £3-£5 from each. The airport bus also stops out side the train station on the last stop so is very easy to get to the hostel.
- **Directions** - From main bus station turn left onto Princes Street then take first right onto Northbridge. At top turn left onto the High St. on the Royal Mile. From train station take the Princes Street exit (up Waverley Steps), at top go right then right again up Northbridge, then left at cross roads, hostel's on the left above the Oxfam Shop. From airport take bus no.100 to city centre, get off at Waverley Bridge.
Walk away from Princes St. towards the roundabout, go over roundabout onto Cockburn Street. At the top of Cockburn Street turn left onto the High St. on the Royal Mile. Cross traffic lights at Northbridge and hostel is on left above Oxfam.

CONTACT: Receptionist
105 High Street, Edinburgh, EH1 1SG
Tel: 0131 557 6120
royalmile@scotlandstophostels.com www.scotlandstophostels.com

CAIRNCROSS HOUSE
UNIVERSITY OF GLASGOW

Cairncross House is in an excellent location within walking distance of the trendy West End and City Centre and is close to public transport. The West End is great for pubs and restaurants and has lots of good value places to eat. Nearby you will find some of Glasgow's top visitor attractions: Art Gallery and Museum, Transport Museum, University of Glasgow and its Visitor Centre, Hunterian Museum and Art Gallery. The City Centre offers great shopping, clubs and pubs.

The Hostel is part of the University of Glasgow's student residence and offers great value for money. Modern, well equipped with bed linen, wash basin in room, cooking facilities, showers and common room.

DETAILS

- **Open** - June to September, 8 am - 10 pm.
- **Number of beds** - 242.
- **Booking** - Advised but not essential, Booking address: Residential Services, University of Glasgow, 73 Great George Street, Glasgow, G12 8RR.
- **Price per night** - £21.25 (inc. VAT) per person.
- **Public Transport** - Buchanan Street Bus Station, Central Station and Queen Street Station are all 2 miles away. The nearest underground station is Kelvinhall (half mile). From George Square take buses 6 or 16, ask for Kelvinhaugh/Radnor St.
- **Directions** - From George St take St Vincent St, which becomes Argyle St after 1 mile. Through traffic lights take third left into Kelvinhaugh St, Cairncross House is on the right. From M8 J19 take A814 to Finnieston. Turn right into Finnieston St, continue to traffic lights and turn left into Argyle St. Kelvinhaugh St is third on the left.

CONTACT:
20 Kelvinhaugh Place, Glasgow, G3 8NH
Tel: 0141 330 4116/2318 or 0141 221 9334
vacationaccom@gla.ac.uk www.glasgow.ac.uk/cvso

Located just off the Royal Mile in the heart of Edinburgh's Old Town, Smart City Hostels, Edinburgh, redefines the hostel experience.

Smart City Hostels is an award winning stylish five-star hostel with great facilities that make it the ideal choice for value accommodation in the heart of Edinburgh. All of the rooms are en-suite, and the hostel can provide private rooms as well as larger dorm style living. The ultimate urban retreat with Bar 50, a fully licensed restaurant and bar, with WiFi, Sky Sports, pool table, and a great atmosphere. Bar 50 is a great area for groups to gather and eat together after a comfy night's sleep in our dorm rooms. Smart City Hostels also has a 24 hour reception, no curfew, and all of Edinburgh's lively night scene and famed attractions on your doorstep. A perfect base for groups, big or small, to explore all the city has to offer.

DETAILS

- **Open** - All year, 24 hours.
- **Number of beds** - 620.
- **Booking** - Not essential, but recommended in summer.
- **Price per night** - From £13.50 per person per night. Group rates available on request.
- **Public Transport** - Airport transfer and Waverley train station 5 minutes walk; St Andrews Bus Station 5-10 minutes' walk.
- **Directions** - From Waverley bridge turn left into Market Street, then turn right into Jeffrey Street. At first set of traffic lights at the Royal Mile turn right. Blackfriars Street is first left and Smart City Hostels is on your right.

CONTACT: Reservations
50 Blackfriars Street, Edinburgh, EH1 1NE
Tel: 0131 524 1989 Fax: 0131 524 1988
info@smartcityhostels.com www.smartcityhostels.com

ALBA HOSTEL
GLASGOW
SCOTLAND

Based in a spacious Victorian building in the west end of Glasgow, Alba Hostel offers a unique backpacker, short stay and hostel experience. It provides safe, comfortable budget accommodation with great facilities, atmosphere and a four star rating from VisitScotland. The rooms are incredibly spacious and clean, the staff are dedicated and very friendly, and no curfew means late nights are no problem. All areas are cleaned daily. It has a great self-catering kitchen, TV lounge, social/dining room and free parking. Irons, sewing kits, hair dryer and towel hire available. Continental breakfast can be provided for £2.

Located in Anniesland in the west end of Glasgow it is close to the city centre with good access to outlying areas such as Loch Lomond and the Highlands of Scotland. Glasgow is a vibrant mix of cultural and stylish attractions and has a great music scene. Top attractions include Kelvingrove Art Gallery, The Burrell Collection, Gallery of Modern Art, Museum of Transport, Botanic Gardens and Glasgow Science Centre. Individuals and groups welcome - backpackers, sports teams, bands on tour, workers, concert-goers etc.

DETAILS

- **Open** - All year, 24 hours.
- **Number of beds** - 2-4 bed, 6-bed and private rooms
- **Booking** - Booking advised but not always necessary by email or website.
- **Price per night** - From £15.00 £17.00 at weekends.
- **Public Transport** - 2 minute walk from Anniesland Rail Station. A short train journey from Central Glasgow for National coach and train connections.
- **Directions** - On the corner of Fifth Avenue.

CONTACT: Reception
6 Fifth Avenue, Anniesland, Glasgow, G12 0AT
Tel: 0141 334 2952, Mob: 07766 284172
bookings@albahostelglasgow.co.uk www.albahostelglasgow.co.uk

EURO HOSTEL
GLASGOW

'Glasgow's Only City Centre Hostel' providing budget en-suite accommodation in Glasgow City Centre, only 2 minutes' walk from Central Station. Ideally suited for international visitors to discover the city's cultural heritage and vibrant nightlife or convenient for guests to stay over after a concert or night out clubbing. The hostel welcomes groups of all sizes throughout the year and makes an ideal choice for sports teams, concert-goers and school/college parties. Facilities include the 'Mint & Lime' bar, games room, chill-out lounges with Big-screen TV and SKY, 24hr reception, internet access, self-catering kitchen, guest laundry, luggage storage and free bike storage.

There are TVs in all the twin and double rooms and FREE WiFi.

DETAILS

- **Open** - All year, all day.
- **Number of beds** - 364: Singles, 2, 4, 8 and 14 person all en-suite
- **Booking** - Individuals with credit card. Groups - 10% deposit required. Book online at www.euro-hostels.co.uk
- **Price per night** - From £13 B&B pp en-suite. Discount for mid week bookings and long stays. Apply for group discounts.
- **Public Transport** - Central Railway Station 2 mins, Queen Street Railway Station 7 mins, Buchanan Bus Station 10 mins, Glasgow Airport 8 miles.
- **Directions** - From the bus station turn right into North Hanover St and right into West George St (past Queen St train station). Turn left into Buchanan St and right down Argyle Street (left if arriving from Central train station). Go down Jamaica St and the hostel is on the corner joining Clyde St.

CONTACT: Reception
318 Clyde Street, Glasgow, G1 4NR
Tel: 0141 222 2828, Fax: 0141 222 2829
glasgow@euro-hostels.co.uk www.euro-hostels.co.uk

Kilmory Lodge Bunkhouse provides ideal group accommodation in a tranquil, rural setting. The Isle of Arran is one of the most accessible Scottish islands, only one hour by ferry from the mainland. It offers the visitor hill-walking, mountaineering, golf, fishing, cycling, pony trekking and a bewildering choice of extreme sports. The bunkhouse is affordable, modern, comfortable and able to sleep up to 23. All the bed linen is supplied, so there's no need to bring anything except your towels and food! There is a great, contemporary kitchen with all you'll need. Attached to the bunkhouse is the village hall which can provide extra rooms and an auditorium at extra cost. Ideal for educational groups, weddings, music workshop groups, clubs or any group needing extra facilities. We look forward to welcoming your family, club, group, school or any combination of these except stag parties! Phone or email with your queries. Registered Scottish Charity SC028200.

DETAILS

- **Open** - All year, 24 hours.
- **Number of beds** - 23: 2 x 8, 1 x 4 (en-suite) 1 x 3 (en-suite).
- **Booking** - Book ahead, 40% deposit. £150 security deposit on arrival.
- **Price per night** - £15 per person for groups of 15+. £20 per person for smaller groups.
- **Public Transport** - Buses stop on demand directly outside the Hall and Bunkhouse. These buses meet all the ferries that arrive and depart from the main ferry terminal at Brodick.
- **Directions** - Bunkhouse attached to Kilmory Public Hall located in village centre.

CONTACT: Jean Clark
Kilmory, Isle of Arran, KA27 8PQ
Tel: 01770 870345
kilmory.hall@btinternet.com www.kilmoryhall.com

BUTE
BACKPACKERS HOSTEL

Bute Backpackers, a friendly independent hostel with panoramic views of Rothesay seafront, has 40 beds with a mixture of single, twin, double and family rooms. The main house has a sea front sun lounge with woodburner and open fire. The self-catering kitchen is equipped to the highest standard and there is a large seafront dining room with catering facilities. Some of the rooms are en suite and there are separate male and female showers and toilets on each level. There is also a separate self-contained cottage dorm with its own fully equipped kitchen and bathroom. Other facilities include Sky TV, internet, WiFi access, drying room and laundry. There is a private car park for twelve cars and secure bike racks. There are regular live music sessions which includes open mic for any budding musos to join the fun. VisitScotland rated as 4 star.

DETAILS

- **Open** - All year, 24hr access, no curfew. Reception 10am - 10pm.
- **Number of beds** - 40: Main House 32 in 14 rooms; Cottage 8.
- **Booking** - Deposit only required for group bookings.
- **Price per night** - From £17.50 per person.
- **Public Transport** - Take train to Wemyes Bay Station and Ferry Port (40 mins from Glasgow Central). Then ferry to Rothesay, Isle of Bute. Hostel 900m from ferry or take a taxi (taxi rank adjacent to port) which costs approximately £2.50.
- **Directions** - Turn right as you leave ferry and walk straight ahead for 200m past the discovery centre and putting green. Continue straight ahead for another 250m and Bute Backpackers is on your left. By car turn right on to main road. Continue for 300m to the mini roundabout . Head straight on for a further 300m and the hostel and access to the private car park is adjacent to the main road on your left.

CONTACT: Reception
The Pier View, 36 Argyle Street, Rothesay, Isle of Bute, PA20 0AX
Tel: 01700 501876
butebackpackers@hotmail.com   www.butebackpackers.co.uk

BALMAHA
BUNKHOUSE / HOSTEL SCOTLAND

Set on the Banks of Loch Lomond right on the West Highland Way, Balmaha Bunkhouse offers 4 star quality assured accommodation at affordable prices. There is a self-catering kitchen and breakfast and bedding are available for a little extra cost. Need more pampering? Then try Bed & Breakfast in the main house with en-suite rooms and breathtaking views over the loch. Boat trips are available on Loch Lomond, or for those with experience, Kayaks and Canadian Canoes can be hired from £20 per day. A catamaran and Topper are also available. Balmaha House is right on the shores of Loch Lomond and just some 5 mins' paddling to the first of the islands (Inchcailloch), where you can hop and explore other islands with castles, deer, capercaillie and even wallabies. There are ancient graveyards with the burial place of Rob Roy`s cousin and some of the most scenic landscapes in the world. Ideal for walkers, sailors, fishermen, and those who just want to get away from it all. We look forward to welcoming you to the romantic, adventurous and beautiful experience of Loch Lomond.

DETAILS

- **Open** - All year, all day.
- **Number of beds** - 14: 1x6, 1x4 (family), 1x2 (double), 1x2 (twin).
- **Booking** - Please phone or email.
- **Price per night** - £15 per person. Sleeping bag hire £2. Breakfast £5 (full) or £3 (cont). B&B in house £35. No credit card facilities, nearest cash point 4 miles.
- **Public Transport** - Bus stop is 100 metres from the hostel.
- **Directions** - The last house in the village on the right hand side opposite the bay and the telephone box.

CONTACT: Bob or Debbie Redley
Balmaha, Loch Lomond, Stirlingshire, G63 0JQ
Tel: 01360 870 218 Mob: 07711 904 902
Balmahabunkhouse@aol.com www.balmahahouse.co.uk

Trossachs Tryst has been purpose-built on its own 8 acre site, set amidst beautiful scenery (on Sustrans route 7c) just outside the bustling tourist town of Callander. The 4 star hostel, which is the only one in the Trossachs area, opened in 1997, is finished to a very high standard and has won accolades in many guide books and websites. The rooms are all en-suite and are either 8, 6 or 4 bedded. The 4 bed family rooms have their own dining facilities and can be used as twin rooms on request. There is a spacious dining/common room, well equipped kitchen, and drying room. A large meeting/recreation room is also available and may be booked separately for conferences, parties, etc. There is an on-site Cycling Centre, which also sells basic provisions. Other activities available locally include hill walking, pony trekking, canoe hire/instruction, fishing and sailing.

DETAILS

- **Open** - All year, (Nov to Feb whole hostel bookings only), reception 8am - 9pm.
- **Number of beds** - 30.
- **Booking** - Booking advised at all times. Groups must book with deposit.
- **Price per night** - £16 to £30 including linen and continental breakfast. Group and family discounts on request.
- **Public Transport** - Nearest train station is at Stirling (15 miles). Nearest Citylink coach stop is at Callander (1.5 miles). Pick up from Callander can usually be arranged.
- **Directions** - GR 606 072. The hostel is situated one mile up Invertrossachs Rd from its junction with the A81 (Glasgow Rd) in Callander.

CONTACT: Mark or Janet
Invertrossachs Road, Callander, Perthshire, FK17 8HW
Tel: 01877 331200, Fax: 01877 331200
info@scottish-hostel.com www.trossachstryst.com

Culdees offers Bunkhouse and family accommodation overlooking Loch Tay, in the heart of Highland Perthshire. Ideal for just a weekend or for longer holidays whether you are a walker, cyclist, a Munro bagger, or a motorist. Culdees is especially popular with family gatherings and reunions. A small conference/ meeting room is also available. The Bunkhouse has a well equipped kitchen with dining area for 16 people. Equipped with a living room, television area and a large music room with a baby grand piano and other instruments, library, three Family Rooms each with a double-bed and two single beds, and one double room. All beds have individual reading lights, duvets, fresh linen and an extra pillow. A two-bedroomed cottage, sleeping 8, plus a double bed-settee in the sitting room, is also available. There is a big open barn, ideal for barbecues and gatherings. All accommodation is interlinked. Tourist Board 3 star recommended. Gold Award for Green Tourism.

DETAILS

- **Open** - All year. Please phone between 08:00-20:00 hrs.
- **Number of beds** - B'nkhouse 16: 4x4, Family Rooms 14: 3x4,1x2, cottage 8: 2x4.
- **Booking** - Book with credit or debit card.
- **Price per night** - From £18pp (bunkhouse), Concessions for young children in family rooms.
- **Public Transport** - Train: Pitlochry 25 miles. Bus: Aberfeldy 9miles. Local bus four days a week and the school bus will drop at hostel track. Taxi from Aberfeldy if stuck.
- **Directions** - From A827 Killin to Kenmore and Aberfeldy road turn off at signpost in Fearnan. In a quarter-mile turn left (Dalchiaran) signposted Culdees, Boreland Farm. OS Map NN718448.

CONTACT: Maryse or John
Culdees, Boreland Farm, Fearnan, nr Aberfeldy, Perthshire, PH15 2PG
Tel: 01887 830519, Mobile 07904 954116
contact@culdeesbunkhouse.co.uk www.culdeesbunkhouse.co.uk

COMRIE
CROFT

Offering self-catering facilities and just over an hour's drive from Edinburgh or Glasgow, the Croft is ideal for individuals, families or groups. Explore the mountains, have a go at adventure sports like high-ropes or white-water rafting, hold a team-building meeting or seminar, tour Scotland's oldest distillery, discover Loch Lomond National Park, swim in their own mill pond, find ruined castles, or simply read a book on the sofa.

Standard or en-suite private rooms, cosy sofa areas, games and movies are all available at the Croft. There is also an eco tent only campsite, shop, bike hire, and the croft's own 230 acre estate offering walks and purpose built mountain bike trails. New for 2012 is a purpose built hide where you can view their resident Ospreys and Red Kite feeding through high-powered scopes. Comrie Croft hold a 'Gold' award in the Green Tourism Business Scheme. Guests arriving by public transport or under their own steam get a discount.

DETAILS

- **Open** - All year, All day.
- **Number of beds** - 56 + 48 + 14 (3 units).
- **Booking** - Recommended.
- **Price per night** - From £15 adults, £7.50 U16, U5 free.
- **Public Transport** - Train stations: Dunblane, Stirling, or Perth. Our own bus stop is served by no. 15 from Perth (approx. every hour). Summer only Citylink service to Oban and Fort William. Ask for Comrie Croft.
- **Directions** - Signposted from A85 between Crieff (5miles) and Comrie (2miles).

CONTACT:
Comrie Croft, By Crieff/Comrie, Perthshire, PH7 4JZ
Tel: 01764 670140
info@comriecroft.com www.comriecroft.com

Pitlochry Backpackers Hotel provides what is without doubt some of the most luxurious backpacker's accommodation in Scotland.

Set in the heart of beautiful rural Perthshire it makes a terrific first stop for any trip into the Highlands. Historic Dunkeld, Blair Castle and numerous whisky distilleries are just a few of the attractions within easy reach, and some of Scotland's finest walking and cycling trails are right on the doorstep.

Pitlochry Backpackers provides all the comforts of a hotel plus the ambience and facilities of a hostel. Twin, double and dorm rooms are available plus a wonderful sunny lounge overlooking the main street.

DETAILS

■ **Open** - March to October, 7.30am-12pm, 4pm-11pm (please check at reception as times may vary).
■ **Number of beds** - 79.
■ **Booking** - Booking in advance not always essential, first night's payment required.
■ **Price per night** - £14 per night. ID required for check-in.
■ **Public Transport** - Buses will drop you off on Atholl Road and the hostel is only 1min walk. The train station exits onto Atholl Road also, only 5 mins' walk.
■ **Directions** - If coming from the south, follow the A9 until you see signposts for Pitlochry. Once in the town you'll reach Atholl Road and the hostel is just on the right-hand side, with a customer car park behind the building – you can get to this by taking the immediate right after the hostel entrance. If coming from the north, once on Atholl Road hostel is on your left, with parking just before the entrance to the left.

CONTACT: Receptionist
134 Atholl Road, Pitlochry, PH16 5AB
Tel: 01796 470044
pitlochry@scotlandstophostels.com www.scotlandstophostels.com

BY THE WAY
HOSTEL AND CAMPSITE

By The Way Hostel and Campsite can be found in the Loch Lomond National Park halfway between Arrochar's peaks and the grandeur of Glencoe. The site is aimed primarily at outdoor enthusiasts and with great walking (the West Highland Way passes by the hostel), climbing, and white water rafting, there is lots to be enthusiastic about (Munro-baggers can find 50 Munros within 20 miles). Accommodation options range from camping (with an indoor cooking/dining area and campers drying room), basic trekker huts/cabins (those using huts/cabins and camping need own cooking utensils etc), and a purpose built four star hostel with twin and double rooms as well as, dormitory accommodation, great self-catering facilities and drying room. For more comfort still there's a three bedroom chalet. By The Way is in Tyndrum with the village pub, shops, café and Tourist Information Centre nearby. The Glasgow to Fort William road is 250m from the site (far from the madding traffic noise) and both the Glasgow Oban and Glasgow Fort William trains stop in Tyndrum.

DETAILS

- **Open** - All year. Camping from April to October, 8am - 10am and 2pm - 8pm.
- **Number of beds** - 26 in hostel; 24 in huts; 50 camping.
- **Booking** - Always phone in advance. Deposit (Visa/Access) guarantees bed.
- **Price per night** - Hostel dorms from £16pp. Huts from £12pp. Camping £8pp
- **Public Transport** - Intercity coach and rail service pickup points in Tyndrum to Edinburgh, Glasgow, Fort William and Oban. Sleeper service to London.
- **Directions** - GR NN 327 302. Travelling on A82 follow sign in village for Tyndrum Lower Station. Hostel is immediately before station.

CONTACT: Kirsty Burnett
Lower Station Road, Tyndrum, FK20 8RY
Tel: 01838 400333
info@TyndrumByTheWay.com www.TyndrumByTheWay.com

Dunolly House is a three storey Victorian house set within its own grounds. The house has a combination of small and larger rooms and can sleep up to 48 people. Situated in the heart of Highland Perthshire Dunolly House is ideally situated for many established walks and tourist attractions. We are not far from Ben Lawers, on the Rob Roy Way, and Schiehallion is a mere 15 miles away. Cyclist are also welcome and many people taking part in the famous Lands End to John O'Groats route choose to break their journey with us.

For those looking for adventure we also have a fantastic range of adrenaline activities on site which can be booked by groups and individuals. Activities include: White Water Rafting, Canyoning, High Ropes, Duckying, Archery and Kayaking.

DETAILS

■ **Open** - All year, 24 hours.
■ **Number of beds** - 48.
■ **Booking** - Booking is normally necessary.
■ **Price per night** - From £14 per person.
■ **Public Transport** - Nearest train station is in Pitlochry (14 miles away). Citylink coaches stop at Ballinluig (11 miles away) and Pitlochry. Local buses to Aberfeldy.
■ **Directions** - Turn off the A9 Road at Ballinluig. Travel for 5 miles. Turn right at the T junction. Travel 6 miles until Aberfeldy. Continue through the main street and we are the last house on the right as you exit Aberfeldy.

CONTACT: Booking Office
Taybridge Drive, Aberfeldy, Perthshire, PH15 2BP
Tel: 01887 820298
info@dunollyadventures.co.uk www.dunollyadventures.co.uk

GULABIN
LODGE

Gulabin Lodge is beautifully situated in the heart of Glenshee at the foot of Beinn Gulabin and is the nearest accommodation to the Glenshee Ski Slopes. The lodge offers excellent accommodation for individuals, families and groups, has under-floor heating throughout and two cosy lounges with log fires for those colder months. All rooms have been tastefully decorated with some rooms having mezzanine platforms which are ideal for families. Based on site at the lodge there are many activities available for all ages and abilities (www.gulabinoutdoors.co.uk) including a Ski School and equipment hire facility for the winter months. The lodge is an ideal base for climbing, walking or mountain biking and mountain bike hire and guided trips are also available. Meals can be provided for groups and also transport to and from aiports and rail stations. Registered 4Star VisitScotland Activity Accommodation provider. AALA Registered L9768/R1801.

DETAILS

- **Open** - All year, 24 hours, arrive by 9pm.
- **Number of beds** - 37:- 9 rooms available.
- **Booking** - Booking advisable.
- **Price per night** - From £15pp self catering. Family rooms from £50. Full board available. Sole use available.
- **Public Transport** - Train and bus stations at Pitlochry (22 miles), Blairgowrie (20 miles), Glasgow (100 miles), Edinburgh (70 miles). Post bus calls half a mile away.
- **Directions** - Gulabin Lodge is on the A93 road at Spittal of Glenshee - 20 miles north of Blairgowrie and 19 miles south of Braemar. Transport can be arranged.

CONTACT: Darren and Tereza
Spittal of Glenshee, By Blairgowrie, PH10 7QE
Tel: 01250 885255 Mobile: 07799 847014
info@gulabinlodge.co.uk   www.gulabinlodge.co.uk

PROSEN HOSTEL

SCOTLAND

Glenprosen is the most intimate of the Angus Glens on the southernmost edge of the Cairngorm National Park. Two Munros, the Mayar and Driesh, link Glenprosen to the Cairngorms plateau. The Minister's Path leads over to Glen Clova, whilst a new footbridge and path along the prettiest stretch of the river Prosen connects to Glenisla and the Cateran Trail in Perthshire. Prosen Hostel was recently converted from an old school to provide accommodation for those using the upgraded East Cairngorms footpath network. Converted to the latest and greenest specification, the living room has a wood burning stove, internet connection, and raised area for admiring the view (and red squirrels) through the school's huge windows. A drying room and laundry facilities complete the cosy welcome. It sleeps a total of 18 in 4 bunkrooms, sleeping 4, 4 and 6 and a family room sleeping 4. The nearby village hall is available to rent for ceilidhs, music sessions, parties and celebrations. STB 4 star.

DETAILS

- **Open** - All year, all day.
- **Number of beds** - 18:1x6, 3x4.
- **Booking** - Book by phone or email.
- **Price per night** - £16 - £20 per person. Minimum periods apply for Christmas and New year.
- **Public Transport** - Trains Dundee; buses Kirriemuir (regular to Dundee and Forfar)
- **Directions** - From Kirriemuir follow B955 signed to Prosen, Clova and Cairngorms National Park. At Dykehead fork left. Carry on for 7 miles until public road ends at telephone kiosk. Turn acute right and follow tarmac 200m uphill to hostel.

CONTACT: Hector or Robert
Prosen Hostel, Balnaboth, Kirriemuir, Angus, DD8 4SA
Tel: 01575 540238/302
sih@prosenhostel.co.uk www.prosenhostel.co.uk

JEREMY INGLIS
OBAN HOSTEL

Jeremy Inglis Oban Hostel is only 150 yards from the station and the bus terminus in Oban.

Prices include a continental breakfast with muesli, toast and home-made jams, marmalade and vegemite. Tea and coffee are available at any time.

The rooms are mostly double and family size so you have some privacy. All linen is included in the price.

Kitchen facilities are provided and the hostel is heated by meter.

WiFi available.

DETAILS

- **Open** - All year, no curfew, access with key.
- **Number of beds** - 37.
- **Booking** - Booking preferred. Deposit in certain circumstances.
- **Price per night** - From £15 per person (in a shared room) including continental breakfast. Single rooms (when available) £22.
- **Public Transport** - Nearest train and Citylink drop off 150 metres from hostel. Ferries to islands 350 metres. For ferry enquiries phone 01631 566688.
- **Directions** - The hostel is in Airds Crescent, one of the streets off Argyll Square. The hostel is on the second floor, pink door.

CONTACT: Jeremy Inglis, Katrin or Michael
21 Airds Crescent, Oban, Argyll, PA34 5SJ
Tel: 01631 565065 Fax: 01631 565933
jeremyinglis@mctavishs.freeserve.co.uk

CORRAN
HOUSE

Corran House is part of a Victorian terrace with magnificent seascapes across the bay to the Isle of Kerrera and the hills of Mull. There is a warm welcome for visitors and reasonably priced accommodation for singles, couples, families and groups. The house has a large self-catering kitchen, spacious TV lounge, comfortable, commodious, well appointed guest rooms and 4 bed dormitories with generous size beds. Most rooms have en-suite facilities. Corran House is well situated for exploring Argyll and visiting the inner Hebrides. It is only a short walk along the sea front to the bus, train and ferry terminals. Downstairs is Markie Dans bar with patio and spectacular views. The pub offers great highland hospitality, tasty meals, live entertainment, widescreen TV, pool table and a late licence all year round to enable the discerning drinker to sample the best range of malt whiskies on the west coast. Pony trekking trips available with prior booking.

DETAILS

- **Open** - All year, reception 10am-9pm. Check in after 3pm.
- **Number of beds** - 36: 7x4: 1x2: 1x6. plus Guest rooms: 11.
- **Booking** - Advisable. Credit card secures bed. Early/late arrival with notice.
- **Price per night** - Bunk room from £15pp. Guest rooms from £25pp.
- **Public Transport** - Oban train, bus and ferry terminals are 900m from the house.
- **Directions** - Corran House overlooks Oban Bay to the west of the town centre. From the Tourist Information and all the Oban transport terminals, with the sea on your left, walk along George Street past the Columba Hotel into Corran Esplanade. Follow the seafront for 300m. Corran House is on your right above Markie Dans Bar.

CONTACT:
1 Victoria Crescent, Corran Esplanade, Oban, Argyll, PA34 5PN
Tel: 01631 566040 Fax: 01631 566854
enquiries@corranhouseoban.co.uk www.corranhouseoban.co.uk

OBAN
BACKPACKERS

Oban Backpackers Plus has become many people's favourite hostel thanks to its friendly atmosphere, excellent facilities and beautiful seaside town setting. There's an enormous self-catering kitchen, a pool table and other games and lots of information from our knowledgeable staff about Oban and Argyll. Oban is a town with spectacular views across to the islands - the view at dusk from McCaig's Tower can provide an amazing sunset. The bustle of fishing boats, ferries, yachts and seabirds make the waterfront a lovely place to be. Ferries leave Oban to the many beautiful Scottish Isles. Ancient standing stones, medieval castles, hairy coos and whisky distilleries are all in the area. The best fish and chips in Scotland are within 200 metres. There is a great minibus available for transfers and our famous custom made tours.

DETAILS

■ **Open** - All year, Reception open 7am - 10.30 pm. Sometimes closed in the middle of day but phone always manned.
■ **Number of beds** - 54: 4 x 6, 1 x 8, 1 x 10, 1 x 12.
■ **Booking** - Booking is strongly recommended but not essential – deposit equivalent to first night's accommodation to be paid in full to confirm the booking.
■ **Price per night** - From £14.90 pp, private rooms from £17.90 pp.
■ **Public Transport** - Close to Oban train station and Citylink buses.
■ **Directions** - From A85 turn left onto Deanery Brae as you come into Oban. Follow the road onto Breadalbane Street. Oban Backpackers is at the bottom of the street on the left, with a big 'Backpackers' sign. By bus or train - walk along the waterfront through town, keeping sea on left. Continue straight up George Street, past cinema on the right, then the Taj Mahal restaurant. Hostel is straight ahead on the right.

CONTACT: Receptionist
Breadalbane Street, Oban, Argyll PA34 5PH
Tel: 01631 567189
info@backpackersplus.com   www.obanbackpackers.com

The Lodge is located on a peaceful and idyllic Inner Hebridean island to the south of Mull which boasts magnificent sandy beaches, ancient forests and beautiful lochs. The place is teeming with wildlife which includes dolphins, seals, otters and many rare species of bird. There are ancient standing stones and a 14th century priory with exceptional carved Celtic tombstones. The famous Colonsay House gardens and café are open to visitors to enjoy twice a week. The hostel offers mountain bikes for hire and tennis racquets to use on the free court. The pub, café, shop and village hall, where there are regular Ceilidhs, are all within three miles. Fresh lobster, crab and langoustines can be bought from fishing boats in the harbour and don't forget the best oysters in the world are grown on Colonsay. The lodge is a refurbished former gamekeeper's house with bothies. It is centrally heated and has 3 large twin, 3 small twin and 1 family room. It has a large dining/cooking/sitting area and a separate sitting room with a log fire. Bed linen provided.

DETAILS

- **Open** - All year, 24 hours.
- **Number of beds** - 16   6 x 2 : 1 x 4.
- **Booking** - Required 24 hours in advance.
- **Price per night** - £20pp twin, £14pp bothy, £18pp 4 bed dorm.
- **Public Transport** - Train and coach in Oban. Ferry to Colonsay takes 2.5 hours.
- **Directions** - Ferry departs Oban 5 times a week April to October, Sun, Mon, Wed, Thurs, Fri (rest of year Mon, Wed, Fri). From Kennacraig and Port Askaig, Islay on Weds. Transport from the harbour can be arranged if required.

CONTACT: The Manager
Colonsay Estate Cottages, Isle of Colonsay, Argyll, PA61 7YP
Tel: 01951 200312
cottages@colonsayestate.co.uk   www.colonsayestate.co.uk

MILLHOUSE
HOSTEL

Tiree is an idyllic Hebridean Island, perfect for outdoor pursuits, wildlife enthusiasts, and those yet to experience the total tranquillity of stunning white beaches and crystal clear seas.

A warm welcome and excellent facilities await you at Millhouse. Bikes are for hire to explore the island, visit the lighthouse museum, 'ping' the ringing stone, find the standing stones, wonder at the Machair flowers or watch the seals. Watersports take place on adjacent Loch Bhasapol, and the secluded Cornaig beach is a ten minute walk away.

There is a resident RSPB warden on the island and a bird hide near the hostel. For walkers, Millhouse is on the Tiree Pilgrimage route linking the ancient chapels and monuments around the island. STB 4 star Hostel.

DETAILS

■ **Open** - Mar-Oct, open in winter by arrangement, open all day (quiet after 11.30pm, check out 9.30am).

■ **Number of beds** - 16/18 : 2 x 2/3 : 2 x 6 plus 3 family rooms : 12 beds: 3 x 4.

■ **Booking** - Advisable, please check vacancies before boarding the ferry.

■ **Price per night** - Twin £18pp, Dorms £15pp, Family £45 - £60 per room.

■ **Public Transport** - Caledonian MacBrayne ferry from Oban to Tiree or Flybe flight from Glasgow. Local Ring and Ride bus 01879 220419.

■ **Directions** - From ferry turn right at T junction, then left at next fork. Continue for 4 miles to Millhouse Hostel.

CONTACT: Judith Boyd
Cornaigmore, Isle of Tiree, Argyll, PA77 6XA
Tel: 01879 220435
tireemillhouse@yahoo.co.uk www.tireemillhouse.co.uk

IONA
HOSTEL

Tucked into the rocky outcrops at the north end of the island, Iona Hostel has spectacular views to Staffa and the Treshnish Isles, and beyond Rhum to the Black Cuillins of Skye. The hostel is situated on the working croft of Lagandorain (the hollow of the otter). This land has been worked for countless generations, creating the familiar Hebridean patchwork of wildflower meadow, crops and grazing land, home to an amazing variety of plants and birds. It offers quiet sanctuary for those that seek it, within easy reach of island activities.

Iona Hostel is new, well-reviewed and recommended. Whether travelling on your own, with friends, or as part of one of our many visiting groups, Iona Hostel offers you a warm welcome - with the best views this side of heaven.
4 star STB. Green Tourism Gold Award.
We regret no dogs are allowed.

DETAILS

- **Open** - All year, closed 11am-1pm for cleaning - no curfew.
- **Number of beds** - 21: 1 x 2 : 2 x 4 : 1 x 5 : 1 x 6.
- **Booking** - Is strongly advised, 50% deposit.
- **Price per night** - £19.50 adult £16.50 under 10s (bedding included).
- **Public Transport** - Caledonian Macbrayne ferry service from Oban or Mull 08705 650000. For buses on Mull 01546 604695. Taxi service on Iona 0781 0325990.
- **Directions** - You cannot bring your car onto Iona, but there is free parking in Fionnphort on Mull at the Columba Centre. Iona Hostel is the last building at the north end of the island, 2 km from the pier and up beyond the abbey.

CONTACT:
Iona Hostel, Iona, Argyll, PA76 6SW
Tel: 01681 700781
info@ionahostel.co.uk www.ionahostel.co.uk

SHIELING
HOLIDAYS

Shieling Holidays is right on the sea, with views to Ben Nevis. There are regular sightings of seals and otters, and sometimes of porpoises, dolphins and eagles. Stroll to the ferry, pub, shops, and swimming pool. Walk to Duart Castle, home of the Chief of Clan Maclean.

Catch the bus for Tobermory; for Iona (where Columba brought Christianity to Scotland) and for Staffa (home of puffins, and inspiration for Mendelssohn's overture 'Fingal's Cave'). Your accommodation is in Shielings, unique carpeted cottage tents, made by them on Mull, which are clean, bright and spacious, and have real beds for 2, 4, or 6.

There are super showers, and communal Shielings with woodburner, TV, payphone and launderette.

DETAILS

- **Open** - April to October, 24 hours (Reception 8am - 10pm).
- **Number of beds** - 18:   6 x 2 : 1 x 6.
- **Booking** - Please email a booking enquiry from our website.
- **Price per night** - £13 pp. Under 15s £9 pp. Bedding £3pp.
- **Public Transport** - From Glasgow, rail (08457 484950) or bus (0871 266 3333) at 12.00, ferry (01680 812343) at 16.00 from Oban, arrive Mull 16.46; back by 10.55 ferry, arrive Glasgow by 1600. Please check times before travel.
- **Directions** - Grid Ref 724 369. From ferry, left on the A849 to Iona. After 400 metres, left opposite church past old pier to reception - 800 metres in all.

CONTACT: David Gracie
Craignure, Isle of Mull, Argyll, PA65 6AY
Tel: 01680 812496
info@shielingholidays.co.uk www.shielingholidays.co.uk

GLENCOE
INDEPENDENT HOSTEL SCOTLAND

Glencoe Independent Hostel is centred around an old highland croft in the heart of Glencoe, offering great value accommodation for groups, families and individuals. It is set in secluded and peaceful woodland midway between Glencoe village and the Clachaig Inn with immediate access to world class cycling, walking, climbing and kayaking and 20 mins from Glencoe Ski Centre and the West Highland Way, 40 minutes from Nevis Range. The hostel has 4 rooms, a lounge with open fire, cooking and dining facilities. The Alpine bunkhouse sleeps 16 in 3 rooms, ideal for outdoor activity and school groups. There are brand new caravans for 4 to 6 people and a log cabin for 2 to 3 people. The site has a top class drying room, bike storage, and mountains all around. Free WiFi in reception.

DETAILS

■ **Open** - All year (phone in Nov and Dec), 9am - 9 pm.
■ **Number of beds** - Hostel: 26, bunkhouse: 16, 4 caravans of 4/6, Log cabin: 2/3.
■ **Booking** - Booking advised in summer. 30% non refundable deposit (min. £10).
■ **Price per night** - From £11.50 to £22 per person.
■ **Public Transport** - 1.5 miles from bus stop in Glencoe Village (crossroads). Citylink buses 914, 915 and 916 from Skye, Fort William, Glasgow. Bus 44 from Fort William and Kinlochleven. For West Highland Way take White Corries near Kingshouse Hotel to Glencoe Crossroads (20 mins) then 1.5 miles walk.
■ **Directions** - From A82 south, take right turn for Clachaig Inn, 1 miles after pub on left. From north, take left turn for Kinlochleven, then immediate right to Glencoe Village. 1 mile out of village on right.

CONTACT: Keith or Davina
Glencoe Independent Hostel, Glencoe, Argyll, PH49 4HX
Tel: 01855 811906
info@glencoehostel.co.uk www.glencoehostel.co.uk

CORRAN
BUNKHOUSE

Corran Bunkhouse 4 star accommodation is situated in a stunning lochside location surrounded by mountains in the magnificent Highlands of Scotland, 8 miles south of Fort William and 7 miles north of Glencoe. The Corran Bunkhouse is made up of two fully equipped self-catering bunkhouses which between them can offer comfortable accommodation for up to 32 people. One bunkhouse sleeps 12 and the other sleeps 20 making Corran Bunkhouse an ideal base for small and large groups. Individual travellers are welcome and the room sizes make the bunkhouse ideal for family groups. All bedrooms have a TV and ensuite facilities. There are fully equipped kitchen/dining areas, drying room, central heating, laundry facilities, private parking and a steam room situated in the smaller bunkhouse. Children and pets welcome. Group discounts. Come and enjoy the many outdoor activities available in the area such as climbing, walking, canoeing, kayaking, cycling and mountain biking.

      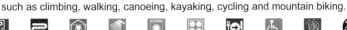

DETAILS

- **Open** - All year, all day (reception 9am -10pm).
- **Number of beds** - 32: 8x2 1x3 2x4 1x5
- **Booking** - Advisable but not necessary - major credit cards accepted.
- **Price per night** - £18 per person, £16 per person for block bookings of 12 or more. £24 for single occupancy. Prices included bedding and power.
- **Public Transport** - Trains at Fort William (8 mile bus or taxi ride to hostel). Regular busses toward Fort William from the south and from Inverness stop 100m from hostel (ask for Onich). Check the Citylink web site for bus details.
- **Directions** - Corran Bunkhouse lies on the Onich side of the Corran/Ardgour Ferry 8 miles south of Fort William on the A82 trunk road from Glasgow to Inverness.

CONTACT: Helen Richardson
Onich, Fort William, PH33 6SE
Tel: 01855 821000
corranbunkhouse@btconnect.com www.corranbunkhouse.co.uk

CALLUNA

Situated within fifteen minutes' walk of Fort William High Street, Calluna is ideal for short or long stays, for individual or groups. The modern accommodation consists of one six-bed flat, an alpine loft (3-5 beds) and two apartments (8 beds each). Bedding is supplied, along with spacious kitchens, comfortable lounges and efficient drying rooms. On the spot advice from Alan Kimber (mountain guide) and an on-site indoor bouldering wall, with over 60 problems set by David Macleod (Britain's best rock and ice climber), make this an ideal all weather climbing venue. Waterproofs, boots, axes, crampons and mountaineering courses are also available (see website for details). Calluna is well known for peace, quiet and fine views over Loch Linnhe to the hills of Ardgour. A popular base for climbing and canoeing groups, families and individual globe trotters. Plenty of parking for mini-buses and trailers. Lecture room available for groups.

DETAILS

- **Open** - All year, 24 hours (keys supplied).
- **Number of beds** - 26: 5 x 2 (twin beds), 4 x 4.
- **Booking** - Phone up beforehand.
- **Price per night** - Dorm beds £16 a night and twin beds £18pp a night.
- **Public Transport** - Fort William train and coach/bus stations are 20 mins walk away. Alan and Sue offer a free lift from the stations when available - just phone.
- **Directions** - From A82 south roundabout (by the Loch and West End Hotel), go uphill on Lundavra Rd, after 500 metres turn left uphil onto Connochie Rd (between four-storey flats). Follow for 200 metres uphill (do not take right turns). Look for sign.

CONTACT: Alan or Sue
Heathercroft, Fort William, Inverness-shire, PH33 6RE
Tel: 01397 700451 Fax: 01397 700489
info@fortwilliamholiday.co.uk www.fortwilliamholiday.co.uk

FORT WILLIAM
BACKPACKERS

Deep in the Highlands, surrounded by spectacular mountain scenery lies Fort William, a mecca for those with a spirit of adventure. You can start (or end) the 'West Highland Way' in Fort William, hike or bike along mountain trails, go for a boat trip on the sea loch or just take it easy amidst the wonderful scenery. Even in winter Fort William stays busy with skiing, snow-boarding, mountaineering and ice-climbing. Nestling on a hillside above the town, with wonderful views, our characterful and comfy hostel provides everything you'll need after a day in the hills. In the evening put your feet up in our elegant lounge in front of a real fire or stroll down to the choice of local pubs. Ben Nevis, Britain's highest mountain, is just around the corner and below it is Glen Nevis, perhaps Scotland's prettiest glen, with wonderful waterfalls and ancient pine forest. Dramatic and eerie, Glencoe awaits a few miles away for an excellent day trip.

DETAILS

- **Open** - All year, all day. Reception 7am-12pm and 5pm-10.30pm (times may vary).
- **Number of beds** - 38.
- **Booking** - Booking not always essential, first nights payment required for booking.
- **Price per night** - £14 per person. ID required for check-in.
- **Public Transport** - Train and bus stations are only 5/10 minute walk from hostel.
- **Directions** - From north on the A82 go right at roundabout towards town centre. Turn left onto Victoria Road, then left at fork onto Alma Road. From south on the A82 go straight over first roundabout, At second roundabout go right onto Belford Road following Inverness signs, then turn right up Victoria Road then into Alma Road at left fork. From stations walk past supermarket, turn left before the underpass, heading onto the Belford Road. The hostel is just a bit further up, on Alma Road on the right.

CONTACT: Receptionist
Alma Road, Fort William, PH33 6HB
Tel: 01397 700 711
fortwilly@scotlandstophostels.com www.scotlandstophostels.com

Bank Street Lodge is situated 100 metres from Fort William High Street which has numerous shops, pubs, restaurants and banks. There is a fully equipped kitchen with cooker, fridge, microwave, cutlery and crockery provided. The common room lounge has a TV, it also provides tables and chairs for eating self prepared meals, and a snack vending machine.

All bedding is provided. Some rooms are en-suite (twins, doubles and family). WiFi is also now available in our lounge/TV room. The Stables Restaurant, at the front of the building, serves fine food for lunches and dinners (also breakfast from May to September) - treat yourself! Fort William is an ideal base from which to enjoy walking, climbing, cycling or mountain biking. The world-renowned Nevis Range Mountain Bike Trails and Ski Centre are only a short distance from the town centre. Three star STB rating.

DETAILS

- **Open** - All year, 24 hour reception
- **Number of beds** - 43: 6 x 4: 4 x 3: 1 x 7.
- **Booking** - Booking advised. Deposit required for long stays or groups.
- **Price per night** - From £16 or £19.00 per person. Group rates available.
- **Public Transport** - Train and bus stations at Fort William, 500 metres from Lodge.
- **Directions** - Head for Town Centre via the underpass, turn left after Tesco supermarket on Bank Street, then head up the hill for 150 metres. Hostel is above the Stables Restaurant. Car parking is available.

CONTACT: Kenny / Reception
Bank Street, Fort William, PH33 6AY
Tel: 01397 700070
bankstreetlodge@btconnect.com www.bankstreetlodge.co.uk

BLACKWATER
HOSTEL & CAMPSITE

Blackwater Hostel is in the centre of the scenic village of Kinlochleven surrounded by the Mamore mountains midway between Glencoe and Ben Nevis. An ideal stopover for families, cyclists, walkers, climbers and those who are walking the West Highland Way. There are high and low-level, half-hour to full-day walks, all with great views, or if you prefer there is a regular bus service from the village to Glencoe, Ballachulish and Fort William. Water sports are available nearby. Ice Factor, Europe's first indoor 14 metre ice/climbing wall is only 200 metres away. This is comfortable, high-quality STB 4 star bunkhouse accommodation. All rooms have en-suite facilities, TV and central heating. Facilities include self-catering kitchens, lounge, dining conference area and drying room. There are supermarkets, pubs and restaurants all within two minutes' walk. The campsite has a drying room, showers and covered area.

DETAILS

- **Open** - All year, 24 hours.
- **Number of beds** - 39 - 2, 3, 4, 8 bedded rooms.
- **Booking** - Essential (between 8am-8pm).
- **Price per night** - £15pp, twin room £35 (including bedding).Sole occupancy £500.
- **Public Transport** - The nearest train station is Fort William and National Express travels from Glasgow to Glencoe and Fort William. Regular bus service to Kinlochleven all day from Glencoe, Ballachulish and Fort William.
- **Directions** - GR 188 618. OS sheet 41. From A82 Glasgow to Fort William road at Glencoe turn right to Kinlochleven. The hostel is situated near the centre of Kinlochleven. Just past the Co-op a large sign with an arrow will point you to Hostel.

CONTACT: Caroline
Lab Road, Kinlochleven, Argyll, PH50 4SG
Tel: 01855 831253 or 0791 9366116
black.water@virgin.net www.blackwaterhostel.co.uk

Coorie Doon is an eco-friendly timber cabin with under floor heating and views onto Ben Nevis, Glen Coe, Aonach Mor and the Mammores. The two en-suite bedrooms can be hired separately and are each fitted with a triple bunk, with a double bed (lower) and a single bunk (upper). There is an open plan kitchen-lounge area, a balcony, drying room and a sauna which is great to relax in after a long day on the hill. The kitchen has everything needed to cook a nourishing meal and the lounge has a sofa, foldaway dining table and chairs. There is also a TV with iPod dock and DVD, CD player, and a selection of reference books and maps. Outside there is parking, a bike bunker and racks and basement lockers which are ideal for storing kayaks, canoes, skis, etc. The deck overlooks a pond and burn abounding with wildlife, (special care needed with small children). The area is ideal for climbing, snowsports, sea or river paddling, walking and biking. Coorie Doon is on the Great Glen Way, near to the West Highland Way and surrounded by forestry tracks. Only 10 mins drive from Nevis Range and 30 mins from Glencoe Mountain Resort. 5 star Hostel VisitScotland

DETAILS

- **Open** - All year, All day, check in 4pm-8pm, check out 10am.
- **Number of beds** - 6: 2x3 (each room as one double and a single bed).
- **Booking** - Full payment should be made at time of booking.
- **Price per night** - Room £60, hostel £110. Includes bedding and fuel. Sauna extra.
- **Public Transport** - Nearest trains at Banavie Stn. On bus routes no. 45 & 46.
- **Directions** - On the A82 take the A830 signed for Mallaig, After about 1 mile, turn right into Banavie, then immediate left onto Old Banavie Road.

CONTACT: Barbara
Coorie Doon, Old Banavie Road, Banavie, Fort William, PH33 7PZ
Tel: 07767 062730
cooriedoon@banavie.com   www.banavie.com

SMIDDY
BUNKHOUSE

A friendly welcome at this comfortable, family run, mountain hostels in a loch-side location overlooking the Caledonian Canal. The pine clad interior gives a cosy, friendly atmosphere. Stunning mountains and water at the doorstep with the meeting of the West Highland Way and Great Glen Way. Hot showers. Fully equipped kitchens available at all times (food available from local shop until 10pm daily). Use of two efficient drying/laundry rooms. Bedding provided. Fully heated for all year round use. Outdoor information, daily weather and snow reports. Advice/instruction available from resident mountain and water based instructors and guides for: winter and summer walking/climbing; river, loch and sea kayaking; dinghy sailing. Hire for sea and river of kayaks/open canoes, dinghy and other equipment. AALA licensed outdoor centre and DofE Approved Activity Provider. Group and family accommodation. Meeting/lecture room facilities available by arrangement.

DETAILS

■ **Open** - All year, all day (with key). Key deposit required.
■ **Number of beds** - 24 : 3x4, 2x6.
■ **Booking** - Book on-line or Telephone to pre-book.
■ **Price per night** - £13.50 - £16.50 (seasonal) pp (incl. bedding).
■ **Public Transport** - Two minutes' walk from Corpach Railway Station on the Mallaig Line. Three miles from Fort William (trains from Glasgow and London).
■ **Directions** - Take A82 north out of Fort William towards Inverness. After one mile take A830 north towards Mallaig and follow for 2 miles to village of Corpach. Turn left before shops, signposted 'Snowgoose Mountain Centre'. The hostel is 30yds on left.

CONTACT: John or Tina
Snowgoose Mountain Centre, Station Road, Corpach, Fort William, PH33 7JH
Tel: 01397 772467
ihg@highland-mountain-guides.co.uk www.highland-mountain-guides.co.uk

FARR COTTAGE
LODGE
SCOTLAND

Farr Cottage is a 4 star hostel situated in Corpach just 4 miles from Fort William town centre, with a breath-taking view of Ben Nevis and across Loch Linnhe, in the outdoor pursuits capital of Scotland. There is a full range of in-house facilities including cable television in the lounge, licensed bar, self-catering facilities, drying room and laundry service. Newly installed central heating and hot showers.

We also organise outdoor pursuits which comprise white water rafting, canyoning, climbing, abseiling, skiing, snowboarding, fishing, golf and many many more! We can provide evening meals, breakfast, picnic lunches and we will ensure you have the break or holiday of a lifetime with us. Our professional team are geared to meet your needs and requirements.

DETAILS

- **Open** - All year.
- **Number of beds** - Cottage 30: 2 x double, 2 x 8,1 x 10. Lodge 6: 2 x twins 2 x singles. Both buildings fully self-contained.
- **Booking** - Advance booking advised.
- **Price per night** - £15pp, From £17pp in double room. Group rates available.
- **Public Transport** - Corpach train station is 200m from the hostel. The nearest Citylink service is three miles away at Fort William. Taxi fare from Fort William centre is approximately £7.50.
- **Directions** - Follow the A82 north from Fort William centre towards Inverness for 1.5 miles. Turn left at the A830 to Mallaig. Follow this road for 1.5 miles into Corpach. We are on the right.

CONTACT: Cliff or Kirsty
Corpach, Fort William, PH33 7LR
Tel: 01397 772315
mail@farrcottage.com www.farrcottage.com

Àite Cruinnichidh, 15 miles northeast of Fort William, occupies a unique sheltered spot adjacent to the Monessie Gorge; explore remote glens, mountain passes and lochs. Numerous easy walks within minutes of the hostel and seven magnificent canoeing rivers within 20 miles. The location is also ideal for climbing (rock and ice), mountain biking, skiing or just relaxing. A warm, peaceful, friendly, country hostel in a converted barn. Àite Cruinnichidh has been renovated to high standards and sleeps 32 in five rooms of four, one of six, one twin and one double/family room en-suite. All bedding supplied. A fully equipped kitchen/dining room, sitting room, excellent showers. Additional facilities: sauna suite, garden, seminar room, dark room, use of maps, advice on walking/cycling routes. Groups and individuals welcome. We do not have wheelchair access but we are glad to accommodate people with all forms of disability whenever we can, and know some sign language.

DETAILS

- **Open** - All year, all day.
- **Number of beds** - 32: 1x6, 5x4, 1x twin, 1x family/double en suite.
- **Booking** - Booking advised, 50% deposit.
- **Price per night** - £15 per person.
- **Public Transport** - Roy Bridge train station and bus stop (2 miles) has several trains and buses to and from Fort William daily. Pick up available from Roy Bridge.
- **Directions** - From Fort William follow A82 for 10 miles to Spean Bridge, turn right onto A86 for 3 miles to Roy Bridge. Pass though village and continue for 2 miles. The hostel is on right 100m after Glenspean Lodge Hotel on left.

CONTACT: Gavin or Nicola
1 Achluachrach, By Roy Bridge, Near Fort William, PH31 4AW
Tel: 01397 712315
gavin@highland-hostel.co.uk   www.highland-hostel.co.uk

INSH HALL
LODGE

Situated between Loch Insh and the foothills of Glenfeshie, Insh Hall Lodge provides comfortable double, twin and family rooms on a room-only or B&B basis. Rooms are equipped with bed linen and TVs. Facilities include large meeting room, laundry/drying room, sauna and mini gym, outdoor volleyball and basketball, as well as private car parking. Meals are available in the Boathouse Restaurant situated by the shore, 120 yds from the lodge.

Loch Insh Watersports provides a range of accessible watersports on-site. This is also the starting point for many local walks, lochside trails and cycle routes. Loch Insh is on Sustrans Route 7 Cycle Way. Anyone staying two nights or more between April and October has free use of the water sports equipment or between November and March has free use of dry ski slope - from 8.30 to 10.00 and from 4.00 to 5.30pm.

DETAILS

- **Open** - All year, All day.
- **Number of beds** - 28: double, twin and family rooms.
- **Booking** - Booking is recommended but not always required. Deposit taken.
- **Price per night** - From £16 - £42 per person.
- **Public Transport** - Trains at Aviemore and Kingussie (7 miles from Loch Insh). Nearest airport is Inverness, approximately one hour north of Loch Insh.
- **Directions** - Situated near Kincraig, 7 miles south of Aviemore, 7 miles north of Kingussie on the B9152, follow signs for Loch Insh Watersports. Local bus routes from Aviemore to Kincraig, approx. 1 mile from the Lodge.

CONTACT: Receptionist
Insh Hall, Kincraig, Inverness-shire, PH21 1NU
Tel: 01540 651272 Fax: 01540 651208
office@lochinsh.com www.lochinsh.com

BEN NEVIS INN
BUNKHOUSE

The Ben Nevis Inn is located in one of the most beautiful and famous areas of Scotland, at the very foot of Ben Nevis, Britain's highest mountain. The Inn sits in Braveheart country at the start of the Ben Nevis path and a mile from the end of the West Highland Way. The bunkhouse offers everything that walkers and mountaineers will need, with self-catering facilities including a large kitchen, comfortable bunks, and a separate drying area. The bathrooms were refurbished in 2010. All bunks have a duvet and all bed linen (no sleeping bags allowed). The bunkroom sleeps 24 divided into three sections and has some great views onto Glen Nevis. The Inn offers an extensive menu with plenty of local produce and something to suit all tastes. There is frequent live music, check out events on the Inn's website. The bunkhouse is 20 minutes' walk from the centre of Fort William which has cafes, provisions shops, outdoor-ware shop, pubs, and a well-equipped and recently refurbished leisure centre with swimming pool.

DETAILS

- **Open** - All year, all day.
- **Number of beds** - 24: 3x8.
- **Booking** - Strongly recommended. Book online with full payment.
- **Price per night** - £15.50 per person per night.
- **Public Transport** - Train station and bus stop in town centre, 2 miles (30 mins walk) from bunkhouse. There is a taxi rank outside the station.
- **Directions** - From A82 in Fort William take road to Inverness. Just before lights turn right onto Achintee Rd towards Claggan. At Spar shop turn right and follow road.

CONTACT:
The Ben Nevis Inn, Claggan, Achintee, Fort William, Inverness-shire, PH33 6TE
Tel: 01397 701227
info@ben-nevis-inn.co.uk www.ben-nevis-inn.co.uk

ARIUNDLE
BUNKHOUSE

The Ariundle Centre is located at the beginning of the Ariundle Oakwoods, close to glorious walks, bird song, climbing, cycling, canoeing and fishing.

It is a friendly family run business with a licensed restaurant, tea room, craft shop and bunkhouse. The 4 star Bunkhouse sleeps 26 people, the rooms are large and airy and there is a drying area and self-catering facilities. Linen is supplied, towels can be hired for 50p. The Bunkhouse is ideal for walkers and climbers. Groups, individuals and families are all welcome and family rooms are available. Cooked breakfasts, morning coffee, light lunches and scrumptious home baking are available in the restaurant and the sandwiches and baking make ideal packed lunches. Candlelit suppers are served using local products, sometimes with a local musician to entertain. The Centre can cater for parties or weddings with guests sleeping in the bunkhouse. The village of Strontian has a petrol station and a well stocked shop.

DETAILS

- **Open** - All year.
- **Number of beds** - 26: 2x8, 2x4,1x2.
- **Booking** - Advance bookings accepted all year
- **Price per night** - From £16 pp. Cont. b/fst £4. Grp. discount for advance payment.
- **Public Transport** - 1 mile from the nearest public transport.
- **Directions** - If travelling from north, east or south the quickest way to arrive at the Centre is to take the A82 to the Corran Ferry and then follow the road to Strontian. (Turn left when you come off the ferry).

CONTACT: Kate Campbell
Ariundle Centre, Strontian, PH36 4JA
Tel: 01967 402279
ariundle@aol.com www.ariundlecentre.co.uk

BRAEMAR LODGE
BUNKHOUSE

Surrounded by the beauty of Deeside, Braemar Lodge Hotel and Bunkhouse is in a quiet setting only a two minute walk from the village itself. Braemar Lodge Hotel was formerly a Victorian shooting lodge and is set in extensive grounds two minutes from the centre of Braemar in the heart of Royal Deeside.

The great value Bunkhouse provides comfortable accommodation for up to 12 people within the hotel grounds. The bunkhouse is equipped with two shower rooms, one of which is suitable for wheelchair access. The bunkhouse also has good drying and laundry facilities, excellent for damp clothes and ski boots. A generous fully equipped kitchen is available for all your self-catering needs. Guests are also welcome to use the hotel's excellent dining facilities if a rest from self-catering is required. All bed linen and towels are supplied for the duration of your stay.

DETAILS

- **Open** - All year, all day.
- **Number of beds** - 12: 3x4.
- **Booking** - Book by phone or email.
- **Price per night** - From £14 per person.
- **Public Transport** - Aberdeen airport 59 miles. Railway stations at Perth (50 miles) and Aberdeen. Buses to Braemar from Aberdeen where the bus and rail station are side by side. Two minute walk to hotel from Braemar village bus stop.
- **Directions** - The hotel is situated on the A93 on the left if you are arriving form the south. Two minutes' walk from the village centre.

CONTACT: Reception
6 Glenshee Rd, Braemar, Aberdeenshire, AB35 5YQ
Tel: 01339 741627 , Fax: 01339 741627
mail@braemarlodge.co.uk www.braemarlodge.co.uk

CRAGGAN OUTDOORS
BUNKHOUSE & BOTHY SCOTLAND

The Bunkhouse and Bothy are part of Craggan Outdoors activity centre which offers one of the widest ranges of outdoor activities available in the Scottish Highlands. The TripAdvisor top-rated outdoor centre in Scotland since 2009 and twice short-listed for 'Best Visitor Experience' in the Highlands & Islands Tourism Awards. The centre accommodates groups from two to sixty plus people, with or without activities. There is a licensed Clubhouse Cafe on-site, with tasty meals and breathtaking views. The Bunkhouse is a light, and airy farmhouse that sleeps up to 27 people in three rooms. It is double-glazed and has a large well equipped kitchen, dining/common room and clean bright bathrooms on a 1:5 ratio. The Bothy is a converted steading with one bunk-room sleeping six people, wheelchair-accessible wet-room, kitchen/dining area and wood burner for cosy evenings. Both buildings are centrally heated and have TV/DVD/CD/MP3, books and games. Located in the Cairngorms National Park at the heart of the central highlands, close to River Spey, Speyside Way, Dava Way and 30 minutes' drive from winter-sports at Cairngorm and The Lecht.

DETAILS

- **Open** - All year. All day
- **Number of beds** - Bunkhouse 27: 1x12,1x11,1x4 Bothy: 6.
- **Booking** - Book by phone or email.
- **Price per night** - From £13 - £19pp. & one-off fee of £6.50 if bedding is required.
- **Public Transport** - Buses: Grantown-on-Spey. Trains: Aviemore and Carrbridge.
- **Directions** - Arrangements made with each group.

CONTACT: Keith Ballam
Craggan Outdoors Bunkhouse & Bothy, Glenbeg, Grantown on Spey, PH26 3NT
Tel: 01479 873 283
info@cragganoutdoors.co.uk www.cragganoutdoors.co.uk

HABITAT
@ BALLATER

Set in the village of Ballater with a range of shops, pubs and restaurants, this is a stunning, purpose built hostel ideal for families, groups and independent travellers. Within the Cairngorms National Park it is a great position for enjoying a variety of outdoor activities.

All rooms are ensuite, ranging from 8 bed dorms to 4 bed rooms suitable for families. Bedding is included.

There's a large kitchen/dining/lounge area with wood burning stove and under-floor heating throughout. There is an excellent drying and laundry room and secure storage for bikes.

Ballater is an ideal location for exploring the Eastern Cairngorms, Royal Deeside and Aberdeenshire.

Habitat@Ballater is a VisitScotland five star hostel.

DETAILS

- **Open** - All year, all day
- **Number of beds** - 37: 2x8, 1x7, 3x4, 1x2. All en-suite.
- **Booking** - Book by phone, email or online.
- **Price per night** - From £18 per person.
- **Public Transport** - From Aberdeen bus station (phone 01224 212266).
- **Directions** - On A93 just west of bridge over river in centre of Ballater.

CONTACT: Harry and Claudia Leith
Bridge Square, Ballater, Aberdeenshire, AB35 5QJ
Tel: 013397 53752
info@habitat-at-ballater.com www.habitat-at-ballater.com

RATTRAY HEAD
ECO-HOSTEL

Rattray Head Eco-Hostel is a former lighthouse shore station among huge dunes on an isolated 11 mile long sandy beach. Come and relax in this gorgeous most easterly part of mainland Scotland, and enjoy one of its driest, sunniest, midge-free areas.

The 1892 granite building has been renovated to form a modern, non-smoking, dog-friendly coastal retreat. The hostel has self-catering kitchens, bunkrooms, and double and family bedrooms. It is part of the SIH network and has a Visit Scotland 3 star grading.

The North Sea Cycle Route (Sustrans 1) is 17 miles inland and passes through historic Aberdeenshire with stone circles, castle ruins and golf courses.

DETAILS

- **Open** - All year, phone in winter, Check-in 4–8pm, check-out 11am. No curfew.
- **Number of beds** - 22: 1x2, 5x4.
- **Booking** - Booking is available with first night as deposit.
- **Price per night** - Bunk £15pp, Triple £17pp, Double/Twin £22.50pp. Includes bedding and drinks.
- **Public Transport** - Airport, coach and train stations at Aberdeen (43 miles). Buses 260, 263 run frequently between Aberdeen and Peterhead. Bus 269 runs hourly between Peterhead and Fraserburgh. Taxi from Peterhead about £17.
- **Directions** - NK103577 Rattray is signed from the A90 Peterhead to Fraserburgh road. The hostel is at the end of the lane near the lighthouse, about 3 miles from the A90.

CONTACT: Rob and Val
Lighthouse Cottages, Rattray Head, Peterhead, Aberdeenshire, AB42 3HA
Tel: 01346 532236
hostel@rattrayhead.net www.rattrayhead.net/hostel

ARDENBEG
BUNKHOUSE

Ideal accommodation for groups and families visiting the stunning Cairngorms National Park, near Aviemore, in the Highlands of Scotland.

Four family/group rooms with private/en suite shower rooms. Two fully equipped kitchen / dining rooms with televisions, stereos. Large, enclosed garden, BBQ, campfire area, play equipment. Outside covered seating area for use from spring to October. Ample off road parking, discount card and free wireless broadband. A superb location for year round activities! Summer/ winter mountaineering, skiing/snowboarding, rock climbing and abseiling, kayaking and canoeing, mountain biking, gorge swimming, orienteering, sailing, windsurfing, golf. Many other local attractions, ideal for families/rest days.

VisitScotland 3 star Hostel, Hospitality Assured.

DETAILS

- **Open** - All year, all day.
- **Number of beds** - 24: 1x4: 2x6: 1x8.
- **Booking** - In advance to avoid disappointment.
- **Price per night** - £18.50 pp for 2 or more nights, £21 for a single night. Private rooms from £48.00
- **Public Transport** - Nearest train station Aviemore. Nearest airport Inverness. Good bus services from both to Grantown Square. Ardenbeg is 2 minutes' walk.
- **Directions** - From the A9 approach Grantown on the A95 passing Dulnain Bridge. At first roundabout turn left into Grantown. Just before traffic lights turn left into Chapel Road. Turn right at the end of road into Grant Rd. Ardenbeg is 2nd on left.

CONTACT: Rebecca
Grant Road, Grantown-on-Spey, Moray, PH26 3LD
Tel: 01479 872824 Fax: 01479 872824
enquiries@ardenbeg.co.uk www.ardenbeg.co.uk

Sharing a car park with the Speyside Way and just yards from the river, the converted Nethy Station offers all that a group of 7-20 could expect from a bunkhouse. It is well equipped, fully central heated and has two public areas. Most rooms have triple bunks and there is a 2 bunk room with unusual access: we call it Narnia, as you get there through a wardrobe! There is also 'The Shed'.

Whether you self-cater or we cook for you as a group, you will have access to the kitchen at all times. We never ask people to share the building so you may sleep, walk, ski, board, hike, ride, fish, etc. at your own convenience.

The bunkhouse is only 200 yards from the centre of Nethy Bridge with its shop, butcher, pub and interpretive centre and half way between two winter sports areas. Dogs are welcome but please do not let them sleep on the beds!

DETAILS

- **Open** - All year, anytime.
- **Number of beds** - 24: 2x9: 3x2.
- **Booking** - Essential (with deposit)
- **Price per night** - £12.50pp May-Sep. £13.50pp Oct–Apr. Minimum of 8 people.

- **Public Transport** - Take train or Citylink coach to Aviemore. Local buses are available from Aviemore to Nethy Bridge Post Office, phone 01479 811566.
- **Directions** - GR 002 207. Hostel is adjacent to the Speyside Way. From the B970, with Post Office on your right, go over the bridge and turn left immediately. Past the butcher turn second right.

CONTACT: Patricia or Richard
Station Road, Nethy Bridge, PH25 3DN
Tel: 01479 821370
info@nethy.org www.nethy.org

SLOCHD MHOR
LODGE

Slochd Mhor Lodge is perfectly situated in spectacular Strathspey in the Cairngorm National Park, halfway between the villages of Carrbridge and Tomatin. The Lodge is on an 'off road' section of the No 7 Sustrans cycle route, surrounded by hills and forests. This is perfect walking country and in winter there are nordic ski trails from the doorstep. Slochd Mhor Lodge offers a genuine welcome in warm cosy surroundings with full central heating. Fully equipped kitchen and a spacious dining area together with large lounge/lecture room with woodburner, TV, WiFi, books and games. Other facilities include a drying room and laundry facilities, some en-suite rooms, a shower and toilet room suitable for wheel-chairs, on-site cycle shop/workshop, MT bike hire and nordic ski hire. Locked bike shed. Free range eggs when available. Coffee and tea. There is an outside seating and BBQ area. Ample parking. Visit Scotland 4 star graded. Silver Green Business Award. Cyclists and Walkers Welcome.

DETAILS

■ **Open** - All year, new arrivals 5-9pm.Checked in gets key.
■ **Number of beds** - 1x10: 1x6: 2x5: 1x2. Maximum 24 people.
■ **Booking** - Booking recommended
■ **Price per night** - £18 for 2 or more nights. £19 for a single night. Family en-suite rooms sleep 5 from £19 each. Juniors from £14, under 2s free. Prices include all bedding and linen. Sole use rates available.
■ **Public Transport** - Nearest bus and train station Carrbridge (4 miles). City Link London/Edinburgh and Glasgow/Inverness stop at Aviemore (11 miles).
■ **Directions** - From south on A9, after mileage board 'Inverness 23' travel 1.5 miles north, take first opening on left marked 'Slochd'. Then first opening on right (¼ mile).

CONTACT: Liz or Ian
Slochd, Carrbridge, Inverness-shire, PH23 3AY
Tel: 01479 841666
Slochd666@aol.com www.slochd.co.uk

INVERNESS
STUDENT HOTEL
SCOTLAND

Inverness, capital of the Highlands, is set amongst some of Scotland's most fascinating attractions. The bustling town centre soon gives way to lochs, hills, forests and glens. Close to Inverness Castle, the intimate and lively Student Hostel enjoys wonderful panoramic views of the town and the mountains beyond. After a hard day's Nessie hunting, our hostel provides a friendly cosy place to unwind, just yards from the city's varied nightlife and a few minutes' walk from the bus and train stations. Visit the beautiful ancient pine forest of Glen Affric, tranquil but deeply historic Culloden Battlefield, the 4,000 year old standing stones at Clava Cairns or stroll down the riverbank to the waterfront to try to glimpse the wild dolphins in the nearby Moray Firth. Famous Loch Ness lies just a few miles upstream and of course has its own special wild animal.

DETAILS

- **Open** - All year, all day, reception 7am-11pm (times may vary).
- **Number of beds** - 57.
- **Booking** - Booking not always essential. First nights payment needed to book.
- **Price per night** - £14 per night. ID required for check-in.
- **Public Transport** - Inverness train station and bus station are a mere 10 minute walk from the hostel. Alternatively jump in a taxi for around £5.
- **Directions** - Head to the city centre and the castle. Hostel is up from Castle Terrace past the castle. Where road forks take the left onto Culduthel Road. Hostel is second building on right. From train/bus station turn left onto Academy St. When you see the Marks and Spencers ahead of you, cross at the traffic lights and go down Inglis St. At the end turn right along the High Street, and then left at the bottom going up Castle St past the castle. Continue up Culduthel Road and hostel is on right.

CONTACT: Receptionist
8 Culduthel Road, Inverness, IV2 4AB
Tel: 01463 236556
inverness@scotlandstophostels.com www.scotlandstophostels.com

MORAG'S LODGE
LOCH NESS

Morag's Lodge is an award winning hostel overlooking Fort Augustus. The perfect base to explore the Loch Ness area. It offers great budget accommodation for backpackers, independent travellers and groups and is an ideal stop-off on The Great Glen Way.

The Lodge has a range of dorms, twins, doubles and private family rooms and most are en-suite. The fantastic facilities include a fully licensed bar, TV lounge, drying room, WiFi, internet access, self-catering kitchen and dining room. The lodge provides breakfast and evening meals with packed lunches on request. Ample car parking is available in the grounds and bike hire is available.
Member of Europe's Famous Hostels.
VisitScotland Grading 4 Stars.
Green Tourism Silver Award.

DETAILS

- **Open** - All year, All day. Check-in from 4.30pm (earlier by arrangement).
- **Number of beds** - 81: 6x6, 1x5, 7x4, 4x2/3.
- **Booking** - Booking recommended.
- **Price per night** - From £19 pp in dorm beds. Doubles/twins from £24pp. Family rooms from £62.00.
- **Public Transport** - Bus stop for Fort William and Inverness only 200m away.
- **Directions** - From Inverness, arrive at Fort Augustus, turn first right up Bunoich Brae. From Fort William, go through village past petrol station and car park. Take next left up Bunoich Brae.

CONTACT: Claire
Bunoich Brae, Fort Augustus, Inverness-shire, PH32 4DG
Tel: 01320 366289
info@moragslodge.com www.moragslodge.com

STRAVAIGERS
LODGE
SCOTLAND

Stravaigers Lodge is an independent, purpose-built, family-run hostel with 30 private rooms sleeping 60 people (no dorms). It offers comfortable, low priced accommodation for individuals, families and groups.

Situated in Fort Augustus on the shores of Loch Ness, the hostel is only five minutes' walk from the Caledonian Canal, Loch Ness and the Great Glen Way. Pubs, restaurants and shops are also within five minutes' walk.

The lodge provides a warm welcome, friendly service and an excellent place to stay. Situated in the beautiful village of Fort Augustus at the southern end of Loch Ness.

DETAILS
- **Open** - April to New Year, 10am onwards.
- **Number of beds** - 60: 30 x 2.
- **Booking** - Notice required for bookings in off peak season.
- **Price per night** - £15 to £20 per person.
- **Public Transport** - Regular air links from London to Inverness and daily bus service from airport via Inverness and Loch Ness to Fort Augustus.
- **Directions** - From the white canal bridge head towards B862 (Whitebridge) and follow for 100metres, hostel is on your right.

CONTACT:
Glendoe Road, Fort Augustus, Inverness-shire, PH32 4BZ
Tel: 01320 366257
stravaigerslodge@aol.com www.highlandbunkhouse.co.uk

LOCH NESS
SCOTLAND BACKPACKERS LODGE

Loch Ness Backpackers is a warm and friendly little hostel with a relaxed atmosphere, good music and no curfew. It has grown from an 18th century farm cottage and barn and provides a warm open fire to greet you on cold nights. The house forms the main area of the hostel with reception, lounges, dining room, kitchen and toilets/showers on the ground floor, and two dormitories and one double room in the upstairs area. A converted barn (the bunkhouse) contains four more dormitories, toilets/showers and a kitchen/dining area/bar and restaurant. There is also a great BBQ area, garden and car park.

Loch Ness Backpackers is within easy walking distance of Loch Ness, Urquhart Castle, three pubs, restaurants, a supermarket, a fish and chip shop, post office, bank, gift shops and bus stops. A perfect location for activity or relaxation amongst spectacular scenery. Horse riding, fishing on the loch and mountain biking can all be arranged locally (great bikes available for hire).

DETAILS

- **Open** - All year, all day.
- **Number of beds** - House 16: Bunkhouse 24: (1x2, 2 x family room, 6 x dorms).
- **Booking** - Check availability on website or by phone.
- **Price per night** - From £15 per person.
- **Public Transport** - Nearest trains at Inverness. Rapsons, Megabus and Citylink buses all pass close to the hostel.
- **Directions** - Near the A82 Inverness to Fort William road. Turn off is next to the stone bridge in Lewiston near the Smiddy pub.

CONTACT: Wendy and Neil MacIntosh
Coiltie Farm House, East Lewiston, Drumnadrochit, Inverness, IV63 6UJ
Tel: 01456 450807
info@lochness-backpackers.com www.lochness-backpackers.com

GREAT GLEN
HOSTEL

Nestled between mountains and lochs in the heart of the "Outdoor Capital of the UK", 20 miles north of Fort William and 10 miles south of Loch Ness, the Great Glen Hostel is an ideal location whether you're touring the Highlands, bagging Munros or paddling rivers and lochs, and it is only a few minutes' walk from the Great Glen Way.

The hostel provides comfortable accommodation in twin, family and dormitory rooms. Hostel facilities include a self-catering kitchen, drying room, laundry, bike and canoe storage, free internet access, hot showers and a hostel store.

The whole hostel is available for exclusive rental for groups throughout the year.

DETAILS

- **Open** - Open all year, all day. Please call first Nov-March.
- **Number of beds** - 50: 3 x 2, 1 x 4, 4 x 5, 2 x 6, 1 x 8.
- **Booking** - Booking recommended. Please telephone in advance or book online.
- **Price per night** - Dorm beds from £16. Twin rooms from £19 per person. Whole hostel available for exclusive hire from £350 per night.
- **Public Transport** - Citylink bus services between Glasgow and the Isle of Skye, and between Fort William and Inverness will stop nearby. Nearest railway station: Spean Bridge. Nearest airport: Inverness.
- **Directions** - We are located 11 miles north of Spean Bridge and 3 miles south of Invergarry on the A82 in a small settlement called South Laggan. Citylink buses stop 100m north of the hostel on the A82. If you are walking the Great Glen Way, stay on the Way until you see signs directing you to the hostel.

CONTACT: Clem or Kirsty
South Laggan, Spean Bridge, Invernesshire, PH34 4EA
Tel: 01809 501430
bookings@greatglenhostel.com www.greatglenhostel.com

Glenfinnan sleeping car provides unique, comfortable accommodation in an historic railway carriage adjacent to Glenfinnan Station. It is an ideal location for the mountains of Lochaber, Rough Bounds, Moidart and Ardgour. It makes a good starting point for bothy expeditions and is a useful stopping-off point on the route to Skye. Why not use it also for extended stays using road or rail for trips to fishing, golf, ferries, cruises, and beach locations.

There is a fully equipped kitchen, showers, a drying room and total hydro-electric heating.
The adjacent dining coach provides excellent meals to give you a break from self-catering.

Your overnight stay includes free admission to the railway museum housed in the railway buildings.

DETAILS

- **Open** - All year, 24 hours.
- **Number of beds** - 10.
- **Booking** - Booking preferred and advisable to avoid disappointment.
- **Price per night** - £14 pp, £120 for exclusive use of whole coach.
- **Public Transport** - Bunkhouse is adjacent to Glenfinnan Railway Station on the West Highland Line (Glasgow-Fort William-Mallaig) and is 100m from a bus stop.
- **Directions** - On the A830, 15 miles from Fort William and 30 miles from Mallaig with ferry connections to the Small Isles and Skye.

CONTACT: John or Hege
Glenfinnan Station, Glenfinnan, nr Fort William, PH37 4LT
Tel: 01397 722295 Fax: 01397 722495
john.barnes8@btconnect.com www.glenfinnanstationmuseum.co.uk

Loch Nevis Bunkhouse/Centre is situated at Ardintigh Bay, a spectacular mountain and loch side location on the south shores Loch Nevis. Eight miles by sea from Mallaig and opposite the Knoydart peninsula, it is accessible only by sea or on foot. The bunkhouse is owned and run by Adventurer, Tom McClean, famous for being the first person to row across the North Atlantic single-handed. The sleeping accommodation is in 5 wooden huts dotted around a 10 acre site. Jocks Lodge provides central amenities with a fully equipped kitchen/dining/recreation room, 2 separate toilet/shower rooms and a drying room for wet kit. The surrounding area is a walker's paradise, there is good sea fishing and freshwater hill lochs provide brown trout. Look out for the playful otters, porpoise and inquisitive seals that inhabit the loch and capture the amazing sight of the sea eagles and other sea birds passing by. Castaway and enjoy adventure and tranquillity at Ardintigh Bay on the edge of the Heavenly Loch.

DETAILS

- **Open** - March to end of September, 24 hours. Telephone only between 9am-7pm.
- **Number of beds** - 24: 6 x 2 : 2 x 6.
- **Booking** - Booking is essential ~ due to remoteness and to popularity.
- **Price per night** - £16pp minimum of 8 people and 2 night stay required. Please enquire for prices for exclusive use of the centre by larger groups.
- **Public Transport** - Trains & Buses to Mallaig or Morar. From Mallaig by boat.
- **Directions** - Enquire to Arrive at Bunkhouse by boat, from Mallaig OR walk to Bunkhouse from Morar. Grid Ref: 777.932 OS Land ranger Map 40. See our website for more details on how to get here.

CONTACT: Tom or Jill McClean
Ardintigh Bay, Loch Nevis, Mallaig, West Highlands. PH41 4PP
Tel: 01687 462274
info@tommcclean.co.uk www.outdoorcentrescotland.co.uk

BACKPACKERS LODGE SCOTLAND

The Backpackers Lodge in Mallaig offers a homely base from which you can explore the Inner Hebrides, the famous white sands of Morar and the remote peninsula of Knoydart. Mallaig is a working fishing village with all the excitement of the boats coming in. You can see the seals playing in the harbour waiting for the boats and whale watching trips are available from the harbour.

The hostel provides excellent budget accommodation with two rooms each with six beds, a drying room, full central heating and fully equipped kitchen/common room. It has three star plus grading with the Scottish Tourist Board.

On site is the Tea Garden Cafe (open from 9am to 6pm) serving quality meals, snacks, speciality coffee and home baking. In the evening The Garden Restaurant (open from 6pm to 9pm) serves home cooked bistro style seafood. Meals available from April to October. See website for pictures of the food and the beautiful countryside around.

DETAILS

- **Open** - All year, 24 hours.
- **Number of beds** - 12: 2 x 6.
- **Booking** - Telephone ahead for availability and bookings.
- **Price per night** - £17 per person.
- **Public Transport** - Mallaig has a train station and services by Citylink coaches. For information on local buses phone 01967 431272.
- **Directions** - From railway station turn right, hostel is two buildings along.

CONTACT:
Harbour View, Mallaig, Inverness-shire, PH41 4PU
Tel: 01687 462764
backpackers@btinternet.com www.mallaigbackpackers.co.uk

KNOYDART
BUNKHOUSE

Knoydart is a remote peninsula on the west coast of Scotland reachable only by boat or long hike. Known as the Rough Bounds because of its remoteness Knoydart is renowned for its secluded beaches, rugged grandeur and blissful tranquillity. It is a haven for hill walkers, mountain bikers, mountaineers and wildlife enthusiasts. A community enterprise, the bunkhouse aims to run on green principals and is owned by the Knoydart Foundation, a community owned organisation. It is 2 mins' walk from the beach and 10 mins from Inverie which has a pub, post office, small shop and the ferry pier. It has 4 bedrooms, a well equipped kitchen, a light and airy dining room, a laundry and a cosy sitting room with a woodburning stove. There is no mobile phone coverage on this part of Knoydart but the bunkhouse has a payphone and broadband internet. CD/DVD/ video player, books, games, bed linen and duvets provided. Explore by yourself or take advantage of the ranger service or deer stalking. Bring your own provisions and a torch. Local wild venison available. Dogs welcome with notice.

DETAILS

- **Open** - All year (except Christmas), all day.
- **Number of beds** - 25: 1x10, 1x7, 1x6, 1x2.
- **Booking** - Always book in advance. 25% or £7.50 pp non-refundable deposit.
- **Price per night** - £15 per adult, £10 for children under 16. Block bookings £325. Special rates for schools, youth groups and Duke of Edinburgh Award Scheme.
- **Public Transport** - Ferry from Mallaig pier to Inverie takes 40 mins. Phone 01687 462320 for details. Private boats are also available for hire (see website for details).
- **Directions** - Bunkhouse is half a mile south east of the centre of Inverie village.

CONTACT: Izzie Prickett
Knoydart Foundation, Inverie, Knoydart, By Mallaig, Inverness-shire PH41 4PL
Tel: 01687 462163
info@knoydart.org www.knoydart-foundation.com

A new conversion of a 19th century building, the Glebe Barn has charm and character whilst providing comfortable accommodation with magnificent views. You can enjoy breathtaking scenery along numerous walks; study fascinating geological formations, or explore varied natural habitats with incredible varieties of plant and animal species. Relax on beautiful sandy beaches, listen to the famous singing sands and watch the eagles soar above the spectacular Sgurr of Eigg. Just a mile away there is a well-stocked shop and café/restaurant with regular traditional music sessions. Facilities at the Barn include a well-equipped kitchen, spacious lounge/dining room (polished maple floor, log fire), a combination of twin, triple, family and dormitory rooms, each with wash hand basins (linen provided), central heating, hot showers plus laundry facilities.

DETAILS

- **Open** - Individuals April to October, Groups all year, all day.
- **Number of beds** - 22: 1 x 2 : 2 x 3 : 1 x 6 : 1 x 8.
- **Booking** - Booking essential prior to boarding ferry. Deposit required.
- **Price per night** - £17 (1-2 nights), £15 (3+ nights). Twin room £38 (1-2 nights), £34 (3+ nights). Sole use (min 14 persons) £16pp (1-2 nights), £13 (3+ nights).
- **Public Transport** - Fort William is the nearest National Express coach stop. The early train from Fort William to Arisaig and Mallaig meets the ferry. Daily summer sailings from Arisaig or Mallaig.
- **Directions** - We try to meet visitors at the pier, but it is not always possible. Follow tarmac road around the shore and up hill until you cross a small stone bridge over a burn. Continue up hill and take first track on right. Taxi/minibus service from pier if required.

CONTACT: Karen or Simon
Isle of Eigg, PH42 4RL
Tel: 01687 482417
simon@glebebarn.co.uk www.glebebarn.co.uk

KINTAIL LODGE
BUNKHOUSES

Kintail Lodge stands at the foot of the Five Sisters of Kintail, right on the shores of Loch Duich. It is an ideal base for touring Skye and the Western Highlands or for bagging some of the 30 Munroes in the area. In the grounds of the hotel there are two budget accommodation units which are especially popular with walkers, climbers and fishermen. The Wee Bunk House has a cosy room with bunks to sleep 6 people and a snack kitchen containing fridge, hot rings, kettle, microwave and basic cooking utensils. There is a shower room with a toilet and the building is wheelchair friendly. The Trekkers' Lodge sleeps 6 people in two twin rooms and two single rooms, each with their own washbasin. There are 2 shower rooms with toilets and a snack kitchen equipped as in the Wee Bunkhouse. After a long day in the hills you can unwind in the relaxed atmosphere of the traditional Kintail Bar, where good food is served and beer is plentiful, or enjoy the lochside garden and patio. Packed lunches available.

DETAILS

- **Open** - All year, all day (restricted winter hours).
- **Number of beds** - Trekkers Lodge 6: 2x2, 2x1, Wee Bunkhouse 6: 1x6.
- **Booking** - Book by phone or email.
- **Price per night** - £15.00pp, 3+ nights £14.50pp, Sole use of Trekkers Lodge £80. Sole use of Wee Bunkhouse £70. Duvet and towel £5.50. Full Scottish Breakfast in the Hotel £11.50.
- **Public Transport** - See Citylink website.
- **Directions** - Kintail Lodge is situated on the A87 between Invergarry and the Skye Bridge.

CONTACT: Reception
Kintail Lodge Hotel, Glenshiel, Kyle of Lochalsh, Ross-shire, IV40 8HL
Tel: 01599 511275
kintaillodgehotel@btinternet.com   www.kintaillodgehotel.co.uk

Flora Macdonald Hostel offers clean, comfortable accommodation in the magnificent surroundings of the Sleat Peninsular in the south of the isle. In this region, also known as the Garden of Skye, visitors may see golden eagles, sea eagles, red and roe deer, otters and lots of other wildlife. It is also of enormous interest to geology students.

The owner Peter Macdonald, a direct descendent of the Lords of the Isles, the Macdonald Chiefs and Robert the Bruce, is a local historian happy to share his knowledge of the area, and breeds rare Eriskay ponies on the family croft.

The hostel has solid pine bunks and is fully centrally heated. It has a modern well equipped kitchen, WiFi, a drying room with washer and tumble dryer, and a conservatory to sit in and enjoy the views.

DETAILS

- **Open** - All year, 9am to 9pm.
- **Number of beds** - 24: 1x10, 3x4, 1x2.
- **Booking** - Booking is not essential but strongly advised. Deposits required with all bookings, at least 1 week in advance.
- **Price per night** - £16 dorm beds, private rooms £42. 20% reduction for block bookings and individual stays in excess of 7 nights.
- **Public Transport** - Regular bus service between Broadford and Armadale (bus stop at end of hostel road by the church).
- **Directions** - 3 miles from Armadale opposite Kilmore church, 22 miles from Skye bridge on the A851.

CONTACT: Peter Macdonald
Kilmore Sleat, By Armadale, Isle of Skye, IV44 8RG
Tel: 01471 844272 or 01471 844440
floramacdonaldhostel@btconnect.com www.skye-hostel.co.uk

BROADFORD
BACKPACKERS

Ideally located for enjoying the Isle of Skye, this child-friendly hostel is clean and cosy, with helpful staff for advice and information. There is a large kitchen for self-catering and a pleasant dining room overlooking the garden. The communal area has a TV and comfortable seating with plenty of board games and tea or coffee. Put in a lovely house cat and you've got yourself a home away from home. There are family rooms sleeping 4 (a double and two single beds), private double and twin rooms and small dorms sleeping 6 or 3. There is a bathroom with bath, a large garden and on-site parking. Cots and high chairs are available. Bedding and linen is provided and towels can be hired. From the hostel it is a short walk to the supermarket, shops, restaurants, beach and regular public transport, which connects Broadford with the rest of Skye and the mainland. Broadford Backpackers makes a perfect base for hiking, climbing, mountain biking and enjoying the spectacular scenery of Skye.

DETAILS

- **Open** - All year, 24 hours.
- **Number of beds** - 37: 2x6, 1x3, 3 x family, 2 x dbl, 3 x twin.
- **Booking** - To book please telephone or email.
- **Price per night** - Dorm: £18.75, Child £14.75; Private Room: Single Bed £23.50, Double Bed £43.50.
- **Public Transport** - Either: ferry from Mallaig to Armadale and a short bus ride; or any bus that is going to Skye will stop at Broadford (regular buses from Glasgow and Inverness); or train to Kyle of Lochalsh and then a short bus ride.
- **Directions** - From west on A87, in Broadford turn right onto High Road, then hostel is on right after 0.3 mile.

CONTACT:
High Road, Broadford, Isle of Skye, IV49 9AA
Tel: 01471 820333
broadfordbackpackers@gmail.com   www.broadford-backpackers.com

Skye Backpackers sits in the picturesque fishing village of Kyleakin, skirted by mountains and sea. A real 'home away from home', the hostel is a sanctuary for any weary traveller. Curl up by the open fire with a good book, or in the summer enjoy the hostel's large garden. Whatever you're looking for - hill walking, sightseeing or the legendary faeries, this island will not disappoint. The pleasant hostel staff can help arrange bus tours and hiking treks.

Kyleakin is on the main bus route and is also easily accessible by boat or from the train station at Kyle on the mainland. The village offers a shop, café, choice of pubs and spectacular scenic views. One of Europe's most dramatic and haunting lands, words can do little justice in describing the awesome beauty of the Isle of Skye. The majestic Cuillin Mountains dominate the rugged landscape, which is peppered with lochs, glens and tiny fishing villages.

DETAILS

- **Open** - All year, all day. Reception 7am-12pm and 5pm-10.30pm (times may vary).
- **Number of beds** - 39.
- **Booking** - Booking in advance not always essential, first nights payment required.
- **Price per night** - £14 per night. ID required for check-in.
- **Public Transport** - Trains at Kyle of Lochalsh, only a short bus ride (approx 10 mins) from the hostel. The bus drops opposite the hostel.
- **Directions** - From Kyle of Lochalsh go over the Skye Bridge then take first exit at roundabout, which takes you into Kyleakin. The hostel is on the right hand side after the Kings Arms Hotel. Park in the car park opposite hostel or in the grounds.

CONTACT: Receptionist
Benmhor, Kyleakin, Isle of Skye, IV41 8PH
Tel: 01599 534510
skye@scotlandstophostels.com www.scotlandstophostels.com

SLIGACHAN
BUNKHOUSE

Sligachan Bunkhouse overlooks the 'Black Cuillins' and is an ideal base for exploring the magnificent mountains of Skye. Several routes up the peaks pass the Bunkhouse and the path to 'Loch Coruisk' can be seen from the verandah. The Bunkhouse is surrounded by peaceful mountain scenery on a track easily accessible by car. It is only a 5 minute walk from the bus stop at Sligachan, which has a regular bus service from the mainland and Portree. The Sligachan Hotel can be seen from the Bunkhouse, about a 5 minute walk, and will provide a hot meal from breakfast through to dinner. The hotel's Seumas Bar has over 300 malt whiskies and is The Good Pub Guide Whisky Pub of the Year for 2011. It also sells its own real ale made at the Cuillin Brewery. The bar makes a great place to relax after a long day's trekking. The Bunkhouse has 4 bedrooms, full kitchen facilities and a lounge with open fire.

DETAILS

- **Open** - March 1st to October 31st, all day.
- **Number of beds** - 20.
- **Booking** - Booking essential for large groups. Deposit required.
- **Price per night** - £16pp. Linen Hire £4. Block bookings £300 per night. Discounts for longer stays.
- **Public Transport** - Train - 1) Fort William to Mallaig, crossing by ferry to Armadale, buses to Sligachan (30m). 2) Inverness to Kyle of Lochalsh, catch bus over Skye Bridge to Kyleakin, connect with bus to Sligachan.
- **Directions** - Inverness: A82 Invermoriston take A887 then A87 to Kyle of Lochalsh, cross Skye Bridge, continue on A87. Fort William: A830 to Mallaig, cross to Skye on ferry, take A851 to Broadford, then A87.

CONTACT: Sligachan Hotel
Sligachan, Isle of Skye, IV47 8SW
Tel: 01478 650204
reservations@sligachan.co.uk www.sligachan.co.uk

SKYEWALKER
HOSTEL

Come and visit the award winning, family run Skyewalker Hostel, rated 4 star by VisitScotland, and experience a warm welcome and true Scottish hospitality. Skyewalker Hostel is ideally situated as a base for exploring the island and offers a very high standard of clean, cosy accommodation at a budget price. There is a range of rooms from 2-bed private rooms to larger dormitories (fresh bed linen provided free of charge), a comfortable lounge and a fully equipped self-catering kitchen. There is also a large garden with BBQ area, giant chess, fantastic glass chill-out dome and off street free parking. The local hotel/pub is a five minute walk from the hostel. Skyewalker hosts regular Scottish folk music sessions and it is also possible to book the whole place for special occasions such as birthdays, family get-togethers, Munro completion parties, etc.

DETAILS

■ **Open** - 1st April - 30th Sept (or all year for group bookings), check in between 3pm and 10pm.
■ **Number of beds** - 40:
■ **Booking** - Book early to save disappointment. Online booking available.
■ **Price per night** - From £16.00 per person.
■ **Public Transport** - Two local buses run each weekday from Portree via Sligachan to Portnalong and back. Citylink coaches from the mainland and north Skye drop off at Sligachan. Please note there is no bus to/from the hostel on Sundays.
■ **Directions** - From Sligachan (in the centre of Skye), take A863 for 5 miles to the turn off for Carbost which takes you onto the B8009. Proceed through Carbost to Portnalong. Alternatively, follow the green signs from Sligachan! GR 348 348

CONTACT: Brian or Lisa
Old School, Portnalong, Isle of Skye, IV47 8SL
Tel: 01478 640250
enquiries@skyewalkerhostel.com www.skyewalkerhostel.com

DUNARD
HOSTEL

Dunard is a warm, friendly, family-run hostel on the beautiful island of Barra in Scotland's Outer Hebrides. The hostel has a cosy living room with a lovely fire, hot showers and spacious kitchen. There are bunk, twin and family bedrooms.

Situated in Castlebay the hostel has views over the castle to beaches and islands beyond. Close to the ferry terminal, a handful of shops, and bars which often fill with live music. During the summer the island is alive for 'Feis Bharraidh' a gaelic festival of music, song and dance. Take time and explore this truly beautiful island with stunning white beaches, quiet bays where otters hunt and seals bask on rocks, dunes and meadows carpeted in flowers, and wild windswept hills home to golden eagles. Join one of our friendly guided sea kayaking trips and paddle amongst sheltered islands for really close-up wildlife encounters (no experience needed). www.clearwaterpaddling.com

DETAILS

■ **Open** - All year, except Christmas and New Year, all day.
■ **Number of beds** - 18: 3x4 3x2.
■ **Booking** - Booking advised,specially in the summer. Booking essential for groups.
■ **Price per night** - £16 per person bunk room and twin cabin. £18 pp twin room. £54 per family room (sleeps 4). £286 sole use.
■ **Public Transport** - The hostel is a 3 minute walk from the Ferry Terminal in Castlebay. If using a local bus ask to be dropped at the hostel.
■ **Directions** - From Ferry terminal in Castlebay head up hill, turn left and we are the third house past the old school (200m from Terminal).

CONTACT: Katie or Chris
Dunard, Castlebay, Isle of Barra, Western Isles, HS9 5XD
Tel: 01871 810443
info@dunardhostel.co.uk www.dunardhostel.co.uk

Nº5 Drinishader is located on the Isle of Harris, Outer Hebrides, 5 miles from Tarbert and 8 miles from the white sandy beaches. Situated above Drinishader Harbour, overlooking the beautiful East Loch Tarbert the hostel and self-catering units provide a variety of accommodation for individuals, families and groups as well as activities. The hostel has a cosy lounge with open fire, a well-equipped kitchen, hot showers and comfortable orthopaedic bunks.

Pick-up services from Tarbert can be arranged if there are no bus services. There is a shop/post office nearby and you can pre-order fresh, delicious home-made bread and cakes to be delivered to your breakfast table. Among the activities guests enjoy are coastal/hill walking, cycling, kayaking, boat trips, sightseeing, bird/wild life watching or simply chilling out. For full information on activities for 2012 please visit our website. Accommodation Activities Hire

DETAILS

- **Open** - March to October, 8am till 11pm.
- **Number of beds** - 28.
- **Booking** - Advisable to confirm beds, may require deposit.
- **Price per night** - From £15 per person.
- **Public Transport** - Caledonian MacBrayne ferries (01876 500337) from Ullapool to Stornoway or from Uig (Skye) to Tarbert. Drinishader is a 10 min bus journey from Tarbert (01851 705050). Bus stop at hostel. There are 5 buses each day.
- **Directions** - From Tarbert follow the A859 south. After 3.5km turn left along the Golden Road. The hostel is located just above the harbour in Drinishader.

CONTACT: Roddy or Warden
Drinishader, Isle Of Harris, HS3 3DX
Tel: 01859 511255
info@number5.biz www.number5.biz

HEB
HOSTEL

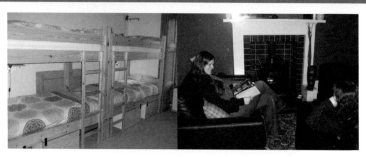

The Heb Hostel is a family-run backpackers' hostel in the heart of Stornoway on the enchanting Isle of Lewis. It is an ideal stop/stay for travellers visiting the Hebrides. Surfers, cyclists, walkers, families and groups are all welcome.

Clean, comfortable, friendly and relaxed - Heb Hostel aims to provide you with a quality stay at budget prices.

There are many facilities, including a common room with TV, peat fire, local guides and information.

DETAILS

■ **Open** - All year, all day. New arrivals phone for access code if warden not around.
■ **Number of beds** - 26: 1x8, 2x7,1x4 (family dorm).
■ **Booking** - Booking is not essential but may be advisable at busier times. Deposits are only required for groups. Payment is due on arrival by cash or cheque.
■ **Price per night** - £16 per person per night. Family dorm £64 for a family, £68 for adults only. 10% discount on booking the whole hostel for more than one night
■ **Public Transport** - By plane: From Glasgow, Edinburgh or Inverness (Flybe), Aberdeen (Eastern Airways), Inverness and Benbecula (Highland Airways). By Ferry (Caledonian McBrayne) Ullapool to Stornoway (Lewis), Uig (Skye) to Tarbert (Harris) or Berneray (Uists) to Leverburgh (Harris)
■ **Directions** - From bus station: exit front door, cross South Beach St and walk up Kenneth St. Pass 1st intersection and we are 2nd on the right. From ferry terminal come out main exit, turn left, follow pedestrian walk-way to the bus station. From Airport take bus to Stornoway bus station.

CONTACT: Christine Macintosh
25 Kenneth St, Stornoway, Isle of Lewis, HS1 2DR
Tel: 01851 709889
christine@hebhostel.com www.hebhostel.com

LAXDALE
BUNKHOUSE
SCOTLAND

Laxdale Bunkhouse is contained within Laxdale Holiday Park which is a small family-run park set in peaceful tree-lined surroundings. Located 1.5 miles away from the town of Stornoway this is an ideal centre from which to tour the islands of Lewis and Harris. Built in 1998, the bunkhouse has four bedrooms with four bunks in each room and caters for backpackers, families or groups looking for convenient, low cost accommodation.

There is a drying room, a spacious fully equipped dining kitchen which provides two cookers, fridge and microwave and a comfortable TV lounge in which to relax. Toilets and showers are located within the building and are suitable for the disabled. Outside there is a covered veranda, picnic table and BBQ area.

DETAILS

- **Open** - All year, 8am - 10pm.
- **Number of beds** - 16: 4x4.
- **Booking** - July and August booking advisable one week in advance.
- **Price per night** - £15pp (high season), £14pp (low season). £210 sole use (high season), £195 sole use (low season).
- **Public Transport** - Buses every 30mins stop close to hostel. Taxi fare from town centre approximately £2.50.
- **Directions** - From Stornoway Ferry Terminal take the A857. Take the second turning on the left past the hospital. Follow camping signs for one mile out of town. The Bunkhouse is located inside the holiday park. From Tarbert or Leverburgh take A859 for 40 miles to Stornoway. Turn left at the roundabout and second left after hospital then as above.

CONTACT:
Laxdale Holiday Park, 6 Laxdale Lane, Stornoway, Isle of Lewis, HS2 0DR
Tel: 01851 706966 / 01851 703234
info@laxdaleholidaypark.com www.laxdaleholidaypark.com

WHITEFALLS
RETREATS

Whitefalls Retreats Bunkhouse and Tigh Iseabail cottage are situated on a small family farm in the secluded Glen Elchaig. Guests come here for peace and quiet and for the superb walks in one of the last of the Highland wildernesses.

It is a wonderful peaceful location to come home to after a day walking the hills of Benula and the majestic Falls of Glomach. Nearer at hand are the numerous Corbetts around the beautiful Loch long and for the sightseer there is Eilean Donan castle and the Isle of Skye only 30 mins' drive.

This is an ideal stop off point on the Cape Wrath Trail, and although they are 8 miles from the nearest shop, the hostel can cater for your needs if you arrive off the hills with no provisions.

A limited number of bikes are available to borrow free of charge.

DETAILS

- **Open** - All year, all day.
- **Number of beds** - Cottage 6: 1x family room, 1x twin, 1x single.   Bunkhouse 9: 1 x family room and 6 x dorm.
- **Booking** - Advisable, groups require deposit. Payment by cash on arrival.
- **Price per night** - from £12.50 dorm to £35 (family room with en suite).
- **Public Transport** - Nearest bus station Dornie 8 miles.
- **Directions** - On A87 take the fourth turning on the right after the castle at Dornie.

CONTACT: William or Sheena
Camusluinie, Nr. Kyle of Lochalsh, IV40 8EA
Tel: 01599 588205
whitefalls@holidayhighlands.co.uk www.holidayhighlands.co.uk

Gerrys Hostel is situated in an excellent mountaineering and wilderness area on the most scenic railway in Britain. It is on the Cape Wrath Trail, The T.G.O. Challenge Route, and is 0.5 miles from Coulin Pass at Craig.

The photo shows the hostel, looking North West. The hostel has a comfortable common room with log fire and library. Meals are available in 15 minutes' drive.

Come and go as you please. No smoking inside or out.

Accommodation for non-smokers.

PLEASE CONTACT THIS HOSTEL BY PHONE OR POST

DETAILS

■ **Open** - All year (check by phone), check in 5pm to 8.30pm (later by arrangement only.)
■ **Number of beds** - 20: 1 x 10 : 2 x 5. Double and twin also.
■ **Booking** - Prepay to secure bed, or phone.
■ **Price per night** - From £15 pp, discount for long stay large groups.
■ **Public Transport** - Achnashellach station is 4km west of the hostel. Nearest Citylink coaches drop off at Inverness. Local bus between Inverness and Lochcarron: Wednesday and Saturday 3pm.
■ **Directions** - GR 037 493. 95 miles north of Fort William, 50 miles west of Inverness on A890.

CONTACT: Gerry Howkins
Craig, Achnashellach, Strathcarron, Wester-Ross, Scotland, IV54 8YU
Tel: 01520 766232
sam@backpackerspress.com www.gerryshostel-achnashellach.co.uk

LEDGOWAN HOTEL
AND BUNKHOUSE

SCOTLAND

Ledgowan Lodge is a traditional country house hotel with cosy log fires, original features and friendly bar open to residents and non-residents. The bunkhouse is adjacent to the hotel and bunkhouse guests have full use of the hotel's facilities. Ledgowan Lodge is perfectly situated for the hill walker, climber or anyone wanting low cost basic overnight accommodation. It is within easy driving distance of the Torridon and Fannich Mountain ranges and Fionn Bheinn Mountain is on the doorstep. The lodge sleeps ten adults in five separate rooms, each with a set of bunk beds, wash hand basin, chest of drawers and thermostatically controlled heating. There is a one off charge for providing pillow, 2 sheets and blankets. There is a bathroom with shower and a toilet. There are new cooking facilities and a refrigerator for self-catering, but it is recommended that guests socialise within the hotel where the welcome provides a restaurant, bar meals, real fires and lively conversation. There is ample car parking in the grounds and an excellent drying room within the hotel. Camping available.

DETAILS

- **Open** - All year, all day.
- **Number of beds** - 10: 5 x 2.
- **Booking** - Book by phone or email.
- **Price per night** - £14pp. £28 for sole use of 2 bed bunkroom. Linen £7 (one off charge). Camper vans and tents £5pp.
- **Public Transport** - Achnasheen Station is one mile from the bunkhouse.
- **Directions** - On the A890, 1 mile south of Achnasheen.

CONTACT: Reception
Legowan Lodge Hotel, Achnasheen, Ross-shire, Scottish Highlands, IV22 2EJ
Tel: 01445 720252
info@ledgowanlodge.co.uk www.ledgowanlodge.co.uk

Walkers, climbers and mountain bikers enjoying the Torridon Mountains and wilderness areas will be delighted to find the Kinlochewe Hotel with its warm, welcoming bar and bunkhouse accommodation. There are over 20 Munros within 20 miles of Kinlochewe and the hotel provides a great base from which to explore them. The Hotel Bar is open all the year round, and serves excellent home-made food at affordable prices. The bar offers a selection of real ales and over 70 malt whiskies. The bunkhouse is ideal for outdoor enthusiasts with a well equipped self-catering kitchen, an efficient drying room, toilets and hot showers. There is one dormitory with 12 bunks (this makes it unsuitable for children). Each bunk has an individual locker and a pillow with pillowcase is provided (please bring your own sleeping bags, towels and padlock for the locker).

DETAILS

- **Open** - All year, 8am - midnight.
- **Number of beds** - 12.
- **Booking** - Essential for groups, deposit required. Advisable for individuals.
- **Price per night** - £14.50 per person.
- **Public Transport** - Nearest train station is in Achnasheen (10 miles away). In summer trains run four times a day (twice a day on Sundays) from Inverness and the lunchtime train can be met by the local Dial-a-Bus which comes to Kinlochewe. Phone 01520 722205 for further details. On Tuesdays, Thursdays and Fridays the 5pm Westerbus from Inverness to Gairloch stops outside the Bunkhouse at 6.45pm.
- **Directions** - Kinlochewe is situated at the junction of the A832 Garve to Gairloch road and the A896 north from Torridon.

CONTACT: Andrew and Gail Staddon
Kinlochewe by Achnasheen, Wester Ross, IV22 2PA
Tel: 01445 760253
bookings@kinlochewehotel.co.uk www.kinlochewehotel.co.uk

RUA REIDH
LIGHTHOUSE

Perched on the cliff tops 12 miles north of Gairloch, Rua Reidh Lighthouse must have one of the most dramatic settings of all the Scottish Hostels. The lighthouse still beams out its light over the Minch to the Outer Isles and Skye, but since its automation the adjoining house, no longer needed for keepers, has been converted into a comfortable independent hostel. The centrally heated house has two sitting rooms with log fires, a self-catering kitchen, a drying room, three private rooms and four dorms (each sleeping four), some rooms with en-suite shower. Meals are available from the main dining room and guided walking is also offered. The area of the lighthouse is unspoiled and makes a perfect place to watch for whales, dolphins, etc.

For an away from it all experience travel to the 'edge of the world' and Rua Reidh Lighthouse.

DETAILS

- **Open** - All year (except last 3 weeks in Jan), 9am - 11pm.
- **Number of beds** - 15: 2 x 4; 1 x 3; 1 x dbl, 1x twin.
- **Booking** - Pre-booking advisable.
- **Price per night** - From £13pp (dorm) to £25pp (private with en-suite facilities)
- **Public Transport** - Nearest train station Achnasheen (40 miles). Nearest Citylink coaches Inverness (80 miles). Westerbus 01445 712255 and Scotbus run a daily connection between Inverness/Gairloch (12 miles from hostel).
- **Directions** - From Gairloch take the road signed Big Sands and Melvaig, follow this road for 12 miles to the lighthouse. The last 3 miles is a private road with 20mph limit.

CONTACT:
Melvaig, Gairloch, IV21 2EA
Tel: 01445 771263
info@ruareidh.co.uk www.ruareidh.co.uk

Sail Mhor Croft is a small rural hostel which is situated at Dundonnell on the shores of Little Loch Broom. The mountain range of An Teallach, which has the reputation of being one of the finest ridge walks in Great Britain, is right on the doorstep and the area is a haven for walkers of all experience as well as for photographers. Whether you wish to climb the summits, walk along the loch side, visit a beautiful sandy beach or just soak up the tranquillity of the area, you know the scenery cannot be beaten anywhere in the country.

The hostel offers accommodation for up to 16 persons in three dorms which are fitted with anti-midge screens. Guests have a choice of using our self-catering facilities or we can provide a full breakfast. It is advisable to ring in advance in order to book yourself a bed, the next self-catering hostel is many miles away.

DETAILS

- **Open** - All year except Xmas, New Year and January, flexible.
- **Number of beds** - 16: 2 x 4: 1 x 8
- **Booking** - Always phone in advance. Groups should book as soon as possible.
- **Price per night** - £15.00 per person, self-catering. £190.00 per night sole use.
- **Public Transport** - Nearest train station is Inverness (60 miles). Nearest City Link bus drop off is Braemore Junction (15 miles). Wester bus passes the hostel 3 times a week; Mon, Wed and Sat. It also provides a service between Gairloch and Ullapool on Thursday afternoon.
- **Directions** - GR 064 893 (sheet 19) 1.5 miles west of Dundonnell Hotel on A832.

CONTACT: Dave or Lynda
Camusnagaul, Dundonnell, Ross-shire, IV23 2QT
Tel: 01854 633224
dave.lynda@sailmhor.co.uk www.sailmhor.co.uk

BADRALLACH
BOTHY AND CAMPSITE

On the tranquil shores of Little Loch Broom overlooking An Teallach, one of Scotland's finest mountain ranges, Badrallach Bothy and Camp Site with its welcoming traditional buildings offers a fine base for walking and climbing in the hills of Wester Ross, Caithness and Sutherland. You can fish in the rivers, hill lochs and sea, or simply watch the flora and fauna including many orchids, golden eagles, otters, porpoises, pine martens, deer and wild goats. Guests often sit around the peat stove in the gas light (there is now electric here too) and discuss life over a dram or two. Hot showers, spotless sanitary accommodation (STB graded 4 star excellent), an unbelievable price (thanks to S.N.H), and the total peace makes the Bothy and camp site (12 tents only) one that visitors return to year after year. There is also a caravan, 4 star cottage and B&B in an iconic Airstream trailer, with breakfast/dinner served in our new eco-crofthouse. Hire canoes, kites, bikes, boats and blokarts.

DETAILS

- **Open** - All year, all times.
- **Number of beds** - 12 plus bedspaces (Alpine style platforms). We have had 20 at a squeeze, mats and sleeping bags required.
- **Booking** - Recommended.
- **Price per night** - £6 pp £1.50 per vehicle. £70 sole use (£150 Xmas & New year).
- **Public Transport** - Westerbus (01445 712255) operate Mon/Wed/Sat between Inverness/Gairloch and drop at road end Dundonnell, 7 miles from hostel. Pick-up can be arranged.
- **Directions** - GR 065 915   Located on the shore of Little Loch Broom 7 miles along a single track road off the A832, one mile east of the Dundonnell Hotel.

CONTACT: Mr/Mrs Stott,
Croft No 9, Badrallach, Dundonnell, Ross-shire, IV23 2QP
Tel: 01854 633281
mail@badrallach.com www.badrallach.com

Stay on a first class train in Rogart in the heart of the Highlands halfway between Inverness and John O'Groats. The three railway carriages have been tastefully converted, with many original features. Two sleep 8, one is subdivided to sleep 4 and 2. There are two beds per room, and a kitchen, dining room, sitting room, showers and toilets. They are heated and non-smoking. All bedding is included. There is also a cosy showman's wagon which sleeps two. Four trains per day in each direction serve this small crofting community which has a shop, post office and pub with restaurant. Glenmorangie and Clynelish distilleries, Dunrobin Castle and Helmsdale's Heritage Centre are easy to reach by train or car. See the silver salmon leap at Lairg and the seabirds and seals in Loch Fleet. Or just enjoy the peace of Rogart.

The climate is good and the midges are less prevalent than in the west! Families welcome. Free use of bikes for guests.

DETAILS

- **Open** - March to September inclusive, 24 hours.
- **Number of beds** - 26: 8 x 2: 1 x 4: 3 x 2.
- **Booking** - Booking is not essential.
- **Price per night** - £15 per person, 12yrs and under £10 per person. (10% discount if you arrive by bike or train).
- **Public Transport** - Wick to Inverness trains stop at the door.
- **Directions** - We are at the railway station, 4 miles from the A9 trunk road, 54 miles north of Inverness.

CONTACT: Kate or Frank
Rogart Station, Pittentrail, Sutherland, Highlands, IV28 3XA
Tel: 01408 641343   Mobile/Text: 07833 641226
kate@sleeperzzz.com www.sleeperzzz.com

BLACK ROCK
BUNKHOUSE

Situated in beautiful Glenglass and sheltered by Ben Wyvis, this comfortable bunkhouse is named after the breathtaking Black Rock Gorge. It is an ideal base for touring the highlands and seeing wildlife, including seals in the Cromarty Firth and dolphins at Cromarty. The bunkhouse is at the eastern end of a hikers' route across Scotland and on the Lands End to John O'Groats route for walkers and cyclists. The Highland Games are held throughout the area. The village has a general shop, Post Office, bus service and an inn (serving good bar meals and breakfasts) 250m away.

Available to groups or individuals, accommodation is in four rooms of four and one room for one. Blankets are available and sheet sleeping bags can be hired. There is a self-catering kitchen and dining area with TV, showers and launderette facilities. There is also a camping ground. All areas of the bunkhouse are easily accessible by wheelchair and suitable for the disabled.

DETAILS

- **Open** - April 1st to October 31st, 24hr access. New arrivals 9am - 9pm.
- **Number of beds** - 17 : 4 x 4, 1 x 1.
- **Booking** - Not always essential. Deposit of 1 night's fee to secure booking.
- **Price per night** - £12- £14 per person. 10% off for groups of 8+.
- **Public Transport** - Nearest train station Dingwall (6 miles) Nearest Citylink drop off Inverness (15 miles). There are local buses hourly.
- **Directions** - Follow A9 north from Inverness, 2 miles north of Cromarty Firth bridge take left turn for Evanton. Follow camping signs.

CONTACT: Lillian
Evanton, Dingwall, Ross-shire, IV16 9UN
Tel: 01349 830917
enquires@blackrockscotland.co.uk www.blackrockscotland.co.uk

HELMSDALE
HOSTEL
SCOTLAND

Set in the scenic coastal village of Helmsdale, halfway between Inverness and John O´Groats, Helmsdale Hostel is an ideal stop when travelling to and from Orkney. On the main Land´s End to John O´Groats route, and surrounded by nearby Marlyn hills, the hostel is popular with cyclists and walkers.

The surrounding area also offers beach walks, bird watching and gold panning opportunties.

The hostel has excellent facilities and all rooms are en-suite. Breakfasts can be provided with prior arrangement. Groups, families and individuals all welcome. There is on-street car parking at the side of the hostel.

DETAILS

■ **Open** - Easter to Sept; other dates by request (all year group booking available). Open during the day.
■ **Number of beds** - 24: 2x8, 2x4
■ **Booking** - Advance booking not essential - book online, by email or phone.
■ **Price per night** - Dorm £17pp, family room from £60.
■ **Public Transport** - Helmsdale is served by the City Link bus service and is on the railway line from Inverness to Thurso.
■ **Directions** - The hostel is situated on the corner of the A9 and Old Caithness Road. Arriving by bus: walk up the slope for 100 metres. The Hostel is after the old church on your left. (200 metres). Arriving by train: Cross over the old bridge, turn right along Dunrobin Street, then left up Stafford Street. Hostel is at the top of the slope on the left (half a mile).

CONTACT: Irene
Helmsdale Hostel, Stafford Street, Helmsdale, Sutherland, KW8 6JR
Tel: 01431 821636   Mob: 07971 516287
irene.drummond@btinternet.com   www.helmsdalehostel.co.uk

BALINTRAID HOUSE
SCOTLAND HIGHLAND RETREAT

Balintraid House is a rambling house in a beautiful location looking directly out onto historic Cromarty Firth. It offers a comfortable alternative to staying in Inverness when driving north or west, or an ideal location to base your Highland holiday. Locally you can see dolphins, seals, swans and migrating birds in the firth. Take a short drive to Shin Falls or Rogie Falls and see salmon leaping up the waterfalls. Explore the Pictish Trail, sample whisky at nearby Glenmorangie or Dalmore Distilleries and enjoy walks to the Fyrish monument, Ben Wyvis and numerous others. Discover original Caledonian forests at Glen Affric. Visit a castle or two. Relax to traditional feis or other music at local venues and hotels.

Facilities include a well-equipped kitchen, central heating, warm duvets and comfy beds, internet access, table tennis, musical instruments and small library. Tea/coffee available. Please note: we have cats.

DETAILS

- **Open** - All year, please phone for access times.
- **Number of beds** - 20: flexible, single/double/family/group dorm.
- **Booking** - Recommended, please advise if arrival time changes.
- **Price per night** - From £18.
- **Public Transport** - Stagecoach stop at house. Trains from Inverness (Thurso/Wick) will stop at Invergordon. Phone for pick up, 3 miles away (charge).
- **Directions** - 26 miles north of Inverness. Turn off A9 for Invergordon and follow coastal road (B817) northwards for 2 miles, passing through small village of Saltburn. After the last house there are two big fields then a clump of trees with two drives on left leading to house.

CONTACT: Anita
Balintraid House, Balintraid, by Invergordon, Ross-shire, IV18 OLY
Tel: 01349 854446
balintraid.house@virgin.net www.balintraidhouse.co.uk

Cornmill Bunkhouse is situated on a traditional croft which has been in the family for many generations. The croft runs ewes, spring-calving cows, and grows winter feed and woodland. The mill was built in the early 1800s and was active until around 1926. It has been converted into 4 star affordable and comfortable accommodation for individuals or groups. The Bunkhouse can sleep up to 14 people. It has a large self-catering kitchen and open-plan sitting room on the first floor, in which the old grinding wheel now serves as a coffee table. There is level access to the first floor at the rear of the building, with an easy going stair down to the ground floor, which has two bunk rooms, a disabled access toilet/wetroom and a toilet with a shower. The first bunk room sleeps 8. The second sleeps 6 and has a patio door looking onto the workings of the old mill with its large wooden cog driving wheels. Activities can be organised for groups including Laser Tagging, Shooting and Clippage. Hen and Stag parties welcome. Come and enjoy this historic setting. 4 star tourist board graded.

DETAILS

- **Open** - All year, advanced notice required 1st Oct - 1st April, all day.
- **Number of beds** - 14: 1x8,1x6.
- **Booking** - Please enquire for availability by phone or email.
- **Price per night** - £15 per person. Discounts available for group bookings.
- **Public Transport** - Forsinard railway station is only 10 miles away. The line runs from Inverness to Wick, stopping at Forsinard three times a day.
- **Directions** - The Cornmill Bunkhouse is located on the A897, 6 miles from Melvich, 20 miles to Thurso, 42 miles to John O'Groats and 34 miles to Helmsdale.

CONTACT: Sandy Murray
Cornmill Bunkhouse, Achumore, Strathhalladale, Sutherland, KW13 6YT
Tel: 01641 571219   Mob: 07808 197350
sandy.murray2@btinternet.com www.achumore.co.uk

INCHNADAMPH
LODGE

Situated at the heart of the dramatic Assynt mountains, Inchnadamph Lodge has been tastefully converted to provide luxury hostel accommodation at a budget price. Twin, family and dormitory (4-8 people) rooms are available and a continental-style breakfast is included. There is a large self-catering kitchen, a games room, a lounge and a dining room (both with real fires). Packed lunches are available on request and bar meals are served at the Inchnadamph Hotel accross the road. At the foot of Ben More Assynt, and overlooking Loch Assynt, you are free to explore one of the wildest areas in the Highlands. Mountains can be climbed from the door! The Inchnadamph Nature Reserve is right by the lodge - home to a wide diversity of birds, plants, animals and full of exciting geological features. Nearby lochs are popular for trout fly fishing. Details and photos are on the website.

DETAILS

- **Open** - All year - phone November - March inclusive, 24 hours.
- **Number of beds** - 38: 8x2: 7x2: 4x2 (dormitory) 12 (twin/double).
- **Booking** - Advised, required Nov-March.
- **Price per night** - £17-£18.50 (dormitory), £24-£27 (twin room) inc. continental breakfast and linen. Group discounts.
- **Public Transport** - Transport is available to our door from Inverness 6 days a week, either by train to Lairg and then postbus, or by coach to Ullapool and minibus to Inchnadamph. Times vary - please call us for details.
- **Directions** - Inchnadamph is 25 miles north of Ullapool on the Lochinver/Durness road. The lodge is the big white building across the river from the hotel.

CONTACT: Chris
Inchnadamph, Assynt, Nr Lochinver, Sutherland, IV27 4HL
Tel: 01571 822218
info@inch-lodge.co.uk www.inch-lodge.co.uk

LAZY CROFTER
BUNKHOUSE

The Lazy Crofter is a small hostel, traditional yet modern with a cosy and informal atmosphere. It offers self-catering accommodation to groups, families and individuals at unbeatable prices. Set between magnificent mountains and stunning seascapes it enjoys wonderful views over the North Atlantic Ocean.

Lazy Crofter Bunkhouse is owned and managed by Robbie and Fiona Mackay who pride themselves on the warm atmosphere and genuine highland hospitality and invite to you come, relax and enjoy a slower pace of life. The Bunkhouse sleeps 20 in a mix of dorms and two-man bunkrooms. The bedrooms are warm, bright and airy; linen is provided and all rooms are fully made-up for your arrival. There's a modern, fully equipped self-catering kitchen, a drying room with American-style washing machine, powerful hot showers, ample parking, bike storage, and secure lockers. A well stocked village store and post office are 100 metres away and it's only a short walk to pubs/restaurants/tourist information and amazing golden beaches.

DETAILS

- **Open** - All year, check in after 12 noon.
- **Number of beds** - 20: 2x8, 2x2.
- **Booking** - Booking is preferred. Deposits required for group bookings.
- **Price per night** - From £16 per person.
- **Public Transport** - Nearest trains at Lairg, just over an hour's drive away. A daily bus service (May- September) leaves Inverness in the morning, driving via Ullapool.
- **Directions** - Grid reference NC 406 679 OS sheet 9.

CONTACT: Fiona
Durine, Durness, Sutherland, Scotland, IV27 4PN
Tel: 01971 511202
fiona@durnesshostel.com www.durnesshostel.com

SANDRAS
HOSTEL

Thurso is the northern-most town on the UK mainland. Caithness has a rich history which can be traced back to its Viking roots. The cliffs are spectacular and every narrow rock ledge is alive with guillemots, kittiwakes, fulmars and posing puffins. The wildlife off shore is equally fascinating where seals and porpoises haunt the surf. A great way to experience both the coast and the wildlife is to take one of the boat trips around the coast.

The Hostel has been upgraded and is a Visit Scotland 4 Star hostel with all rooms ensuite. Using their own backpacking experience the owners have developed a level of comfort and service which ranks it amongst the top places to stay for families, individuals and couples wanting privacy in the twin / double rooms. Surfing, pony trekking, fishing, quad biking and coastal walks are all available in the area.

DETAILS

- **Open** - All year, 24 hours
- **Number of beds** - 30: 4 x 4 - 1 x 6 - 3 x 2 (or 3) beds
- **Booking** - Advisable, deposit please for groups.
- **Price per night** - Dorm £16pp. Double/Twin £38. Family room £60 (4 people), £70 (5 people). Breakfast is included in the price.
- **Public Transport** - Train Station 10 minutes walk. Bus stop 2 minutes walk.
- **Directions** - From Train station follow Princes Street downhill to Sandras. Buses stop on St George Street. Walk uphill (2 mins) 1st right, 1st left and 1st right again to Princes Street. By car or bike follow A9 to Olrig St, take junction opposite Bank onto bottom end of Princes Street.

CONTACT: George or James
24-26 Princes Street, Thurso, Caithness, KW14 7BQ
Tel: (01847) 894575
sandras-backpackers@ukf.net www.sandras-backpackers.co.uk

HAMNAVOE
HOSTEL

On the Stromness waterfront, a short distance from the ferry terminal, Hamnavoe Hostel makes an ideal base for your visit to Orkney. It has single, twin and family rooms with one recently upgraded to en-suite. The rooms have easy access to the shower, bathroom and toilet on each floor. They are fitted with wash hand basins, pine bunk beds and have stunning views out across Hamnavoe. The light and airy kitchen has two cookers, microwave, double fridge, freezer, toasters, kettle and sandwich toaster. The large dining table has fantastic views over the harbour and marina. The lounge has comfortable seating, freeview TV, video, stereo and a stock of books, cards and games. There is a small laundry room with coin operated washing machine, tumble drier and iron. There is a pay phone and WiFi internet connection. Entry is by a coded door lock and individual rooms have keys. Free long stay car park. Come and visit the nearby islands of Graemsay and Hoy, check out the World Heritage Sites or just relax in the tranquillity of island life.

DETAILS

■ **Open** - All year, all day, no curfew, check in from 2pm and check out by 10am. Reconfirm your booking by 7pm on the scheduled date of arrival.
■ **Number of beds** - 13: 1x4, 1x1, 4x2.
■ **Booking** - Book with deposit of first night, re-confirm by 7pm on the arrival day.
■ **Price per night** - From £18pp. Private rooms £21.
■ **Public Transport** - Orkney Ferries run to Stromness Ferry terminal. There is a regular bus service to and from the town of Stronmness from the terminal.
■ **Directions** - On the waterfront a short walk from Stromness ferry terminal.

CONTACT: Mr George Argo
10a North End Road, Stromness, Orkney, KW16 3AG
Tel: 01856 851202
info@hamnavoehostel.co.uk www.hamnavoehostel.co.uk

BROWNS
HOSTEL AND HOUSE

Brown's Hostel makes an ideal base for your stay in Orkney, situated close to all ammenities and just 3 minutes' walk from the bus and ferry terminal. Stromness is a small friendly town full of character, has a museum and newly extended art centre, has diving courses, free fishing in the lochs, etc. and there are festivals run throughout the year. The Hostel is within walking/cycling distance of the many popular historical sites. We now offer 2 separate units sleeping 8 and 10.

The ground floor Hostel has single, twin and a family room, and a cosy fully equipped kitchen / living room. The House has a spacious kitchen/dining/sitting room, a family bedroom, single and twin/double bedrooms. Both have computer access and WiFi. There is a shed available for cycle storage and free car parking up the lane from the hostel.

DETAILS

- **Open** - All year, all day. No curfew, keys provided.
- **Number of beds** - 18: 3x1; 2x2; 1x3; 2x4.
- **Booking** - Booking advisable especially if wanting private rooms.
- **Price per night** - From £15.
- **Public Transport** - Train or bus to Thurso, bus 2 miles to Scrabster then boat to Stromness. Alternatively from Gills Bay to St Margarets Hope by boat or John O'Groats by boat to Burwick then bus to Stromness via Kirkwall.
- **Directions** - Browns accommodation is just three minutes' walk along the street from the Stromness ferry terminal and bus stop.

CONTACT: Sylvia Brown
45/47 Victoria Street, Stromness, Orkney, KW16 3BS
Tel: 01856 850661
info@brownshostel.co.uk www.brownsselfcatering.co.uk

Birsay Hostel in the northwest corner of the Orkney mainland offers comfortable accommodation for up to 28 in 5 bedrooms. It is an ideal venue for outdoor education trips, weddings, workshops, clubs or family gatherings. It has a well equipped kitchen, dining area and small lounge, drying room, disabled access, and all bed linen is provided. There is a camp site in the extensive grounds with a level firm grassy site for touring caravans, motor homes and tents. Dogs allowed on the campsite but not in the hostel. The centre is close to spectacular coastline including the RSPB reserve of Marwick Head. Nearby at the Brough of Birsay you can see the remains of early Christian and Norse settlements on a tidal island, The Centre is convenient for visiting Orkney's 5,500 year old Neolithic Heartland (UNESCO World Heritage site), with the Ring of Brodgar, the Standing Stones of Stenness, the tomb of Maeshowe, and Skara Brae.

DETAILS

- **Open** - All year (excl. Christmas and New Year), 6-7pm.
- **Number of beds** - 28: 2x4, 1x2, 1x6, 1x12 plus camping.
- **Booking** - Bookings preferred. For group bookings 25% deposit required with balance payable 28 days prior to arrival.
- **Price per night** - From £14.50 (adult), £10.95 (junior), £3.95 (under 3s). Family rooms (£35.45). Private rooms and sole use of hostel available - contact for details.
- **Public Transport** - For buses from Kirkwall and Stromness contact Orkney Coaches (01856 870555). Ferries from Scrabster, (Northlink Ferries 01856 872044), to Gills Bay, (Pentland Ferries 01856 831226). Foot passenger ferries from John O'Groats, summer only (John O'Groats Ferry 01955 611353).
- **Directions** - OS sheet 7 GR 253267.

CONTACT: Recreation Department
Birsay, Orkney, KW17 2LY
Tel: 01856 873535 ext. 2417
leisure.culture@orkney.gov.uk   www.hostelsorkney.co.uk

HOY CENTRE

Surrounded by magnificent scenery the Hoy Centre is ideally situated for a peaceful and relaxing holiday and is an ideal venue for outdoor education trips, weddings, workshops, clubs or family gatherings. It offers high quality, four star accommodation, all rooms are ensuite with shower, twin beds and a bunk bed, chairs, lockers and bedding. One room is equipped for wheelchair access and the centre is all on one level. It has a well equipped kitchen, comfortable lounge area, a spacious dining hall and washing and drying facilities. Under floor heating ensures a comfortable temperature at all times. Much of Hoy is an RSPB reserve comprising 3,500ha of upland heath and cliffs with a large variety of wildlife including arctic hares. Off the west coast is The Old Man of Hoy - Orkney's most famous landmark and a great place to see puffins. The dramatic hills and cliffs offer excellent walking and climbing. The nearest shop is 20 miles so guests need to bring their own provisions. Catering is available for groups. The Centre has Visit Scotland Walkers and Groups Welcome awards.

DETAILS

- **Open** - All year, all day.
- **Number of beds** - 32: 8x4.
- **Booking** - Preferred. Groups send 25% deposit, balance 28 days prior to arrival
- **Price per night** - From £15.75(adult), £12.15(child), £3.95(under 3). Family rooms from £38.10. Private rooms and sole use of Centre available - contact for details.
- **Public Transport** - Short walk from Moaness Pier (pedestrian ferry from Stromness) www.orkneyferries.co.uk (01856 872044). Taxis/minibuses are available.
- **Directions** - Car ferry arrives from Houton to Lyness, which is 16km from centre.

CONTACT: Recreation Department
Hoy Centre, Hoy, Orkney, KW16 3NJ
Tel: 01856 873535 ext 2417
leisure.culture@orkney.gov.uk   www.hostelsorkney.co.uk

RACKWICK
OUTDOOR CENTRE

Rackwick Hostel is in the scenic Rackwick Valley in the north of Hoy. Much of North Hoy is owned by the RSPB, where a large variety of birds live and breed. Off the west coast of the reserve towers The Old Man of Hoy, a 137m sea stack, Orkney's most famous landmark and a great place to see puffins. Local wild flowers and bird life make this a must for naturalists to visit.

The hostel overlooks Rackwick Bay considered one of the most beautiful places in Orkney. The hostel sleeps 8 in two rooms, two pairs of bunks per room. All bedding is provided. There's a small kitchen with a good range of utensils, and a separate eating area. Free car parking and storage to the rear of the hostel for bikes. Walkers and Cyclist Welcome Scheme awarded.

DETAILS

- **Open** - April to September. Signing in by arrangement with warden.
- **Number of beds** - 8: 2x4.
- **Booking** - Booking is preferred. 25% deposit required for groups with balance payable 28 days prior to arrival.
- **Price per night** - From £12.55 (adults), £10.95 (juniors) £3.35 (under 3s). Family and exclusive rooms available
- **Public Transport** - Passenger ferry from Stromness to Moaness Pier (about 10 km away). Private hire and taxis are normally available at the pier, or alternatively the walk to the hostel is via the scenic Rackwick valley which takes approximately 2 hours. Car ferry from Kirkwall to Lyness, about 21 km away. (Orkney ferries 01856 872 044/www.orkneyferries.co.uk).
- **Directions** - In Rackwick village on the NW coast, OS sheet7 GR199998.

CONTACT: Recreation Department
Rackwick, Hoy, Orkney, KW16 3NJ
Tel: 01856 873535 ext. 2417
leisure.culture@orkney.gov.uk   www.hostelsorkney.co.uk

ORCADES
HOSTEL

SCOTLAND

Welcome to Orcades Hostel in Kirkwall. A warm and friendly welcome awaits you at this modern, comfortable 4 star hostel which makes an excellent base for exploring the beautiful Orkney isles. The family who run the hostel have carefully considered the guest's comfort to create a homely feel. Accommodation is in doubles, twins, 4, 5 and 6 bedded rooms (mixed or single sex). All of the bedrooms have en-suite toilet/shower rooms, TVs and all bedding is provided. There is a stylish kitchen fully equipped, including oils and spices for cooking. The lounge has a DVD player, XBOX 360, lots of board games and books and free internet access. There is WiFi throughout the building. Drying facilities, bike storage and lockers are available. Outside is a large garden with ponds, picnic benches and a BBQ area. Stag and Hen groups are not welcome.

DETAILS

■ **Open** - All year, Check in after 2pm. Check out by 10.30 on day of departure.
■ **Number of beds** - 17+: double, twin, 4, 5 and 6 bed rooms.
■ **Booking** - Book by email or phone. Credit or debit card details must be given to secure bookings.
■ **Price per night** - £18pppn in a shared room. £25 pppn double/twin room or £40 single occupancy. Private room prices may be a little cheaper in the winter months.
■ **Public Transport** - Kirkwall is the centre for buses on mainland Orkney and the harbour is the hub for ferries to the Northern Isles.
■ **Directions** - Take Pickaquoy Rd from roundabout at the west side of the waterfront. Proceed for 300m, turn left onto Muddisdale Rd, and hostel is after 500m.

CONTACT: Geira or Erik
Muddisdale Road, Kirkwall, KW15 1RS
Tel: 01856 873745
orcadeshostel@hotmail.co.uk www.orcadeshostel.com

PEEDIE
HOSTEL

The Peedie Hostel (Peedie is an Orcadian word meaning "small") is a quaint hostel overlooking the harbour in the town of Kirkwall, and lies within easy strolling distance of the Main Street and many local attractions.

Kirkwall is the heart of the Orkney Archipelago and the hub of nearly all transport within the isles. The Peedie Hostel is within 300m of the island's main bus station and within 200m of the inner and outer North Isles ferry terminals, making it the ideal base for your Orkney adventure. It is close to many local amenities, including pubs, restaurants shops and supermarkets. The Peedie Hostel has one single room, five double rooms, two 4 bed dorm rooms (or family rooms) and a self-contained Bothy which sleeps 4. Shared facilities include three kitchens and three shower/bathrooms. All rooms have TVs and most enjoy views over the bay. All rooms are heated. Each room has its own key and the hostel and its facilities are open 24/7 giving guests complete freedom during their stay. We also understand that travel to and from Orkney sometimes involves checking in or out at odd times and this can be accommodated.

DETAILS

- **Open** - All year, all day.
- **Number of beds** - 23: 1x1, 5x2, 2x4 plus Bothy (sleeps 4).
- **Booking** - Bookings can be made by phone, email or letter.
- **Price per night** - £15 pp. (supplement for single occupancy).
- **Public Transport** - 200m to North Isle & Shapinsay ferries. 300m to bus station.
- **Directions** - Situated on the sea front on Ayre Road.

CONTACT: Julia Wild
1 Ayre Houses, Ayre Road, Kirkwall, Orkney, KW15 1QX
Tel: 01856 875477 Fax: 01856 872817
kirkwallpeediehostel@talk21.com www.kirkwallhostel.co.uk

AYRES ROCK
HOSTEL
SCOTLAND

Sanday is the perfect place to take time out, with long stretches of unspoilt sandy beaches, an abundance of birds, seals and other wildlife, glittering seas, clear air and spectacular skies. Those lucky enough to live here enjoy a rare quality of life in a small, friendly and safe community. Ayre's Rock Hostel has accreditation by Visit Scotland and is rated at four stars. There are two twin rooms and one family ensuite room. A brand new conservatory and lounge area with expansive views over the Holms of Ire & Westray offers a comfortable place to relax after a day's exploration. A kitchen is available for self-catering, continental breakfast included for hostel guests. Camping Pods one, two or three berth are available new this season, use of campers' facilities and free cycle hire for Hostel guests. Evening meals can be provided by arrangement. Takeaways are also available from the Ayre's Rock Chip Shop when open.

DETAILS

- **Open** - All year, 8am to 10pm.
- **Number of beds** - 8 : 2x2, 1x4.
- **Booking** - Book by phone or email.
- **Price per night** - From £15pp. Twin room single occupancy £18. Group bookings from £50. C'ping Pods from £10pp. Cooked B'fast £5, evening meals from £8.
- **Public Transport** -   Direct ferry from Kirkwall Pier to the Loth terminal in Sanday takes 1 hr 20 mins minutes. Passenger fares approx £14 rtn. Flying direct from Kirkwall airport to Sanday takes 11 minutes and a return flight approx £65. For local buses and taxi phone 01857 600410.
- **Directions** - 6 miles from Loth ferry terminal and 2 miles from Sanday air field.

CONTACT: Julie or Paul
Ayre, Coo Road, Sanday, Orkney KW17 2AY
Tel: 01857 600410
allanpaul67@googlemail.com www.ayres-rock-sanday-orkney.co.uk

OBSERVATORY
HOSTEL

The North Ronaldsay Bird Observatory is situated at the south west corner of the island with outstanding views and an adjacent shell sand beach. Seals and the unique seaweed-eating sheep are abundant along the coast which skirts the 34 acres of croft managed by the observatory. The observatory sees spectacular bird migration through the island in spring and autumn. It offers a special attraction for those interested in wildlife, but welcomes all visitors. The Observatory Hostel consists of three dormitories and a self-catering kitchen in a converted barn and byre of the croft. The Byre sleeps four in two bunks and has en-suite washing, shower and toilet facilities. It is particularly suitable for family use. The Barn also sleeps four and shares facilities with the Bøl which has a single bunk sleeping two. Adjacent is the Observatory Guest House (3 star) which has a lounge bar and meals which are available to hostellers.

DETAILS

- **Open** - All year, 24 hours, open all day, no curfews.
- **Number of beds** - 10: 2x4, 1x2; house: 8: 2x4 and private rooms.
- **Booking** - Advance booking essential.
- **Price per night** - Hostel £14.50-£15.50. Half board in hostel from £31. Guest House private rooms £47.50-£59.50 half board.
- **Public Transport** - Loganair flights from Kirkwall (Orkney) leave daily. Ferry from Kirkwall on Fridays and between May-Sept also on Tuesdays (subject to tides and weather). Small boats may be chartered. Orkney can be reached by vehicle ferries from Aberdeen, Thurso (Scrabster) and Gill's Bay, and a passenger summer service from John O'Groats.
- **Directions** - Situated at the south west corner of the island

CONTACT: Duty Warden
NRBO, North Ronaldsay, Orkney Islands, KW17 2BE
Tel: 01857 633200 Fax: 01857 633207
bookings@nrbo.prestel.co.uk www.nrbo.co.uk

Papa Stour is a beautiful unspoilt island with spectacular cliffs and caves, ideal for walkers, bird watchers and photographers, or just to enjoy the fresh air and peace. Spot the seals, otters and the occasional dolphin, or visit sights of historical interest. There are long hours of daylight in the summer and in the autumn and winter you can spy the northern lights. Glimpse the untamed wildness of this remote corner of the world.

Hurdiback is a comfortable bunkhouse on a working croft, overlooking a picturesque bay. There are two bedrooms and a kitchen/sitting room. Equipment includes electric cooker, microwave, toaster, kettle and fridge. Heating, bed-linen, quilts and towels are included in the price and cots are available. We can order in your groceries with a couple of weeks' notice and there is complimentary tea and coffee at the hostel.

DETAILS

- **Open** - All year, all day.
- **Number of beds** - 8: 2 x 4.
- **Booking** - Advisable, groups require deposit.
- **Price per night** - Adults £20pp, 5-16 yrs and OAPS £10pp, under 5's free.
- **Public Transport** - Ferry (booking required 01957 722 259) West Burrafirth to Papa Stour return. Bus (booking required 01595 860 266) Margaret public/private bus. By air use Direct Flight Ltd 01595 840246.
- **Directions** - Hurdiback is a short walk/drive from the ferry pier, or airport pick-up on request.

CONTACT: Peter or Esther
Hurdiback, Papa Stour, Shetland, ZE2 9PW
Tel: 01595 873227 or 0808 1920 006 (freephone) Fax: 01595 873229
enquiries@hurdibackhostel.co.uk www.hurdibackhostel.co.uk

The Shetland camping böd network offers low cost accommodation in nine historic buildings with fantastic scenery - giving the opportunity to tour these beautiful islands, staying in böds en route. Due to the böd's historic nature, no two buildings are the same and facilities vary. The smallest böd sleeps four and the largest sixteen. Electricity, hot water and showers are available in six of the nine buildings and solid fuel stoves and mains water in all. Each böd has a story to tell, for example Voe Sail Loft was once a knitwear workshop, where the jumpers for Sir Edmund Hillary's expedition to reach the peak of Mount Everest in 1953 were produced. Seven out of nine have local meals available within two miles and seven out of nine have (variable) facilities for less able people. Under 16s must be accompanied by an adult. No pets allowed. Explore Shetland, bed down in a böd. For further info log onto: www.camping-bods.co.uk.

DETAILS

- **Open** - 1st March – 31st October. The böds are unmanned but a custodian is contactable until 9pm, please call to arrange entry.
- **Number of beds** - 4 to 16 (depending on böd).
- **Booking** - Booking is not essential however, as böds are unmanned it is best to book in advance to ensure the custodian is available before arrival.
- **Price per night** - £8 to £10 pppn. Group discounts are also available.
- **Public Transport** - Information on public transport within Shetland: www.shetland.gov.uk/transport/ Information on cycle and car hire: http://visit.shetland.org/car-and-bike-hire
- **Directions** - Ferry from Aberdeen to Shetland (NorthLink). Flights to Shetland from Orkney, Inverness, Aberdeen, Edinburgh and Glasgow (Flybe).

CONTACT: Reception
For info: Shetland Amenity Trust, Garthspool, Lerwick, Shetland, ZE1 0NY
Tel: 01595 694688
info@shetlandamenity.org www.camping-bods.co.uk

GARDIESFAULD
HOSTEL

Gardiesfauld Hostel is on Unst, the most northerly of the Shetland Isles. The island has spectacular cliffs sculpted by the Atlantic Ocean on the west and secluded, sandy beaches on the east with rocky outcrops where seals and otters appear. The Gulf Stream provides a moderate climate and offers an invigorating chance to relax in a community where crime is unknown. During the summer enjoy long hours of daylight and the twilight of the "simmer dim" while in winter the long nights provide the backdrop for a vibrant cultural life. Situated on the picturesque shore at Uyeasound, this refurbished hostel combines superb facilities with a relaxed atmosphere. There is a kitchen, dining room, lounge, conservatory, coin operated laundry, showers (coin operated) and rooms with en-suite facilities. A 5 berth caravan site has also been added.

DETAILS

- **Open** - April to September, Open in winter for pre-booked groups, , all day
- **Number of beds** - 35: 1 x 11, 2 x 6, 2 x 5, 1x 2
- **Booking** - Book by phone or email
- **Price per night** - Adults £13pp, children (under 16) £8pp. Camping from £6 a tent, caravan hook ups £12.
- **Public Transport** - Ferry from Aberdeen to Shetland (Northlink Ferries). The bus meets the ferry and continues to Unst. Ask for Uyeasound. Flights to Lerwick (BA). From Fetlar catch 7:55am ferry from Oddsta (Bus meets ferry)
- **Directions** - Take the A970 north from Lerwick to Voe then the A968 north to Toft . Take the ferry from Toft to Ulsta in Yell. Take the A968 north to Gutcher. Take the ferry from Gutcher to Belmont. Follow the A968 north and head into Uyeasound (B9084). Follow the road to the pier and look out for the hostel sign board.

CONTACT: Warden
Uyeasound, Unst, Shetland, ZE2 9DW
Tel: 01957 755279
enquiries@gardiesfauld.shetland.co.uk www.gardiesfauld.shetland.co.uk

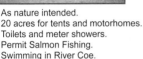

IRELAND			
KENMARE FAILTE	Kenmare	+353 64 6642333.	www.kenmare.eu/failtehostel
THE RITZ	Killybegs	+353 (0) 74 9731309	www.theritz-killybegs.com
JAMAICA INN	Sixmile-bridge	+ 353 (0) 61 369220	www.jamaicainn.ie
KINLAY HOUSE	Cork	+353 21 4508 966	www.kinlayhousecork.ie
GERMANY			
FIVE ELEMENTS	Frankfurt	+ 49 (0)69 24005885	www.5elementshostel.de
GENERATOR	Berlin	+ 49 30 417 2400	www.generatorhostels.com
ODYSSEE GLOBETROTTER	Berlin	+49 (0)30 29000081	www.globetrotterhostel.de
HEART OF GOLD	Berlin	+49 (0) 30 2900 3300	www.heartofgold-hostel.de
HOSTEL EOL 777	Sachsen	+ 49 (0) 15257196915	www.hosteleol777.com
SWITZERLAND			
CITY BACKPACKER	Zurich	+41 44 251 9015	www.city-backpacker.ch
BERN BACKPACKERS	Bern	+41 31 311 37 71	www.bernbackpackers.ch
ITALY			
PERUGIA FARMHOUSE	Perugia	+39 339 5620005	www.perugia-farmhouse.it

CZECH REPUBLIC

ARPACAY	Prague	+42 0/251 552 297	www.arpacayhostel.com
PRAGUE SQUARE	Prague	+420 224 240 859	www.praguesquarehostel.com
OLD PRAGUE	Prague	+420 224 829 058	www.oldpraguehostel.com

ESTONIA

TARTU STUDENT VILLA	Tartu	+372 58078527	www.hot.ee/apartment/

ROMANIA

HOSTEL EOL 777	Constanta	+40 727 555556	www.hosteleol777.com

COSTA RICA

LA COLINA LODGE	Monteverde	50626455009	www.lacolinalodge.com

CANADA

HOSTELS CANADA	Vancouver	+1 604 684-3713	www.stclairvancouver.com

USA

OBI HOSTEL	San Diego	1-800-339-7263	www.californiahostel.com

31 hostels in 27 cities all over Switzerland

6677 Aurigeno, **Baracca Backpacker**, +41 (0)79 207 15 54

3011 Bern, **Backpackers - Hotel Glocke**, +41 (0)31 311 37 71, info@bernbackpackers.ch

8784 Braunwald, **adrenalin backpackers hostel**, +41 (0)79 347 29 05, info@adrenalin.gl

6558 Cabbiolo/Lostallo, **Humanita Backpackers**, +41 (0)91 830 14 81, info@humanita.ch

7002 Chur, **JBN Just be Nice Hostel**, +41 (0)81 284 10 10, info@justbenice.ch

7075 Churwalden, **Basis Hostel**, +41(0)81 356 22 31, hostelbasis@krone-churwalden.ch

7180 Disentis, **Cucagna Hostel**, +41 (0)81 929 55 55, hostel@cucagna.ch

1202 Genève, **City Hostel Geneva**, +41 (0)22 901 15 00, info@cityhostel.ch

3826 Gimmelwald, **Mountain Hostel**, +41 (0)33 855 17 04, mountainhostel@tcnet.ch

3818 Grindelwald, **Downtown Lodge**, +41 (0)33 828 77 30, downtown-lodge@jungfrau.ch

3818 Grindelwald, **Mountain Hostel Grindelwald**, +41 (0)33 854 38 38, info@mountainhostel.ch

1882 Gryon, **Chalet Martin**, +41 (0)79 724 63 74, info@gryon.com

3800 Interlaken, **Backpackers Villa Sonnenhof**, +41 (0)33 826 71 71, mail@villa.ch

3800 Interlaken, **Happy Inn Lodge**, +41 (0)33 822 32 25, info@happy-inn.com

3800 Interlaken, **River Lodge**, +41 (0)33 822 44 24, welcome@riverlodge.ch

3800 Interlaken/Matten, **Balmer's Herberge**, +41 (0)33 822 19 61, mail@balmers.com

3800 Interlaken/Unterseen, **Lazy Falken Backpacker**, +41 (0)33 822 30 43, info@lazyfalken.ch

7031 Laax-Cons, **Backpacker Deluxe Capricorn**, 41 (0)81 921 21 20, info@caprilounge.ch

3550 Langnau i.E., **Emme Lodge**, +41 (0)34 402 45 26, info@emmelodge.ch

1007 Lausanne, **Guesthouse & Backpacker**, +41 (0)21 601 80 00, info@lausanne-guesthouse.ch

3822 Lauterbrunnen, **Valley Hostel**, +41 (0)33 855 20 08, info@valleyhostel.ch

6005 Luzern, **Backpackers Lucerne**, +41 (0)41 360 04 20, www.backpackerslucerne.ch

6000 Luzern 6, **Lion Lodge Luzern**, +41 (0)41 410 01 44, info@lionlodge.ch

2560 Nidau b. Biel, **Lago Lodge**, +41 (0)32 331 37 32, sleep@lagolodge.ch

6430 Schwyz, **hirschen backpackers.hotel.pub**, +41 (0)41 811 12 76, info@hirschen-schwyz.ch

7554 Sent, **Backpacker Hotel Swissroof**, +41 (0)81 864 17 22, info@swissroof.ch

7500 St. Moritz, **Randolins Backpackers**, +41 (0)81 830 83 83, welcome@randolins-backpackers.ch

9657 Unterwasser, **Saentis Lodge**, +41 (0)71 998 50 20, saentis@beutler-hotels.ch

1800 Vevey-Montreux, **Riviera Lodge**, +41 (0)21 923 80 40, info@rivieralodge.ch

6484 Wassen, **Gotthardbackpacker**, +41 (0)79 306 54 23, www.gotthardbackpacker.ch

8001 Zürich, **City Backpacker/Hotel Biber**, +41 (0)44 251 90 15, sleep@city-backpacker.ch

60 independent
quality hostels

in **38** cities all
over Germany

Backpackers Hostels Canada
Auberges Backpackers Canada

Visit Canada!
Visit ... www.backpackers.ca

Wake up in the (BEST) IRISH HOSTELS

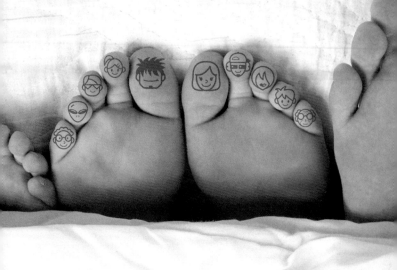

{ Beds for all AGES! }

Book Online at
www.hostels-ireland.com

The network of IRISH TOURIST BOARD approved hostels all over IRELAND

INDEPENDENT HOLIDAY
HOSTELS
OF IRELAND

Lakeland
Camping Barns

www.lakelandcampingbarns.co.uk

Dry camping in prime locations around the English Lake District. Camping barns offer the opportunity to stay in restored farm buildings at affordable prices. Experience Cumbria's stunning lakes and lofty peaks literally from your doorstep. All the barns are unique and offer differing facilities. Visit our website to take our virtual tours.

We look forward to welcoming you and your families and friends in 2012.

Barn	Facilities	Page
St John's-in-the-Vale Camping Barn		200
Tarn Flatt Camping Barn		217
Bents Camping Barn		177
Catbells Camping Barn		209
Swallow Barn Camping Barn		215
Murt Barn Camping Barn		
Cragg Barn Camping Barn		214
Dinah Hoggus Camping Barn		
Fell End Camping Barn		187
Hudscales Camping Barn		208
Wythmoor Farm Camping Barn		186
Swirral Camping Barn		203

SYMBOLS

	Breakfast bookable in advance
	Shop (miles)
	Pub (miles)
	Shower
	Pets by arrangement
	Electric lighting
	Toilets not in main building
	Hot water
	Campfire
	Powerpoints
	Disabled facilities
	Wood burning stove
	BBQ aea
	Cooking facilites
	Heating

BREAK FOR THE BORDER

BUNKHOUSESINWALES.CO.UK

WALKING & CYCLING TRAILS

For Brilliant Bunkhouses
in the Brecon Beacons
and Mid & South Wales
for accommodation that's fun and different visit
www.bunkhousesinwales.co.uk

BUY DIRECT FROM THE MANUFACTURER

"Titan" Three tier bunk bed

"Trident" 3' over 4'6" Family or "Luxury" bunk

"Neptune" Double bunk bed

NEW HOSTEL "PACKS" AVAILABLE WHATEVER YOUR REQUIREMENTS!!

BUNKS – DOUBLES, TRIPLES, OR SINGLE OVER DOUBLES IN YOUR CHOICE OF COLOUR

MATTRESSES – FOAM CORE OR SPRING INTERIOR IN A VARIETY OF FINISHES

LINEN PACKS – SHEETS, DUVETS, PILLOWS, PILLOW CASES

ALL ITEMS ARE OF CONTRACT QUALITY AND CONFORM TO RELEVANT BRITISH STANDARDS

CHARTERBRAE - YOUR ONE-STOP SHOP FOR HOSTEL FURNISHINGS

SHEETS – FITTED AND FLAT, PILLOW CASES, PILLOWS, DUVETS, ALL AVAILABLE IN A RANGE OF COLOURS.

CONTACT US NOW ON

0121 520 5353

OR VISIT

WWW.CBBEDS.CO.UK

TO SEE OUR FULL COMPREHENSIVE RANGE OF BUNKS AND BEDS FOR ALL OCCASIONS AND VIEW OUR FACTORY TOUR

We can also provide folding beds for the peak times you need the extra sleeping platforms.

 commercial & agricultural | insurance brokers

The Specialists in Hostel Insurance

FOR A NON-OBLIGATORY QUOTATION, CONTACT MIKE PATERSON

Commercial & Agricultural Insurance Brokers, Erskine House, 6b Commerce Street, Arbroath, Angus, DD11 1WB

TEL: 01241 870303
FAX: 01241 877592
EMAIL: mail@caib.co.uk
www.caib.co.uk

Flexible covers tailored to your requirements

Competitive premiums

Competitive finance rates

Free Hostel Risk Management Guide with all policies

Authorised and Regulated by the Financial Services Authority

'Our social network'
Philippe, Anna, Leo, Leah & Rob

Escaping their everyday routine - follow our athletes' adventure: www.facebook.com/berghaus

Independent Hostels UK
www.independenthostelsuk.com

The UK's network of independently managed hostels, bunkhouses, camping barns and group accommodation

In partnership with

Did you know?

The IHUK  network is now larger than the Youth Hostel Association.

What is the IHUK Network?

Independent Hostels UK, in partnership with Berghaus, is the UK's network of independently managed bunkhouses, hostels, camping barns and group accommodation in England, Scotland & Wales. With over 330 member hostels the network is comparable in size to the Youth Hostel Association in the UK (YHA plus SYHA).

The network aims to promote all of the accommodation providers equally from small rural setups all the way to the large city hostels by offering a broad marketing package that targets the UK's outdoor market and independent travellers.

Independent Hostels UK was established under grant funding from the government and is now a self supporting membership body guided by a small committee of member directors.

The network of hostels has grown dramatically since it first started out as a small collection of 14 listed in the very first Independent Hostel Guide (IHG). The handbook of IHUK now lists over 330 hostels, bunkhouses, camping barns and group accommodation centres and approximately 10,000 copies are distributed each year.

Meet the Directors

Jon Beavan.

Owner of Dalesbridge, a complex of group accommodation, individual small bunkhouses and campsite. Jon is a master of diversification and has a strong belief in the benefits provided by networking information and lobbying as a group.

James Powell

James embarked on the new venture of Llandudno Hostel after being inspired by travelling extensively in Britain, America, Australia and Asia. James has an interest in the independent hostels' community and hopes to see others develop their business through the help and support given by an established strong network.

Carl Borum

Owner of Snowdon Lodge (a well established historic group accommodation centre) Carl has many years of experience in marketing, operating/owning several businesses in the hospitality sector. This expertise ensures IHUK makes the most of its marketing potential and helps the network stay sustainable and grow.

Clint Maskell

Sales/marketing manager at Hatters Hostels UK, a chain of budget accommodation with properties in Liverpool, Manchester and Birmingham, Clint offers first hand experience in digital marketing and the UK backpackers' market.

Comments from our members

"A very wise choice and has led to many enquiries!"
Ken Davies, Woodside Lodges Bunkhouse

"They are one of the most efficient and reliable advertisers that I know. I get many enquiries and bookings from visitors using either the printed publication or the website. Their customer service is second to none. Well worth the money!"
Ann (Bottrill), Braich Goch Bunkhouse & Inn

"The best thing we've found with Independent Hostels is the constant interaction between yourselves and the individual hostels like ourselves and all the promotion that you put in to it"
John Adams, Woodhouse Farm

"We advertise with you because the IHG book and website package offer great value for money"
Andrew Donaldson, Comrie Croft

"Thanks for your work with the Independent Hostels, we continue to get lots of enquiries through it, more importantly usually groups of nice people!"
Sue, Spring Hill Farm

"Sam and her team promote the guide extensively... hits on our link from IHG continue to grow."
Neil Macintosh Loch Ness Backpackers

Passion for the outdoors runs through Berghaus, with over 40 years of British heritage. It's what drives us to create the best outdoor products and push the boundaries of innovation. Our athletes, some of the world's best, continually test our gear to the extreme so that you can get out there with the confidence to have fun, enjoy every adventure and make the most of life!

INDEX

INDEX